ג'אן רמי

לכבוד בוגר בבר-אבא קץ
נתן שאול ני
בברכת הצלחה ואיחול
שיוון הדרך לבריך הוא נתן שאול
יוצלח ושבוי לברוא'

# The Eternal Heritage

# The Eternal Heritage

## An Anthology of Torah Thought

Exodus I
Shemoth — Yithro

By
**Avraham M. Goldstein**

Published by Bash Publications, Inc.
New York

# THE ETERNAL HERITAGE

**FIRST EDITION**
First Impression — DECEMBER 1990

Published by bp

Copyright © 1990 by Avraham M. Goldstein
**ALL RIGHTS RESERVED**

This book, or parts thereof, may not be reproduced, stored, or copied in any form without written permission from the copyright holder, except by a reviewer who wishes to quote brief passages in connection with a review written for inclusion in magazines or newspapers.

**THE RIGHTS OF THE COPYRIGHT HOLDER
WILL BE STRICTLY ENFORCED.**

ISBN 0—932351—07—7 (Casebound Edition)

Distributed by: **HaChai Distributions**
705 Foster Avenue ● Brooklyn, New York 11230
(718) 692-3900

Printed in the U.S.A.

*dedicated to my
dear wife,
Dawn*

# Acknowledgments

It is a happy task to acknowledge the many people who helped in the production of the third volume of The Eternal Heritage.

I would like to thank my *rosh yeshiva,* HaRav Yechiel Perr, who assisted in the clarification of problematic commentaries. I also express my gratitude to HaRav Moshe Brown, *rosh kollel* at Kollel Birchas Yaakov, in Far Rockaway, and to HaRav Aharon Brafman. Special thanks are in order to HaRav Avrohom Kleinkaufman, for his time and for the unrestricted use of his impressive Torah library.

In addition, I discussed parts of this volume with several of my fellow students in the Derech Ayson Rabbinical Seminary, and I appreciate their help.

It was a joy to work with my editor, Fayge Silverman, whose talents shone in both the literary and artistic fields. Along with editing the manuscript, she redesigned the graphics of The Eternal Heritage.

My brother, Yair S. Goldstein, edited portions of the manuscript, and was always helpful with his advice. Thanks are also due to Judy Bendet, for editing parts of the book; as in the past, her skills were amply demonstrated.

My mother, Shulamit Goldstein, proofread the manuscript, as did Mrs. Faygie Weinbaum. I greatly appreciate their assistance.

Esther Lipschitz and Hallie Cantor typeset the English text, while Billa Tessler typeset the verses in Hebrew.

My wife, Dawn, proofread the English verses and provided helpful suggestions throughout the production process. I also thank her for once again tolerating my difficult working hours. It is to her that this volume is dedicated, with the hope that we and our children, Elisheva Bracha and Yitzchak, will continue to enjoy the fruits of God's blessings.

Whatever errors remain in The Eternal Heritage are my responsibility, and I would be grateful to anyone who brings any mistakes to my attention. Such correspondence should be sent to the publisher.

I reserve a special acknowledgment to Mayer Bendet. It is his foresight that has led to the appearance of all three volumes of this series.

Finally, I thank the Almighty for allowing me to have a small share in the work of making the thoughts of our Sages more accessible. I pray that I will have the merit to produce more such work in the future.

A. M. G.

Cheshvan 5751
November 1990

# Notes

There are several important points which need to be made regarding the procedures used in the production of The Eternal Heritage.

The text of the verses is based on The Living Torah, by the late Rabbi Aryeh Kaplan. The Living Torah translated the Torah into modern English, while remaining faithful to the meaning of the text. There have been changes made in instances when the author felt that such substitutes enhanced the precision of the translation.

There are several Torah anthologies in Hebrew from which The Eternal Heritage has drawn. The best of them is Iturei Torah. Also of note are MeOtzareinu HaYashan, Ma'ayanah shel Torah, and MiMa'ayanoth HaNetzach.

Under no circumstances is the reader to use any portion of this book to determine Jewish law. Questions concerning halacha must be addressed to a competent Orthodox rabbi.

Hebrew contains two letters, *heth* and *chaf*, which are pronounced as in the German *ach*. In The Eternal Heritage, both letters are generally spelled *ch*.

Biblical names are usually translated into their English equivalents. Thus, the patriarch Avraham is identified as Abraham, Moshe as Moses, etc. Exceptions to this rule have been made on occasions when the English name seemed awkward. For example, Chanoch is not identified as Enoch, and Lavan is not called Laban.

The Sages of the Talmudic era, and later authorities and commentators as well, are called by their Hebrew names. As an example, the Talmudic figure R. Yehuda is not called R. Judah.

The spelling for the various European towns from which many of the commentators hail has been taken from the Encyclopaedia Judaica. Generally, when a town has both a Yiddish and a European name, the European name has been used.

The selections appearing in The Eternal Heritage may, for the most part, be put in two categories: those which have tag lines at the end identifying their authors, and those whose authors are identified within the piece, but are not signed. The ones which have tag lines are presented as it was felt the author would have conveyed his thoughts were he writing in English. On rare occasions, it was deemed necessary to insert information not present in the Hebrew, for the purpose of clarification. Such information is enclosed in brackets.

Pieces which do not have tag lines are presented as a summary by The Eternal Heritage of the views expressed by one or more commentaries. These selections are not to be taken as an attempt to put the author's thoughts into English as he would have written them, but, rather, as a summary of his thoughts from the vantage point of an independent observer. When information not present in the Hebrew is inserted here, it is placed within parentheses.

I have included my own views on a number of occasions. Thoughts that are unattributed may be taken as my ideas.

Additionally, I have included a number of thoughts propounded by my *rosh yeshiva*, HaRav Yechiel Perr, *shlita*, which he has presented over the course of many years in his Friday lectures on the Torah.

## Additional Notes

In order to enhance readability, the third volume of The Eternal Heritage has been redesigned, with new typefaces.

The reader should note that pieces which comment on the same verse are separated by a solid box ■. The end of a verse is marked by three solid boxes ■ ■ ■. In the previous volumes, the same style held; however, the boxes were hollow. In cases where two pieces are closely connected, there is no box.

When a citation is made from another verse in the same chapter, only the verse is given (e.g., verse 23). When the verse cited occurs elsewhere in the same book of the Torah, the chapter and verse are given (e.g., 6:12). When the citation is from another book, the book, chapter, and verse are noted (e.g., Deuteronomy 28:3).

## Table of Contents

| 1 | Shemoth | 13 |
| 2 | VaEra | 107 |
| 3 | Bo | 181 |
| 4 | Beshalach | 259 |
| 5 | Yithro | 325 |

# 1
# Shemoth

וְאֵלֶּה שְׁמוֹת בְּנֵי יִשְׂרָאֵל הַבָּאִים מִצְרָיְמָה אֵת יַעֲקֹב אִישׁ וּבֵיתוֹ בָּאוּ.
*These are the names of the children of Israel who came to Egypt with Jacob, each with his family. (1:1)*

"These are the names of the children of Israel" — The term *b'nai Yisrael* can mean "the children of Israel" — the entire nation — or it can mean "the sons of Israel," of Jacob. Either reading poses a problem. If, on the one hand, we translate *b'nai Yisrael* as "the children of Israel" — the nation of Israel — then the subsequent verses, which list the names of Jacob's children, present a difficulty. The present verse having stated that "These are the names of the children of Israel," one would expect that *all* the people of Israel, not only Jacob's sons, would be named. And yet, the Torah continues by listing only Jacob's sons. On the other hand, if *b'nai Yisrael* means "the sons of Israel," Jacob's sons specifically, then the subsequent verses, which enumerate his sons, are comprehensible. However, the present verse is problematic. Once it says that "These are the names of the sons of Israel," why does the Torah have to state that they came to Egypt "with Jacob"? Whereas Jacob is already identified by the word "Israel," it should have continued that they came to Egypt "with *him.*"

It appears that the correct translation of *b'nai Yisrael* is "the children of Israel," the *nation* of Israel. And while the following verses list only Jacob's sons, they are actually referring to each son and his household — Reuven and his household, Simeon and his household, etc. In this way, the verses do discuss the entire nation of Israel.

This corresponds with the final words of the present verse, that they came "each with his family" — Reuven with his family, Simeon with his family, and so on. *(Ha'amek Davar)*

■

Rashi says that God listed the sons here, at their death, to publicize His love for them, in that they are compared with the stars. Just as God brings out the stars by number and name (Isaiah 40:26), so did He escort the sons of Jacob in life and in death by name.

Sefath Emeth sees here an allusion to the special mission of the Jews. The stars were created in order to provide light during the night. Similarly, the Jews were created in order to bring God's light to the places which are spiritually dark.

■

Why does the Torah deem it necessary to restate the names of Jacob's children? These are already well known to us. Moreover, the names of everyone who immigrated to Egypt are listed earlier (Genesis 46:8-27). Why is this repetition required?

The Sages say that one's name reflects the essence of his character, that it alludes to his deeds (Berachoth 7b). Drawing on this, the Midrash states, regarding the sons, that "their names are good and their deeds are good" (Bereshith Rabbah 71), and proceeds to connect Reuven and Simeon's names to their character; their names served to glorify their actions.

Now, Rashi says here that the Torah enumerates the sons at the time of their death — although they were enumerated when they were alive — as an indication that God loves them. Scripture is speaking of the sons at their hour of death. By repeating their names, it is informing us that there was no change in the character of the sons throughout their stay in Egypt. Just as their deeds in Canaan had been exemplary, and had befitted their names, so were their

## Shemoth

deeds in Egypt exemplary. This was the case despite the fact that Egypt was a land steeped in impurity.

Literally, the verse reads, "*And* these are the names." The conjunction connotes continuity. Just as the sons' first years were good, so were their final years good. *(Be'er Mayim Chaim)*

■

The Torah wishes to emphasize that the Israelites began to increase prolifically. Therefore, it must first repeat that the generation which came to Egypt numbered only seventy souls. Only after that generation passed on (verse 6) did the population begin to increase (verse 7). *(Rashbam)*

■

"These are the names of the children of Israel who came to Egypt" — In specifying the reasons why the Israelites merited redemption, the Rabbis include the fact that "they did not change their names" (VaYikra Rabbah 32). Thus, Scripture says here that these were the names with which the Israelites came to Egypt and these were the names they kept.

What is the importance of the fact that they kept their names?

A name testifies to the essence of something, and we find that this was Adam's wisdom. Scripture says of him, "Whatever the man called each living thing would be its name" (Genesis 2:19). Adam was able to discern the innate characteristics of each creature, and knew how to reflect those characteristics in its name.

This principle is also seen later in the present portion. Moses said to God, "They will ask me what His name is. What shall I tell them?" (3:13). He asked: If the Israelites inquire as to God's essential nature — with what name that nature would be reflected — what was he to tell them? In truth, however, God's essence cannot be captured in a name; He is above such categorization. Nobody knows God's essence; we know only of His existence. God responded, "I will be what I will be" (Ibid., verse 14) — I exist in perpetuity. I was, I am, and I will be.

The Israelites did not change their names. They protected their essence. Even in Egypt, they did not abandon the recognition of themselves as essentially Israelite — that they were offspring of Reuven, Simeon, and the rest of Jacob's sons.

*(R. Shlomo Yosef Zevin)*

■

"These are the names" — Jacob's sons were worthy of having their names mentioned individually, with each one's name testifying to his particular characteristics.

While they were alive, Jacob's sons influenced their surroundings, and the Jewish people retained their good character. However, after Jacob's sons died, the remaining righteous people of the generation were not as lofty spiritually. Still, as long as "everyone else in that generation" (verse 6) — any one of the seventy people who came down to Egypt — remained alive, the Jews did not completely depart from the correct path. But when all had perished, the Jews descended to the level of animals (verse 7 — *vayishretzu,* "[they] increased abundantly," is rooted in *sheretz,* "creature").

*(Sforno)*

■

"The children of Israel who came" — The literal translation of *haba'im,* "who came," is "who are coming." This is problematic, since Jacob's family came to Egypt many years earlier. Why are these words in present tense, making it seem that they just now came to Egypt?

Da'ath Zekenim MiBa'alei HaTosafoth explains that the Israelites' status underwent a change with the death of Joseph. While Joseph was alive, the Israelites were not subject to taxes. Now, however, a tax was placed upon them. In a sense, it was as if they were just coming to Egypt, as they now faced a new situation.

■ ■ ■

וַיָּקָם מֶלֶךְ־חָדָשׁ עַל־מִצְרָיִם אֲשֶׁר לֹא־יָדַע אֶת־יוֹסֵף.

A new king, who had not known Joseph, came to power in Egypt. (1:8)

Had the new Pharaoh been aware of the events that transpired during Joseph's time, he would have seen that all the attempts to harm Joseph — whether by his brothers or by Potiphar — had

## Shemoth

backfired; he had risen to power because of them. Pharaoh would thus have been afraid to subjugate and oppress the Israelites, since an attempt to do so would doubtless have led to their redemption.

*(Imrei Aish)*

■ ■ ■

הָבָה נִתְחַכְּמָה לוֹ פֶּן־יִרְבֶּה וְהָיָה כִּי־תִקְרֶאנָה מִלְחָמָה וְנוֹסַף גַּם־הוּא עַל־שֹׂנְאֵינוּ וְנִלְחַם־בָּנוּ וְעָלָה מִן־הָאָרֶץ.

"... We must deal wisely with them. Otherwise, they may increase so much that if there is war they will join our enemies and fight against us, and leave the land." (1:10)

Literally, the verse reads, "We must deal wisely with *him*," *lo*. The Talmud objects that it should read *lahem*, "with them," the Jews of the land. It then explains that Pharaoh was referring to the savior of Israel, Moses. He said that the Egyptians should "deal wisely with" — conceive a plan against — "him," the Jews' redeemer (Sotah 11a).

It is possible to explain this as follows: Rashi says later (6:16) that we are informed of Levi's life span, 137 years, so that we can calculate the actual time of the Israelites' servitude. Levi was the last of Jacob's sons to die, and the slavery did not commence until all the sons had perished.

Now, Levi was forty-three years of age when he came to Egypt (see Ibn Ezra on 2:2). Thus, he resided there for ninety-four years. The Israelites lived in Egypt for 210 years (Rashi on 12:40). Therefore, 116 years remained from the time of Levi's death until the Jews left Egypt. Moses was eighty years old when the Israelites left Egypt (7:7), and so there were thirty-six years between Levi's death and Moses' birth. The Midrash states that the Egyptians schemed against the Israelites until Moses was born. *Lo*, "with him," has a numerical value of thirty-six, and serves as an allusion to this.

*(R. Pinchas Eliyahu of Lutomiersk)*

■

Pharaoh and his advisors elected not to openly attack the Israelites — to kill them by the sword — opting instead for a surreptitious war. It would have reflected very poorly on Egypt to attempt to exterminate the very people it had invited to immigrate to the country (Genesis 45:17-18). Additionally, the general populace would not have permitted Pharaoh to commit such a crime. Moreover, the Jews were large in number and would have fought back, causing a great civil war.

Therefore, Pharaoh plotted to thin out the Jewish population in a manner which even the Jews themselves would not detect. In order to deceive them, he first imposed a tax upon them. Since the citizens of a land are expected to participate in supporting it, the tax made the Jews believe that they were welcome as citizens of Egypt.

Pharaoh then told the midwives to kill the newborn Jewish males. This was to be done without even the knowledge of the women who gave birth. Next, Pharaoh commanded the entire Egyptian nation to throw all the Jewish male infants into the river (verse 22). Again, Pharaoh did not want his executioners involved. If a Jew would complain that his son had been murdered, Pharaoh would respond that the complainant should procure witnesses to the killing, after which revenge could be exacted. With this license granted to them, the Egyptians searched the houses of the Jews at night and brought the children out and killed them. This is why Yocheved was unable to keep her son Moses hidden (2:3).

This decree against the firstborn sons did not last very long. When Aaron was born, there evidently was not yet an edict [as there is no indication that he was hidden], and once Moses was born it was apparently rescinded, as Moses was permitted to live after he was rescued from the river by Pharaoh's daughter. It may be that Pharaoh's daughter, her mercy having been kindled regarding Moses, prevailed upon her father to abolish the decree. Alternatively, word may have spread that the king had been the instigator of the violence against the Jews, and he therefore was forced to rescind the decree. Or perhaps Pharaoh's astrologers told him to cease the killing.

When Moses and Aaron demanded that Pharaoh release the Israelites, Pharaoh responded by increasing the quota of bricks that the slaves were to produce. The Israelites complained to Moses and Aaron that "You have placed a sword in their hands to kill us" (5:21).

## Shemoth

The Israelites believed that Pharaoh would use Moses' protestations as a basis for an accusation that they were rebelling against the monarchy. Pharaoh would no longer need to resort to a surreptitious means of attack, and could proceed to declare an open war against the Israelites. *(Ramban)*

■ ■ ■

וְכַאֲשֶׁר יְעַנּוּ אֹתוֹ כֵּן יִרְבֶּה וְכֵן יִפְרֹץ וַיָּקֻצוּ מִפְּנֵי בְּנֵי יִשְׂרָאֵל.
*But the more [the Egyptians] oppressed them, the more [the Israelites] proliferated and spread. [The Egyptians] came to loathe the Israelites. (1:12)*

Rashi explains that the Egyptians loathed their own lives.

What practical difference does it make if the Egyptians did or did not despise themselves?

We are taught here that only someone who regards his own life as worthless is capable of embittering someone else's life. One who respects himself also respects others. Because the Egyptians loathed themselves, they were capable of afflicting the Israelites.

*(Mei Marom)*

■ ■ ■

וַיַּעֲבִדוּ מִצְרַיִם אֶת־בְּנֵי יִשְׂרָאֵל בְּפָרֶךְ.
*The Egyptians started to make the Israelites do hard labor. (1:13)*

The word *befarech*, which denotes hard labor, is the subject of a Talmudic dispute. R. Shmuel b. Nachmani translates it literally, as labor which causes one's body to break. The word *befarech* is rooted in the word *perichah*, "breaking." R. Eleazar, however, says that *befarech* is a contraction of *befeh rach*, "with soft-spokenness," and means that Pharaoh did not, at first, subject the Israelites to back-breaking slavery. Rather, he used a gentle approach to convince them to do work (Sotah 11a).

Rashi, in his commentary on the Talmud, explains the latter view by saying that, at first, the Egyptians paid the Israelites a salary for the work they did. The purpose of this was to acclimate the Jews to hard labor. Once this had been accomplished, the Egyptians forced the Israelites to work without pay.

## The Eternal Heritage

The Midrash relates that Pharaoh told the Jews to do him a favor and work along with him for one day. Now, no one, seeing Pharaoh himself working, would refrain from joining him. The Israelites, who were strong-bodied, assisted him and, working with all their strength, achieved a considerable output. That night, Pharaoh told the Jews to count the number of bricks they had made during the day. When they reported the total, Pharaoh told them that this amount would be their required daily output from then on.

■ ■ ■

וַיֹּאמֶר מֶלֶךְ מִצְרַיִם לַמְיַלְּדֹת הָעִבְרִיֹּת אֲשֶׁר שֵׁם הָאַחַת שִׁפְרָה וְשֵׁם הַשֵּׁנִית פּוּעָה.

*The king of Egypt spoke to the Hebrew midwives, whose names were Shifrah and Puah.* (1:15)

There exists a dispute among the Sages regarding the identity and nationality of Shifrah and Puah, the midwives. Rashi says that Shifrah was Yocheved, Moses' mother, and Puah was Miriam, Moses' sister. Rashi says that Yocheved is called Shifrah because, in her capacity of midwife, she improved, or made beautiful, the newly born children. (Shifrah is rooted in the word *shippur*, improvement or betterment.) Puah was the name given Miriam because she would speak and call aloud to the babies. (*Puah* is rooted in the word *pa'oh*, "crying aloud" — see Isaiah 42:14.) The source for Rashi's view is the Talmud (Sotah 11b), where another opinion regarding Puah is also recorded: that she was Elisheva, the sister of Nachshon and wife of Aaron (6:23).

Yet a third view is put forth, by Da'ath Zekenim MiBa'alei HaTosafoth: that there actually was only one midwife — Yocheved. Although Puah was Miriam, she was still a young girl at this juncture and could not have been a midwife. She did, however, speak to the infants, and it is her role in that capacity which is noted in the present verse.

Kli Yekar proposes that the midwives were Egyptian women, not Yocheved, Miriam, or Elisheva. He translates the verse to read:

## Shemoth

"The king of Egypt spoke to those who birthed the Hebrew women." This is also the view of Malbim.

After noting this opinion, Kli Yekar proceeds to ponder the Sages' view that the midwives were Yocheved and Miriam. He wonders why the Talmud assumes that Shifrah was Yocheved and Miriam was Puah, when perhaps the converse was true. Moreover, why does Scripture find it necessary to point out the change of names? He responds that the name Shifrah is more likely associated with Yocheved. At the age of 130, she had become youthful again and borne Moses (Rashi on 2:1). Puah is more likely associated with Miriam. Miriam was a prophetess (15:20), who foresaw her mother bearing the child who would redeem the Israelites (Sotah 12b). The word *nevu'ah*, "prophecy," refers to speech (see Rashi on 7:1). The word *Puah* also indicates speech, and so the Sages understood that Miriam and Puah were one and the same. Thus, both the miracle which occurred to Yocheved and the prophecy spoken by Miriam were for the purpose of bringing forth the savior of the Israelites.

Kli Yekar says that it is now evident why the Torah noted the new names of Yocheved and Miriam. Both of these women were involved, as indicated by the names Shifrah and Puah, with Moses, Israel's redeemer. The Torah is demonstrating that Pharaoh's strategy for forestalling Israel's redemption, the killing of its sons, was doomed to failure. Pharaoh had entrusted this task to the very people whom God had called upon to herald the redemption — Miriam by predicting Moses' birth, and Yocheved by bearing him. Hence, such an effort by Pharaoh certainly could not succeed.

Abravanel avers that it is impossible for Pharaoh to have called upon only two midwives. The Israelites were numerous, and certainly were not reliant upon only two midwives. Further, it cannot be — he says — that Shifrah and Puah were but the chief midwives (which is Ibn Ezra's opinion), because Scripture makes no mention that they had this status, as it does earlier regarding Pharaoh's chief wine steward, chief baker, and chief butcher (Genesis 37:36, 40:2). Moreover, even if these women were the chief midwives, commanding them to kill the children would have been pointless without telling their underlings as well, and we find no

## The Eternal Heritage

inference that Pharaoh ordered these midwives to so instruct the other midwives.

Therefore, Abravanel explains that the custom in Egypt was to have two midwives assisting at each birth. One was involved in the actual birthing of the child. The other was assigned to encourage the mother by speaking with her and by praying. The former was called Shifrah — she improved the status of the child — and the latter was called Puah, as her task was to speak. There were many sets of midwives; in each set, one woman was named Shifrah and the other Puah. These were not genuine names, but the titles of positions. Pharaoh now called in all of the midwives, not just two of them. He commanded every Shifrah and Puah regarding the male infants. And these women were Egyptians, for Pharaoh would not have relied on Hebrew women to heed his order.

Abravanel concludes that in the end his plan backfired, since the midwives, although Egyptian, saved the Hebrew infants.

∎ ∎ ∎

וַיֹּאמֶר בְּיַלֶּדְכֶן אֶת־הָעִבְרִיּוֹת וּרְאִיתֶן עַל־הָאָבְנָיִם אִם־בֵּן הוּא וַהֲמִתֶּן אֹתוֹ וְאִם־בַּת הִוא וָחָיָה.

[He] said, "When you deliver Hebrew women, you must look at the birth stool. If [the infant] is a boy, kill it, but if it is a girl, let it live." (1:16)

The word *ure'ithem*, "you must look," occurs three times in the Torah: in the present verse; *Ure'ithem eth ha'aretz*, "See what kind of land" is the Land of Canaan, in Moses' charge to the spies (Numbers 13:18); and *ure'ithem otho*, "when you see it," in reference to *tsitsith*, the ritual fringes (Ibid., 15:39).

This alludes to the Sages' assertion that if one considers three things he will not sin: whence he originated; where he will finally come to rest; and before Whom he will one day be forced to give an account of his actions (Avoth 3:1). Where did he originate? At the "birth stool." Where will he have a final resting place? Under the "land." Before Whom will he be judged? Before "Him" (*ure'ithem otho* may be rendered "when you see Him," God).

(R. Shmuel Shmelke of Nikolsburg)
∎

22

## Shemoth

Cursed are the wicked, for they try to best one another in their decrees against the Jewish people.

Cain killed Abel. Then Esau came along and said that Cain was a fool for killing Abel before their father Adam had died. Whereas Adam was capable of having more children [thereby thwarting Cain's attempt to be the sole possessor of the earth], to murder Abel before Adam had died was purposeless. Adam would simply produce a replacement. I, said Esau, will not commit the same error. I will wait until Isaac, my father, dies before I kill Jacob (Genesis 27:41).

Pharaoh came along and asserted that Esau had reasoned foolishly. Was he not aware that Jacob could beget many children during the time that Isaac was alive? Even if Jacob had subsequently been killed by Esau, his children would have perpetuated his name. Instead, Pharaoh said, I will destroy the male sons of Israel while they are infants — "If [the infant] is a boy, kill it."

Haman came along and pointed out that Pharaoh was a fool. Pharaoh had said that "if it is a girl, let it live." Haman asked: Did Pharaoh not know that one man can have children with many women, thus perpetuating the Jewish people? I, said Haman, will not make the same mistake. Haman decreed that all the Jews — men *and* women — were to be exterminated in one day (Esther 3:13), thus wiping them out.

In the future, Gog will say that all his predecessors were fools. They had tried to annihilate the Jewish people, neglecting the fact that as long as God exists His children will continue to exist. I — Gog shall say — will do battle with the God of Israel: "The kings of the earth will stand, and the nobles will be gathered together, against God and His Messiah" (Psalms 2:2).

However, "He who abides in the heavens will laugh; God will mock them" (Ibid., verse 4).

*(MeOtzareinu HaYashan,*
*in the name of Midrash HaGadol)*

## The Eternal Heritage

וַתִּירֶאןָ הַמְיַלְּדֹת אֶת־הָאֱלֹהִים וְלֹא עָשׂוּ כַּאֲשֶׁר דִּבֶּר אֲלֵיהֶן מֶלֶךְ מִצְרָיִם וַתְּחַיֶּיןָ אֶת־הַיְלָדִים.

*The midwives feared God, and did not do as the Egyptian king had ordered them. Rather, they allowed the infant boys to live. (1:17)*

"The midwives feared God" — Scripture is teaching us that one who is willing to risk his life for others in a circumstance where nobody will find out about his noble deed will not be able to withstand the temptation to save himself if he does not possess fear of Heaven. If the midwives had not feared God, they would have been unable to defy Pharaoh, as nobody knew of the risk they were taking. When one is faced with such a choice in private, the only check upon him is fear of God.

Now, the midwives not only saved the children, but fed them. Still, when announcing their reward (verse 21), the Torah attributes it to their fear of Heaven, for that was the critical factor.

*(Emeth LeYaakov)*

■

"The midwives feared God," and ignored Pharaoh's orders. Now, one may ask why the midwives did not simply resign their positions. They would thereby have satisfied God's demands by not participating in the murder of Jewish children, while not endangering themselves by ignoring Pharaoh's order. However, they feared that their replacements might heed Pharaoh's order. Instead of permitting the Jewish children to be imperiled, they put themselves at risk by defying Pharaoh. Moreover, as Rashi says, they supplied the birthing women with food.

*(Chafetz Chaim)*

In a similar vein, a young God-fearing man was offered a position as a rabbi in a certain town. He was reluctant to accept, feeling that he was not competent enough in deciding matters of Jewish law. R. Yisrael Salanter advised him to assume the post, arguing that if he did not accept it someone who was not God-fearing might be offered the position instead.

*(R. Shmuel Greiniman, in his commentary on Chafetz Chaim)*

■

## Shemoth

Why is it necessary for Scripture to repeat the same thought? Having said that the midwives "did not do as the Egyptian king had ordered," it is seemingly superfluous to add that "they allowed the infant boys to live."

The Sages say that the latter statement is not just a repetition of the former, and does not refer to the midwives' disregard of Pharaoh's order. Rather, it is testimony that they were extremely diligent in protecting the Jewish children — the midwives strove to provide the children with food and water (Sotah 11b). However, if this is the explanation for the verse's verbosity, we must explain why they had just begun now to supply sustenance to the infants. No hint is given that they did so earlier, before the decree was announced.

Two answers are possible. It may be that the midwives had provided food all along. Scripture seeks to emphasize that "The midwives feared God," not only regarding the decree, but even regarding the provision of food, and they therefore continued to provide such sustenance. Another answer is that perhaps at first the midwives did not bring food and water to the infants. However, upon the institution of the decree, they feared that any death among the infants — even one from natural causes, such as lack of nourishment — would be blamed on them. To free themselves from any suspicion, they began to provide food and water for the infants.

This may explain why the Torah states that "The midwives feared *eth haElokim,* God," when it could have said that they feared *haElokim*, which also means God. [*Eth* is superfluous, as it has no literal meaning, being only a stylistic embellishment.] However, *eth* is often understood as an amplification, and may be present here to include the Israelites. The midwives feared God *and* the Israelites, and so took measures to assert their innocence.

The verse states that the midwives "did not do as the Egyptian king had ordered them." *Ka'asher*, "as," could have been written *asher*, with the explanation that they did not do *what* Pharaoh commanded them. *Ka'asher* can be translated to mean "like." Thus, the explanation is that not only did they not do *as* Pharaoh commanded, but they did not do anything *similar* to what he ordered, either.

## The Eternal Heritage

Or, *ka'asher* may be translated as "when." Generally, when a king first promulgates a decree, it is scrupulously observed. As time goes by, this observance decreases. The midwives ignored Pharaoh's orders even at the outset, "*when* the Egyptian king had ordered them." Indeed, they went out of their way to subvert his injunction, supplying food and water to assist in keeping the Jewish infants alive. *(Ohr HaChayyim)*

∎

"The midwives . . . did not do as the Egyptian king had ordered them." The Midrash says that Pharaoh desired to have intercourse with the midwives, but they "did not do as the Egyptian king" had requested.

The Sages assert that the nations of the world mocked the Jews, saying that whereas the Egyptians dominated the bodies of the Jews — through slavery — they certainly must have had license with the Israelite women (Rashi on Numbers 26:5). Pharaoh, too, assumed that the great increase in the Israelite population had occurred by the union of Israelite women with Egyptian men. Just such an example was the son of Shlomith, daughter of Divri; this son grew up to curse God (Leviticus 24:10, 11). His father was an Egyptian, the man Moses killed after spotting him striking a Jew (Ibid., verse 10, in Rashi). Pharaoh held that if the Israelite children were born of Egyptian men it would be improper to exterminate them.

Pharaoh decided to test his theory on the midwives. If they were unwilling to have relations with him, even though he was "the Egyptian king," it would stand to reason that the rest of the Israelite women would resist the advances of their masters, who were not royal. Seeing that indeed the midwives did not heed his wishes, Pharaoh ordered the death of the Israelite males.

*(Chatham Sofer)*

∎ ∎ ∎

וַיֵּיטֶב אֱלֹהִים לַמְיַלְּדֹת וַיִּרֶב הָעָם וַיַּעַצְמוּ מְאֹד.
וַיְהִי כִּי־יָרְאוּ הַמְיַלְּדֹת אֶת־הָאֱלֹהִים וַיַּעַשׂ לָהֶם בָּתִּים.

*God was good to the midwives, and the people increased and became very numerous.*

## Shemoth

*Because the midwives had feared God, He made houses for them.* (1:20, 21)

The Torah states that God was good to the midwives. Rashi says that the benefit God provided for them was that "He made houses for them." God rewarded them by establishing the houses of the priests and Levites from Yocheved, Levi's daughter, and the royal house from Miriam.

Da'ath Zekenim MiBa'alei HaTosafoth disputes Rashi's view that the "houses" were the benefit earned by the midwives. Da'ath Zekenim objects that there is a thought that interrupts "God was good to the midwives" and "He made houses for them" — that thought being: "the people increased and became very numerous."

Da'ath Zekenim offers a different explanation of these verses, saying that when the midwives had told Pharaoh that the Israelite women were capable of giving birth without their assistance (verse 19, as explained by Rashi), Pharaoh did not believe them. However, when the Israelites started to multiply quickly, Pharaoh conceded that the midwives were correct. It would have been impossible for the two midwives to have assisted in so many births, so evidently the midwives were not needed by the Jewish women. The midwives' reward was that Pharaoh believed them, and this came about because "the people increased and became very numerous."

■

"He made houses for them" — While the simple explanation of the verse is that *God* made houses for the midwives, Malbim says that it was *Pharaoh* who made the houses for Yocheved and Miriam. Pharaoh observed that they feared God, and he suspected that if they were allowed to travel as they wished they would somehow succeed in evading his decree. Therefore, Pharaoh "made houses for them." He established homes where the midwives had to stay under guard. The guards were aware whenever the midwives were called for a birthing procedure. This allowed Pharaoh to better observe the actions of the midwives.

(Malbim's view paraphrases that of Abravanel, differing in minor points.)

■ ■ ■

## The Eternal Heritage

וַיֵּלֶךְ אִישׁ מִבֵּית לֵוִי וַיִּקַּח אֶת־בַּת־לֵוִי.

A *man of the house of Levi went and married Levi's daughter.* (2:1)

Why does the Torah not identify Moses' parents more precisely, by saying that Amram married Yocheved? Additionally, why does the Torah choose to stress that a "man" took a "daughter"?

Moses was the man of God, the one who went up to the heavens to receive the Torah. God was concerned that, at a future date, it might be claimed that Moses was not human. Some men might begin to worship him as a god. In order to preclude this possibility, Scripture chose here, at the description of Moses' birth, to assert that he was the son of a "man" and a "daughter." Moses, the leader of all the prophets, was human. *(Kehillath Yitzchak)*

■

Why does the Torah neglect to mention the names of Moses' parents, referring to them only as a "man" and a "daughter"?

This is done to teach us that every Jewish couple — any man and woman — is capable of producing an offspring who will be a savior of Israel.

*(Sefer Yuchsin)*

■

"A daughter of Levi" — She became youthful looking, although she was 130 years of age (Rashi).

Rashi is attempting to explain why Yocheved is called a *bath*, which indicates a young woman, when she was actually quite old at the time she bore Aaron and Moses. Rashi's view is consistent with his opinion earlier (Genesis 46:15) that Yocheved was born at the time that Jacob and his sons immigrated to Egypt. Since the Israelites lived in Egypt for 210 years, and Moses was eighty years old at the time of the Exodus, Yocheved was 130 when she gave birth to Moses.

Ibn Ezra (Ibid., verse 23) disagrees with Rashi, asserting that Scripture takes great pains to comment on Sarah's birthing of Isaac at the advanced age of ninety. Certainly, then, if Yocheved had been 130 at this juncture, Scripture would have made explicit mention of it. (For an extended discussion of this dispute, and a

## Shemoth

retort by Ramban to Ibn Ezra's view, see The Eternal Heritage, Genesis II, 46:15.)

The Maggid of Dubno responds to Ibn Ezra's question with a parable:

A group of fund-raisers was gathered together at an inn. They entered into a discussion about their profession, and agreed that it had taken a great downturn. Even rich men were doling out mere pittances.

One man, however, boasted that he had recently received a large sum — one ruble — from a wealthy donor. The others, astonished, asked for the details of when and where the donation had occurred. The man related that he had come to a particular town on Purim, during the holiday's festive meal, and had been given the ruble by the wealthy man.

The others laughed derisively. They said that such a donation on another date would have been noteworthy. Purim, however, is a day on which people are exceedingly happy. Everyone, even the stingiest of men, is willing to make a donation on Purim.

The same, said the Maggid of Dubno, applied to Yocheved and Sarah. During the latter's day, her bearing of Isaac at the age of ninety was truly miraculous. Women were accustomed then to giving birth at an earlier age. But Yocheved lived at a time when all the Israelite women were giving birth in an unnatural fashion — they were bearing sextuplets (Rashi on 1:7). Furthermore, these children were all healthy — "Their population increased and they became very mighty" (Ibid.). As everyone was experiencing miracles, there was no need to mention that Yocheved had also been the beneficiary of a miracle.

■

The Talmud asks: Is it possible that a woman 130 years of age would be termed a *bath*, a "daughter"? R. Yehuda answers that Yocheved became youthful again (Sotah 12a).

Why is the term "daughter" problematic? Does the fact that Yocheved was 130 years old change her status as "Levi's daughter"?

The Talmud is not bothered by the mere fact that, at 130 years of age, Yocheved is termed a *bath;* it is troubled on a different score.

## The Eternal Heritage

Two of the Sages mentioned in Ethics of the Fathers, *Pirkei Avoth*, are Ben Bag Bag and Ben Hei Hei (5:22, 23), "son of Bag Bag" and "son of Hei Hei." Tosafoth Yom Tov writes that these two men were young and not ordained when they made the statements quoted in their names, and were therefore called by the names of their more well-known fathers, Bag Bag and Hei Hei.

The Talmud's thrust here is similar. Why would a 130-year-old woman be called "Levi's daughter"? At her age, Yocheved had certainly acquired her own reputation. Why, then, was she identified by her father Levi's name and not her own name?

*(R. Avraham Polkaver)*

■ ■ ■

וַתַּהַר הָאִשָּׁה וַתֵּלֶד בֵּן וַתֵּרֶא אֹתוֹ כִּי־טוֹב הוּא וַתִּצְפְּנֵהוּ שְׁלֹשָׁה יְרָחִים.
*The woman became pregnant and had a son. She realized that he was good, and she hid him for three months.* (2:2)

According to the Sages, Moses was born on the seventh day of Adar. Moses was hidden until the sixth day of Sivan, which completes three months from the seventh day of Adar. The sixth of Sivan coincides with the day the Jews were given the Torah at Mount Sinai (Sotah 12b).

This, says Alshich, is why the Torah says that Moses was *tov*, "good." The Torah is also called *tov*, "good," as it says, "I have given you a good gift" (Proverbs 4:2). Yocheved saw that her house filled with light when Moses was born (Rashi). Whereas light symbolizes the Torah (Proverbs 6:23), she concluded that, until the sixth of Sivan, the merit of Moses' receiving the Torah would protect him, and so she was unafraid to keep him hidden in the house for three months.

■

The Talmud (Sotah 12b) says that Pharaoh's astrologers foresaw the leader of the Israelites meeting his downfall due to water. For this reason, Pharaoh ordered the Hebrew males thrown into the Nile. When Moses was hidden there, the astrologers no longer saw this sign, and concluded that their task had been accomplished. They erred, however, in thinking the Nile was the water in question,

## Shemoth

when actually Moses' downfall occurred at the waters of Merivah (Numbers 20:12).

The Talmud continues by quoting R. Chanina b. Papa, who says that Moses was hidden on the twenty-first day of Nissan, the date of the Red Sea crossing. The angels asked God: Is it possible that the one who is destined to sing at the Red Sea on this day should be smitten on the same day?

R. Acha b. Chanina, however, says that this was the sixth of Sivan. The angels asked: Is it possible that the one who will accept the Torah on this day should be smitten on the same day?

The Talmud continues that it is given that Moses was born on the seventh of Adar. According to R. Acha b. Chanina, the present verse, in saying "she hid him for three months," is quite understandable. The sixth of Sivan follows the seventh of Adar by three months. However, what of R. Chanina b. Papa's view? The time from 7 Adar to 21 Nissan is a month and a half, not three months. The Talmud answers that he would maintain that this was a leap year, in which the month of Adar was repeated. While there were not three full months, there was most of Adar I, all of Adar II, and most of Nissan. This may be correctly described as "three months."

Maharsha contends that R. Chanina b. Papa and R. Acha b. Chanina dispute the Talmud's earlier view that the Egyptians did not realize Moses' downfall was to be the waters of Merivah. This was not the incident they envisioned. Rather, they saw the Israelite redeemer succumbing to the Nile waters, and thus ordered the drowning of all the males. And Moses should have died in the Nile. However, the angels interceded in his behalf, citing as cause of his rescue either his status as singer of praise to God or that of his being the lawgiver. The decree that Moses die at the Nile was voided because of this intercession.

■ ■ ■

וַתֵּתַצַּב אֲחֹתוֹ מֵרָחֹק לְדֵעָה מַה־יֵּעָשֶׂה לוֹ.
*[The child's] sister stood at a distance to see what would happen to him.* (2:4)

The Talmud says that when Miriam later contracted leprosy she was rewarded for her vigil over Moses. The Israelites did not commence traveling until she had been cured and her banishment had ended (Numbers 12:15). Although Miriam had watched Moses for only an hour, and the Israelites delayed their journey for an entire week on her account, the principle is that a reward exceeds in scope the deed it recompenses (Sotah 9b, 11a).

This principle is derived from Scripture's pronouncements regarding the effect of one's actions upon his descendants. It is written that good deeds reverberate for two thousand generations, while evil deeds have a malevolent effect for four generations (34:7, and Rashi). Thus, good deeds obtain a reward 500 times the magnitude of the punishment meted out for evil deeds (Tosefta Sotah, Ch. 4).

Tosafoth (Sotah 11a) points out that Miriam did not actually stand watch over Moses for an entire hour. If that had been the case, then the seven days the Israelites waited for her would not have been five-hundredfold the amount of time she spent. Rather, says Tosafoth, she tarried for a quarter of an hour or a third of an hour.

Tosafoth is bothered by the Talmud's implication that Miriam was compensated *in full* for her good deed by the delay of the Israelites' journey. Whereas this could not be the case if she had watched Moses for a full hour, Tosafoth explains that she watched him for a shorter time.

Maharsha points out that, while the figure of a third of an hour would yield approximately a five-hundredfold reward (actually the figure is 504), the figure of a quarter-hour would yield considerably more. He asserts that if one uses this figure one must also assume that a misdeed results in a punishment of a somewhat larger magnitude than itself, so that the five hundred-to-one ratio is maintained.

Iyun Yaakov objects that neither figure yields precisely a five-hundredfold reward, and so proposes an alternative. He says that to consider the full seven days which the Israelites delayed their journey a reward for Miriam is an error. Only six days may be calculated as the reward, since one of the seven days was the Sabbath, and travel is prohibited on the Sabbath. Thus, the fact that the Israelites tarried on the Sabbath was not due to Miriam's

## Shemoth

banishment. There is, in addition, the requirement to add on at least a small amount of time to the Sabbath from the time periods preceding and following it. Hence, Miriam's reward was actually a fraction less than six days. Now, if Miriam watched over Moses for twenty minutes (a third of an hour), of which there are seventy-two periods per day, seventy-two times six yields 432, of which two periods may be subtracted in consideration of the time one must add to the Sabbath. Thus, we have a figure seventy less than 500. If she watched Moses for fifteen minutes (a quarter-hour), of which there are ninety-six periods in a day, ninety-six times six yields 576. Subtracting six periods for the time appended on to the Sabbath, one is left with 570, seventy periods more than the reward coming to her. (The amounts subtracted for the time added to the Sabbath are obviously arbitrary.) Iyun Yaakov asserts that Miriam watched Moses for seventeen-and-a-half minutes — precisely half the time between a third of an hour and a quarter-hour. This is what Tosafoth means when he uses these figures. Indeed, says Iyun Yaakov, one may read Tosafoth to say "between a third- and a quarter-hour" instead of "a third- *or* a quarter-hour."

Tosafoth continues by pointing out that the penalty for the Israelites' believing the evil report of the men Moses sent to spy out Canaan was "one year for each day" (Numbers 14:34). The spies spent forty days on their mission, and so the Israelites were compelled to remain in the desert for forty years. We see, insists Tosafoth, that the magnitude of punishment in the incident of the spies exceeded the magnitude of reward received by Miriam. How, then, can it be maintained that the magnitude of reward exceeds that of punishment?

Tosafoth's reasoning is perplexing. Miriam received a five-hundredfold reward. The Israelites were punished three hundred sixty-fivefold — one year for every day. How can Tosafoth maintain that here is proof that one is punished to a greater degree than one is rewarded? If anything, the converse has been proved!

Maharsha proposes that Tosafoth does not mean to say that the punishment of the Israelites exceeded the reward of Miriam. Tosafoth merely intends to question the Tosefta's declaration that reward is meted out at a five hundred-to-one ratio in respect to punishment. If Miriam was rewarded five-hundredfold, and the Israelites were penalized three hundred sixty-fivefold, the difference between reward and punishment is evidently much smaller.

The fact is, however, that Tosafoth quite clearly says that the case of the Israelites demonstrates that punishment is meted out in greater magnitude than reward, and so Maharsha's explanation is difficult to accept.

Retzuf Ahavah explains Tosafoth's question along the lines of Maharsha's view. However, Retzuf Ahavah goes even further, asserting that there occurred a printer's error in our text of Tosafoth. Our text reads: "If so, the measure of punishment (of the spies) exceeded the measure of reward of Miriam." Retzuf Ahavah amends as follows: "If so, the measure of reward of Miriam was not five hundred times the measure of punishment (of the spies)."

While Tosafoth does not attempt to answer this question, Tosafoth Yom Tov says that the case of the spies was a unique one. In reality, death should have immediately overcome the Israelites for believing the spies' report. However, God was generous to the Israelites and permitted each Jew to live until the age of sixty. To do so, He had to extend the period of their wandering for forty years, since the penalty had been pronounced upon every Israelite who had attained the age of twenty (Ibid., verse 29). Thus, the actual punishment would have been of a much briefer duration than forty years. The length of time the Israelites spent in the desert was to enable them to live longer.

Etz Yosef adopts a similar stance to that of Tosafoth Yom Tov. Etz Yosef refers to the Midrash Tanchuma (Parshath BeShalach, Ch. 1), which lists two reasons why God kept the Israelites in the desert for forty years. Firstly, God desired that they be immersed in Torah life by the time they came to Canaan. Otherwise, every man would have settled his land and spent all his time working it, leaving no time for Torah study. Secondly, when the Canaanites heard that the Israelites were coming, they destroyed the crops and trees of the land. God had promised Abraham that the Israelites would inherit a land of plenty, and so He delayed their arrival until the Canaanites regrew their fields. It is thus evident that the forty years the Israelites tarried in the desert were not a punishment for the sin of the spies; they were kept in the desert for their own good.

Given this, Etz Yosef maintains that the punishment of the Israelites for believing the spies was to have continued for only forty days. They were all to have perished during that period, a length of time commensurate with the length of time the spies sinned. However, only those Israelites above the age of twenty were consigned to death. Since the youth had to be kept in the desert until forty years had elapsed, God dealt kindly with the others, allowing each to live until the age of sixty.

Etz Yosef continues that this explanation serves as well to resolve a problem with the text of God's oath to keep the Israelites in the desert for forty years. God said their punishment would be (in the literal reading) "a day for a year, a day for a year." If the punishment were a year in the desert for each day of sinning, God should have decreed "a year for a day," not "a day for a year." Rather, the penalty was forty days of death. However, instead of running consecutively, these forty days were to be spread over forty years. "A day for a year" is explained thusly: One of the forty days of punishment would fall during each of the next forty years. And that day was the ninth of Av, on which, according to the Midrash Eichah, each year those Israelites who had turned sixty died.

With this, Tosafoth's problem is resolved, as the punishment of the Israelites was forty days of death, commensurate with the forty days they sinned — a ratio of one-to-one.

■ ■ ■

וַתֵּרֶד בַּת־פַּרְעֹה לִרְחֹץ עַל־הַיְאֹר וְנַעֲרֹתֶיהָ הֹלְכֹת עַל־יַד הַיְאֹר וַתֵּרֶא אֶת־הַתֵּבָה בְּתוֹךְ הַסּוּף וַתִּשְׁלַח אֶת־אֲמָתָהּ וַתִּקָּחֶהָ.

*Pharaoh's daughter went to bathe in the Nile, while her maidens walked along the Nile's bank. She saw the box among the reeds, and sent her maiden, who fetched it.* (2:5)

Why does the verse say that Pharaoh's daughter went to bathe *al ha'ye'or,* literally, "above the Nile"? Moreover, the Sages say that she desired to wash off, to cleanse herself from, the idols of her father's house (Megillah 13a). Why did she choose this particular moment to distance herself from idolatry? Finally, why do the Sages say that she cleansed herself of the idols of her father's house? Why don't they say simply that she cleansed herself of idol worship?

To answer these questions, a further question must be posed. It states earlier that a new king ascended the throne in Egypt, who had not known Joseph (1:8). Why was it necessary to point out that the new Pharaoh did not know Joseph? The answer is that Joseph had informed the Egyptians that Jacob gave Pharaoh the blessing that the Nile would rise to greet him. Egypt would be blessed with sufficient water due to Jacob (Rashi on Genesis 47:10). When Jacob came, the famine ceased. Knowing this, the Egyptians bore no ill will toward the Jews; it was due to the patriarch of the Jews that Egypt had been blessed. And certainly the Egyptians would not have consented to drown the children of Israel in the Nile, the very body of water which had been blessed due to Jacob. No one would have tolerated such an affront to the conscience.

However, Pharaoh was a "new king" in the sense that his decrees were new — different (Rashi on 1:8). He proclaimed himself a god. He said that he had created the Nile, that he was its owner, and that for this reason it rose at his feet — not due to any blessing given Pharaoh by Jacob. This is the meaning of the statement that Pharaoh did not know Joseph; he denied Joseph's assertion that Jacob was responsible for Egypt's fruitfulness. Pharaoh was then able to advocate the oppression of the Jews (Ibid., verse 10). Whereas the Jews had not benefited the Egyptians, the Egyptians were not bound by conscience to desist from harming them.

In its description of Pharaoh's dreams, Scripture states that he was standing *al ha'ye'or* "above the Nile," instead of "at the Nile" (Genesis 41:1). R. Bachya says that this was an allusion to the fact that Pharaoh would, in the future, assert that he had created the Nile.

The questions can now be answered. Pharaoh's daughter did not, at this juncture, abandon all idol worship. She forsook only the idol

## Shemoth

worship of her father's house — the worship of Pharaoh as a god. She bathed *al ha'ye'or*, on the Nile — she rejected her father's claim that he was *al ha'ye'or*, above the Nile, that he was a god and had created it. Rather, she believed that the Nile had been blessed due to Jacob. Therefore, she saved the Hebrew child who was floating on the river, considering it abominable for the Egyptians to use the very object which had been blessed by Jacob to harm one of Jacob's descendants. *(Chatham Sofer)*

∎

Rashi advances two explanations for how Bithyah (Pharaoh's daughter's name — see Chronicles I 4:18) fetched Moses. Either she sent her maiden to take the box out of the river, or she stretched her hand out and took the box. *Amathah* may be translated "her maiden" or "her hand." The opinion that says she stretched out her hand maintains that a miracle occurred whereby her arm became elongated to the length of several cubits — *amathah* may be understood to imply *amoth*, cubits (Sotah 12b).

It is asked: How did Pharaoh's daughter know that God would stretch her arm miraculously, enabling her to rescue Moses? R. Yitzchak of Warka explains that one who earnestly desires to assist someone in need does not first consider whether his efforts will be successful. He goes ahead and makes the attempt — he extends his hand. *(MeOtzareinu HaYashan)*

∎

The word *amathah* is translated by Rashi as "her maidservant." Rashi notes that one Talmudic Sage (Sotah 12b) takes *amathah* to mean "her (Bithyah's) hand," which was extended several *amoth*, cubits, in order to enable her to reach Moses.

An *amah*, cubit, is the unit of measure equivalent to the distance from the elbow to the tip of the middle finger. The source for this measurement is thus the arm, and so it would not be inappropriate to term the arm or hand an *amah*. But the Talmud notes that this is not a common usage, as *yadah* is the term generally used to denote "her hand." The deviation from the common usage is taken as a sign that Bithyah's arm was miraculously extended several cubits. In this particular case, given the supernatural event, there was a reason to eschew *yadah* in favor of *amathah* — in order to stress the extension, by several *amoth*, of Bithyah's arm.

Although Rashi takes note of the Rabbinic exposition of *amathah*, he objects that the construction of *amathah* is not in consonance with it. Were *amathah* to denote "her hand," and not "her maidservant," the *mem* should have been punctuated differently. It should have carried a *dagesh chazak*, a hard dot, with an accompanying hard pronunciation. Since the *mem* is *rafah*, soft, the word can only refer to a maidservant.

Radak, however, records an alternate reading for *amathah*. Says Radak: "There is a dispute regarding the reading of this word, for some read it with a *dagesh chazak*." This being the case, the translation of *amathah* would be "her hand." Indeed, Radak continues that Sa'adiah Gaon, in his Arabic translation of the Torah, renders the verse: "She put out her arm."

■ ■ ■

וַתִּפְתַּח וַתִּרְאֵהוּ אֶת־הַיֶּלֶד וְהִנֵּה־נַעַר בֹּכֶה וַתַּחְמֹל עָלָיו וַתֹּאמֶר מִיַּלְדֵי הָעִבְרִים זֶה.

She opened it and saw the boy. He was crying. She had pity on him, and said, "He is of the Hebrew boys." (2:6)

*Vatir'ehu*, literally, "she saw him," should be written *vateire*, "she saw," since the next words, *eth hayeled*, mean "the boy." What is the purpose of the repetition, that she saw "him, the boy"? The Talmud answers that Pharaoh's daughter saw the Divine Presence with Moses (Sotah 12b). But what nuance in the word *vatir'ehu* would indicate that the Divine Presence was with Moses?

It seems that this is based on the Talmudic assertion (Shabbath 104a) that *hu* is one of God's names. Similarly, the Mishnah records the word *hu* in the phrase *ani vahu hoshiah na* (Sukkah 45a). The verse states, *vatir'ehu*, which can be translated, "she saw *hu*, God."

(Vilna Gaon)

With Vilna Gaon's explanation of this verse, we may resolve a

## Shemoth

dispute regarding the pronunciation of the phrase *ani vahu hoshiah na*. These words are part of the liturgy of Hoshana Rabba. In some prayer books, the reading is *ani vaho hoshiah na*. However, it is evident that Vilna Gaon is of the opinion that the proper reading is *vahu*.

Further proof that the word is pronounced *hu* may be adduced, *inter alia*, from Torah Temimah's explanation of a Talmudic gloss by Rashi (Shabbath 133b). Commenting on the phrase "This is my God and I will glorify Him" (15:2), the Talmud instructs, "Glorify Him means one should seek to imitate Him. Just as He is gracious and merciful, so should you be gracious and merciful." Rashi says that the word *anvehu*, "I will glorify Him," is being read by the Talmud as a contraction of *ani vahu*, "I and He" — that is, men should seek to cleave to God's ways. Torah Temimah avers that Rashi bases himself on the words *ani vahu hoshiah na*, where we find that God's name is composed of the letters *heh* and *vav*, in the word *hu*. Thus, while Torah Temimah's intent here is not to discuss the pronunciation of the word, it is evident that he believes Rashi held it to be *hu*, not *ho*.

■

The verse terms Moses a *na'ar*, a lad, although he was only an infant. Rashi comments that he had the voice of a lad.

R. Yitzchak of Torchin says that the fact that an unnatural event — an infant crying as if he were a lad — occurred here was what made Pharaoh's daughter realize that Moses was of Israelite stock. It indicated that this child belonged to the nation that has lived and continued to exist only through extra-natural means.

■

"She had pity on him" — Ohr HaChayyim is of the opinion that Pharaoh's daughter was bent on saving Moses all along. When she saw the box in which Moses had been put, she understood that a child was in it, and set out to save him. This is indicated by the present verse's statement that she opened the box and saw "the boy." Had it said that she saw "a boy," the implication would have been that the sight was unexpected. "*The* boy" infers that she saw precisely what she believed she would find — she saw "the boy" that she had known would be in the box.

Since her decision to rescue Moses had been made before she opened the box, the "pity" which she felt upon opening it must refer to something beyond his rescue. Ohr HaChayyim explains that, out of mercy, she desired to breastfeed Moses. Proof of this comes from the following verse, where Miriam offered to find a nursing woman for Moses. And the Sages say (Sotah 12b) that Pharaoh's daughter brought Moses to many Egyptian women, but Moses would not suck.

Ohr HaChayyim continues that the words "He is of the Hebrew boys" need amplification. What did Pharaoh's daughter mean to add when she said this? Since it was the Israelite children who were being hidden, was it not obvious that this child was a Hebrew? On the other hand — Ohr HaChayyim continues — if the necessity to specify Moses' nationality was based on the Sages' comment that, beginning with that particular day, Egyptian male infants were also to be drowned, how indeed did she know that Moses was a Hebrew? Now, we might explain that she knew he was a Hebrew because he refused to be nursed by Egyptian women. Nonetheless, it seems pointless for Pharaoh's daughter to have made an issue of Moses' ancestry.

Ohr HaChayyim offers two solutions for this problem. It may be that, although Pharaoh's daughter knew that there was a baby in the box, she was uncertain about its ethnicity. She believed it might be Egyptian, and due to this doubt she saved Moses. Had she known that the child was a Hebrew, she would not have rescued it. Thus, her assertion that Moses was a Hebrew serves as an indicator that she had not intended to save an Israelite baby. She had acted to save what she believed was an Egyptian, but would not have saved Moses otherwise, as she would have pitied only her own countryman.

While it is true that Pharaoh's daughter kept Moses and sought a nurse for him, that is not necessarily evidence that she had known he was an Israelite. The Sages say that she had come to the Nile to bathe because she had contracted leprosy, and was healed when she

## Shemoth

touched Moses' box. Additionally, she saw that Moses was a unique child. These were good enough reasons for her to raise him despite her not intending to save an Israelite.

Alternatively, she had known there was a Hebrew child in the box, and nevertheless rescued it. In saying that Moses was a Hebrew, she was giving the reason for his refusal to suck from Egyptian women.

■

How did Pharaoh's daughter know that this was a Hebrew child?

One of the identifying signs of Jews is that they are merciful folk (Yevamoth 79a). Now, it is stated that when one sees a righteous person, a *tzaddik*, the holiness of the *tzaddik* affects the observer. Pharaoh's daughter saw the child and "had pity on him." It was thus evident to her that this was a Hebrew child, that her compassion for him was ignited by her seeing him and his holiness affecting her.

(*R. Aharon Halberstam of Sanz*)

■ ■ ■

וַיִּגְדַּל הַיֶּלֶד וַתְּבִאֵהוּ לְבַת־פַּרְעֹה וַיְהִי־לָהּ לְבֵן וַתִּקְרָא שְׁמוֹ מֹשֶׁה וַתֹּאמֶר כִּי מִן־הַמַּיִם מְשִׁיתִהוּ.

*When he had grown older, [his mother] brought him to Pharaoh's daughter. She adopted him as her own son and named him Moses (Moshe), because she said, "I took him out (meshithihu) from the water." (2:10)*

A *maskil* (someone influenced by the Enlightenment) asked R. Yisrael of Ruzhin how he could justify having an extravagant court, one that exhibited splendor, royalty, and wealth to excess. Wasn't a *tzaddik* required to live a life of moderation and thereby serve as an example to others?

In response, R. Yisrael pointed out that the Torah tells us that Moses was raised in a palace, by Pharaoh's daughter. Why was it important that Moses experience such a life style, instead of growing up among his brethren in an atmosphere of poverty? The answer, said R. Yisrael, is that had Moses been poor he might have overlooked God's promise to give the Jews wealth as they departed

Egypt (Genesis 15:14). Having been raised in a poor environment, he might have considered freedom alone to be sufficient — he would have felt wealthy in that he was free. It was necessary for him to experience wealth so that he would insist on the Jews being given riches when they prepared to leave Egypt. [The same, then, was true of R. Yisrael's court. His wealth would cause him to demand that, at the time of the final redemption, the Jews be supplied with riches.] *(MeOtzareinu HaYashan)*

■ ■ ■

וַיִּפֶן כֹּה וָכֹה וַיַּרְא כִּי אֵין אִישׁ וַיַּךְ אֶת־הַמִּצְרִי וַיִּטְמְנֵהוּ בַּחוֹל.
*[Moses] looked all around and saw that no one was [there]. He killed the Egyptian and hid the body in the sand. (2:12)*

Rashi (on verse 14) says that Moses killed the Egyptian by pronouncing God's Ineffable Name. Ramban disagrees, and says that Moses struck the Egyptian, killing him.

■

Moses "saw that no one was [there]." Rashi comments that Moses peered into the future and saw that nobody who was to descend from the Egyptian would convert to Judaism. Therefore, Moses proceeded to kill him. What forced Rashi to eschew the simple meaning of these words: that Moses looked around to make sure nobody would observe him killing the Egyptian? Had someone been there, he would have been afraid to do so and would have desisted, as one is not required to endanger himself in order to save his fellow man.

It must be that Rashi could not explain it this way because there were indeed people watching the scene unfold: Dathan and Aviram were there (verse 14). Rashi had to advance a different explanation, that Moses looked into the future to examine the Egyptian's descendants.

This, however, also demands scrutiny. If someone merits the death penalty, is the court of law trying the case obligated to examine the quality of the defendant's descendants?

The answer is that this particular case differed from general cases. Moses killed the Egyptian by pronouncing God's name. He used a

*Shemoth*

metaphysical means, and thus had to use the yardstick used by the Heavenly Court before he meted out justice to the Egyptian. God's court does take into account the quality of one's descendants before pronouncing sentence. As an example, the Talmud says that Hezekiah did not attempt to have children because he foresaw that they would not be virtuous, but was admonished by Isaiah that such a consideration was a matter for God, not for men (Berachoth 10a). Apparently, God takes the future into account.

Once we say that Moses used God's name to kill the Egyptian, we may refine the explanation for why Rashi did not say that Moses looked about to make sure nobody was observing him. Rashi cannot accept the simple explanation, because whereas Moses did not physically assault the Egyptian, an observer would not have been able to implicate Moses. He would not have feared arrest. It must be, then, that Dathan and Aviram heard Moses use God's name, and understood that this caused the Egyptian's death. [That Dathan and Aviram knew what the weapon had been is apparent from the fact that Moses' use of God's name is gleaned from their conversation with him (Rashi on verse 14).] Alternatively, as Mizrachi says, they watched Moses hide the dead man in the sand and, not having seen him use force, deduced that he used God's name.

*(R. Yaakov Kamenetsky)*

Mizrachi asks why Moses peered into the future before killing the Egyptian. If the man deserved to die for having had relations with Shlomith and for hitting her husband, what difference did it make whether the Egyptian was destined to have a child who would convert to Judaism?

Similarly — asks Mizrachi — we find that, although two nations, Moab and Midian, caused the Israelites to engage in illicit sexual relations at Shittim (Numbers 25:1, 31: 16), only Midian was punished, all its males being slain. God spared Moab because Ruth was destined to descend from that nation (Bava Kamma 38b).

Mizrachi (as explained by Gur Aryeh) answers that Moses did not have actual evidence that the Egyptian had had relations with Shlomith. Moses knew this through Divine Inspiration. Therefore, if

Moses saw, also with Divine Inspiration, a convert among the Egyptian's descendants, Moses could not have killed him. If Moses relied on Divine Inspiration to execute the Egyptian, he had to spare him if there was mitigating information supplied by the same prophecy.

Divrei David answers the question differently, saying that there is a difference between death at the hands of a court and death at the hand of Heaven. A court does not have the right to deal with the future when judging a case. However, the Heavenly Court does take the future into account. Since the Sages say that Moses killed the Egyptian by speaking God's Ineffable Name (Rashi on verse 14), this case constituted death at Heaven's hand, and so Moses had to consider the future.

This means that R. Yaakov Kamenetsky and Divrei David are in agreement.

Their view seems to be in opposition to that of Moshav Zekenim. The Torah says that when Ishmael was dying of thirst in the desert he was spared "because God has heard the voice of the boy where he is" (Genesis 21:17). The Midrash and Talmud (Rosh HaShanah 16b) take the words "where he is" to mean that Ishmael was saved because he was presently righteous. God declined to condemn him based on the fact that in the future the Ishmaelites would cause Jews to die during the latter's expulsion from the Land of Israel by Nebuchadnezzar.

Moshav Zekenim objects that a rebellious son *(ben sorer u'moreh)* is executed as a youth for committing minor crimes, because the Torah foresees that he will grow up to become a major criminal. Why is a rebellious son judged based on the future, while Ishmael was not? Moshav Zekenim answers that when death is meted out by Heaven the future is not considered. However, when a human court considers a case, it does take the future into account. Therefore, the rebellious son, who is judged by a court, is condemned, while Ishmael was spared.

Thus, the views of Moshav Zekenim and Divrei David are in diametric opposition.

■

## Shemoth

Rashi says that Moses foresaw that none of the Egyptian's descendants would convert to Judaism.

The man who cursed God (Leviticus 10:11) was the son of this Egyptian and Shlomith, daughter of Divri, who was the wife of the man the Egyptian had beaten. The previous night, the Egyptian had supplanted the man in his bed. On this day, realizing that Shlomith's husband suspected he had engaged in relations with her, he took to beating the man (Rashi on verse 11). While one may see this as a contradiction in Rashi — was not the blasphemer a convert? — it is evident that Rashi is not inconsistent. The blasphemer was conceived on the night before the Egyptian's death, when he copulated with Shlomith. Moses looked into the future to see if the Egyptian's life should be spared because his continued existence would yield the benefit of a descendant who would convert to Judaism. Whereas the blasphemer had already been conceived, there was no benefit regarding him which would accrue by sparing the life of the Egyptian.

Divrei David, however, proposes an alternative answer. Even if the Egyptian's already-conceived child were a reason for granting him clemency, this would apply only if the child would become a righteous Jew. Wicked Jews are, in a certain sense, not part of the "nation of Israel." As the Talmud states regarding the commandment "Do not curse a leader of your people" (22:27), it does not apply to wicked men, as they are not termed "your people" (Bava Bathra 4a). Whereas the Egyptian's son grew to be a blasphemer, he was not qualified to spare his father.

■ ■ ■

וַיֵּצֵא בַּיּוֹם הַשֵּׁנִי וְהִנֵּה שְׁנֵי־אֲנָשִׁים עִבְרִים נִצִּים וַיֹּאמֶר לָרָשָׁע לָמָּה תַכֶּה רֵעֶךָ.

[Moses] went out the next day, and he saw two Hebrew men fighting. He asked of the evil one, "Why are you beating your brother?" (2:13)

"Your friend" infers one to whom you are similar. He is evil just as you are "the evil one" (Rashi).

*The Eternal Heritage*

What does Rashi wish to point out when he says that Moses scolded one of the men for hitting someone evil like he was?

Rambam states in Mishneh Torah that it is not forbidden to strike a wicked person (Hilchoth Chovel U'Mazik 5:1). This being the case, Moses should not have scolded the assailant. However, it is obvious that only a righteous person is not prohibited from striking an evil one. Someone evil has no right to assault an evil man.

This was Moses' assertion — that whereas the assailant was also evil, he had no right to strike his friend.

*(R. Yisrael Yehoshua Trunk of Kutno)*

∎

Rashi says that Moses asserted both men were evil.

Moses was not astonished that a wicked man was perpetrating an assault. Such is the behavior of evil men. Moses was, however, surprised that the victim was also evil. Generally, assailants will victimize righteous people, as such men are not versed in the ways of the wicked and are unable to respond successfully to an attack. It is rare for an assault to be made upon a wicked man, and this was cause for comment on Moses' part.

*(Ya'alath Chen)*

∎ ∎ ∎

וַיֹּאמֶר מִי שָׂמְךָ לְאִישׁ שַׂר וְשֹׁפֵט עָלֵינוּ הַלְהָרְגֵנִי אַתָּה אֹמֵר כַּאֲשֶׁר הָרַגְתָּ אֶת־הַמִּצְרִי וַיִּירָא מֹשֶׁה וַיֹּאמַר אָכֵן נוֹדַע הַדָּבָר.

He replied, "Who made you our prince and judge? Do you intend to kill me as you killed the Egyptian?" Moses was frightened. "The incident is known," he said. (2:14)

In describing the assault by the Egyptian on the Israelite, the Torah says that Moses saw the assailant "beating a Hebrew man from among his brothers" (verse 11, according to the literal reading). Binah LaIttim asks why the verse has to state that the Israelite was Moses' brother. If he was an Israelite, then he was by definition a brother of Moses.

Binah LaIttim therefore says that the word *me'echav*, "from among his brothers," is used to indicate that the Egyptian selected

## Shemoth

the Hebrew from among the Israelites who were present, that there were witnesses to the incident, but that they made no attempt to save their fellow Israelite.

Moses was astonished that the Israelites had not defended their brother, but decided that this inaction was due to fear on their part; having been slaves for so long, they had doubtless lost the ability to fight.

But the next day Moses observed two Israelites fighting.

Furthermore, they accused him of killing the Egyptian; the Israelites considered Moses' attack an evil act.

Observing all this, Moses said, "Now it is known." Now, declared Moses, I see the truth. The reason for the Israelites' inaction was not an unwillingness to fight, but rather an inability to recognize the difference between justice and injustice.

■ ■ ■

וַיִּשְׁמַע פַּרְעֹה אֶת־הַדָּבָר הַזֶּה וַיְבַקֵּשׁ לַהֲרֹג אֶת־מֹשֶׁה וַיִּבְרַח מֹשֶׁה מִפְּנֵי פַרְעֹה וַיֵּשֶׁב בְּאֶרֶץ־מִדְיָן וַיֵּשֶׁב עַל־הַבְּאֵר.

*Pharaoh heard about the affair and sought to put Moses to death. Moses fled from Pharaoh. He settled in Midian, and he sat by the well. (2:15)*

"He sat by the well" — Moses knew that Jacob had found his mate Rachel at a well, and so he too sat by a well (Rashi).

Why was it at this particular juncture — when Moses was fleeing from Pharaoh — that he chose to apply the lesson he had learned from Jacob and sat by the well? Why had he not done this before?

After the portion describing the bringing of Isaac upon the altar, Scripture relates that Abraham was told that his brother Nachor had produced children, among whom was Rebecca, who became Isaac's wife (Genesis 22:20-24). The Rabbis say that Abraham had regretted not marrying Isaac off earlier. Had Isaac died at Mount Moriah, his branch of the family would have ceased. Therefore, Abraham prayed that Isaac find a mate, and was immediately informed of Rebecca's birth.

Moses feared that Pharaoh would chase after him and kill him, thereby wiping out his family. Taking his lesson from Jacob, who had met his wife at a well, Moses now went to a well.

*(Yeshuoth Yaakov)*

■

Divrei David points out that although Moses sat by the well due to the example set by Jacob the latter apparently had not had an example to copy. How did Jacob know to go to a well in order to find his mate?

Divrei David answers that indeed Jacob did not have an example to follow, but that nonetheless one cannot pose an objection to his action. Jacob was attracted to the well by the unusual occurrence there — he saw that all the shepherds had gathered before the well was opened (Genesis 29:2, 3). There was nothing, however, to attract Moses to this particular well. (The shepherds and Jethro's daughters had not yet arrived.) Moses' action thus needs explanation, so Rashi says that he took his example from Jacob.

Levush HaOhrah responds that Jacob did have an example which he copied. Eliezer, Abraham's servant, had found Rebecca, Isaac's mate, at a well (Genesis 24:11). As for Eliezer, he was not following anyone's example. His case was pure happenstance. He had desired to water his camels and went to the well for that purpose.

Levush HaOhrah continues that one may not object to Jacob learning from a case that involved coincidence. Jacob did not glean from Eliezer anything more than that the young women went to the town well to draw water. And Jacob went to seek out such a girl, but God brought him one who went to water her flocks.

Now, given the fact that both Eliezer and Jacob had set examples, why is Rashi certain that Moses copied Jacob? Perhaps his role model was Eliezer. To this Levush HaOhrah answers that while Eliezer had found a girl who had come to draw water Jacob found a girl who went to water the flocks. Moses had to take into account both possibilities. His mate might be either a water-drawer or a waterer of the flocks. The reality was that Jethro's daughters went to water the flocks, as was the case with Jacob, not with Eliezer. Therefore, Rashi says that Moses took his lesson from Jacob.

■ ■ ■

## Shemoth

וַתֹּאמַרְןָ אִישׁ מִצְרִי הִצִּילָנוּ מִיַּד הָרֹעִים וְגַם דָּלֹה דָלָה לָנוּ וַיַּשְׁקְ אֶת־הַצֹּאן.

*[Jethro's daughters] replied, "An Egyptian man rescued us from the shepherds. He also drew water for us and watered the sheep." (2:19)*

The Midrash asks: Was Moses then an Egyptian that he is termed an "Egyptian man"? It answers that the Egyptian man referred to by the daughters of Jethro was not Moses, but the man Moses had killed in Egypt. Jethro's daughters thanked Moses for rescuing them. Moses responded that it was actually the Egyptian man he had killed who had brought about their rescue. Moses had come to the defense of the Jew whom the Egyptian had assaulted, and killed him. Pharaoh had attempted to arrest Moses, and so Moses had fled. It was through all of this that he had come to be at the well.

Jethro's daughters told their father that an "Egyptian man" — the man Moses killed — had triggered the sequence of events that resulted in their rescue.

The Midrash continues that based on the description of Moses given by his daughters Jethro concluded he was a descendant of Jacob. The daughters said that the waters had been blessed due to Moses, and that he had watered all of the flocks, including those of the shepherds. This coincided with Jacob's story, in which the well whose stone he uncovered was blessed.

R. Yaakov Kamenetsky avers that when Moses departed Pharaoh's palace to circulate in the world at large his entire purpose in doing so was to help oppressed people free themselves from their oppressors. On the first day, he spotted an Egyptian man striking a Jew, and so he killed the Egyptian. On the next day, he saw two Jews fighting, and he immediately rebuked the antagonist. He was then forced to flee. Now, it is the nature of fugitives that they strive to avoid involvement in controversies which concern the citizens of the place where they have taken refuge. This was demonstrated in Lot's case. Upon arriving in Sodom, Lot scolded the Sodomites, and was taken to task for his interference in local affairs (Genesis 19:9). However, seeing Jethro's daughters suffering at the hands of the shepherds, Moses did not desist from defending them. The essence

## The Eternal Heritage

of Moses was the pursuit of righteousness and justice. Because of this quality, Moses was selected to be the giver of the Torah, all of whose laws are righteous.

R. Yaakov continues that this corresponds with Moses' words to Jethro's daughters — that the Egyptian had saved them. Moses asserted that there was no reason for them to feel indebted to him. His nature was to love justice. He simply could not tolerate the perversion of justice, and thus had no alternative but to rescue them. His nature would permit nothing less. He then related that the same had occurred with the Egyptian, and they told all of this to their father. Jethro did not invite Moses to dine with them and arrange Moses' marriage to Tzipporah simply out of gratitude, but because he recognized the nature of Moses' makeup.

R. Yaakov adds that Jethro was the quintessential lover of justice and righteousness. The Talmud relates that Jethro knew of Pharaoh's plot against the Jewish male children, and fled Egypt. In reward, his descendants merited sitting in the Sanhedrin, the high court of justice (Sotah 11a). Jethro was unable to tolerate the injustice of Pharaoh's decree. It was this very attribute which he immediately recognized in Moses. God rewards a man corresponding to his deeds, and so Jethro merited being the catalyst for the inclusion in the Torah of a portion regarding a new court system (18:13-26). Moreover, this portion was named in his honor. Finally, his descendants merited sitting in the Sanhedrin.

■ ■ ■

וַיֹּאמֶר אֶל־בְּנֹתָיו וְאַיּוֹ לָמָּה זֶּה עֲזַבְתֶּן אֶת־הָאִישׁ קִרְאֶן לוֹ וְיֹאכַל לָחֶם.
[Jethro] said to his daughters, "Where is he now? Why did you abandon the man? Fetch him, and let him have food." (2:20)

Jethro said, literally, "let him eat bread, *lechem.*" Rashi comments that Jethro thought Moses might be a suitable marriage partner for one of his daughters, and indicated this with the word *lechem*, a euphemism for one's wife. Rashi cites as proof Joseph's admonition to his master's wife regarding his being forbidden to her. Joseph said that Potiphar had given him administration over everything in

## Shemoth

his house, "except for the bread *(lechem)* he ate" — i.e., Potiphar's wife (Genesis 39:6).

Chatham Sofer is puzzled by Jethro's choice of language. Why did he deem it proper to state his interest in Moses metaphorically? Moreover, from the tone of the verse it seems that Jethro was cross with his daughters for having not invited Moses into the house. If Jethro was concerned not about making certain that Moses had food, but about a possible opportunity for one of his daughters to find a husband, why was he angry? Was there any great sin on their part in not showing interest in Moses? Finally, it is not the custom for a woman to be presumptuous and ask a man to her house for the purpose of marriage. Again, why was Jethro so upset?

Chatham Sofer answers that Jethro did not desire to marry his daughters to an idol worshiper. Jethro had been excommunicated by the citizens of Midian because he had ceased to practice idolatry (Rashi on verse 16). He was thus resigned to the probability that his daughters would remain single. Jethro now heard that Moses, having been informed by the shepherds of the reason for Jethro's excommunication, nevertheless proceeded to save his daughters from them. It was evident to Jethro that Moses too had separated himself from idol worship. Given the circumstances, Jethro felt that his daughters should have entertained the possibility of Moses as a husband. To find a man who did not practice idolatry in Midian was rare. It was for this reason that Jethro was disturbed.

Still — says Chatham Sofer — one may defend Jethro's daughters on the ground that they suspected Moses of deception. Perhaps he had set his sights on one of the daughters — Jethro had been, after all, the priest of Midian (verse 16) — and had defended them in order to make them believe that he was not an idol worshiper. Moses was an Egyptian — as they said, "An Egyptian man rescued us" — and the Egyptians were idol worshipers. To determine whether or not this was true, Jethro pointed out that they should have invited Moses to come and eat with them. It says earlier that the Egyptians would not eat with the Hebrews (Genesis 43:32). The Targum explains that the Egyptians worshiped the animals which the Hebrews consumed, thereby making a common meal uncomfortable. If Moses were an idol worshiper — posited Jethro — he would decline the invitation to break bread with Jethro's family, which had denounced idolatry. If he accepted the invitation, then here lay a sterling opportunity for marriage.

This was why Jethro was angered that his daughters had not invited Moses to dine with them, and why he phrased his interest in Moses as a son-in-law metaphorically.

■ ■ ■

וַיּוֹאֶל מֹשֶׁה לָשֶׁבֶת אֶת־הָאִישׁ וַיִּתֵּן אֶת־צִפֹּרָה בִתּוֹ לְמֹשֶׁה.

*Moses desired to live with the man. He gave to Moses his daughter Tzipporah [as a wife]. (2:21)*

How old was Moses when he arrived in Midian? The Torah tells us that Moses was eighty years old when he first demanded that Pharaoh free the Israelites (7:7); a majority of his life was behind him. Where was it spent?

There are a number of opinions regarding this. One opinion holds that Moses was twelve years old when he killed the Egyptian. Another opinion contends that he was eighteen. Yet another view is that he was twenty, and a fourth opinion is that he was forty.

Ramban believes that Moses was twelve, and that he spent most of the next sixty-eight years fleeing from place to place.

The opinion that Moses was eighteen is found in Yalkut Shimoni. It relates that Moses fled to a country called Cush, presumably in Africa, where he served for nine years as a king's deputy, finally becoming king himself at the age of twenty-seven. Moses ruled for forty years, but was then deposed, because he had never been intimate with his Cushite wife and because he was not an idol worshiper.

Moses came to Midian at the age of sixty-seven, but was imprisoned for ten years. After being freed he married Tzipporah, at the age of seventy-seven.

R. Yehuda, who maintains that Moses was twenty when he fled Egypt, believes that he was in Midian for sixty years. R. Nechemiah,

## Shemoth

who holds Moses was forty when he left Egypt, says that he was in Midian for forty years.

■

The Midrash sees in the word *Vayoel*, "He desired," the root *alah*, "oath." As it says regarding Saul (Samuel I, 14:24), "Saul put an oath (*Vayoel*) upon the people." The meaning here is that Moses swore to Jethro that he would not leave Midian without the latter's permission. According to the Midrash, Jethro told Moses that he knew that Jacob had married Lavan's daughters, only to leave Charan without seeking permission from Lavan. In order to prevent Moses from following Jacob's example and leaving Midian after marrying Tzipporah, Jethro first forced Moses to swear that he would remain until permission was granted for him to depart.

Etz Yosef says that Jethro's fear was rooted in the fact that Moses had already demonstrated a determination to copy Jacob. Moses had set himself by a well in search of a wife, just as Jacob had done. Jethro believed that Moses might continue in Jacob's footsteps by leaving without permission.

■

"Moses desired to live with the man." When Moses met Jethro and came to know him on a personal basis, Moses realized that Jethro was not truly a "priest of Midian" (verse 16). He was, rather, a "*man*" — someone possessing fine attributes, someone who was seeking the true God.     *(Oznayim LaTorah)*

■ ■ ■

וַיְהִי בַיָּמִים הָרַבִּים הָהֵם וַיָּמָת מֶלֶךְ מִצְרַיִם וַיֵּאָנְחוּ בְנֵי־יִשְׂרָאֵל מִן־הָעֲבֹדָה וַיִּזְעָקוּ וַתַּעַל שַׁוְעָתָם אֶל־הָאֱלֹהִים מִן־הָעֲבֹדָה.

*A long time passed, and the king of Egypt died. The Israelites groaned due to their subjugation, and cried out. Their pleas, due to their slavery, went up before God.* (2:23)

Why was it at this time that the Israelites groaned due to their servitude? Weren't they being oppressed until now as well?

While Pharaoh was alive, the Israelites believed that it was he who was responsible for their agony. They were certain that his death would bring a new Pharaoh who would improve their situation. Now Pharaoh died, but nothing changed. Therefore, the Israelites groaned — with the realization that their desire had been a vain one. All the Pharaohs were identical. Only God could redeem them.

*(R. Yitzchak of Volozhin)*

Sha'ar HaShamayim answers the same question differently. He says that as long as Pharaoh was alive he forbade the Jews to express anguish; they had to appear contented. However, Pharaoh's death was the cause of grief among the Egyptians. The Jews were able to utilize this opportunity to pour out their hearts, to lament their suffering, although on the surface it appeared that they too were mourning the death of Pharaoh.

■

The Midrash asserts that Pharaoh did not die at this time. Rather, he became afflicted with leprosy, and a leper is considered dead (Nedarim 64b). Why does the Midrash discount the literal meaning of Scripture?

Vilna Gaon points out that, on the words "David's time to die was approaching" (Kings I, 2:1), the Midrash notes that David is not referred to as "King David." This is because "there is no dominion on the day of death" (Ecclesiastes 8:8).

In the present verse, it states that the "king of Egypt" died. If Pharaoh had actually perished, he should not, according to this Midrash, have been termed a "king." Hence, it is explained that he did not actually die, but contracted leprosy.

Panim Yafoth answers the question in a different fashion. He observes that Scripture's custom, when recording a king's passing, is to immediately note the ascension of his successor. In Pharaoh's case, no such mention is made. Apparently, then, Pharaoh did not actually die.

■

The sentence structure in the present verse seems awkward. Would it not have been simpler to say that "The Israelites groaned

## Shemoth

and cried out due to their subjugation"? Why is the groaning connected with the slavery — they "groaned due to their subjugation" — while their crying out is mentioned independent of the slavery?

The groaning was indeed due to the oppression the Israelites were suffering. However, their cry — their expressed desire to be redeemed — was unrelated to their subjugation. They believed that they were entitled to be redeemed by God due to the nature of their conduct — they considered themselves righteous. Therefore, the verse does not connect their cry with the oppression they were undergoing.

However, God knew that the Israelites were sinners. Independent of their servitude, they did not merit being redeemed from Egypt. It was only because the Egyptians had imposed a particularly cruel servitude upon the Israelites that they were to be redeemed. As Scripture states, "A great wrath I will expend upon the tranquil nations, since I was angry a little and they went overboard to do evil" (Zachariah 1:15). Thus, the conclusion of the present verse is that "their pleas, due to their slavery, went up before God."

An alternative explanation is that there were two groups among the Jews. The righteous group asked God to free them because the oppression was too great — "The Israelites groaned due to their subjugation." Groaning is an expression of the heart, and the principal mode of prayer comes from the heart. The less righteous group did not pray for redemption. They merely "cried out," protested to God that He had to redeem them.

The verse concludes that "Their pleas, due to their slavery, went up before God." God responded to the group that prayed to Him because of their oppression.

*(Kli Yekar)*

■

"The king of Egypt died" — Rashi cites the Midrash, which says that Pharaoh contracted leprosy, and would slaughter Jewish infants and wash in their blood to try and cure himself.

Mizrachi questions this Midrash, noting that if the Israelites

## The Eternal Heritage

groaned due to this particular decree Scripture should not have attributed the groaning to their subjugation.

However, based on Targum Yonathan's exposition of the verse, we can understand the Midrash. Targum Yonathan says that Pharaoh specifically slew firstborn Israelite children in order to bathe in their blood. Now, before the sin of the Golden Calf, it was the firstborn who served as priests. When the Israelites saw that Pharaoh was killing their firstborn sons, they understood that he was trying to undermine their ability to perform the sacrificial service. This is why they groaned and cried out. (*Avodah*, "subjugation," can also be translated as the "service." Thus, the verse is saying, "The Israelites groaned due to" the undermining of the sacrificial "service.") When God realized that the Israelites were crying because of Pharaoh's tampering with the priestly service, His compassion was aroused, and He heeded their pleas.

*(Emeth LeYaakov)*

■ ■ ■

וּמֹשֶׁה הָיָה רֹעֶה אֶת־צֹאן יִתְרוֹ חֹתְנוֹ כֹּהֵן מִדְיָן וַיִּנְהַג אֶת־הַצֹּאן אַחַר הַמִּדְבָּר וַיָּבֹא אֶל־הַר הָאֱלֹהִים חֹרֵבָה.

*Moses was tending the flock of his father-in-law Jethro, the Priest of Midian. He led the flock to the edge of the desert, and he came to God's mountain, in Horeb.* (3:1)

The Torah wishes to inform us why Moses merited being Israel's shepherd. It was because Moses was the faithful, compassionate shepherd of Jethro's flock.

The Midrash relates that once a kid left the flock, and Moses ran after it. The kid came to a pool of water and began to drink. When Moses caught up, he said that he hadn't realized the kid had fled due to thirst, and that the kid must be weary. He lifted the kid upon his shoulder and carried it along. God said: Because you have demonstrated such compassion in leading the flock owned by a human being, you shall become My shepherd.

■

The Midrash says that there were two great men who were tested by God regarding a minor matter. God found them upstanding and

## Shemoth

elevated them to a position of greatness. David was given flocks to tend, and he led them to the wilderness so that they would not graze on private pastures. Moses was also tested in this manner, and brought Jethro's flocks to the desert for the same reason.

The Sages examined the depth of the shepherd's soul and found that it is his nature to justify pasturing on private property. The shepherd's reasoning is that he is not stealing for his own gain, but in order to feed the sheep which are dependent upon him. Since he lacks the wherewithal to provide for them, they would otherwise suffer the agony of hunger. It is forbidden by the Torah to cause such agony to animals, and so the community must feed them.

This is the shepherd's line of reasoning. However, the prohibition to steal is not waived in such a situation. Whether or not one is stealing for his own benefit is irrelevant. Moses and David proved their honesty by desisting from stealing even when they served as shepherds.

The moral for the leaders of the Jewish people is that they are forbidden to steal or use underhanded methods in order to benefit their constituents. They must keep in mind that a shepherd, as a consequence of his actions, becomes unfit to serve as a witness (Bava Metzia 5b). *(Tal Mishpat)*

Tal Mishpat's explanation is puzzling. The halacha is that a shepherd who tends his own flock is rendered unfit to give testimony. One who tends the flocks of others is not rendered unfit, because it is not expected that he will steal in order to benefit others. Whereas Moses was tending Jethro's flock, there should have been no assumption that he would graze the sheep on private property. The fact that he did not do so should not have proved that he possessed qualities above and beyond those of the average shepherd.

■ ■ ■

וַיַּרְא ה' כִּי סָר לִרְאוֹת וַיִּקְרָא אֵלָיו אֱלֹהִים מִתּוֹךְ הַסְּנֶה וַיֹּאמֶר מֹשֶׁה מֹשֶׁה וַיֹּאמֶר הִנֵּנִי.

*God saw that [Moses] was coming to investigate. God called to him from inside the bush, saying, "Moses, Moses." He replied, "Yes?"* (3:4)

The Zohar relates that R. Shimon b. Yochai heard his name being called: "Shimon, Shimon." He said, "Who would be calling me Shimon, if not for God?"

It is asked: Wasn't R. Shimon displaying arrogance and boastfulness by assuming that it was God who was calling to him?

Iturei Torah advances the view of R. Yisrael of Ruzhin that, quite the contrary, it was R. Shimon's *humility* which led him to conclude that he had heard God's voice. Everyone called him "Rabbi Shimon," and this appellation caused him great distress; he did not believe himself worthy of the title "Rabbi." He thought his friends were in error.

Now he heard someone calling him simply "Shimon," not "Rabbi Shimon." In his humility, he assumed this could only be God calling. God knows one's true character, and He alone would be aware that R. Shimon did not deserve the appellation "Rabbi."

■ ■ ■

וַיֹּאמֶר אַל־תִּקְרַב הֲלֹם שַׁל־נְעָלֶיךָ מֵעַל רַגְלֶיךָ כִּי הַמָּקוֹם אֲשֶׁר אַתָּה עוֹמֵד עָלָיו אַדְמַת־קֹדֶשׁ הוּא.

*[God] said, "Do not come any closer. Take your shoes off your feet, for the place upon which you are standing is holy ground."* (3:5)

The wilderness is a place rampant with poisonous snakes and scorpions. It is very dangerous to walk there without shoes, and one who does so and dies has, in effect, committed suicide.

Therefore, when God ordered Moses to remove his shoes, He immediately added that "the place upon which you are standing is holy ground." In a holy place, serpents and scorpions are unable to cause injury. As the Sages say (Avoth 5:5): "It never happened that a snake or scorpion caused injury in Jerusalem." Thus, Moses was not in danger. *(Eduth Bihosef)*

■

The commentators have pointed out that there are certain differences between God's appearance to Moses, with His directive

## Shemoth

that Moses remove his shoes, and His revelation to Joshua, who was similarly instructed. In Moses' case, he was ordered to remove both of his shoes. Joshua was told to remove only one shoe. Additionally, in Moses' case, Scripture states that he was standing on "holy ground," while regarding Joshua the word "ground" is omitted; it says, "for the place upon which you are standing is holy" (Joshua 5:15).

Rabbeinu Bachya, as well as other exponents of Scripture, have stated that the act of removing the shoes was a symbol of the separation of Moses and Joshua from materialism. Moses was more removed from materialism than Joshua. This was indicated by Moses being asked to take off both shoes, while Joshua had to remove only one shoe. With this view in mind, we will resolve the difficulties mentioned above.

The Sages have said that Moses' face resembled the sun, while Joshua's face is compared to the moon. The moon is lit from one side, while the second side is dark. Similarly, Joshua's intellectual aspect was "lit" — it had been spiritually purified. However, his physical aspect was dark; he was not entirely divorced of materialistic desires. By contrast, Moses was like the sun. He was lit on both sides. He had purified his physical aspect as well as his intellectual one, so much so that his skin glowed (34:29). This came about because he had tarried on Mount Sinai for forty days and nights without eating or drinking. Moses had absorbed the *ziv haShechinah*, the glory of the Divine Presence, during that period of time. All this testified to Moses' removal from physical wants.

Thus, God told Moses to remove both his shoes. This symbolized the pristine state of his two aspects — intellectual and physical. This also explains why God described the place upon which Moses was standing as "holy ground." God wished to emphasize that even Moses' "ground" — his physical aspect [Man being composed of the earth] — was holy. God now had to add that Moses was not to "come any closer." Since Moses was in such a holy state, he had to be warned not to try to advance nearer and look at God. Even the angels cannot observe God, and so certainly a human being, regardless of his spiritual level, cannot do so.

## The Eternal Heritage

The Sages comment that when Moses was born his entire house was filled with light (Rashi on 2:2). This too was an indication that Moses would be "lit" in all his aspects.

However, Joshua was lit only in his intellectual aspect, and so he was told to remove only one shoe. Moreover, it is not stated that he was standing on "holy ground," because the ground within him — his physical aspect — had not been sanctified. And there was no need to warn him not to peer at God. There was no possibility of his doing so, because the lack of spiritual perfection in his physical aspect served as a screen between himself and God. He was incapable of seeing God.

This may also explain why God called Moses' name twice (verse 4). God was calling to both of his aspects, because they were both holy. *(Kli Yekar)*

■

Moses was ordered to remove both of his shoes. By contrast, when Joshua was in a similar situation, he was told only, "Remove your shoe" (Joshua 5:15). What is the difference between the two cases?

R. Yitzchak Rosenthal refers to the Midrash, which says that God used Moses' father's voice when speaking from the bush. Moses said, "I am here. What does Father want?" God replied, "I am not your father, but the God of your father." Since God said He was the God of Amram, Moses' father, and Moses knew that God does not associate His name with living people (Rashi on Genesis 31:42), Moses realized that his father must have died.

R. Yitzchak continues that Rashi says God and Moses were at the bush for seven days (4:10). It may be, then, that Moses had to remove his shoes not only due to the holiness of the ground upon which he was standing, but because the laws of *shivah*, mourning, applied to him. During the mourning period both shoes must be removed.

In Joshua's case, however, the removal of footwear was only in order that he not tread with shoes on holy ground. Hence, he was told to remove one shoe, as it was technically possible for him to keep one shoe on while standing on his shoeless foot.

## Shemoth

Regarding a priest doing the Temple service, the Talmud (Zevachim 24a) says: If he has one foot on a utensil and one on the ground, or one on a rock and one on the ground, we examine the situation. As long as he would be able to remain standing if the utensil or rock were removed, the service is fit. If not, the service is profaned.

We observe that, since the floor of the Temple sanctifies the priest for the service, nothing may separate the priest from the floor. Still, if one leg is not on the floor at all, it does not necessarily render his service unfit. The same may hold even if he has a shoe on the uplifted foot.  *(Har Tzvi)*

■

God gave Moses two commands. He told Moses, "Do not come any closer." Then He added, "Take your shoes off your feet." Not only could Moses not approach further, but he already was standing on holy ground, and thus had to remove his shoes.

Moses was at this moment transgressing God's wishes by standing with his shoes on. Why, then, did God first order him not to come closer and then tell him to take his shoes off? Wasn't the immediate issue the fact that Moses was wearing his shoes? Shouldn't the command to remove them have taken precedence?

God's primary concern is with the negative commandments, because the transgression of these harms the sinner. Positive commandments are given so that one should pursue good, and the neglect to do them does not engender punishment (with the exception of a few, such as the Paschal sacrifice and circumcision). God now gave Moses a negative command — not to approach further — and a positive one: to remove his shoes. Had Moses continued to approach, he would have transgressed the negative command. By contrast, had he not removed his shoes, while he would have been displaying a lack of respect toward God, he would still merely have been violating a positive command. God always lends primacy to negative commandments. As it says about the laws, one must be careful in "safeguarding and doing them" (Deuteronomy 7:12). *Shemirah,* "safeguarding," always connotes negative commandments (Shevuoth 4a), and it precedes *asiyah*, the "doing" of the positive commandments. Therefore, God first issued the primary order and then the secondary one.

However, we must still explain why God allowed Moses to be on this holy ground with his shoes. Had God told Moses earlier to remove his shoes — before Moses arrived at Horeb — this infraction would have been avoided.

We can answer that this alone would not have been sufficient reason for God to speak to Moses. Only together with the stricture against advancing further was there sufficient basis for God to address Moses. Alternatively, it may be that Horeb was not sanctified until this moment. God desired to speak to Moses at this juncture, and so He sanctified Horeb for that purpose. Thus, God could not have instructed Moses earlier to remove his shoes, for the place was not yet holy, and so no restrictions applied. This may serve to explain why the verse says, literally, "the place upon which you are standing, *this (hu)* is holy ground." It is unnecessary to add the word *hu*, "this." The indication may be that it was only now that the ground became holy. *(Ohr HaChayyim)*

■ ■ ■

וַיֹּאמֶר ה' רָאֹה רָאִיתִי אֶת־עֳנִי עַמִּי אֲשֶׁר בְּמִצְרָיִם וְאֶת־צַעֲקָתָם שָׁמַעְתִּי מִפְּנֵי נֹגְשָׂיו כִּי יָדַעְתִּי אֶת־מַכְאֹבָיו.

*God said, "I have indeed seen the suffering of my people in Egypt. I have heard their cry due to the slave-drivers, and I am aware of their pain. . . ." (3:7)*

"In Egypt" — In all their other exiles the Jews have been scattered throughout many lands. However, in the Egyptian exile they were all in one place: Goshen. This is because the other diasporas occurred after the giving of the Torah. In those cases the Jews had the Torah to bind them together despite their dispersion. The Egyptian exile took place before the Torah was given. Lacking its binding force, the Jews needed to be together, else they would have been unable to survive. *(R. Avraham of Sochachev)*

■ ■ ■

## Shemoth

וָאֵרֵד לְהַצִּילוֹ מִיַּד מִצְרַיִם וּלְהַעֲלֹתוֹ מִן־הָאָרֶץ הַהִוא אֶל־אֶרֶץ טוֹבָה וּרְחָבָה אֶל־אֶרֶץ זָבַת חָלָב וּדְבָשׁ אֶל־מְקוֹם הַכְּנַעֲנִי וְהַחִתִּי וְהָאֱמֹרִי וְהַפְּרִזִּי וְהַחִוִּי וְהַיְבוּסִי.

". . . I have come down to rescue them from Egypt, and to bring them up out of that land to a good, spacious land, to a land flowing with milk and honey — to the place of the Canaanites, Hittites, Amorites, Perizites, Hivites, and Jebusites. . . ." (3:8)

Oznayim LaTorah points out that God did not come down to investigate if there was a basis for the despair of the Israelites. By comparison, when God heard of the cry against Sodom, He went to investigate the situation (Genesis 18:21). Indeed, such is God's general policy: to come down and inquire about evildoing before He passes judgment.

That, however, is the case only regarding the nations of the world. When the Jewish people cry out, God's response is different. He told Moses, "I am aware of their pain" (verse 7). God accompanies the Jews when they are in distress (Psalms 91:15). This, as the Sages point out, was why God appeared to Moses in a bush. The bush — a lowly object — demonstrated that God was in exile along with the Israelites. In fact, God told as much to Jacob: "I will go down to Egypt with you" (Genesis 46:4).

Therefore, says Oznayim LaTorah, God had no need to determine the veracity of the Jews' cries. He was already with them, and so knew of their suffering.

■

God informed Moses here that, from the days of the patriarchs, the Land of Israel was already the possession of the Jewish people. God did not term it the "land of the Canaanites," which would have indicated that at present it was Canaanite property. It was called, rather, the *"place* of the Canaanites" — the site at which the Canaanites happened to be residing.

*(Oznayim LaTorah)*

■ ■ ■

## The Eternal Heritage

וַיֹּאמֶר מֹשֶׁה אֶל־הָאֱלֹהִים מִי אָנֹכִי כִּי אֵלֵךְ אֶל־פַּרְעֹה וְכִי אוֹצִיא אֶת־בְּנֵי יִשְׂרָאֵל מִמִּצְרָיִם.

*Moses said to God, "Who am I that I should go to Pharaoh, and that I should take the Israelites out of Egypt?" (3:11)*

"Who am I" — Why should I be considered important enough to talk with a king? "That I should take the Israelites out of Egypt" — What did the Israelites do that would merit a miracle being performed to free them? (Rashi).

When Chatham Sofer was elderly and sick, his son Shimon used to read to his father the various halachic questions and responsa that had been sent him from all over the Jewish world. One day, R. Shimon read a letter from a particular rabbi, and read not only the halachic portions of the letter, but also the words of praise for Chatham Sofer which served as the letter's preface. Chatham Sofer sighed upon hearing these laudatory words.

R. Shimon asked: Why are you upset, Father? Are you unaware that you are today reckoned the leader of the Jewish people, the *gadol hador*?

Chatham Sofer replied: It is for this very reason that I am upset — that our generation is so spiritually impoverished that I am considered its leader.

R. Shimon pointed out that Moses had experienced the same emotion, and that Rashi's gloss on the present verse had now become clear to him. In his great humility, Moses wondered why he should be considered important enough to speak to Pharaoh in the capacity of the Israelites' leader. Moreover, if the Israelites had reached the point that he was considered their leader, it was clear that they had descended to an extremely low level of spirituality. That being the case, why did they merit having a miracle performed for them to redeem them?

*(MeOtzareinu HaYashan)*

∎

Moses told God: You promised Abraham, "I will also bring judgment against the nation that enslaves them" (Genesis 15:14). You said that You Yourself would contest with Pharaoh. If You send

## Shemoth

me, how will Your promise to have a direct hand in the redemption be fulfilled?

God responded, "I will be with you" (verse 12). You are My agent, and I will speak through you. In this fashion, I will directly battle Pharaoh. *(Likutei Yehoshua)*

■ ■ ■

וַיֹּאמֶר כִּי־אֶהְיֶה עִמָּךְ וְזֶה־לְּךָ הָאוֹת כִּי אָנֹכִי שְׁלַחְתִּיךָ בְּהוֹצִיאֲךָ אֶת־הָעָם מִמִּצְרַיִם תַּעַבְדוּן אֶת־הָאֱלֹהִים עַל הָהָר הַזֶּה.

*He replied, "Because I will be with you. And this is the proof that I have sent you — when you take the nation out of Egypt, you will worship God on this mountain."* (3:12)

"This is the proof that I have sent you" — God said, "This" — the fact that you, Moses, said, "Who am I that I should go to Pharaoh" (verse 11) — is the reason I selected you to be My messenger.

God chooses only humble people for His agents. That was why He selected Mount Sinai from among the other mountains as the site at which the Torah would be given. Sinai was smaller than the other mountains; they took pride in their height, but Sinai was humble (Sotah 5a).

This is also why God now told Moses that "when you take the nation out of Egypt, you will worship God on *this* mountain." The fact that this particular mountain was chosen for the giving of the Torah was a further symbol for why Moses was chosen to redeem Israel — because of his humility.

*(Avnei Ezel)*

■

Among the disciples of the Rebbe of Lublin were two brothers. One of the brothers had a large following of chassidim, while the other had no following at all.

Once the brothers were together, and the latter asked the former: Aren't we equals in Torah study and Chassiduth? Didn't we both sit in the shadow of the same rebbe? Why, then, do you have so many disciples while I have none?

His brother responded: Believe me, my brother, I have asked

myself the same question — why I have disciples and you don't. However, these questions that we ask themselves provide the answer. The very fact that I don't understand why I *do* have disciples, while you don't comprehend why you *do not* have a following, is the reason that I have adherents and you don't.

Humility itself is a reason for God to elevate someone.

*(Ma'ayanah shel Torah)*

■ ■ ■

וַיֹּאמֶר אֱלֹהִים אֶל־מֹשֶׁה אֶהְיֶה אֲשֶׁר אֶהְיֶה וַיֹּאמֶר כֹּה תֹאמַר לִבְנֵי יִשְׂרָאֵל אֶהְיֶה שְׁלָחַנִי אֲלֵיכֶם.

God replied to Moses, "I Will Be Who I Will Be." [God] continued, "This is what you must say to the Israelites: 'I Will Be sent me to you.' " (3:14)

"I Will Be Who I Will Be" — The Talmud states that God said to Moses: Tell the Israelites that I am with them in this diaspora and I will similarly be with them in future diasporas. Moses responded: It is enough to deal with each adversity as it occurs. Why must I tell the Israelites that they will face future exiles? God answered: I Will Be sent me to you (Berachoth 9b).

In the simple explanation, God was actually responding to Moses' query regarding who Moses was to say had dispatched him to the Israelites. God said that *Ehyeh*, "I Will Be," had sent him. One of God's names is thus *Ehyeh*. However, the Talmud understands *ehyeh* as taking its usual, verbal form — that it is not God's name; God was simply telling Moses that He would be with the Israelites. God first told Moses that "I will be who I will be." The repetition denoted that He would be with the Israelites in future exiles as well. (This coincides with the Sages' declaration that the Divine Presence abides with the Jews when they are in exile [Megillah 29a].) Moses asserted that it would be wrong, at this traumatic time, to mention the fact that there would be future diasporas as well. God agreed and said, "I will be sent me to you." The lack of repetition indicated that Moses was not to refer to the future exiles which would befall the Jews.

Maharsha points out that the basis for interjecting an objection by

## Shemoth

Moses into the verse is the fact that Scripture divides God's statement into two sections with the words "God continued."

The Talmud's version of this dialogue infers that God changed His mind regarding the message Moses was to convey to the Israelites, and this is how Rashi on the present verse explains it. However, the Midrash records a different version of the conversation. According to the Midrash, as explained by Maharsha, God responded to Moses that he was to tell the Israelites, "I will be sent me to you," because "I am informing *you* [about the other exiles], but I am not informing *them*." God had not intended that Moses tell the Israelites about future diasporas. That piece of information was meant exclusively for Moses. He misunderstood God, and objected, prompting God to issue a clarification.

It is conceivable, however, that the Talmud does not disagree with the Midrash, as the description in the Talmud of the dialogue is somewhat vague. It is possible that the Talmud also believes that Moses misunderstood God, and that God did not change His mind regarding what to tell the Israelites.

Chatham Sofer, accepting the view that God did at first intend to tell the Israelites about the future diasporas, points out that He certainly knew, at the outset, that the Israelites would be distressed were they told now about future diasporas. Why, then, did God first command Moses to so inform them?

Chatham Sofer resolves this problem based on the two reasons given by the Sages for why God came to redeem the Israelites prematurely. They had, after all, been destined for a servitude lasting 400 years (Genesis 15:13), but left Egypt after 210 years (Rashi, Ibid.). The Sages say that the future exiles which the Jews were to endure compensated for the shortened period they spent in Egypt. Alternatively, the extraordinary harshness of the Egyptian diaspora was equivalent to 400 years of the less rigid servitude to which the Israelites should have been subjected.

Moses asserted to God that the Israelites would not believe his proclamation that their redemption was near (4:1). They had been raised with the expectation that redemption was still a distant event. God responded that Moses should inform them that there would be future diasporas, which would compensate for the early redemption from Egypt. Moses replied with the plea that God spare the Israelites the knowledge of such future troubles: "It is enough to deal with each trouble in its time." Moses insisted that the extraordinary oppression suffered by the Israelites should be accounted "enough trouble" to compensate for the early redemption. God accepted Moses' plea, and told him that there was indeed enough suffering in the Egyptian exile to fulfill the Israelites' obligation. Thus, if not for their later sins, the Jews would not have suffered the other exiles — having already completed their sentence of servitude.

■

R. Avraham Mordechai of Gur sees in the term *ehyeh asher ehyeh* an allusion to *emeth*, "truth," which is God's seal (Shabbath 55a). *Emeth* has a numerical value of 441. *Ehyeh*'s value is twenty-one. Twenty-one squared — reflecting the doubling of *ehyeh* in God's name — is 441.

In response to Moses' query as to how he was to identify God to the Israelites — as to which of His names indicated that He was reliable to keep His word to liberate them — God said His name is *Ehyeh Asher Ehyeh*, which connotes *emeth*, truth.

R. Avraham Mordechai adds that the connection between *emeth* and *ehyeh* is inferred by the liturgist who composed the High Holidays hymn *Vechol Ma'aminin*. One stanza reads: "And all believe He is the true *(emeth)* judge, who is named *Ehyeh Asher Ehyeh*." *(Iturei Torah)*

■

Why did God tell Moses that His name was *Ehyeh Asher Ehyeh*, "I Will Be Who I Will Be," only to proceed to say that Moses was to identify Him to the Israelites as *Ehyeh* — "*I Will Be* sent me to you"? Secondly, why does Scripture say that "God told Moses" His name? Whereas we know God was speaking to Moses, it should have said, "God told *him*." Why is Moses identified by name?

The name *Ehyeh*, "I Will Be," connotes the fact that God would be allied with the Israelites — He would *be* with them. Moses had

## Shemoth

two concerns regarding his mission to Pharaoh. He worried that he might come to harm, and he also was concerned that Pharaoh would not heed his demand to free the Israelites. The Israelites had only one fear — that Pharaoh would not free them. Moses' personal safety was not a matter of particular concern to them. God thus told Moses that His name was *Ehyeh Asher Ehyeh*. The repetition of *Ehyeh* was an indication that God would be with Moses in protecting him from harm as well as in making his mission a success. The Israelites, however, needed support regarding only one matter, and so there was no need to repeat *Ehyeh* to them.

Another view is that *asher ehyeh*, which can be translated as "because I will be," is not an integral part of God's name. His name is *Ehyeh*. *Asher ehyeh* is the reason that God is called *Ehyeh*: He is eternal — He "will be" — and so He is named "I Will Be." However, it was not necessary to convey the reason for God's name to the Israelites, and so they were told His name, *Ehyeh*, without the reason for it: *asher ehyeh*.

As for God's command to tell the Israelites that He is the "God of Abraham, the God of Isaac, and the God of Jacob" (verse 15), this was an indication that God was not to be called *Ehyeh*, but rather the "God of Abraham . . ." This is Scripture's intent when it says, "This is My eternal name, and this is how I am to be recalled for all generations." *Ehyeh* is God's "eternal name," as it infers His continued existence. The verse may be translated thusly: "This is My name because I exist for eternity." And "the God of Abraham, the God of Isaac, and the God of Jacob" is how God "is to be recalled for all generations." The reason is that this name goes beyond a description of God's eternal nature. It asserts that God will, for eternity, associate His name with every person who fears Him, just as He associated His name separately with each of the patriarchs ["the God of Abraham," "the God of Isaac," "the God of Jacob"].

*(Kli Yekar)*

■

The Talmud (Shevuoth 35a) lists nine names of God which, it asserts, one is prohibited to destroy (for example, by erasing them).

Among these names is *Ehyeh Asher Ehyeh*, "I Will Be Who I Will Be." The other eight names are *El, Eloah* (in accordance with Vilna Gaon's reading of the Talmudic text), *Elohim, Eloheichem, Adonai,* the Tetragrammaton *(YHVH), Shaddai,* and *Tzva'oth.*

Rambam, in his Mishneh Torah (Hilchoth Yesodei HaTorah 6:2), rules that there are seven names which one may not destroy. However, he proceeds to record eight such names: the Tetragrammaton, *Adonai, El, Eloah, Elohim, Elohei, Shaddai,* and *Tzva'oth.*

Kessef Mishneh, noting the inconsistency between Rambam's list of eight names and his statement that there are seven names, avers that the Tetragrammaton and *Adonai* are reckoned as one and the same, because the Tetragrammaton is also pronounced *Adonai,* although it has a different spelling than the latter.

The text of Mishneh Torah supports Kessef Mishneh, as it reads, "There are seven names: the name written [with the letters] *yud, heh, vav, heh* (the Tetragrammaton), which is the Ineffable Name, or the one written [with the letters] *aleph, daleth, nun, yud (Adonai)* . . ." The conjunction "or" would appear to indicate that these two are interchangeable — one name with two spellings. Kessef Mishneh notes, however, that another text of Mishneh Torah does not include *Elohei* on the list of names. There would thus be seven names, without the need to identify the Tetragrammaton and *Adonai* as one and the same.

Lechem Mishneh reads no inconsistency at all in Rambam's list. He does not have *El* or *Elohei* in his version of Rambam's text, while he adds *Ehyeh*. Thus, there are only seven names, and the Tetragrammaton and *Adonai* are two names, not one. This text of Rambam's work is from the Venice edition, which is noted as well by Kessef Mishneh, and which Kessef Mishneh describes as "the correct text." It resolves, Kessef Mishneh continues, not only the inconsistency in number which exists in the text we have in our editions, but another problem as well. The Talmud includes *Ehyeh Asher Ehyeh* on its list of names, but *Ehyeh* is omitted from the eight-name compilation in our edition of Mishneh Torah; the Venice edition has *Ehyeh.*

*Shemoth*

The Venice edition's list includes the Tetragrammaton, *Adonai, Eloah, Elohim, Ehyeh, Shaddai,* and *Tzva'oth*. As for the fact that it does not include *El* and *Elohei*, Kessef Mishneh asserts that they are subsumed, respectively, under the names *Eloah* and *Elohim*.

(Kessef Mishneh, objects, however, that *Eloah* is actually a form of *Elohim*, and should be subsumed under it. He gives no answer.)

If one assumes that *El* and *Elohei* are actually on the Venice list, being included in the names *Eloah* and *Elohim*, then that edition's compilation corresponds with the Talmud's list, with one exception: the Talmud has the name *Eloheichem*, while Rambam has the name *Elohei*. This, though, is not problematic, as the two names are actually one and the same. *Elohei* is in the construct state. It is always connected with another word, or suffixed, as it means "the God of." The Talmud chose to record the word as it would appear with one of its suffixes — *Eloheichem*, "your (plural) God." Rambam recorded the name without a suffix.

Indeed, with this explanation, a gloss by Vilna Gaon becomes comprehensible. The Vilna edition of the Talmud — which is the standard edition — has the names *Elohecha* and *Eloheichem* on its list. It has neither *Elohei* nor *Eloah*. Vilna Gaon instructs one to read *Eloah* in place of *Elohecha*. This is because *Elohecha* ("your [singular] God"), like *Eloheichem*, is a suffixed form of *Elohei*. There is no reason that both *Elohecha* and *Eloheichem* should be listed, while *Eloah* is omitted.

It is interesting to note that R. Chananel, in his commentary on the Talmud, records a completely different list from any described above. His list consists of *El, Elohim, Eloheichem, Eloheihem, Elohecha, Ehyeh Asher Ehyeh, Shaddai,* and *Tzva'oth*. Three forms of *Elohei* are listed: *Eloheichem, Eloheihem* ("their God"), and *Elohecha*. It is obvious, however, that R. Chananel's list is not meant to be exhaustive, as it omits the Tetragrammaton and *Adonai*, both of which he describes several lines further as among the names which may not be destroyed.

■

In the previous verse, Moses asked God to tell him His name so

## The Eternal Heritage

that Moses could relay it to the Israelites. Why did God have to use a new name — *Ehyeh*?

R. Yisrael HaDarshan explains that Moses asserted he was unable to pronounce any of God's names. Moses said that he was "heavy of mouth and heavy of tongue" (4:10). According to R. Chananel, who is cited by R. Bachya, Moses had difficulty pronouncing the letters that are formed with the teeth and those that are formed with the tongue. The letters *daleth, teth, lamed, nun,* and *tav* are formed with the teeth. The letters *zayin, samech, shin, resh,* and *tzaddi* are formed by using the tongue. R. Yisrael HaDarshan points out that all of God's names known to Moses at this point (e.g., *El, Shaddai*) contained at least one of these letters. Moses told God that he found it difficult to pronounce these names. Therefore, God gave him a name which had none of these letters: *Ehyeh*, which contains the letters *aleph, heh,* and *yud*.

■ ■ ■

לֵךְ וְאָסַפְתָּ אֶת־זִקְנֵי יִשְׂרָאֵל וְאָמַרְתָּ אֲלֵהֶם ה' אֱלֹהֵי אֲבֹתֵיכֶם נִרְאָה אֵלַי אֱלֹהֵי אַבְרָהָם יִצְחָק וְיַעֲקֹב לֵאמֹר פָּקֹד פָּקַדְתִּי אֶתְכֶם וְאֶת־הֶעָשׂוּי לָכֶם בְּמִצְרָיִם.

"... *Go, gather the elders of Israel, and say to them: God, the Lord of your fathers, has appeared to me — the God of Abraham, Isaac, and Jacob. He said, 'I have surely remembered you and what is being done to you in Egypt. . . .'*" (3:16)

"The elders of Israel" — R. Chama b. R. Chanina said: From the time of our forefathers the people of Israel have never lacked a house of study. When they were in Egypt, we see that they had a house of study, as it says, "Go, gather together the elders of Israel" (Yoma 28b).

Torah Temimah explains that, in general, as a person becomes older he acquires more and more wisdom and knowledge, due to his life experience. As Job's friend Elihu, son of Barachel, stated, "I said, 'Days speak, and a multitude of years conveys wisdom'" (Job 32:7). And it says there as well (12:12), "In the elderly there is wisdom." Therefore, the Talmud asserts that only wise men are termed *zaken*, "elderly" (Kiddushin 32b). If an elderly person has not acquired more knowledge than his younger counterpart, then there is no advantage to his having aged. Being termed a *zaken* is a type of praise — that one has utilized his life experience to gain knowledge — not simply a description of one's age.

Thus, says Torah Temimah, the Talmud gleans from the present verse that the Israelites had a house of study even during their enslavement in Egypt. If the Torah describes some of the Israelites as elderly, it can only be because they were knowledgeable men, having studied the Torah.

Torah Temimah adds that God occasionally grants to a youth the kind of knowledge that is generally acquired only by a *zaken*. Such a young man is also termed a *zaken*, despite his tender age. Joseph is an example. Joseph is described as Jacob's *ben zekunim*, literally, the "child of his old age." The Targum translates *ben zekunim* as *bar chakim*, a "wise son." The Targum understands the word *zekunim* as a description of Joseph, not of Jacob. If Joseph is portrayed as a *zaken* although he was only seventeen years of age at the time, it must be that he already possessed the attributes of wisdom which are the hallmark of elderly people.

■

God said: If you use these words (*pakod pakadti*, "I have surely remembered," the word "remembered" being repeated), the Israelites will believe you, as they have a tradition, dating back to Jacob and Joseph, that they will be redeemed with these words. Jacob said, "God will surely remember *(pakod yifkod)* you" (Genesis 50:24), as did Joseph (Ibid., verse 25) (Rashi on verse 18).

Why were the Israelites to be redeemed specifically with the terminology of "remembering"? We may answer that the word *pakod* can have different connotations. It may indicate bad tidings: "keeping in mind *(poked)* the sin of the fathers" (20:5). Or it may herald a pleasant event: "God remembered *(pakad)* Sarah" (Genesis 21:1). The redemption of the Israelites from Egypt involved both bad and good aspects. It contained retribution for the Egyptians due to their sins, while rewarding the Israelites for the fact that their forefathers had walked in God's footsteps. Thus, this terminology is all-encompassing, and is therefore an exalted language.

This also serves to explain why there exists in the description of the redemption a doubling of the word *pakod* — (*pakod yifkod* and *pakod pakadti*). The dual language refers to the dual aspects of the word. *(Maharal)*

Rashi says that Jacob used the language of *pakod* when he said, "God will surely remember you." In reality, Scripture does not record Jacob making this statement. Joseph, however, used this style of language twice (Genesis 50:24, 25). Ramban posits that the fact that the Torah mentions this language twice in connection with Joseph is seen by Rashi as an indication that Jacob gave this sign to Joseph.

However, the source for Rashi's view, Shemoth Rabbah, states only that Joseph used this language. No mention is made of Jacob.

Ramban asks why there was such certainty that the Israelites would accept Moses as their redeemer merely on the basis of the words *pakod pakadti*. Was it not possible that Moses was an imposter and, having heard the tradition that the redeemer would use these words, was attempting to deceive the Israelites?

Ramban gives two answers. Firstly, he says that the tradition may have been that the first person to use these words would truly be the redeemer. Joseph had been told this by Jacob, who was a prophet. God knew that nobody would precede the redeemer in using this language, and gave this information to Jacob. Secondly, Ramban advances the view of R. Chama (Shemoth Rabbah 5) that Moses was only twelve years of age when he fled Egypt. God caused him to leave his father's house at this early age so that when he came to the Israelites as the redeemer they would accept him. They would not say that he was deceiving them based on the traditional sign of the redeemer, for he had been too young to be told the sign.

■ ■ ■

וְשָׁמְעוּ לְקֹלֶךָ וּבָאתָ אַתָּה וְזִקְנֵי יִשְׂרָאֵל אֶל־מֶלֶךְ מִצְרַיִם וַאֲמַרְתֶּם אֵלָיו ה׳

## Shemoth

אֱלֹהֵי הָעִבְרִיִּים נִקְרָה עָלֵינוּ וְעַתָּה נֵלֲכָה־נָּא דֶּרֶךְ שְׁלֹשֶׁת יָמִים בַּמִּדְבָּר וְנִזְבְּחָה לַה׳ אֱלֹהֵינוּ.

"... They will heed your words. Then you and the elders of Israel will go to the king of Egypt. You will tell him, 'God, the Lord of the Hebrews, has revealed Himself to us. Now we request that you allow us to take a three-day journey into the wilderness to sacrifice to God our Lord.' ..." (3:18)

R. Yaakov Kamenetsky wonders: Although God had Moses ask Pharaoh to allow the Jews a leave of three days so that they might worship God in the desert, there is no indication that this was God's actual plan. In truth, He did not intend for the Israelites to return to Egypt. How is it possible that Moses was sent to Pharaoh with the implied message that the Israelites would return to Egypt? Isn't God's seal "truth" (Shabbath 55a)? Moreover, isn't it said about Moses that he "is trusted throughout My house" (Numbers 12:7)? How could Moses have told a lie?

R. Yaakov poses yet another question. Why did God send Moses to Pharaoh, only to have Pharaoh increase the oppression of the Israelites, which brought about a harsh rejoinder to God on Moses' part — "Why do You mistreat this people?" (5:22) — which in turn caused God to be angry with Moses?

R. Yaakov explains that God did not actually intend, at the outset, for the Jews to leave Egypt now. God Himself had declared that the Israelites would be slaves for 400 years, but the Sages say that the Israelites were in Egypt for only 210 years. It is evident — says R. Yaakov — that the Sages believe that God had originally intended a 400-year slavery. While they say that the 400 years is counted from the birth of Isaac, this is only a rationalization for shortening the exile. The early exit from Egypt occurred, say the Sages, because the Israelites had sunk to such a low spiritual level that a prolongation of their stay in Egypt would have resulted in their remaining there forever.

R. Yaakov continues that God now wanted the Israelites to worship Him outside of Egypt for three days. His goal was to restore within them the foundation of faith in Him. Once that was done, they would have been able to return to Egypt and complete the 400-year sentence. However, Pharaoh did not permit them to leave even for this short span of time. Therefore, God was forced to free them now. In order to fulfill their sentence, He mandated that they suffer enough affliction within the next six months to offset the 191 years which would not be spent in Egypt (this being the 209th year of servitude). That is why Pharaoh increased the hardship of the servitude upon the Israelites.

This explains the following verses. God tells Moses that "I know that the Egyptian king will not allow you to leave unless he is forced to do so. I will then display My power . . . Then [Pharaoh] will let you leave." At first, God had only desired that the Israelites be allowed to leave on a temporary basis. However, due to Pharaoh's refusal to accede to this request, God had to set the Israelites free permanently. (R. Yaakov understands *lahaloch*, "to leave," to connote a temporary journey and *yeshalach*, "will let leave," to indicate a permanent departure.)

All the questions are now answered. No lie was intended by Moses, as the Israelites were indeed to have returned after three days. And the oppression was increased after Moses visited Pharaoh in order to allow the Israelites to leave Egypt earlier than scheduled.

▪

It is necessary to clarify why God told the Israelites to lie to the Egyptians. The Israelites were to say that they wished to take a three-day journey, although their intent was to leave Egypt permanently. The Israelites were also told to ask the Egyptians to lend them valuable items, although God did not intend for the Israelites to return them (verse 22).

In reality, the Israelites were entitled to be given the Egyptians' valuables as payment for the services the Israelites had provided while enslaved (see Sanhedrin 91a). And God could certainly have used another method to take out the Israelites. But He wanted to deceive the Egyptians, so that they would chase the Israelites in the wilderness. This would lead to the Egyptian defeat at the Red Sea, thereby causing God to be glorified (14:4). Had the Israelites been allowed to leave with the understanding that they would not be returning at all, and had the Egyptians not lent their valuables to the Israelites, the Egyptians would not have felt justified in pursuing them.

Proof of this is the Sages' assertion that during the Plague of Darkness the Israelites searched the Egyptians' houses and belongings to locate their valuables. When the Israelites later came to the Egyptians asking to borrow these valuables, the Egyptians could not deny their existence, as the Israelites were able to pinpoint their locales. The Israelites could have simply taken the valuables during the days of darkness. The fact that they refrained from doing so is evidence that God desired that the valuables be lent rather than taken or given.

It remains unclear, however, why God needed to arrange the scenario whereby the Egyptians chased the Israelites into the wilderness. Wouldn't it have been simpler for Him to flood Egypt with the waters of the Nile — the very waters with which the Egyptians had sinned by drowning the Israelites' firstborn sons? Furthermore, by doing that, God would have wiped out the women and children as well as the men. And the Israelites could have then taken the Egyptians' gold and silver.

There are two possible solutions to this problem. Firstly, it may be that such a scenario would not have produced the worldwide glorification of God which occurred by His splitting of the Red Sea and drowning of the Egyptians therein. Secondly, God dispenses punishment in the same measure as the sin which has been committed. The Talmud (Sotah 11a) asserts that the Egyptians enslaved the Israelites in a gradual fashion. They first enticed the Israelites to work voluntarily, and only later made them slaves. God punished the Egyptians measure for measure with their crime. At first, the Israelites asked for a three-day respite, not a permanent leave, and they asked only to borrow the Egyptians' valuables and clothing. Later, the harsh reality became evident: that the Israelites were not returning, and were keeping the valuables. Therefore, the Egyptians gave chase to the Israelites.

*(Ohr HaChayyim)*

"We request that you allow us to take a three-day journey" — The Israelites were not actually to return after three days. Yet this was not an act of deception, says Oznayim LaTorah. He points out that the Sages say, "Whoever accepts the yoke of Torah has the yoke of the king removed from him" (Avoth 3:5). Once the Israelites became God's servants, Pharaoh could no longer have a hold on them.

Oznayim LaTorah (on 5:3) adds that God dealt with Pharaoh commensurate with the latter's comportment. Pharaoh first invited the Israelites to live in Egypt on a temporary basis — so that they might have sustenance during the famine that raged in Joseph's time. The king then made them slaves forever. In response, God had the Israelites request a three-day leave, which He intended to use as a springboard for their permanent departure.

■ ■ ■

וַאֲנִי יָדַעְתִּי כִּי לֹא־יִתֵּן אֶתְכֶם מֶלֶךְ מִצְרַיִם לַהֲלֹךְ וְלֹא בְּיָד חֲזָקָה.
". . . Now, I know that the Egyptian king will not allow you to leave unless he is forced to do so. . . ." (3:19)

There were three possible ways for the Israelites to leave Egypt. Firstly, Pharaoh could have decided to allow them to leave. Secondly, they could have waged war against Egypt and left by use of force. Finally, God could have set them free through the use of miracles.

God now informed Moses that the first two options would not come to pass. "The Egyptian king will not allow you to leave" — of his own volition. And the Israelites were too weak to defeat Pharaoh in a war — "and not by force" (an alternative translation of *velo beyad chazakah*, "unless he is forced to do so"). Therefore, only the third possibility remained: a supernatural intervention — "I will . . . smite Egypt through all the miraculous deeds that I will perform in its midst" (verse 20).   *(R. Shimon Sofer)*

■

"The Egyptian king will not allow you to leave unless he is forced to do so." Meshech Chochmah links this verse with Rambam's

## Shemoth

understanding of the rule which mandates forcing a husband, in certain circumstances, to give his wife a writ of divorcement. The halacha is that a divorce must be granted willingly. Therefore, the husband is compelled, by force if necessary, to say that he is giving the divorce of his own volition.

The difficulty is that the fact that one has been forced to say that he is willingly divorcing his wife does not seem to resolve the problem at hand: the necessity for him to actually *desire* the divorce. If the husband does not truly wish to grant the divorce, how can his speaking the contrary make the divorce valid?

Rambam explains that a person wants, in his heart of hearts, to do God's will. It is only one's surface emotions and desires that prevent him from doing so. When he is instructed to state that he desires to divorce his wife in a case where the halacha mandates a divorce, the act of compulsion is used to remove his surface emotions and reveal his true will. Thus, he ultimately does grant the divorce willingly.

Meshech Chochmah avers that such was not the case with Pharaoh. The Egyptian king's aversion to freeing the Hebrews was not a resolve grounded merely in superficial emotions and reasons. It was his inner, true desire as well — despite the fact that God wanted the Israelites freed. The verse may be translated: "The Egyptian king will not allow you to leave *even* if he is forced to do so." Even were he forced to pronounce his consent that the Israelites depart, it would not reflect his true will. Pharaoh did not wish, even in his heart of hearts, to do God's will.

■ ■ ■

וְשָׁאֲלָה אִשָּׁה מִשְּׁכֶנְתָּהּ וּמִגָּרַת בֵּיתָהּ כְּלֵי־כֶסֶף וּכְלֵי זָהָב וּשְׂמָלֹת וְשַׂמְתֶּם
עַל־בְּנֵיכֶם וְעַל־בְּנֹתֵיכֶם וְנִצַּלְתֶּם אֶת־מִצְרָיִם.

". . . Every woman shall borrow articles of silver and gold, as well as clothing, from her neighbor or the woman living with her. You shall put these on your sons and daughters. You will thus drain Egypt [of its wealth]." (3:22)

*Vesha'alah ishah*, "Every woman shall borrow" — Kli Yekar advances the view of some commentators that *vesha'alah* does not mean "borrowing" in this instance. If this were the translation, how could God have instructed the Israelites to engage in deception — "borrowing" without any intention of returning the items to the Egyptians? Rather, it denotes the giving of a gift. A similar usage of the word is found regarding King Solomon (Kings I, 3:5). Thus, the Israelites were to request presents of the Egyptians.

Later it says that "God allowed the people to find favor in the eyes of the Egyptians, and they lent to them, *va'yashilum*" (12:36). This word (of the same root as *vesha'alah*) is not to be translated "they lent to them," but rather "they gave them presents." The Egyptians pressed the Israelites to take gifts due to the overwhelming favor which the Israelites had incurred with them.

Kli Yekar proceeds to point out a lack of symmetry in Scripture. In the present verse, God asserted that the Israelites were to receive "silver and gold, as well as clothing." When God later gave Moses the actual command regarding this, He made no mention of clothing. Only silver and gold were mentioned (11:2). Finally, in describing what actually transpired, the Torah says that the Israelites *did* obtain clothing along with silver and gold objects (12:35).

Secondly — wonders Kli Yekar — why does God tell Moses, in the present verse, that "You shall put these on your sons and daughters"? Is it God's intention merely to give advice? And if so, why is the counsel limited to what the Israelites were to do with the clothing? Why didn't He advise them concerning the best use for the silver and gold?

Kli Yekar answers that the Plague of the Killing of the Firstborn led to the suspicion that an infectious disease was rampant in Egypt. The clothing owned by the Egyptians might have become contaminated, making it dangerous to wear. Therefore, in instructing Moses later, God did not need to tell him that the Israelites were to ask for clothing. The Egyptians volunteered their clothing to the Israelites, hoping that the desert wind would carry away any bacteria that were present. But God knew that the Israelites would hesitate to accept clothing from the Egyptians, due to the worry of contamination. To alleviate this fear, He told Moses,

## Shemoth

"You shall put these on your sons and daughters." There was no reason for any fear on their part.

This — says Kli Yekar — accords with the Sages' assertion that the Egyptians forced items upon the Israelites (*va'yashilum* may be translated as "they forced them to borrow" [Berachoth 9b]). Thus, the Israelites did receive clothing, as stated in Scripture, but it was at the behest of the Egyptians. And the present verse is not an order by God regarding what the Israelites were to request, but merely a description of what would occur. The Israelites would receive silver, gold, and clothing, but not all of these were given because the Israelites asked for them, as the clothing was given at the insistence of the Egyptians.

Kli Yekar suggests that Scripture alludes to this difference between the silver and gold and the clothing. The word *chen*, "favor," is mentioned in connection with the present subject on three occasions (verse 21, 11:3, 12:36). The numerical value of *chen*, multiplied by three, is 174, which is equal to the sum of the numerical value of the words *kessef*, silver, and *zahav*, gold. This indicates that only the silver and gold were given the Israelites due to the favor which they found in the eyes of the Egyptians. The clothing was not given due to this, as it would have been given to the Israelites regardless of the way the Egyptians felt about them.

Kli Yekar adds that another inconsistency can now be resolved. The present verse states that "Every *woman* shall borrow," but when God issues the command to the Israelites, He says, "Let each *man* borrow" (11:2). Kli Yekar explains that God's command made reference only to gold and silver. Men and women alike were interested in acquiring these items (and so the masculine gender is used, as always when men and women together are the subject). Here, however, God is describing what was actually to transpire. It was the Egyptian women who were interested in giving clothing to the Israelites. The clothing had belonged to their husbands, who had died during the Plague of the Killing of the Firstborn. This was the clothing that was conceivably contaminated. The Egyptian women gave the Israelite women these articles of clothing (which, says Kli Yekar, were evidently those worn on the upper part of the body, making them suitable for women as well as men). Therefore, the present verse says: "Every woman shall borrow."

■ ■ ■

וַיַּעַן מֹשֶׁה וַיֹּאמֶר וְהֵן לֹא־יַאֲמִינוּ לִי וְלֹא יִשְׁמְעוּ בְּקֹלִי כִּי יֹאמְרוּ לֹא־נִרְאָה אֵלֶיךָ ה׳.

*Moses spoke up and said, "But they will not believe me — they will not accept what I say. They will say, 'God did not appear to you.'"* (4:1)

It is necessary to explain why Moses suspected that the Israelites would not believe him regarding their redemption. After all, God had promised him that they would heed his words (3:18). Further, why did Moses repeat his claim, saying first that "they will not believe me" and then that "they will not accept what I say"? Moreover, Moses did not phrase his suspicion as a possibility — "perhaps they will not believe me" — but as a certainty. Why was he sure the Israelites would not believe him?

Rambam writes that one who lacks wisdom or is imperfect physically does not qualify to be a prophet. Kessef Mishneh objects that Rambam should have included among the criteria wealth, might, and humility, since these are listed as prerequisites for prophecy in the Talmud (Nedarim 38a). Kessef Mishneh answers that these criteria are demanded for one who is to be a prophet on a permanent basis. By contrast, Rambam is describing the qualifications of one who is a prophet only occasionally.

Because of his great humility, Moses felt that he lacked the requirements to qualify for prophecy. Not only did he not possess the attributes demanded of a permanent prophet, but he lacked even the lesser ones demanded of an occasional prophet. Moses thus told God that the Israelites would certainly not believe he had been the receptor of a prophecy, and that they would have every right to doubt his word.

As regards a permanent prophet, Moses said that he lacked the aspect of wealth. This is evident from the fact that he was merely a shepherd of his father-in-law's flocks. He became wealthy only at a later stage, from the slivers which were left over of the tablets he

## Shemoth

had made (Rashi on 34:1). As regards a temporary prophet, Moses said that he was unable to speak clearly. This constituted a physical defect, which disqualified him from receiving any prophecy at all.

This explains why Moses repeated his suspicion — "they will not believe me," and "they will not accept what I say." The second statement referred to his inability to speak well. Moses also did not believe he had wisdom. Thus, he concluded, the Israelites would assert that "God did not appear to you," that he was ineligible for prophecy.

Now, Moses did not express his fear until this juncture, saying earlier only that he needed to know God's name in order to convey it to the Israelites when they would ask who had sent him (3:13). It seems that earlier he did not entertain the same doubts he now had. The explanation may be that, in asking God to reveal to him His name, Moses expected that he would simultaneously come to understand God's hidden aspects and wondrous ways. Moses hoped to acquire, in that moment of revelation, all the spiritual and physical tools needed to qualify for prophecy. However, God did not, when revealing His name, also reveal His hidden aspects.

Alternatively, Moses may not, until this moment, have thought to raise the issue of whether or not the Israelites would believe him. But God now told Moses something he had not known heretofore: that Pharaoh would not free the Israelites when Moses came to him (3:19). Moses said that if this were true then the Israelites also would "not believe me." When Moses would persist, only to find Pharaoh still adamant, the Israelites would "not accept what I say." They would aver that "God did not appear to you," for if God were truly the sender of the message then Pharaoh would not have refused to heed His word. It would be evident to them that God had not sent Moses. *(Ohr HaChayyim)*

■ ■ ■

וַיֹּאמֶר מֹשֶׁה אֶל־ה' בִּי אֲדֹנָי לֹא אִישׁ דְּבָרִים אָנֹכִי גַּם מִתְּמוֹל גַּם מִשִּׁלְשֹׁם גַּם מֵאָז דַּבֶּרְךָ אֶל־עַבְדֶּךָ כִּי כְבַד־פֶּה וּכְבַד לָשׁוֹן אָנֹכִי.

*Moses said to God, "I beg You, O God, I am not a man of words — not yesterday,*

## The Eternal Heritage

*not the day before, not from the very first time You spoke to Your servant. This is because I am heavy of mouth and heavy of tongue."* (4:10)

Moses was given a speech defect by God so that it would not be said that his success in persuading the Israelites to accept the Torah was due to his oratorical powers. The defect was proof that his success came solely from the fact that the Divine Presence spoke from within him. *(Derashoth HaRan)*

■

Why did Moses emphasize that he was unable to speak well "yesterday" and "the day before"? Why would yesterday's conditions play a role here?

There are people who are able to speak extemporaneously, even before kings. Other find it difficult to speak without preparation, and need time to arrange their thoughts. But there are some people who, due to an inborn speech defect or some other reason, will be unable to express their thoughts properly regardless of how much they prepare.

As Rashi says, Moses had by now been arguing with God for seven days. Moses had had the time to determine how he would speak to Pharaoh, and recognized that he simply could not make a proper presentation.

This is the significance of the fact that Moses couldn't speak "yesterday" and "the day before." He realized that even with preparation he was not a good speaker. Therefore, he told God to send someone else to Pharaoh. *(Kthav Sofer)*

■ ■ ■

וַיֹּאמֶר בִּי אֲדֹנָי שְׁלַח־נָא בְּיַד־תִּשְׁלָח.

*[Moses] said, "I beg You, O Lord! Please send someone else whom You would wish to send."* (4:13)

Moses told God to send the one whom He usually would call upon to be His messenger — Aaron (Rashi).

Why did Moses refuse to be God's messenger in bringing the Israelites out of Egypt — feeling that Aaron deserved the honor —

## Shemoth

while he did not protest God's plan to have him accept the Torah? The reception of the Torah, through which Moses became the Jews' chief sage, was certainly a more important function.

The answer is that Moses saw how all the tall mountains asked God to reveal the Torah from upon them. However, God selected Mount Sinai for Revelation precisely because it was a mountain with a low elevation — a symbol of humility (Sotah 5a). Moses was also aware that the Torah is only perpetuated through someone who humbles himself (Derech Eretz Zuta 8). Now, Moses believed himself to be at a lower level than any other man (Numbers 12:3). Therefore, when God told him to receive the Torah, Moses accepted the responsibility willingly.

This is the explanation of the Mishnah's statement that "Moses received the Torah at Mount Sinai" (Avoth 1:1). If one wonders why Moses did not protest his selection by God to receive the Torah, the explanation is that Moses received the Torah "from Sinai." He took his lesson from the fact that God chose the smallest of mountains for the Lawgiving.

*(R. Yaakov Yosef of Polonnoye)*

■ ■ ■

וַיִּחַר־אַף ה' בְּמשֶׁה וַיֹּאמֶר הֲלֹא אַהֲרֹן אָחִיךָ הַלֵּוִי יָדַעְתִּי כִּי־דַבֵּר יְדַבֵּר הוּא וְגַם הִנֵּה־הוּא יֹצֵא לִקְרָאתֶךָ וְרָאֲךָ וְשָׂמַח בְּלִבּוֹ.

*God became angry with Moses. He said, "Is not Aaron the Levite your brother? I know that he is capable of speaking. He will come out to meet you, and when he sees you his heart will be glad. . . ." (4:14)*

**Vayichar af Ado-nai,** "God became angry" — R. Yehoshua b. Karcha said that every instance in the Torah of *charon af,* "anger," incurs a consequence. Here, however, we find no consequence, no punishment, despite the fact that God was angry. R. Shimon rejoined that here too there was a consequence. God said that "Aaron the Levite" would greet Moses. Aaron had been destined to be only a Levite, while the priests were to have descended from Moses' stock. Now, however, Aaron would be the priest, while Moses would be reckoned merely a Levite (Zevachim 102a).

## The Eternal Heritage

Oznayim LaTorah asserts that Moses was punished in corresponding measure to his sin *(middah kenegged middah)*. The Talmud states that the priests are God's agents (Yoma 19a). Hence, Moses, who refused to become God's agent to redeem the Jews, was deprived of the right to serve in a priestly capacity, with the task of performing the service before God in the Tabernacle and Temple.

■ ■ ■

וְאֶת־הַמַּטֶּה הַזֶּה תִּקַּח בְּיָדֶךָ אֲשֶׁר תַּעֲשֶׂה־בּוֹ אֶת־הָאֹתֹת.

"... Take this staff in your hand, as with it you will perform the signs." (4:17)

God certainly could have given Moses the ability to perform signs without the medium of a staff. Why was the staff necessary?

When a messenger arrives carrying with him no tangible object given him by the sender, there is a tendency to disbelieve him. As an example, the Talmud states that, if someone arrives in a town and claims that a particular woman's husband has died, he is not permitted to marry the widow, for he may have lied in order to secure her hand in marriage. However, if he brings a writ of divorcement, a *get,* he is allowed to marry the divorcee. The difference between the cases, says the Talmud, lies in the tangibility of the writ of divorcement (Yevamoth 25a). Here, too, when Moses brought with him the wondrous staff, the Israelites believed he was sent to be their redeemer. The staff was tangible evidence of Moses' agency.

It is for the same reason that God gave Moses the Two Tablets on Mount Sinai. Actually, the entire Torah was given by God to Moses on the mountain, and he wrote it all in a book. But when Moses descended with the Two Tablets written by God's hand — "The Tablets were made by God, and the script was God's script, engraved on the Tablets" (32:16) — the Jews believed in Moses and his Torah.

*(Oznayim LaTorah)*

■

"As with it you will perform the signs" — At this point God had

## Shemoth

only given Moses one feat to perform with the staff: to turn it into a serpent before the Israelites (verse 3). Yet the verse mentions "signs," in the plural. Ramban and Ibn Ezra say that God was referring also to the signs and wonders later to be performed with the staff — turning it into a serpent before Pharaoh as well as before the Israelites (7:10), and using it for the plagues of Blood, Frogs, Lice, Hail, Locusts, and Darkness.

Ramban avers that God did specify to Moses the various tasks of the staff. However, Scripture did not bother to detail this here, and it was included in God's general declaration regarding "all the miraculous deeds that I will perform in their midst" (3:20).

■ ■ ■

וַיֵּלֶךְ מֹשֶׁה וַיָּשָׁב אֶל־יֶתֶר חֹתְנוֹ וַיֹּאמֶר לוֹ אֵלְכָה־נָּא וְאָשׁוּבָה אֶל־אַחַי אֲשֶׁר־בְּמִצְרַיִם וְאֶרְאֶה הַעוֹדָם חַיִּים וַיֹּאמֶר יִתְרוֹ לְמֹשֶׁה לֵךְ לְשָׁלוֹם.

Moses left and returned to his father-in-law Jethro. [Moses] said to him, "Please let me leave, so that I may return to my brethren in Egypt and see if they are still alive. Jethro replied to Moses, "Go in peace." (4:18)

*Lech leshalom*, "Go in peace," is literally translated as "go to peace." R. Avin HaLevi said that one who takes leave of his friend should not tell him, *lech beshalom*, "go in peace," but should say, *lech leshalom*, "go to peace." This is evident from Jethro's manner of speaking, as he told Moses, "Go to peace" — *lech leshalom* — and Moses was successful in his mission to Egypt. By contrast, King David told Avshalom, "Go in peace," *lech beshalom* (Samuel II, 15:9), and Avshalom was hanged.

R. Avin also said that one who takes leave of a dead person should not say to him: *lech leshalom*, but should rather say: *lech beshalom*, "go in peace." This is proved from God's assurance to Abraham (Genesis 15:15): "You shall join your fathers in peace *(beshalom)*. You will be buried at a good old age" (Berachoth 64a).

Why must a dead person be spoken to differently than a living person? Ein Yaakov explains that, as is known, a person's task in life is to strive to do God's will. After he dies, he collects his reward in the World to Come, in the realm of true peace. One may thus not tell a dead person to "go to peace," as the implication would be that he should continue to seek avenues by which to arrive at peace. These avenues are open only to living beings, in the present world. Rather, he should "go *in* peace." He should go with the peace for which he has striven all his life. He now has the peace which he earned.

Conversely, a living being must be told to "go *to* peace." The advice to him is that he should continue to do God's will. He should continue to seek out the means by which to find peace and completeness (*shalom* implies both peace and completeness, *shlemuth*). He must not be told to "go in peace," as the inference would be that he is to be satisfied with the level of *shalom* he has achieved — that he should go with the peace he has already gained, and not strive for greater perfection.

Maharsha disputes Ein Yaakov's interpretation, objecting that the verses cited by the Talmud — regarding Moses, Avshalom, and Abraham — do not relate to the pursuance and achievement of *shlemuth*. Instead, Maharsha explains that during one's life he is always pursuing the successful accomplishment of his goals wherever he goes. After one dies, he no longer engages in actions, and thus has no success orientation.

Therefore, when speaking to a living person, one should say: *lech leshalom*, "go to peace." He is given the blessing that he should find the success he seeks wherever he goes. He should not be told: *lech beshalom*, "go in peace," as the blessing would be that he should travel in peace. He would be blessed only that he should travel and arrive at his destination in peace, not that he should be successful in his pursuits once he arrives there. *Lech leshalom* is thus only a partial blessing.

The converse applies when one is addressing a deceased person. To bless him that he should "go *to* peace" is pointless, as he has no pursuits in the grave. The only significant blessing for him is that he should "go *in* peace," that his journey to his final resting place should be a peaceful one. He should merit joining his fathers in peace, as God promised Abraham.

Although Maharsha does not elaborate and apply his reasoning to the cases of Moses and Avshalom, his view is quite evident. Jethro told Moses, "Go to peace." Moses was a living being, and was being blessed that his mission in Egypt should succeed. David told Avshalom, "Go in peace." This was an inappropriate blessing for a man who was yet alive, and the end result was that Avshalom met his death.

Rabbeinu Nissim (Moed Kattan 29b) takes a similar approach regarding the implication of *lech beshalom* — that only the journey will be peaceful. Thus, one whose death is imminent may be told: *lech beshalom*. He is afraid, and is thus blessed that his departure from the world will be a peaceful event. R. Nissim adds that the Sages were addressing themselves to people who are superstitious. For those who do not take such nuances to heart, the language by which they are addressed has no effect.

Torah Temimah (on Genesis 15:15) notes that the halachic decisors do not, in the main, make a record of the Talmud's admonitions regarding *lech beshalom* and *lech leshalom*. Only Magen Avraham (Orach Chaim 110) and Rambam (Hilchoth Evel 4:4) make reference to this issue, and the latter seems to mention it only in passing. Why is this law omitted?

Torah Temimah notes further that we find cases where going *beshalom* is used in reference to a living person, and yet has no ill effect. Examples can be found in Genesis 28:21, regarding Jacob, and in Exodus 18:23, where Jethro, whose statement in the present verse is one of the Talmud's bases for its pronouncement, uses the term in regard to the people of Israel. Other instances are found in Joshua 10:21, Samuel I, 29:7, Jeremiah 43:12, and Chronicles II, 18:16. Finally, we find in the Talmud that R. Gamliel invited R. Yehoshua to enter his house *beshalom* (Rosh HaShanah 25a). Why is Avshalom's case unique, in that it serves as proof that one should not speak about the living in this fashion? Perhaps it was coincidental that he met with misfortune.

Torah Temimah answers this question by noting the view that a person who is not superstitious has no need to fear repercussions from the use of the term *lech beshalom*. It may be, says Torah Temimah, that the cases noted above prompted this opinion. There is indeed no effect on people who are not superstitious, and so there is no reason for the term *lech beshalom* to be avoided. The Talmud addressed itself only to people who are bent on finding bases for their superstitions.

Torah Temimah asserts that for the same reason the difference between *lech leshalom* and *lech beshalom* goes generally unrecorded in the halachic codes. Firstly, the medieval Sages always attempted to eradicate mention of superstition, as it is inappropriate for the Jewish people to be steeped in superstition. Secondly, there is no ill effect upon righteous people from the use of *lech beshalom*. Therefore, the codifiers omitted this ruling.

Iyun Yaakov poses the same objection as does Torah Temimah — that we find cases where *beshalom* was used without ill effect. Iyun Yaakov answers that there may actually be no difference between *beshalom* and *leshalom*. However, we do find that on one occasion — Avshalom's — tragedy occurred, despite the fact that David had blessed him. From this it is apparent that, although there may be no malevolent intent, there is an unfortunate aspect to the word *beshalom*, as it may refer to the peace of the World to Come. Therefore, if one tells his friend: *lech beshalom*, the friend may see this as a curse instead of a blessing. Instead, one should say: *lech leshalom*, "go to peace."

The Talmud continues that Torah scholars promote *shalom*, "peace," in the world. Iyun Yaakov says that the blessing *lech leshalom* infers that one should go and make peace among mankind. Such a person is a *shliach mitzvah,* an agent sent to perform a righteous deed, and it is stated that such an agent is protected from harm while going to and returning from his mission. This, says Iyun Yaakov, is why we find no instance where a righteous person told a friend, "go to peace," and harm befell the friend. But one who takes leave of a dead person is not to say that his friend should "go to peace." Whereas this phrase carries the implication that one is to go about making peace, something a dead person is unable to do, such an expression would amount to a taunt.

■ ■ ■

## Shemoth

וַיֹּאמֶר ה' אֶל־מֹשֶׁה בְּמִדְיָן לֵךְ שֻׁב מִצְרָיִם כִּי־מֵתוּ כָּל־הָאֲנָשִׁים הַמְבַקְשִׁים אֶת־נַפְשֶׁךָ.

*God told Moses in Midian, "Go return to Egypt, as all the men who are seeking to kill you have died." (4:19)*

"All the men who are seeking to kill you have died" — The Talmud says that the people to whom God was referring were Dathan and Aviram, the same two who revealed to Pharaoh that Moses had killed the Egyptian. Dathan and Aviram were actually still alive, but they had become poor, and a poor person is considered dead (Nedarim 64b).

Had Dathan and Aviram actually perished, God should have told Moses that the men "who *sought* to kill you" died. Instead, He used the present tense, declaring that the men "who *are seeking* to kill you" died. The inference was that Dathan and Aviram were still alive, and still desirous of Moses' death. However, they had become poor, and a poor person is considered dead, because people ignore what he has to say. Hence, Moses had no need to fear Dathan and Aviram any longer. *(Iturei Torah, citing Vilna Gaon)*

■

R. Yonathan Eybeschuetz suffered a great deal from people who spoke badly of him. He pointed out that God instructed Moses to return to Egypt, comforting him with the message that Dathan and Aviram had died. But what of Pharaoh, who had tried to execute Moses based on the report delivered to him by Dathan and Aviram that Moses had killed the Egyptian? Was not Pharaoh still alive? [This is based on the Midrash's view that, when Scripture says that Pharaoh died (2:23), it means he contracted leprosy.] It appears, said R. Yonathan, that the evil speech of Jews — Dathan and Aviram — is more dangerous than the sword of Pharaoh.

*(Cited by Iturei Torah)*

■

The Talmud states that the men who were "seeking to kill" Moses were Dathan and Aviram, the two who had told Pharaoh that Moses had executed the Egyptian who had been hitting a Jew (Rashi on

## The Eternal Heritage

2:13, 15). Dathan and Aviram had not actually died, but had become poor, and a poor man is considered dead.

Da'ath Zekenim MiBa'alei HaTosafoth wonders why the Talmud is certain that Dathan and Aviram had become poor. There are three other categories of men who are compared with the dead — lepers, blind men, and people who have no children (Nedarim 64b). Perhaps Dathan and Aviram belonged in one of those categories.

Da'ath Zekenim answers that there is no evidence that Dathan and Aviram were lepers, for had they been they would have been expelled from the camp of the Israelites, and we do not find that this occurred. We also know that they were not blind, since Scripture says, in the rebellion of Korach, that Dathan and Aviram had eyes (Numbers 16:12-14). Finally, the Torah records that they had children (Ibid., verse 27), thus eliminating that as a possibility.

Nevertheless, Da'ath Zekenim persists in positing that perhaps Dathan and Aviram had one of the aforementioned afflictions. The Sages say that all the sick people among the Israelites were healed at Mount Sinai. Whereas the present circumstance occurred before the Israelites went to Sinai, perhaps Dathan and Aviram had been lepers, or blind, but were later healed at Sinai.

Da'ath Zekenim answers that if such had been the case they would have again fallen sick after the worship of the Golden Calf.

Da'ath Zekenim proceeds to ask that perhaps at present Dathan and Aviram had not yet had children, seeing that the verse which mentions their children occurs later in Scripture. Why, again, is the Talmud so certain that they are reckoned as dead because they had become poor? Perhaps they were wealthy, but had no children.

Da'ath Zekenim answers that, concerning childlessness, one is considered dead only if he will never have children. Regardless of whether or not they had offspring at the present time, the fact that Dathan and Aviram eventually begot children precluded their being termed dead on this account.

To emphasize the impossibility of understanding their circumstance in any other fashion, Da'ath Zekenim adds that if Dathan and Aviram were wealthy, but had encountered leprosy, blindness, or childlessness, their ability to harm Moses would not

*Shemoth*

have been impaired. They still would have had the means to hire someone to kill Moses. How, then, could God have told Moses that he no longer had anything to fear from these men? Moses' security would have been ensured only if they had become poor and thereby lost their influence.

Finally, Da'ath Zekenim points out that *meithu*, "they died," has essentially the same numerical value as *yardu minichseihem*, "they became poor," the term used by the Talmud to describe Dathan and Aviram's financial situation. The value of the former is 446, and of the latter is 445, and it is accepted that the connection established by the equivalence of numerical values holds even if there is a variance of one between them. This too serves as evidence that Dathan and Aviram became poor.

■ ■ ■

וַיִּקַּח מֹשֶׁה אֶת־אִשְׁתּוֹ וְאֶת־בָּנָיו וַיַּרְכִּבֵם עַל־הַחֲמֹר וַיָּשָׁב אַרְצָה מִצְרָיִם וַיִּקַּח מֹשֶׁה אֶת־מַטֵּה הָאֱלֹהִים בְּיָדוֹ.

**Moses took his wife and sons, and, putting them on a donkey, set out to return to Egypt. Moses took God's staff in his hand. (4:20)**

Moses brought his family to Egypt in order to strengthen the Israelites' faith in the coming redemption. The people would comment that, whereas Moses himself was moving his wife and children to Egypt, this was a sign that he truly knew they would shortly be redeemed. He would not otherwise have brought them to Egypt. *(R. Yosef ibn Caspi)*

■ ■ ■

וְאָמַרְתָּ אֶל־פַּרְעֹה כֹּה אָמַר ה' בְּנִי בְכֹרִי יִשְׂרָאֵל. וָאֹמַר אֵלֶיךָ שַׁלַּח אֶת־בְּנִי וְיַעַבְדֵנִי וַתְּמָאֵן לְשַׁלְּחוֹ הִנֵּה אָנֹכִי הֹרֵג אֶת־בִּנְךָ בְּכֹרֶךָ.

*". . . You must say to Pharaoh, 'This is what God says: Israel is My son, My firstborn.*
*"'I have told you to let My son go so that he may serve Me. If you refuse to send him, I will kill your firstborn son.'" (4:22, 23)*

At this time, according to the Midrash, God affirmed Esau's sale of his birthright to Jacob.

## The Eternal Heritage

Why does God bring up the sale of the birthright specifically at this point?

The Midrash (Bereshith Rabbah 63) tells us that Jacob strove to acquire the birthright because he foresaw that the priestly service was to be performed by the firstborn. [This was only for a short time, as this responsibility was, very soon after the giving of the Torah, transferred to Aaron and his descendants.] Jacob saw that Esau, who was evil, did not deserve to have title to the position of priest. Now, God had told Abraham, "It is through Isaac that you will gain posterity" (Genesis 21:12). The verse literally reads: "*Within* Isaac you will gain posterity." Only part of Isaac's seed, the Sages say, would be considered Abraham's descendants. Jacob bought the birthright so that it would be in his branch of the family, not in Esau's, that God's blessings to Abraham would take effect. Had Jacob not done so, Esau would have inherited God's promises, as it is the firstborn's right to take the prime possessions of his father.

Along with the benefits promised by God came a liability — that Abraham's descendants would be slaves for 400 years (Ibid., 15:13). This was the burden only of the branch of the family which was to succeed Abraham, and Jacob assumed this responsibility when he acquired the birthright. Jacob's liability in the agreement was not merely to supply Esau with bread and lentils (Ibid., 25:34), but also to assume any responsibilities which would have been shouldered by Esau in his capacity of firstborn son to Isaac.

Jacob agreed to assume the burden of slavery so that he might acquire the benefits of the birthright, including the right to perform the sacrificial service. Therefore, Pharaoh certainly had no right to prevent the Israelites from sacrificing to God. This is the Torah's intent here, when it says, "Israel is My son, My firstborn. I have told you to let My son go so that he may serve Me." Pharaoh was ordered by God to allow the Israelites to serve Him by performing sacrifices (5:1). Pharaoh's refusal to do so was undermining the basis of the Egyptians' right to enslave the Israelites. If they were not to be permitted to perform sacrifices, they were similarly not subject to slavery. Therefore, Pharaoh's enslavement of the Israelites was an impediment to Israel's acquisition of its rights as the firstborn, and

## Shemoth

so [in corresponding measure] God would kill Pharaoh's firstborn son. *(R. Yosef Dov Soloveichik of Brisk)*

■

"Israel is My son, My firstborn." A firstborn son has greater importance than one's other children, and receives a double portion of the inheritance. This importance stems from the fact that it is this son who gives his father the status of a father.

The same holds true with God and the people of Israel. By recognizing God and promoting faith in Him, it is they who made Him into the Father of the world. It is for this reason that God describes Israel as "My son, My firstborn."

*(Meshech Chochmah)*

■ ■ ■

וַיְהִי בַדֶּרֶךְ בַּמָּלוֹן וַיִּפְגְּשֵׁהוּ ה' וַיְבַקֵּשׁ הֲמִיתוֹ.
*They were at the lodging place on the road, and God confronted Moses, seeking to kill him. (4:24)*

Our Sages say that Moses deserved to die because he delayed the circumcision of his son Eliezer. Now, this delay was the result of Moses' wish to immediately fulfill God's desire that he redeem the Israelites. It was for this purpose that Moses was hastening back to Egypt. Yet, because Moses neglected, without malicious intent, to perform one mitzvah, circumcision, the redemption of the Israelites, and all that was to transpire through that redemption, were jeopardized.

We see from this that the complete observance of all the commandments is a prerequisite for one who is working toward Israel's redemption. The redemption — with all its happy consequences — cannot come about, even through the true redeemer, if even one of the Torah's commandments is not being properly kept.
*(Ma'ayanah shel Torah, citing one of the Mussarists)*

An alternative may be proposed to explain why the redemption of the Israelites was jeopardized because Moses delayed the circumcision of his son.

## The Eternal Heritage

The purpose of the redemption from Egypt was to consecrate the Israelites as a holy nation, chosen above all other peoples. The Israelites were to become God's treasured community (19:5). The commandment which, more than any other, symbolizes the uniqueness of Israel is circumcision. Indeed, it was the only commandment which the children of Israel had to observe at this point in history, having not yet received the Torah. Hence, for Moses to abrogate this commandment, however benignly, undermined the purpose of the very redemption which he was to initiate. If Israel's uniqueness was not being demonstrated by Moses, the redemption which was meant to solidify that uniqueness could not transpire.

■ ■ ■

וַתִּקַּח צִפֹּרָה צֹר וַתִּכְרֹת אֶת־עָרְלַת בְּנָהּ וַתַּגַּע לְרַגְלָיו וַתֹּאמֶר כִּי חֲתַן־דָּמִים אַתָּה לִי.

*Tzipporah took a stone knife and cut off her son's foreskin. She threw it at [Moses'] feet and said, "You are the murderer of my husband." (4:25)*

The Talmud says that Rav and R. Yochanan differ about whether a woman can perform a circumcision, with Rav forbidding and R. Yochanan permitting.

The Talmud then asks: Can anyone maintain that a woman may not act as a *moheleth* (circumciser)? Does it not say, "Tzipporah took *(Vatikach)* a stone knife [and cut off her son's foreskin]"? It answers: Read *Vatakach*, "She caused to be taken." It continues: Does it not say, *vatichroth*, she "cut off"? It answers: Read *vatachreith*, "she caused to be cut off" — she told someone else to cut off the foreskin. (Perhaps Gershom, her older son, performed the circumcision; however, according to one Midrash, he was only about two years old at this time. It is possible that the innkeeper or some other traveler did the circumcision. The general assumption is that Eliezer was the child circumcised here. However, one Midrash says that Gershom was not circumcised when Moses lived with Jethro, so perhaps it was he who was now circumcised.) Another possibility is that she began the circumcision and Moses finished it (Avodah Zarah 27a).

## Shemoth

R. Tzvi Pesach Frank points to an inconsistency in Rashi's commentary on the Talmud. In explaining *Vatakach*, Rashi says that Tzipporah appointed a *shaliach*, an agent, to take the knife, while in explaining *vatachreith* (which he reads *vatachroth*, probably in error) he says she "told someone else" to cut off the foreskin. Why doesn't Rashi use the same language to explain both words?

R. Tzvi Pesach answers that Rashi's view is based on the law that one who cannot legally perform a particular function is not qualified to select an agent to fulfill that function. Tzipporah had the legal right to pick up the knife, and so she was able to ask someone to do likewise for her. This is why, regarding the knife, Rashi says that she appointed someone to pick it up. However, being a woman, she could not perform the circumcision itself, and so she also could not appoint someone to act in her stead. Hence, Rashi says only that she "told someone else" to circumcise Eliezer. The circumciser was not her agent, but acted of his own mind, albeit at her request.

R. Tzvi Pesach says that, given the above, there is no need to amend the word *Vatikach* to have it read *Vatakach*. Since the rule is that if one appoints an agent to act in his stead the agent embodies his sender — it is exactly as if the sender has performed the deed — it makes no difference if it was Tzipporah herself who picked up the knife or if it was the *mohel*. Either way, she is credited as the doer of the deed. It is thus entirely proper to say that she "took," *Vatikach*, the knife, even if her agent actually took it. It is only *vatichroth* which must be amended to read in the causative form, since the actual cutting could not be done by Tzipporah.

This, continues R. Tzvi Pesach, makes it difficult to understand the reading of the Talmudic text which is advanced by R. Yaakov Emden. R. Yaakov Emden vowelizes these two words, and *Vatikach* is vowelized as *Vatakach*. R. Tzvi Pesach asserts that this is an unnecessary emendation.

In truth, however, it would seem more problematic to read *Vatikach*, along with R. Tzvi Pesach. If the word is not being amended, what is the Talmud's response to the question of how

Tzipporah was able to pick up the knife? The response would be: "Read *Vatikach*," and the explanation would be that one may leave the text unamended, because regardless of who picked up the knife, Tzipporah is credited for doing so. This is not the common style in the Talmud. When it wishes to leave a word as written, it does not say, "Read . . ." This choice of words indicates a change in the reading, not a justification of the present reading. Hence, R. Yaakov Emden is correct in his view that *Vatikach* is amended by the Talmud to *Vatakach*.

The Rishonim — the medieval commentators on the Talmud — disagree regarding the eligibility of a woman to act as a *moheleth*. Tosafoth rules in accordance with Rav, who does not allow a woman to act as a *moheleth*. Despite the fact that Rav's disputant is R. Yochanan, and a disagreement between the two is generally resolved in the latter's favor, Tosafoth contends that the Talmud's tone here dictates differently. However, Ba'al Halachoth Gedoloth, quoted by Tosafoth, rules in accordance with R. Yochanan, that a woman may perform a circumcision. Rambam rules similarly (Hilchoth Milah 2:1).

Shulchan Aruch also declares that a woman may be a *moheleth* (Yoreh Deah 264:1). However, R. Moshe Isserles (Rema) says, "Some say that a woman does not circumcise," and asserts that the custom is that women do not perform circumcisions if a man is available to perform the procedure.

Shach wonders how Rema's view differs from that of Shulchan Aruch. Shulchan Aruch himself writes that, while all are fit to act as circumcisers — even slaves, women, minors, and males who are uncircumcised because their brothers died during circumcision — it is preferable to select a male for the task. What, then, is Rema adding by saying that it is preferable for a male to perform a circumcision? If his opinion is that a woman may perform circumcision but that a male is preferred, then he is just reiterating Shulchan Aruch's words, which is not Rema's style. If, on the other hand, he believes a woman may not be a *moheleth*, then it is imprecise to say that the "custom" is to find a male. It would not be due to custom, but due to law, that a man is needed.

Two explanations may be proposed to clarify Rema's words. First, it should be noted that Taz understands Rema to be recording the opinion of Rav — that a woman is ineligible to perform circumcision. And yet, Taz is apparently not bothered by Rema's dictate that the "custom" is to seek out a man for the task. It is possible that Taz understands Rema as introducing Rav's view without accepting it as law. Rema writes only, "Some say a woman does not circumcise." He does not say that R. Yochanan's lenient view is rejected. However, where a male is available, it is preferable, in light of the strict view, that he act as the *mohel*.

Given the above approach, Rema would differ from Shulchan Aruch in that the latter, who makes no mention of Rav's opinion, gives it no decisive credence at all. Despite this, a male is preferred, according to Shulchan Aruch, for reasons unexplained. One may conjecture that this is similar to the case of *shechitah*, ritual slaughter. Although women may act as slaughterers, Rema writes that a man is preferred for the task, since it is not the custom for women to be *shochatoth*. (This is only an example, not a comparison, as Shulchan Aruch himself maintains that there is no difference between the sexes regarding *shechitah*.)

In a second resolution to the difficulty in Rema's words, we may assume that he and Shulchan Aruch are in agreement regarding the necessity to acknowledge the strict view — Rav's enjoinment of circumcision by a woman. However, they differ in how much impact Rav's opinion has. This may be deduced from a careful analysis of the phrasing each codifier uses. Shulchan Aruch declares, "If there is an adult male who knows how to circumcise, he takes precedence over all others." Rema says, "The custom is to take the preferred course of seeking out a male." Shulchan Aruch is explicit in demanding from the male who is to replace the woman, minor, etc., only the ability to circumcise. It appears that as long as the male has that ability he should replace the female, even if the woman is more adept at the task (assuming, of course, that the difference in ability will pose no health risk to the infant). Rema does not discuss such a minimum standard for the male. He may believe that one should seek out a male only if the male is better in ability, or, perhaps, equal in ability, to the prospective female circumciser. If there is not a man more capable than she — or, if the narrower proposition is correct, equal to her — then there is not a reason to have a man perform the circumcision.

■

*Chathan damim,* "the murderer of my husband," is more literally translated "a bloody bridegroom." Radak suggests that, just as we term a groom on his wedding day a *chathan,* so, in Biblical times, were newborn sons referred to by the term *chathan* on the day of their circumcision.

To Radak, *chathan* indicates a renewal of joy — an emotion experienced on the wedding day and at the circumcision of a baby.

■ ■ ■

וַיֹּאמֶר ה' אֶל־אַהֲרֹן לֵךְ לִקְרַאת מֹשֶׁה הַמִּדְבָּרָה וַיֵּלֶךְ וַיִּפְגְּשֵׁהוּ בְּהַר הָאֱלֹהִים וַיִּשַּׁק־לוֹ.

*God said to Aaron, "Go meet Moses in the desert." He went and met him at God's mountain, and kissed him. (4:27)*

Sforno says that Aaron kissed Moses as if he were kissing a holy object.

Aaron certainly had a very powerful love for his brother, and he desired to kiss Moses in a way that would express this love. After all, they had not seen each other for a number of years. However, Aaron suppressed this love and kissed Moses as he would kiss a holy object. He expressed the spiritual love one has when greeting a holy object, such as a Torah scroll. Neither Aaron's emotional love for Moses, nor his joy at seeing Moses' glory as a messenger of God, was involved in Aaron's greeting. Instead, he embraced and kissed the holy scroll which stood before him. *(Ohr Yahel)*

■ ■ ■

וַיַּאֲמֵן הָעָם וַיִּשְׁמְעוּ כִּי־פָקַד ה' אֶת־בְּנֵי יִשְׂרָאֵל וְכִי רָאָה אֶת־עָנְיָם וַיִּקְּדוּ וַיִּשְׁתַּחֲוּוּ.

*The people believed. They accepted the message that God had remembered the*

## Shemoth

*Israelites, and that He had seen their misery. They bowed their heads and prostrated themselves.* (4:31)

It is astonishing — writes R. Yaakov Kamenetsky — that now the Israelites were so ready to believe Moses' message that God was about to redeem them. Later, however, after Pharaoh increased their workload, they would not hearken to Moses, due to the oppression they were suffering. Were they not, at the present time, also burdened with "broken spirits and the hard labor" (6:9)?

R. Yaakov proposes that the Israelites felt that Pharaoh's wickedness was unnatural. Logic dictated that a nation which had been invited to move to Egypt, and which had brought relief from famine to the Egyptians, would be treated in a dignified manner. The harsh slavery imposed upon the Israelites was contrary to the accepted norm of conduct. The Israelites reasoned that they must be undergoing a punishment from Heaven. Their redemption would thus come at the moment that God chose to have mercy upon them. He would then send messengers to Pharaoh with word that the Israelites were to be freed, and Pharaoh would readily comply.

However, to the Israelites' disbelief, Pharaoh did not heed the demand of Moses and Aaron, God's messengers, and he refused to release the Israelites. Indeed, he imposed an even harsher regimen upon them. They then realized that it was truly Pharaoh's desire to enslave them, against all logic, and so they lost hope of redemption and did not believe Moses' message of salvation.

R. Yaakov continues that God subjected the Israelites to this continued and increased slavery in order to impress upon them the fact that the kindness of the nations is worthless. The Israelites were to rely only on God for redemption — here and in the future — not on the good will of others.

This — adds R. Yaakov (on Deuteronomy 32:36) — is the meaning of the Talmud's assertion (Sanhedrin 97a) that the Messiah will not arrive until the Jews lose hope of redemption. (The Talmud bases this comment on Scripture's statement in Deuteronomy (Ibid.) that "God will then take up the cause of His people," when they have "no protection or help.") How can it be that the Jews will give up hope

## The Eternal Heritage

of Messiah's coming? After all, the expectation of Messiah's arrival is one of the principles of Jewish faith. Can a basis for redemption be conditional upon the eradication from Israel of belief in that very redemption? This is inconceivable.

R. Yaakov explains the Talmud's assertion to mean that as long as the Israelites expect their redemption to take place along natural lines — through the mercy of the nations of the world, who will give the Jews a homeland and other accoutrements of freedom — the Messiah will not come. This is because the Jews are hated more than any other nation, and the kindness of the nations is not truly kindness. Only when the Jews abandon the hope of such a redemption, when they understand that they have "no protection or help," and that God alone can redeem them, will the Messiah come.

■ ■ ■

וַיֹּאמֶר אֲלֵהֶם מֶלֶךְ מִצְרַיִם לָמָּה מֹשֶׁה וְאַהֲרֹן תַּפְרִיעוּ אֶת־הָעָם מִמַּעֲשָׂיו לְכוּ לְסִבְלֹתֵיכֶם.

*The Egyptian king said to them, "Why, Moses and Aaron, are you distracting the people from their work? Get back to your own business." (5:4)*

It has been a custom throughout history for a country to extend special privileges to the leaders of its oppressed minorities. The intention is that these leaders will be content and will refrain from protesting the evil perpetrated upon their brethren.

It seems that this was Pharaoh's practice as well. The Sages say that Moses and Aaron — indeed, the entire Tribe of Levi — were exempt from the servitude imposed upon the Israelites. Despite this, Moses and Aaron demanded that their nation be freed. Pharaoh was angered. He asked: "Why, Moses and Aaron, are you distracting the people from their work?" Haven't I appeased you by giving you special rights? Why do you interfere with my policies regarding the Israelites?

*(MeOtzareinu HaYashan)*

■ ■ ■

## Shemoth

לֹא תֹאסִפוּן לָתֵת תֶּבֶן לָעָם לִלְבֹּן הַלְּבֵנִים כִּתְמוֹל שִׁלְשֹׁם הֵם יֵלְכוּ וְקֹשְׁשׁוּ לָהֶם תֶּבֶן.

"Do not continue to give the people straw to make the bricks, as it was before. They will go and gather their own straw. . . ." (5:7)

Why did Pharaoh decree that the Israelites would now have to seek their own straw? Why didn't he simply increase the amount of bricks they were expected to make each day?

Pharaoh's goal was to embitter the lives of the Israelites. He knew that worry and heartbreak are much more oppressive than even the harshest labor. Therefore, he preferred to impose upon them the worry of finding straw rather than merely adding to their labor.

*(R. Chanoch Henoch of Aleksandrow)*

■ ■ ■

וַיָּשָׁב מֹשֶׁה אֶל־ה' וַיֹּאמַר אֲדֹנָי לָמָה הֲרֵעֹתָה לָעָם הַזֶּה לָמָּה זֶּה שְׁלַחְתָּנִי.

Moses returned to God and said, "O Lord, why do You mistreat this people? Why did You send me? . . ." (5:22)

Moses was humble and believed he did not deserve to be the Israelites' savior. Therefore, he affixed the blame for the increased oppression of the Israelites upon himself. He cried: "Why did You send me?" If God had dispatched someone more suitable, Pharaoh would not have hardened his position.

God responded, "Now you will see what I will do to Pharaoh" (6:1). Now — seeing how humble you are — you are truly worthy of redeeming the Israelites, and you will see the redemption come to fruition.

*(Cited by Ma'ayanah shel Torah)*

■ ■ ■

וּמֵאָז בָּאתִי אֶל־פַּרְעֹה לְדַבֵּר בִּשְׁמֶךָ הֵרַע לָעָם הַזֶּה וְהַצֵּל לֹא־הִצַּלְתָּ אֶת־עַמֶּךָ.

". . . From the moment I came to Pharaoh to speak in Your name he made things worse for the people. You have done nothing to rescue Your people." (5:23)

R. Levi Yitzchak of Berdichev says that every Jew who seeks relief for the people of Israel should address God in the manner

## The Eternal Heritage

Moses did. Moses said, "From the moment I came to Pharaoh to speak in Your name he made things worse for the people." One should assert to God that the Jews are hated because they "come to Pharaoh to speak in Your name" — due to the fact that they speak God's words. It is therefore God's fault that the Jews are oppressed, and so it is His responsibility to redeem them.

■ ■ ■

וַיֹּאמֶר ה' אֶל־מֹשֶׁה עַתָּה תִרְאֶה אֲשֶׁר אֶעֱשֶׂה לְפַרְעֹה כִּי בְיָד חֲזָקָה יְשַׁלְּחֵם וּבְיָד חֲזָקָה יְגָרְשֵׁם מֵאַרְצוֹ.

*God said to Moses, "Now you will see what I will do to Pharaoh. He will be forced to let [the Israelites] go — he will be forced to drive them out of his land." (6:1)*

The Talmud says that the Messiah will not arrive until the Israelites give up hope of redemption (Sanhedrin 97a).

A similar thing occurred in Egypt. The situation had deteriorated to such an extent that not only the Israelites had lost hope of salvation — "You have destroyed our reputation with Pharaoh and his advisors. You have placed a sword in their hands to kill us" (5:21) — but even Moses had despaired, saying, "Why do You mistreat Your people? Why did You send me?" (Ibid., verse 22). With the pessimism of the Jews so pronounced, God said, "Now you will see . . ." Now that the condition for redemption had been met, the Israelites would be rescued.

*(Pardes Yosef)*

■

The verse refers twice to *yad chazakah,* "force" (lit., "strong hand"). Rashi, according to Mizrachi, says that the first application of force would be against Pharaoh — "He will be forced to let [the Israelites] go." God would compel Pharaoh, by virtue of the plagues, to free the Israelites. The second instance of force applied to the Israelites. Pharaoh would make them depart Egypt hastily, without allowing them time to bake bread (12:33-34).

Sifthei Chachamim disagrees with Mizrachi's view of the second clause. Sifthei Chachamim contends that God would be the applier of force in both clauses. Because God would exert a strong hand over the Egyptians, they would drive the Israelites out of their land.

At any rate, according to Rashi the first clause — "He will be forced to let them go" — refers to the "strong hand" God would apply to the Egyptians with the plagues. Rashbam disputes Rashi's explanation, stating that the "strong hand" to which Scripture refers is that of the Egyptians, the one alluded to in the words "The Egyptians were insistent with the people that they should hurry and leave" (12:33).

■

Why must Scripture first state that the Egyptians will send the Israelites away and then say that Pharaoh will drive out the Israelites from his land? Isn't this repetitive? Furthermore, the Torah says that Pharaoh will "drive them out of his land." Why would it be necessary to drive away the Israelites? Wouldn't they be anxious to leave Egypt?

The Talmud records that the enslavement of the Israelites actually ceased six months before they departed Egypt (Rosh HaShanah 11a). The redemption was a two-step process, and the present verse alludes to the two stages. First, Pharaoh would "let them go." He would free them from the obligation to serve the Egyptians. *Yeshalcheim*, "He will . . . let them go," is to be understood in the same fashion as *lachofshi yeshalchenu*, "he shall set him free," stated in regard to the freeing of a Canaanite slave (21:26), which refers to the dispensation with servitude. However, as we often find with the Jews, when they obtain a respite from their troubles, however minor the respite may be, they tend to be satisfied and abandon the hope of a complete salvation. When the slavery ceased, six months before the departure from Egypt, the Israelites lost sight of that larger goal. They were content to remain in Egypt as free men. Therefore, there would be a necessity to drive them out of Egypt, against their will.

*(R. Yitzchak Yaakov Reines)*

# 2
# VaEra

וַיְדַבֵּר אֱלֹהִים אֶל־מֹשֶׁה וַיֹּאמֶר אֵלָיו אֲנִי ה׳.
*God spoke to Moses and said to him, "I am God. . . ."* (6:2)

The present verse uses *Elokim*, God's name denoting justice — "*Elokim* spoke to Moses." God then proceeds to discuss Israel's redemption. In the previous verse, where God tells Moses that He will punish Pharaoh, *Ado-nai*, the name of God denoting mercy, is used — "*Ado-nai* said to Moses." Why is the name denoting justice used in connection with a merciful event, while the converse occurs with the name indicating mercy?

Alshich explains the usage of God's different names by making reference to the Sages' dictum that righteous people cause the attribute of justice to become merciful (Sukkah 14a). The opposite obtains with wicked people. Thus, when God told Moses that Pharaoh would be punished, He used the name *Ado-nai*, denoting the attribute of mercy, which Pharaoh had caused to become strict. And in discussing the Israelites, God went by His name of justice, which would become merciful — "*Elokim* spoke to Moses and said to him, 'I am *Ado-nai*.'"

■

God spoke harshly to Moses because he had criticized God regarding the condition of the Israelites (Rashi).

## The Eternal Heritage

Mizrachi advances two possible bases upon which Rashi built his statement. Firstly, Scripture uses God's name denoting justice — *Elokim*. Alternatively, the word *Vayedaber* ("spoke") connotes a harsh tone (see Rashi on Numbers 12:1).

■ ■ ■

וָאֵרָא אֶל־אַבְרָהָם אֶל־יִצְחָק וְאֶל־יַעֲקֹב בְּאֵל שַׁדָּי וּשְׁמִי ה' לֹא נוֹדַעְתִּי לָהֶם.

". . . I revealed Myself to Abraham, to Isaac, and to Jacob as God Almighty (El Shaddai), and did not allow them to know Me by the name God (YHVH). . . ." (6:3)

Scripture mentions Abraham, Isaac, and Jacob separately — "*to* Abraham, *to* Isaac, and *to* Jacob," rather than "to Abraham, Isaac, and Jacob." This is because each of the patriarchs possessed a unique distinction.

Abraham's distinction was that he recognized God before God ever made Himself known to him. Now, someone who observes God's conduct and comports himself in the same manner is not considered praiseworthy. After all, anyone with intelligence would choose to act in accordance with the ways of God, as they are obviously the components of absolute good. Abraham's arrival at recognition of God occurred before he was able to perceive God's characteristics and conduct.

Isaac's uniqueness was that he readily allowed himself to be brought onto the altar. Jacob's mark of distinction was that all his children were righteous, unlike Abraham, who bore Ishmael, and Isaac, who bore Esau.

God now told Moses that, despite the singular greatness of each of the patriarchs, He had not revealed Himself to them at a high level. He had revealed Himself only with the name *E-l Shad-dai*, which is a lower level of revelation than the one Moses had experienced. God had revealed Himself to Moses at the level of the Tetragrammaton *(YHVH)* — "I am God" (verse 2). Moses was being reprimanded for showing ingratitude to God. Although he had surpassed the patriarchs, experiencing a closer connection with God, he had not spoken with God in a befitting manner. [Instead, Moses had complained that God had sent him to Pharaoh, ostensibly to improve the Israelites' situation, but that Pharaoh had proceeded to increase their oppression (5:22, 23).]

While we do find that the Tetragrammaton was used by God in speaking to the patriarchs [e.g., Genesis 15:7, 28:13], there was a difference between the patriarchs and Moses. God did reveal to the patriarchs the Tetragrammaton as His name, but they did not merit understanding the lofty level which the Tetragrammaton represents. This is the meaning of God's assertion that He "did not allow t' ɔm to know Me by the name God."

*(Ohr HaChayyim)*

■

The verse begins by using a term that denotes seeing — *Va'era*, literally, "I allowed Myself to be seen" — and ends with a term that denotes knowing: *lo nodati lahem*, "I did not allow them to know Me." Why isn't the Torah more consistent in its phraseology? Either the end of the verse should also have spoken of seeing — *lo nireithi lahem*, "I did not allow them to see Me" — or the start of the verse should have been phrased in terms of knowing — *va'evada*, "I made Myself known."

*Re'iyah*, the terminology for "seeing," indicates a greater certainty regarding a matter than does *yediah*, "knowing." It is possible for one to think he has knowledge of something, based on intellectual conclusion or through hearing about it, and yet it turns out that he has erred. But when one witnesses something with his own eyes, the likelihood of error vanishes. The best verification of something is when one witnesses it himself.

The name *E-l Shad-dai* is to be understood as Rashi explains regarding the verse "May God Almighty *(E-l Shad-dai)* grant that the man have pity on you" (Genesis 43:14). Jacob told his sons, "He who said to the world: *dai* ['Sufficient' — God provided the world with all its needs] should say *dai* regarding my troubles." The patriarchs faced difficulties throughout much or all of their lives. Abraham was first thrown into a furnace by Nimrod. Then he was forced to travel about, and his wife was taken from him by the Pharaoh. Isaac's wife was also taken, and the Philistines sealed the wells he had dug. [Actually, Isaac found that Abraham's wells had been sealed, and he redug them (Genesis 26:18). Isaac's difficulties were with the Philistine shepherds, who fought with him concerning the ownership of several wells.] Moreover, Isaac was considered a sojourner. As for Jacob, he encountered more troubles than his fathers. Nevertheless, God pronounced an end, *dai*, to their difficulties, and this is reflected in the name *E-l Shad-dai*. The patriarchs were eyewitnesses to the fact that God had shielded them from their problems.

The Tetragrammaton has a different connotation. It is the name that reflects God's attribute of mercy, so that one encounters no difficulties in his life. Not only were the patriarchs not eyewitnesses to this attribute, but they were not able to know of it due to any intellectual calculation.

The change in terminology in the present verse now becomes comprehensible. God told Moses that the troubles one may encounter were known to the patriarchs not circumstantially — intellectually, or by hearing of them — but empirically. They saw trouble with their own eyes; they themselves were confronted by it. Conversely, not only did they fail to observe God's pure attribute of mercy with their eyes, but they did not even have any knowledge of it. Therefore, while God had told the patriarchs of the Tetragrammaton, He had not displayed His mercy to them.

The following verses continue with this theme. Furthermore, said God, He had established a covenant with the patriarchs — that they would inherit the Land of Canaan (verse 4) — but this too had not come to pass in their lifetimes. Finally, God had heard the groaning of the Israelites due to the slavery (verse 5).

Now, however, the Israelites would directly experience the mercy of God, as represented by the Tetragrammaton, and would be free from bondage and brought to Canaan, while their masters would be punished (verses 6-8).

*(Kli Yekar)*

## VaEra

"[I] did not allow them to know Me by the name God" — as I promised to them, but did not fulfill it (Rashi).

Why, indeed, were the patriarchs silent? Why didn't they challenge God regarding the fact that He had not fulfilled His promises, while Moses did challenge God?

The answer is that, for the patriarchs, the promise that they would inherit Canaan applied only to themselves, as there was not yet an Israelite nation. When a matter affects just a person himself, he is not as diligent in pursuing it as when it affects others.

By Moses' time the promise applied to all the Israelites, and so Moses demanded to know why it had not been kept.

*(Yalkut Yehuda)*

■ ■ ■

לָכֵן אֱמֹר לִבְנֵי-יִשְׂרָאֵל אֲנִי ה' וְהוֹצֵאתִי אֶתְכֶם מִתַּחַת סִבְלֹת מִצְרַיִם וְהִצַּלְתִּי אֶתְכֶם מֵעֲבֹדָתָם וְגָאַלְתִּי אֶתְכֶם בִּזְרוֹעַ נְטוּיָה וּבִשְׁפָטִים גְּדֹלִים. וְלָקַחְתִּי אֶתְכֶם לִי לְעָם וְהָיִיתִי לָכֶם לֵאלֹהִים וִידַעְתֶּם כִּי אֲנִי ה' אֱלֹהֵיכֶם הַמּוֹצִיא אֶתְכֶם מִתַּחַת סִבְלוֹת מִצְרָיִם.

"... Therefore, say to the Israelites [in My name], 'I am God. I will take you away from the forced labor of Egypt and I will rescue you from their bondage. I will redeem you with an outstretched arm and with great judgments.

"I will take you to Myself as a nation, and I will be your God. You will know that I am God your Lord, who is bringing you out from under the Egyptian subjugation. . . .'" (6:6, 7)

The Jerusalem Talmud asks: Where in Scripture do we find an allusion to the four cups of wine which are drunk at the Passover Seder? Four answers are given. R. Yochanan responds in the name of R. Banyah that the present verses have four references to redemption. The four references are: "I will take you away," "I will rescue you," "I will redeem you," and "I will take you to Myself." These allude to the four cups. R. Yehoshua b. Levi says that the four cups correspond to the four cups that are mentioned regarding Pharaoh (Genesis 40:11, 13). R. Levi avers that the four cups represent the four kingdoms which, during history, subjugated Israel — Babylonia, Persia, Greece, and Rome. The Sages maintain that the four cups symbolize the four cups — measures — of retribution that God will one day force the nations of the world to drink, corresponding to which there will be four cups of consolation which the Jews will drink (Pesachim 10:1).

There is apparently a difference of opinion between the reason given by R. Banyah and the reasons proposed by the other Sages. According to R. Banyah, the four cups of wine which are consumed at the Seder have a direct link with the redemption from Egypt. However, the other opinions do not see the source for the four cups in the present verses' description of the redemption, finding other bases for the practice. It seems that according to these views the four cups are not a symbol of the redemption from Egyptian bondage.

With the above in mind, we may postulate that a legal difference as well will arise from this dispute. As a foreword, we take note of the description by the Alter Rebbe (R. Shneur Zalman of Lyady), in his Shulchan Aruch HaRav, of the laws of *hasebah* — reclining while at the Seder (Hilchoth Pesach 472:14): When must one recline? While eating the matzoh . . . the sandwich of matzoh and *maror* [*korech*], and the *afikoman*, and while drinking the four cups, since all of these things are a reminder of the redemption and freeing of the Israelites, as the four cups were established by the Sages to represent the four references to redemption mentioned in the portion VaEra: "I will take you away from the forced labor of Egypt," "I will redeem you," "I will take you to Myself," and "I will rescue you." And the *afikoman* and sandwich are a reminder of the Paschal sacrifice, which was eaten in a manner signifying freedom. Therefore, they require reclining in a fashion that indicates freedom. But one may eat the rest of the meal without reclining . . . However, if one reclines during the entire meal, he is praiseworthy, and has performed the commandment in the preferred manner.

This is the statement of the Alter Rebbe. We see that he relates the obligation to recline while eating matzoh, *korech*, and the *afikoman*, and while drinking the wine, to the fact that they symbolize the Israelites' redemption and freedom.

## VaEra

There are three problems which must be addressed. Firstly, earlier in the same section he explains that reclination is required because "in every generation one must demonstrate that it is as if he himself left the bondage of Egypt . . . Therefore, one must perform all of the evening's functions in a manner indicating freedom." Given this, there should be no need to give a special reason why the matzoh and wine must be consumed while reclining. To the contrary, a basis should be advanced for the exemption which is granted regarding the rest of the meal.

Secondly, why does the Alter Rebbe mention that the four expressions of redemption are "mentioned in the portion of VaEra"? He does not generally record the location of the verses that he quotes.

Finally, the Alter Rebbe changes the order of the four expressions as they are found in Scripture and in the Talmud. He removes "I will rescue you" from the second position to the fourth position. Why is the sequence altered?

The above difficulties may be resolved by first examining the nature of the obligation to recline. This may be not a separate law among the laws of the Seder, but merely a corollary to the requirements to consume matzoh and wine. In other words, just as there are stipulations regarding the amount and kind of matzoh and wine which are to be used, so is there a stipulation regarding the manner in which they are to be eaten — while reclining.

Alternatively, the obligation to recline may be a law unto itself. A person is mandated, on Passover night, to demonstrate that he is a free man by reclining. He is to recline while performing other mandated rituals — eating matzoh and drinking wine — but this is essentially a separate requirement. It is not merely a component of the other rituals.

The difference between these two outlooks would have a bearing if one consumed the required amount of matzoh in an upright position. If reclination is an integral part of the commandment to eat matzoh, then he has not satisfied the requirement, due to the Rabbinic stipulation that one must recline. (He has, however, fulfilled the Biblical requirement.) Conversely, if reclination is a separate law, then, while he has not fulfilled the obligation to recline, he *has* fulfilled the obligation to eat matzoh. Now, the halacha is that one who has not consumed the matzoh while reclining must eat it again, in a reclining position. While this would seem to support the thesis that reclination is an integral part of the obligation to eat matzoh, that is not the case. Even if reclination is a separate obligation, it must be done while the matzoh is being consumed, and so the Sages mandated that one must again eat the matzoh — not to fulfill the commandment to eat matzoh, but to properly execute the commandment to recline.

While in this case one would have to eat the matzoh a second time regardless of the nature of the mitzvah to recline, a practical difference between the two theses exists respective to the blessing which is made over the mitzvah to eat matzoh. If the obligation to consume matzoh a second time, this time in a position of reclination, is merely for the purpose of properly fulfilling the requirement to recline — while the requirement to eat matzoh has already been satisfied — then one would not repeat the blessing over the matzoh. However, if the purpose in eating again is to fulfill the commandment to eat matzoh, which having first been done in an upright position has not yet been properly accomplished, then one would have to repeat the blessing.

Another practical difference would obtain if the person in question is now in a situation where he would not have to recline — if, for example, he is at the table of his rabbi. If he did not fulfill the obligation to consume matzoh earlier, because he had not reclined, then he would have to eat matzoh a second time; but he would not have to do this in a reclining position, because there is no obligation to recline at his rabbi's table. However, if he did fulfill the obligation to eat matzoh, then there would be no purpose in eating again, while reclining, because he is currently exempt from reclining.

There are proofs which substantiate each position. The Talmud says: "A butler who consumed matzoh while reclining has fulfilled his obligation. If he was reclining, this is the case, but if he was not reclining, this is not the case" (Pesachim 108a). The implication is that if the butler did not recline he did not satisfy the obligation to eat matzoh, and that reclination is subsumed under the mitzvah to eat matzoh. If the obligation in question is the one to recline, then there would be no purpose in saying that "if he was not reclining" he did not fulfill his obligation. It would go beyond saying that, if there were a separate mitzvah to recline and one did not recline, then he did not satisfy the requirement. This is evidence that reclination is part and parcel of the commandment to eat matzoh.

Further, Rosh wonders whether one who drank the third and fourth cups of wine in an upright position should drink again, since doing so would make it appear that he is adding to the number of cups one must drink. Rosh avers that since he did not drink in the prescribed manner — while reclining — it is evident that what he drank was not to be counted among the four cups, and so he should drink again. Rosh clearly believes that reclination is part of the ritual of drinking the four cups of wine. And the same would logically hold with matzoh.

However, proof may be evinced that there is a separate mitzvah to recline, from the Alter Rebbe's declaration that one who reclines during the entire Seder is praiseworthy, and has fulfilled the mitzvah in the preferred manner. Now, if reclination is part of the matzoh ritual, why is one praised for reclining during the rest of the meal, when it is purposeless? It would seem that reclination is itself a mitzvah, one whose main fulfillment comes about while consuming the matzoh, but which nevertheless is a meritorious act when done throughout the entire Seder.

But one can refute this proof. The entire meal is part of the holiday celebration. It may be that reclination is not a commandment unto itself. It may be part of the matzoh ritual in an indispensable sense and part of the holiday ritual in a more elastic sense — being praiseworthy, but not mandatory.

There is, however, other proof that reclination is a separate ritual. Rambam writes: "In every generation one *is required* to demonstrate that he himself has today left the bondage of Egypt . . . Therefore, when he dines on this night he must eat and drink while reclining, which is a mannerism indicating freedom" (Hilchoth Chametz U'Matzoh 7:6, 7). It is not Rambam's general policy to give the reason for his decisions. Therefore, it would appear that, in saying one must demonstrate that he has left Egypt, Rambam is not merely giving a *reason* for the obligation to recline, but holds that this demonstration is an *obligation in itself*. This is why he writes that one "is required" to *demonstrate his freedom*, not just that one is required to recline. Now, whereas this requirement is independent of the requirement to partake of matzoh, it is obvious that the manner by which freedom is demonstrated — reclination — is independent as well.

In order to resolve the conflicting evidence, one can say that there are two aspects to reclination. There *is* a unique requirement to recline. But it is also a part of the matzoh ritual. Hence, when one consumes matzoh while reclining, he satisfies the obligation to eat the matzoh while reclining, and also satisfies the obligation to recline as a ritual unto itself. And while even this independent mitzvah finds its ultimate fulfillment when one is consuming the matzoh and wine, there is a secondary fulfillment if one reclines throughout the rest of the Seder — it is praiseworthy, and one who does so fulfills the obligation in the preferred manner.

This clarifies the words of the Alter Rebbe. After recording the obligation to recline using Rambam's language, he adds, "Therefore, one must perform all of the evening's functions in a manner that indicates freedom." This refers to the requirement to recline in its independent aspect. Later, in enumerating the specific rituals for which reclination is mandated — matzoh, *korech*, and wine — he is referring to reclination as a component of these rituals. As he concludes, "Therefore, [the rituals] require reclining in a fashion that indicates freedom." The reason is that "all [these rituals] symbolize redemption and freedom" — because they stand as symbols of redemption and freedom, it is imperative that one recline in order to properly execute them.

In discussing the four cups of wine, the Alter Rebbe explains that they "were established by the Sages to represent the four references to redemption mentioned in the portion VaEra." It is because the cups represent the redemption that one must recline during their consumption. This would not be the case regarding any of the other

## VaEra

reasons proffered for the drinking of the four cups — the four cups of Pharaoh, the four exiles, and the four cups of retribution which God will make the nations drink. None of these reasons would serve to explain the requirement to recline.

This is why the Alter Rebbe goes out of his way to mention that the languages of redemption are found in the portion VaEra. It is not his intention to cite the source of the redemption verses. Rather, he wishes to emphasize that these verses appear in the section of the Torah which relates the story of the Exodus, as it is due to this episode of redemption that one must recline while drinking the four cups.

There is, however, additional significance to the four cups. The Alter Rebbe states: "One must drink the four cups in the proper order [according to the Seder ritual]. That is, between the first and second cups, and between the third and fourth cups, one is to recite the Haggadah and Hallel respectively, and between the second and third cups one engages in the eating of the matzoh and the Grace after meals" (Ibid., Subsection 16). This is because (in the words of Beth Yosef, the commentary written by R. Yosef Caro on the Tur code before he authored Shulchan Aruch) "[the Sages] established each cup for its particular purpose." It seems, then, that the four cups were established not only as a symbol of redemption, but that each cup also has its unique function in the Seder ritual. For this reason the Alter Rebbe alters the sequence of the four languages of redemption, moving "I will rescue you" from the second position to the fourth. The four expressions — "I will take you away," "I will redeem you," "I will take you to Myself," and "I will rescue you" — correspond, in this order, to the various aspects of the Seder.

The first cup is the one upon which *Kiddush*, the sanctification service, is recited. In the *Kiddush* one says, "in commemoration of the Exodus from Egypt." This corresponds to "I will take you away from the forced labor of Egypt." The second cup is the one before which the main body of the Haggadah is read. The difference between the commandment to discuss the Exodus on Passover night and the commandment to mention the Exodus every day is that on Passover night the Exodus must be discussed at length. This corresponds to "I will redeem you with an outstretched arm and with great judgments" — which refers to the miracles that heralded the redemption. And the blessing over the second cup concludes: "who redeemed us and redeemed our forefathers from Egypt . . . Blessed be You, God, who redeemed Israel."

The third cup is the one upon which the Grace after the meal is said. An indispensable part of the text of Grace is: "We thank You . . . for Your Torah which You taught us." This thought corresponds to "I will take you to Myself as a nation, and I will be your God." This statement alludes to the giving of the Torah, as is evident from Scripture's words: "Today you have become a nation to God, your Lord" (Deuteronomy 27:9). [This verse refers to the giving of the completed Torah to the Israelites, which occurred on the day Moses told this to them. See Ramban, Ibid., 29:1, Rashi, Ibid., verse 9, R. Bachya on the present verse, and Meiri on Pesachim 99b.]

The final cup is the one with which Hallel is completed. The emphasis of this cup is on the future redemption, as is seen from the inclusion of a paragraph which calls on God to pour out His wrath upon the nations [see R. Bachya on verse 6]. "I will rescue you from their bondage" alludes to this future redemption. The manner of rescue is not indicated, and we find the same idea expressed by Rambam regarding the final redemption: "As for all these things . . . no one will know how they will transpire until they occur" (Hilchoth Melachim 12:2).

Thus, the parts of the Seder which are connected to each of the four cups correspond to the four expressions of redemption in the order given by the Alter Rebbe and are each related to aspects of redemption and freedom.

*(R. Menachem Mendel Schneerson,
the Lubavitcher Rebbe)*

■

Whence do we derive the requirement for four cups of wine on Passover? R. Yochanan says: They correspond to the four redemptions — "I will take you away," "I will rescue you," "I will redeem you," and "I will take you to Myself" (Jerusalem Talmud, Pesachim 10:1).

Torah Temimah points out that the other sources which record this thought use the phrase "four languages of redemption," while the Jerusalem Talmud uses the phrase "four redemptions." He opines that the latter is the preferred terminology, for the former would indicate that there was one redemption, whose occurrence was expressed in four different ways. Why would we establish a ritual of drinking four cups of wine to thank God for one redemption? Why should it matter that Scripture defined the redemption in four ways? It was still but one redemption.

The latter terminology, by contrast, indicates that there were four redemptions, not just one, and so it would be appropriate to express our gratitude for each instance.

Torah Temimah continues by listing the four redemptions. The first was the alleviation of the extreme oppression — "I will take you away from the forced labor of Egypt." At this point, the yoke of slavery was eased, but the Israelites were still required to labor. The second redemption was the freeing of the Israelites from all work — "I will rescue you from their bondage."

However, they were still nominally Pharaoh's servants. The third redemption removed this yoke — "I will redeem you with an outstretched arm."

With all this, the Israelites were still not God's special people, so that was the focus of the fourth redemption — "I will take you to Myself as a nation."

Now, there is actually a fifth redemption that is mentioned here, in the next verse — "I will bring you to the land." And yet, a fifth cup was not instituted in the Seder ritual. Torah Temimah suggests that, whereas that redemption was not permanent — since the Israelites were eventually exiled from the Land of Israel — it would have been inappropriate to symbolize it with a cup of wine. Nonetheless, we do pour a fifth cup — the Cup of Elijah — and Torah Temimah sees that as a symbol of our pining for the Messiah, at which time we will be restored — permanently — to our land.

■

## The Eternal Heritage

"Who is bringing *(hamotzi)* you out from under the Egyptian subjugation" — The Talmud (Berachoth 38a) asserts that *hamotzi*, "who is bringing," actually denotes past tense: "who brought." God told the Israelites, "When I bring you out, I will perform feats on your behalf so that you will know that it is I who brought you out of Egypt." R. Nechemiah, however, opines that *motzi* denotes past tense, while *hamotzi* indicates present tense. R. Nechemiah adduces proof for his view from the present verse, understanding it according to the simple explanation: "who is bringing." This debate is relevant to the blessing pronounced over bread: "who brought out bread from the ground." The Sages maintain that one says *hamotzi*, while R. Nechemiah contends that one says *motzi*. The halacha is in accordance with the Sages.

Tosafoth asks that, whereas R. Nechemiah's view is that *hamotzi* indicates present tense, and everyone, according to the Talmud, agrees that *motzi* refers to the past, the blessing should have been coined with the term *motzi*, thereby satisfying all opinions. He answers by referring to the Jerusalem Talmud (Berachoth 6:1), which says that *motzi* is not used because it begins with the letter *mem*. The word preceding *motzi*, *ha'olam*, ends with a *mem*. Were *motzi* to follow *ha'olam*, people might merge the two words. They might say: *ha'olamotzi*. This is to be avoided if at all possible, and so *hamotzi* was coined in the blessing, although it does not satisfy R. Nechemiah's opinion.

Torah Temimah points out that in other blessings we do not find the use of the prefix *ha*. For example, we say: "who created *(borei)* different kinds of sustenance," not *haborei*. Similarly, we say: "who created *(borei)* the fruit of the vine." The dispute between the Sages and R. Nechemiah regarding the tense of the word *hamotzi* would also apply to the word *haborei*. It seems, then, that in the case of *haborei* the prefix *ha* was not used in the blessings because the preceding word, *ha'olam*, and *borei* would not be accidentally fused together. *Ha'olam* ends with a *mem*, while *borei* begins with a *beth*. Since all concur that *borei* denotes past tense, it, not *haborei*, was used in coining these blessings.

Why does the Babylonian Talmud not advance this line of

## VaEra

reasoning, as did the Jerusalem Talmud? Torah Temimah submits that the Babylonian Talmud may have observed that there are blessings in which the word after *ha'olam* (which is in the standard part of all blessings) *does* begin with a *mem*. Examples are: "who clothes *(malbish)* the naked" and "who frees *(matir)* the imprisoned." The Sages did not concern themselves, in these cases, with the possibility that *malbish* and *matir* would be merged with *ha'olam*. It would follow that this is not a concern in the case of *motzi*, either. For this reason, the Babylonian Talmud eschewed the fusing of words as a reason for using the word *hamotzi*. This, however, leads back to the question raised earlier: Why didn't the Babylonian Talmud coin the word *motzi* in the blessing over bread?

Torah Temimah answers that the Talmud did not find it necessary to deal with R. Nechemiah's stance — that *hamotzi* is in present tense — because his is a minority opinion. Hence, Tosafoth and Torah Temimah differ in their view of the Babylonian Talmud's reasoning. Tosafoth believes that R. Nechemiah's viewpoint was rejected because it might lead to a merging of the words in the blessing, while Torah Temimah believes it was rejected because it is a minority opinion.

Torah Temimah continues by asking why the present verse is not given a simple reading by the Talmud, wherein *hamotzi* would refer to the present. Why is a convoluted translation given, so that *hamotzi* is in past tense? Is not "who is bringing you out" a smoother phrasing than "who brought you out"?

Torah Temimah solves this problem by referring to another Talmudic discussion. Scripture states, "They will go out and see the carcasses of the people who sinned against Me" (Isaiah 66:24). The Talmud asserts that *haposh'im* — *posh'im* with the *ha* prefix — is to be translated: "who are sinning" — in the present tense rather than in the past tense. R. Cahana demurs that, if *haposh'im* is understood to denote present tense, so should the case be with *hamotzi* and *hama'aleh*. R. Cahana is referring to the word *hamotzi* in Leviticus 22:33 — "who brought *(hamotzi)* you out of Egypt." There, when the Israelites were in the desert, the Exodus was an event of the past, and so R. Cahana contends that the verse can be understood in no other way. He is referring also to "who brought you out *(hama'aleh)* of Egypt," in Leviticus 11:45, where, again, the Israelites were already in the desert, and so *ma'aleh* with the *ha* prefix can be translated only in the past tense. Rather, says R. Cahana, just as *hamotzi* and *hama'aleh* denote past tense, so is *haposh'im* in past tense: "who sinned," not "who are sinning." R. Cahana's opinion is not refuted by the Talmud. Hence, concludes Torah Temimah, it is evident that the Talmud has no doubt that *hamotzi* is in past tense, and so R. Nechemiah's view is to be discarded.

■

The word *sivloth*, "hard labor," may be understood to denote "tolerance." Chiddushei HaRim says that a nation can be redeemed only after it learns to despise the exile in which it is mired. The Israelites had to loathe their position as slaves before God could bring them out of Egypt. "I will take you away from the patience of Egypt," God told Moses. God would change the attitude of the Israelites toward their condition from one of tolerance to one of loathing, after which redemption would be possible.

Also translating *sivloth* as "tolerance," R. Simcha Bunem of Pshischa adopts the opposite position. He says that the Israelites had become so accustomed to slavery that they perceived it as a natural state. God saw that they were bearing the burden of slavery with tolerance, and that this was a situation that posed grave danger for them. If the Israelites were so entrenched that they were unaware of their position, they had to be redeemed, else they would be lost forever.

■

"I will take you to Myself as a nation" (verse 7) — that is, through the giving of the Torah at Mount Sinai. Chiddushei HaRim says that the Ten Plagues visited upon Egypt transformed the ten *ma'amaroth* into the ten *dibroth*, the Ten Commandments. The Sages point out (Avoth 5:1) that God created the world with ten *ma'amaroth*, pronouncements — in Genesis 1:3-29, Scripture states "God said," *vayomer,* nine times, and the words "In the beginning,

## VaEra

God created the heaven and the earth" (Ibid., 1:1) count as the tenth pronouncement. The world was created by ten commands of God. However, God's involvement is hidden in nature. One is so accustomed to the natural order that God's presence as the Creator is not felt when observing nature.

The Ten Plagues revealed God's presence. The use of supernatural means made it clear that there is a God, who is capable of changing nature when He so desires. The plagues thus paved the way for the Revelation at Mount Sinai and the giving of the Ten Commandments — an event that was the ultimate *giluy Elokim*, manifestation of God.

Hence, the "great judgments" — the Ten Plagues — led to "I will take you to Myself as a nation" — at Mount Sinai, when the Ten Commandments were given.

■ ■ ■

וְהֵבֵאתִי אֶתְכֶם אֶל־הָאָרֶץ אֲשֶׁר נָשָׂאתִי אֶת־יָדִי לָתֵת אֹתָהּ לְאַבְרָהָם לְיִצְחָק וּלְיַעֲקֹב וְנָתַתִּי אֹתָהּ לָכֶם מוֹרָשָׁה אֲנִי ה׳.

". . . I will bring you to the land regarding which I raised My hand [in oath] that I would give it to Abraham, Isaac, and Jacob. I will give it to you as an inheritance. I am God." (6:8)

Chatham Sofer says that when a person becomes accustomed to something remarkable he loses his appreciation for the extraordinary nature of that thing. For example, one is used to seeing ants. Now, an ant is an incredibly wondrous creature, about which King Solomon said, "See its ways and become wise" (Proverbs 6:6). Despite its minuscule size, it has all the limbs necessary to carry out its functions. Still, the commonality of the ant diminishes its extraordinariness in the eyes of men. By contrast, if one sees an elephant, one is struck by its uniqueness and praises God as its Creator.

The same, says Chatham Sofer, was the case with the Israelites. During their stay in Egypt they were accustomed to seeing foods grow in the natural way, and found nothing remarkable in the fact that a small seed grows, over the years, to become an enormous tree.

Therefore, when they left Egypt and entered the desert, and were fed manna from heaven and an unnatural amount of fowl (Numbers 11:31), they were astonished. They came to recognize God's greatness through the manna.

However, their children who were born in the desert, and who were the ones who merited entering the Land of Israel, had no experience with natural food growth. Their lifelong sources of sustenance were the manna and fowl which God provided for the Israelites. They saw nothing special about the manna and fowl, and did not perceive them as indicators of God's greatness. When they arrived in Canaan and witnessed plant growth, they were overwhelmed, and came to understand the wonders of God.

Chatham Sofer asserts that this was the thrust of God's statement to Moses in the present verse. "I will bring you to the land . . . I am God." Those who would enter Canaan would come to recognize God's awesomeness only due to their leaving the desert and inheriting Canaan.

■

"I will bring you to the land" — It is difficult to understand how God could have told the Israelites that He would bring them into Canaan, when in reality only their children entered Canaan; all the men who were above twenty years of age at the departure from Egypt perished in the wilderness. Moreover, God began His statement with the word *lachein,* "therefore" (verse 6), and the Sages say that *lachein* denotes an oath. If God promised to bring the Israelites into Canaan, how could He later renege — when the spies sinned — and sentence them to die in the desert?

We may answer that in this statement — in which God promised to rescue the Israelites from slavery, bring them out of Egypt, take them as His own people, and bring them into Canaan — there is an interjection before the final part of the promise is made. Before saying He would bring the Israelites into Canaan, God says, "You will know that I am God." The first clauses of the oath [regarding the redemption of the Israelites and God's taking them to be His people] were independent of the fulfillment of any condition on the

## VaEra

part of the Israelites. But the final clause [concerning the entry into Canaan] was dependent on the Israelites accepting God as their Lord. God's promise to bring the Israelites into Canaan was thus a conditional one, and, at the incident of the spies, they violated the condition. *(Ohr HaChayyim)*

■ ■ ■

וַיְדַבֵּר מֹשֶׁה כֵּן אֶל־בְּנֵי יִשְׂרָאֵל וְלֹא שָׁמְעוּ אֶל־מֹשֶׁה מִקֹּצֶר רוּחַ וּמֵעֲבֹדָה קָשָׁה.

*Moses related this to the Israelites, but they did not accept [his] words, due to their broken spirits and the hard labor. (6:9)*

"Their broken spirits and the hard labor" — There were two reasons why the Israelites left Egypt after 210 years, instead of having to stay there 400 years. One reason was that the Israelites had become so mired in the impurity of Egypt that if they had tarried longer they would have become completely assimilated. They would not have been able to maintain their identity as a nation and leave as the people of Israel. This situation is alluded to by "broken spirits" — their lack of spirituality. The second reason was that the oppression they had endured was so great that it amounted to the equivalent of 400 actual years; this is alluded to by "hard labor."

The Torah is informing us that the Israelites did not accept either reason as a basis for an early redemption. They believed that, regardless of their spiritual crisis or the intolerable oppression, they would remain slaves until 400 years had passed.

*(Pardes Yosef)*

■ ■ ■

וַיְדַבֵּר מֹשֶׁה לִפְנֵי ה' לֵאמֹר הֵן בְּנֵי־יִשְׂרָאֵל לֹא־שָׁמְעוּ אֵלַי וְאֵיךְ יִשְׁמָעֵנִי פַרְעֹה וַאֲנִי עֲרַל שְׂפָתָיִם.

*Moses spoke before God, saying, "The Israelites did not listen to me. How, then, can I expect Pharaoh to listen to me? I have a speech impediment." (6:12)*

After the First Zionist Congress, R. Shmuel Mohilever brought together numerous Zionist representatives for an assembly in

Bialystok. R. Shmuel, a leading religious Zionist, made two requests of the assembled: that they keep their heads covered, in accordance with Jewish tradition; and that all speakers address the gathering in Yiddish.

One of the attendees, Dr. Cohen-Bernstein [the reference is probably to Jacob Bernstein-Cohen, a famous early Zionist], protested that while everyone was willing to cover his head, there were many there who simply were unable to speak Yiddish fluently. He suggested that those who preferred to speak in Russian be allowed to do so, with an interpreter available to translate for those who didn't understand the language.

R. Shmuel responded that he had not requested that Yiddish be spoken because some of the assembled did not understand Russian. Rather, his purpose was to expedite the subject matter at hand. He pointed out that God sent Moses to speak for the Israelites even though Moses had a speech impediment. Would it not have been better to dispatch a more eloquent individual on such a crucial mission? However — said R. Shmuel — the opposite is the case. If a trained speaker had come to Pharaoh, he would have delivered an eloquent discourse on the importance of freedom, righteousness, and kindness. The primary reason for his being sent to Pharaoh — to free the Israelites — would have been forgotten. But Moses was unable to speak eloquently, and so he delivered God's message to Pharaoh in simple, succinct fashion: "Let My people leave" (5:1).

R. Shmuel asserted that the same held for this assembly in Bialystok. He knew that those attending were good public speakers, and that if they spoke in Russian they would wax eloquent about the virtues of the Land of Israel. They would neglect to concentrate on the subject at hand: the establishment of a Jewish national home. He thus desired that they talk in Yiddish, a tongue with which they were less comfortable, so that they would speak briefly and to the point.

*(MeOtzareinu HaYashan)*

■

Moses wished to give the Israelites the benefit of the doubt. He asserted that the reason they were unwilling to listen to him was not that they rejected God's word. Rather, it was because he had a

## VaEra

"speech impediment." He was not gifted as a speaker and so was unable to influence them.

*(Sefath Emeth, cited by Iturei Torah)*

■ ■ ■

וַיְדַבֵּר ה' אֶל־מֹשֶׁה וְאֶל־אַהֲרֹן וַיְצַוֵּם אֶל־בְּנֵי יִשְׂרָאֵל וְאֶל־פַּרְעֹה מֶלֶךְ מִצְרָיִם לְהוֹצִיא אֶת־בְּנֵי־יִשְׂרָאֵל מֵאֶרֶץ מִצְרָיִם.

*God then spoke to Moses and Aaron. He gave them instructions regarding the Israelites and Pharaoh, king of Egypt — in order that they might bring the Israelites out of Egypt. (6:13)*

The Midrash (Bemidbar Rabbah 13) says that there were three tribes — Reuven, Simeon, and Levi — which occupied a position of leadership in Egypt. Meshech Chochmah conjectures that these three tribes possessed their own Israelite slaves, whom they purchased from the monarchy.

Meshech Chochmah says that God wanted the Israelites to free their own slaves before Pharaoh was forced to let them leave Egypt. Otherwise, how could the Israelites ask Pharaoh to desist from doing something which they themselves were doing?

Thus, the present verse says that God commanded Moses and Aaron "regarding the Israelites and Pharaoh." Not only Pharaoh, but the Israelites as well had to be ordered to "bring the Israelites out" of bondage. The following chapter records the genealogy only of Reuven, Simeon, and Levi, as it was these three tribes which were culpable for holding slaves.

Meshech Chochmah refers to the Jerusalem Talmud's comment on the words "He gave them instructions regarding the Israelites." The Talmud says that the Israelites were commanded regarding the subject of freeing one's slaves (Rosh HaShanah 3:5). This, says Meshech Chochmah, refers to the slaves held by the Israelites in Egypt, not merely to the general subject of Hebrew servantry.

After the Torah discusses the genealogy of Reuven, Simeon, and Levi, it continues that Moses and Aaron were to "Bring the Israelites out of Egypt *al tzivotham*, by their hosts" (verse 26). *Al tzivotham* implies that each tribe was to leave as an entity unto itself. This

## The Eternal Heritage

could only be accomplished if those who were enslaving members of other tribes would free those servants and allow them to return to their tribes.

Meshech Chochmah adds that, according to the Midrash, there were four reasons why the Israelites were redeemed from Egypt: because they kept their Hebrew names, language, and distinct identity; and because they saw themselves only as temporary dwellers in the land as they awaited the redemption — a redemption which Jacob, in his blessings, had promised would result in each tribe inheriting its own land in Canaan (see Genesis 49:13, where Zebulun's boundary is mentioned). Three tribes, however, were rebuked rather than blessed by Jacob — Reuven, Simeon, and Levi. These three tribes also did not receive their own portions in the Land of Israel. Reuven took land on the eastern side of the Jordan River, Levi had no land at all, and Simeon was given a portion within Judah's boundaries. Had they been subjected to slavery, they might not have been able to withstand the pressure to assimilate. They could not look forward to acquiring their own parcel of land in Canaan, and so did not have as great a vested interest as the other tribes in retaining their identity. Therefore, they did not become slaves, but instead achieved a certain status.

■■■

אֵלֶּה רָאשֵׁי בֵית־אֲבֹתָם בְּנֵי רְאוּבֵן בְּכֹר יִשְׂרָאֵל חֲנוֹךְ וּפַלּוּא חֶצְרוֹן וְכַרְמִי אֵלֶּה מִשְׁפְּחֹת רְאוּבֵן.

*These are the heads of their clans. The sons of Reuven, Israel's firstborn, were Chanoch, Pallu, Chetzron, and Carmi. These are the families of Reuven. (6:14)*

Ramban says that the Torah did not begin recording this genealogy with the Tribe of Levi — although the purpose here is to delineate Moses and Aaron's ancestry — because that might have led one to believe that the Tribe of Levi would henceforth, in Moses' honor, have the rights of the firstborn.

Still, the genealogies of Reuven and Simeon are described skeletally, while Levi's tribe is discussed in great detail. Only the

## VaEra

children of Reuven and Simeon who went to Egypt with Jacob are mentioned. In Levi's case, his grandchildren, who were born in Egypt, are noted, as are the life spans of himself and some of his descendants. Therefore, Scripture deviates in introducing Levi's genealogy, stating: "These are the names of the sons of Levi *according to their generations*" (verse 16) — inferring that a fuller description is to follow, due to the superiority of that tribe.

Kli Yekar records a different reason why the Torah bothers to mention the descendants of Reuven and Simeon when the purpose of this section is to detail the ancestry of Moses and Aaron. God first sought a leader for the Israelites among Reuven and Simeon's tribes, as these two were Jacob's oldest sons. He found nobody among them who was qualified, and so He searched among Levi's descendants. When He discovered Moses and Aaron, He concluded His search.

Sforno appears to elaborate on this view. Taking note of the fact that only Reuven and Simeon's sons are recorded, while the entire chain of descent from Levi until Moses is noted, Sforno asserts that Reuven and Simeon did not have progeny who merited being the leaders of Israel. Only their sons were qualified, having been raised by Reuven and Simeon themselves, but by this time these sons had died. Levi's case was different. Levi outlived his brothers (Rashi on verse 16). He was able to help raise and influence his children and grandchildren, including Kehath, Moses' grandfather, and Amram, Moses' father. The result was that Moses and Aaron, who merited being the leaders of Israel, came from Levi.

■

"[God] gave them instructions regarding the Israelites . . ." (verse 13). "These are the heads of their clans." This in itself constituted God's charge to Moses regarding the Israelites. Moses was to point out to them that they came from a distinguished lineage, and that it was unbecoming for such a nation to be held in bondage.

*(R. Chanoch Henoch of Aleksandrow)*

■ ■ ■

## The Eternal Heritage

וַיִּקַּח אַהֲרֹן אֶת־אֱלִישֶׁבַע בַּת־עַמִּינָדָב אֲחוֹת נַחְשׁוֹן לוֹ לְאִשָּׁה וַתֵּלֶד לוֹ אֶת־נָדָב וְאֶת־אֲבִיהוּא אֶת־אֶלְעָזָר וְאֶת־אִיתָמָר.

*Aaron took Elisheva, daughter of Aminadav and sister of Nachshon, as a wife. She bore him Nadav, Avihu, Eleazar, and Ithamar. (6:23)*

"Aaron took Elisheva, daughter of Aminadav and sister of Nachshon" — The Talmud (Bava Bathra 110a) asks: Whereas Elisheva was Aminadav's daughter, do we not know that she was Nachshon's sister? It answers that the inclusion of the words "sister of Nachshon" teaches that one who wishes to marry should investigate the character of his prospective bride's brothers, as one's children tend to be similar to his brothers-in-law.

Scripture describes in like fashion the marriage of Esau to Machalath. It says that she was the "daughter of Ishmael, the son of Abraham, sister of Nevayoth" (Genesis 28:9). The Talmud (Megillah 17a) points out that the words "sister of Nevayoth" are superfluous. Since Machalath is described as Ishmael's daughter, we already know that she was Nevayoth's sister, as Scripture says that Ishmael was Nevayoth's father (Genesis 25:13). In answer, the Talmud asserts that the Torah desires to reveal to us Jacob's age at the time he left Canaan to go to Charan. Esau's marriage to Machalath occurred at that juncture. Ishmael had betrothed Machalath to Esau, but Ishmael died before the wedding. Therefore, Nevayoth, Machalath's brother, gave her to Esau in marriage. Ishmael died at the age of 137 (Ibid., verse 17). Jacob was born when Ishmael was seventy-four years old (as Isaac was sixty when Jacob was born [Ibid., verse 26], and Ishmael was fourteen years older than Isaac). Thus, when Ishmael was 137, Jacob was sixty-three.

Maharsha wonders why the Talmud chooses different explanations for two similar cases: that of Machalath and that of Elisheva. Why doesn't the Talmud assert that Aminadav died and Nachshon gave Elisheva in marriage to Aaron?

Maharsha answers that the same explanation cannot be given in Elisheva's case. The Talmud's statement that Ishmael died after Machalath's betrothal but before her nuptials is based on the fact

## VaEra

that the verse describing her marriage starts with the words "Esau went to Ishmael." Evidently, Ishmael was still alive when Esau came in search of a wife. The interjection of Nevayoth later in the verse is an indication that Ishmael died after Esau had arrived, but before the wedding. No such indication is given regarding Aminadav and Nachshon.

Additionally, says Maharsha, there is a purpose for Scripture to allude to Ishmael's death at that point — since it took place when Jacob left his father's house, we are able to deduce Jacob's age at the time. In our case, however, it would make no difference if Aminadav died at this time. Hence, a different explanation must be given for Nachshon's being mentioned.

As for why the Talmud does not explain Machalath's case in the same fashion that Elisheva's is explained, Maharsha says that it is not reasonable to conclude that the wicked Esau was concerned with the character of Machalath's brother.

■ ■ ■

הוּא אַהֲרֹן וּמֹשֶׁה אֲשֶׁר אָמַר ה' לָהֶם הוֹצִיאוּ אֶת־בְּנֵי יִשְׂרָאֵל מֵאֶרֶץ מִצְרַיִם עַל־צִבְאֹתָם.
הֵם הַמְדַבְּרִים אֶל־פַּרְעֹה מֶלֶךְ־מִצְרַיִם לְהוֹצִיא אֶת־בְּנֵי־יִשְׂרָאֵל מִמִּצְרָיִם הוּא מֹשֶׁה וְאַהֲרֹן.

*These were Aaron and Moses, to whom God said, "Bring the Israelites out of Egypt by their hosts."*
*They are the ones who spoke to Pharaoh, king of Egypt, in order to bring the Jews out of Egypt. These were Moses and Aaron. (6:26, 27)*

The first verse mentions Aaron before Moses: "These were Aaron and Moses." The second verse places Moses before Aaron: "These were Moses and Aaron."

Kli Yekar explains that as far as the mission to rescue the Israelites is concerned it would seem that Moses was the principal actor. It was to Moses that God revealed Himself in the bush, with the word that he was to lead the Israelites out of Egypt. One would have thought that Aaron was a secondary player in the rescue. To dispel this notion, the first verse, which discusses bringing the Israelites out of Egypt, mentions Aaron before Moses; Aaron was as important as Moses in freeing the Israelites.

The task of speaking to Pharaoh seemed to fall primarily upon Aaron, since Moses possessed a speech impediment. In reality, though, Moses was equal to Aaron in this mission, and so the second verse, which notes that they spoke to Pharaoh on behalf of the Israelites, mentions Moses before Aaron.

Kli Yekar proposes a second explanation for Scripture's inverting the order of Moses and Aaron's names. We find that until this time it was Aaron who had the mission of guiding the Israelites to the path of righteousness, in order that they would merit leaving Egypt. That is why, when God told Moses to lead the Israelites out of Egypt, Moses asked Him to send "someone else whom You would wish to send." Moses was referring to Aaron (Rashi on 4:13). It was thus appropriate to record Aaron's name before Moses' name in the first verse, which speaks about bringing the Israelites out of Egypt. This is a general statement, referring to the entire process of redemption, in which Aaron was the primary leader.

The second verse discusses the particular mission in which Moses and Aaron were now involved. Moses, who was directly commanded by God regarding this mission, was the principal actor in this phase. This mission revolved around the pleas to Pharaoh to free the Israelites, and so in the second verse, which discusses this latter phase — "They were the ones who spoke to Pharaoh" — Moses is mentioned before Aaron.

■

Sometimes Aaron is mentioned before Moses, and sometimes Moses is mentioned before Aaron. This is to indicate that they were equals (Rashi).

Chatham Sofer points out that the equation of Moses and Aaron does not suggest that they were identical. They had different skills. Moses was unmatched as a prophet (Deuteronomy 34:10). Aaron was unrivaled as a pursuer of peace (Avoth 1:12). However, because

## VaEra

each was outstanding in his own field, they were equal in status.

Chatham Sofer continues that each one's distinguishing characteristic is alluded to by the present verses. In the first verse, Aaron's name is noted first. This verse speaks of bringing the Israelites out of Egypt. Aaron was closer to the Israelites than Moses, due to his constant peacemaking between husband and wife and between one man and his fellow. It is thus appropriate that he be mentioned first in regard to the Israelites. In the second verse, the subject is the mission to Pharaoh. Moses was God's main prophet, and so it is proper to mention him first when describing the confrontation with Pharaoh and the performance of miracles which were to lead to the release of the Israelites.

R. Simcha Bunem of Pshischa advances another reason why the names of Moses and Aaron are reversed in the two verses. R. Simcha Bunem says that Aaron had been with the Israelites throughout their bondage, while Moses grew up in Pharaoh's house, and afterwards left Egypt for many years — until he was eighty years old. Therefore, in the first verse, which refers to the Israelites, Aaron is mentioned first.

The second verse speaks of the mission to Pharaoh. The king knew Moses, because the latter had been raised in the palace, and so Moses was more important than Aaron when it came to speaking to Pharaoh.

■

Rashi's source for the statement that Moses and Aaron were equals is the Tosefta in Tractate Kerithuth. Torah Temimah wonders why this statement is relegated to the Tosefta, which incorporates addenda to the Mishnah, rather than being included in the Mishnah itself, which lists various items that are equivalent to each other (Kerithuth 28a).

Torah Temimah gives two answers. Firstly, he points out that the Mishnah lists subjects which are halachically oriented — e.g., the equivalence of different sacrifices, and the requirement to fear one's father and mother equally. The relative status of Moses and Aaron has no legal ramifications, and so it is left to the Tosefta to discuss it.

Torah Temimah's second answer is more novel. He proposes that Moses and Aaron were not of equal stature. Moses was superior to Aaron. This superiority is evident in several ways. It was Moses, not Aaron, who went up on Mount Sinai to commune with God. Moreover, Moses stayed on the mountain without food or drink for forty days and nights (Deuteronomy 9:9). It was Moses whom Scripture describes as being unsurpassed in humility (Numbers 12:3), and as being the supreme prophet (Deuteronomy 34:10). Finally, the Tosefta states (Megillah 3:13) that it is appropriate for the Megillah reader to be greater than the translator (in Talmudic times an interpreter explained the Scriptural readings), but it is inappropriate for the interpreter to be greater than the reader. The Tosefta brings proof for this assertion from God's statement to Moses that Aaron would assist him in speaking to Pharaoh (7:1). Moses is clearly depicted as being greater than Aaron. For this reason the Mishnah does not include Moses and Aaron among its pairs of equal subjects.

What, then, does the Tosefta mean when it describes Moses and Aaron as equals? Torah Temimah explains that it is only regarding the mission to rescue the Jews that they were equals. This is gleaned from the fact that Aaron is mentioned first in the verse which discusses freeing the Jews, while Moses is mentioned first in discussing their confrontation with Pharaoh. Now, since Aaron was the primary speaker to the king, it would seem more appropriate to mention him first in the latter verse. Conversely, Moses, who certainly had the chief role in taking the Israelites out of Egypt, should have had priority in the former verse. The fact that Scripture inverts the names in each verse is taken by the Tosefta as a sign that Moses and Aaron were equally deserving of having the primary role in both undertakings. In the particular missions of speaking to Pharaoh and redeeming the Israelites, Moses and Aaron were equal.

■ ■ ■

## VaEra

וַיְדַבֵּר ה' אֶל־מֹשֶׁה לֵּאמֹר אֲנִי ה' דַּבֵּר אֶל־פַּרְעֹה מֶלֶךְ מִצְרַיִם אֵת כָּל־אֲשֶׁר אֲנִי דֹּבֵר אֵלֶיךָ.

*God spoke to Moses, saying, "I am God. Relate to Pharaoh, king of Egypt, all that I am saying to you." (6:29)*

Earlier Moses had worried that because the Israelites had refused to believe him Pharaoh would also not believe him (verse 12). The Sages (Bereshith Rabbah 32) say that this is one of ten cases in Scripture where there is an inference from minor to major *(kal vachomer)*.

There is, however, a refutation to this inference. The Israelites were able to exercise their free will in rejecting Moses' words. But a king does not possess free will (Proverbs 21:1). As it says, "Assyria is the rod of My anger" (Isaiah 10:5). God directs kings in their actions, and He had the ability to make Pharaoh decide to free the Israelites. Thus, God ordered Moses: "Relate to Pharaoh, king of Egypt, all that I am saying to you." If God desired it, Pharaoh would heed His wishes.

Therefore, Moses now (verse 30) raised only the second point he had made earlier (verse 12) — that he had a speech impediment. He did not repeat his concern that Pharaoh would not listen to him. The inference from minor to major had been refuted. God then responded that Aaron would speak to Pharaoh, and so the speech impediment would not present a difficulty either (7:1).

*(Meshech Chochmah)*

■ ■ ■

אַתָּה תְדַבֵּר אֵת כָּל־אֲשֶׁר אֲצַוֶּךָּ וְאַהֲרֹן אָחִיךָ יְדַבֵּר אֶל־פַּרְעֹה וְשִׁלַּח אֶת־בְּנֵי־יִשְׂרָאֵל מֵאַרְצוֹ.

*". . . You will speak everything I command you to, and your brother Aaron will relate it to Pharaoh. He will then let the Israelites leave his land. . . ." (7:2)*

"You will speak everything I command you to" — Rashi says that Moses was to proclaim each of God's messages once, in brief. Aaron was then to repeat and explain the message until Pharaoh understood it.

## The Eternal Heritage

Ibn Ezra contends that Moses was not to speak to Pharaoh at all. He was to relay God's message to Aaron, who would then speak to Pharaoh.

■ ■ ■

וַאֲנִי אַקְשֶׁה אֶת־לֵב פַּרְעֹה וְהִרְבֵּיתִי אֶת־אֹתֹתַי וְאֶת־מוֹפְתַי בְּאֶרֶץ מִצְרָיִם.

"... I will harden Pharaoh's heart, and will multiply My signs and wonders in Egypt...." (7:3)

Bina LaIttim points to an apparent philosophical contradiction. On the one hand, God says here that He will harden Pharaoh's heart, thereby apparently taking away the option of repentance. On the other hand, the Sages say, regarding the Plague of Hail, that Pharaoh was given advance warning so that he might consider repenting (9:18). From that it would seem that Pharaoh did indeed have the choice to heed God's will and free the Israelites.

Bina LaIttim answers that God does not force someone to act against his own wishes. Pharaoh was not stripped of his free will, and he could have repented. However, Pharaoh was of the opinion that there was a conflict between the concept of an all-powerful God and the concept of free will. Pharaoh held that, by definition, such a God had to be in control of the acts of men. If God wanted a person to act in a specific way, then He would force the person to heed His wishes, as this is part of being all-powerful; there would not be free will. The fact that there was free will was a sign that an all-powerful God did not exist.

This is the thrust of God's statement here to Moses. Having (in the previous verse) commanded Moses and Aaron to speak to Pharaoh in His name, God continued, "I will harden Pharaoh's heart." God meant that the very fact that Moses and Aaron would speak for Him would cause Pharaoh to be obstinate. Pharaoh would assert that evidently Moses was lying, that he was not bringing the message of an all-powerful God, for, were that truly the case, Pharaoh could not refuse to abide by God's wishes. Furthermore, there would be no necessity for God to send a messenger to Pharaoh; God should simply force Pharaoh to agree with Him.

## VaEra

Indeed, Pharaoh alluded to this earlier, when he told Moses, "Who is God that I should obey Him?" (5:2). Pharaoh asked: What kind of God is it who cannot do everything by Himself? Why should I listen to such a God?

This answers the question, as God did not take Pharaoh's free will away.

■

How could God proceed to punish Pharaoh after removing his free will to choose whether or not to release the Israelites?

Pharaoh's free will was not taken from him, and he did continue to have the option to free the Israelites. God hardened Pharaoh's heart only in the sense that He prevented the warnings and plagues from making an impression upon the king. Pharaoh was left with the free will he possessed before the warnings and plagues were administered. This accords with the halacha that a non-Jew is liable for death for transgressing one of the Seven Noahide Laws even if he has not been warned to desist from sinning.

This is also consistent with Rambam's explanation for how a writ of divorcement, when obtained coercively from a recalcitrant husband, is effective, although the law mandates that such a writ be given with the husband's free will. Rambam asserts that the coercion merely removes the external forces which are convincing the husband not to divorce his spouse. Once those forces are neutralized, the husband proceeds with the divorce willingly; he does what he truly desires to do: heed the will of God and the Sages.

Similarly, God hardened Pharaoh's heart so that the external forces which might have influenced him to free the Israelites — the warnings and plagues — were neutralized. Pharaoh could now decide based on his actual desire — which, it turned out, was to keep the Israelites enslaved. As for the warnings and plagues, their purpose was not to change Pharaoh's mind, but to proclaim God's greatness throughout the world.

*(Oznayim LaTorah)*

■

Why did God immediately tell Moses that Pharaoh would be

## The Eternal Heritage

unwilling to free the Israelites, instead of letting Moses find out in due course?

God suspected that if Moses and Aaron went to Pharaoh and found him obstinate they would be reluctant to continue their mission. Therefore, He informed Moses in advance that such would be Pharaoh's response. *(Sha'ar Bath Rabbim)*

■ ■ ■

וְלֹא־יִשְׁמַע אֲלֵכֶם פַּרְעֹה וְנָתַתִּי אֶת־יָדִי בְּמִצְרָיִם וְהוֹצֵאתִי אֶת־צִבְאֹתַי אֶת־עַמִּי בְנֵי־יִשְׂרָאֵל מֵאֶרֶץ מִצְרַיִם בִּשְׁפָטִים גְּדֹלִים.

"*. . . Pharaoh will not listen to you. I will then send My hand against Egypt, and will take out My hosts, My people the Israelites, from Egypt with great acts of judgment. . . .*" (7:4)

"Pharaoh will not listen to you." Having already informed Moses that Pharaoh's heart would be made obstinate (verse 3), why was it necessary to add that the king would not listen to Moses? This seems to be repetitive. Secondly, what does God mean when He says that "I will then send My hand against Egypt"? Having just said that He would "multiply My signs and wonders in Egypt," what is He now adding?

God first told Moses that He would harden Pharaoh's heart and bring tribulations upon Egypt. God is not, in the present verse, referring to the same obstinacy and tribulations, but to what would transpire *after* the tribulations. "Pharaoh will not listen to you" — despite having been visited by the plagues, Pharaoh would persist in his obstinacy. Indeed, it would be intensified. Pharaoh would refuse even to hear Moses out; he would not permit Moses to speak with him. As Pharaoh later told Moses, "Don't you dare see me again!" (10:28).

God continued that "I will then send My hand against Egypt." Pharaoh would have pushed God to His limit in refusing to speak to Moses, and so it would be time for God to send His "hand." This refers to the killing of the firstborn Egyptian males, as the hand is used to symbolize the concept of killing: "with a drawn sword in his hand" (Numbers 22:23). That plague was inflicted by God directly,

## VaEra

by His hand. As the Haggadah states, it was brought not by angels or messengers, but by "God in His glory, by Himself."

During the Plague of the Killing of the Firstborn, God would "take out My hosts, My people the Israelites, from Egypt."

*(Ohr HaChayyim)*

■ ■ ■

וַיַּעַשׂ מֹשֶׁה וְאַהֲרֹן כַּאֲשֶׁר צִוָּה ה' אֹתָם כֵּן עָשׂוּ.
*Moses and Aaron did as God had commanded them — this is what they did. (7:6)*

This verse is apparently repetitive. Having said that "Moses and Aaron did as God had commanded them," why does the Torah have to add that "this is what they did"?

The Torah wishes to indicate that Moses and Aaron fulfilled their mission on two levels. Firstly, they did all that they *believed* God had commanded — in accordance with their ability to comprehend the Divine will. That is the thrust of the words "this is what they did." Secondly, they were truly able to perceive God's wishes. Not only did they do as they *thought* God had commanded, but their comprehension of His words was accurate. "Moses and Aaron did as God had commanded them" — God's actual intent was heeded.

A second explanation is that Moses and Aaron did "as God had commanded them"; they had no ulterior motives for obeying God. Thus, the first part of the verse testifies to their thought processes, their undiluted desire to serve God, while the end of the verse records their action — "this is what they did."

*(Ohr HaChayyim)*

■ ■ ■

וּמֹשֶׁה בֶּן־שְׁמֹנִים שָׁנָה וְאַהֲרֹן בֶּן־שָׁלֹשׁ וּשְׁמֹנִים שָׁנָה בְּדַבְּרָם אֶל־פַּרְעֹה.
*Moses was eighty years old and Aaron was eighty-three years old when they spoke to Pharaoh. (7:7)*

Why does the Torah inform us here of the ages of Moses and Aaron?

It is commonly believed that revolutions are the province of young people. Youth help bring about change. The Torah is asserting that such is not necessarily the case. When God desires it, even elderly people can foment revolution.

*(Sha'arei Yerushalayim)*

■ ■ ■

כִּי יְדַבֵּר אֲלֵכֶם פַּרְעֹה לֵאמֹר תְּנוּ לָכֶם מוֹפֵת וְאָמַרְתָּ אֶל־אַהֲרֹן קַח אֶת־מַטְּךָ וְהַשְׁלֵךְ לִפְנֵי־פַרְעֹה יְהִי לְתַנִּין.

"When Pharaoh speaks to you, he will tell you to prove yourself with a miraculous sign. You (Moses) must then tell Aaron, 'Take your staff and throw it down before Pharaoh. Let it become a viper.'" (7:9)

A Torah scholar must have within himself two contradictory characteristics. He must be a merciful man, just as God is merciful. But he must also be capable of harshness: "A Torah scholar who does not exact vengeance like a serpent is not a Torah scholar" (Yoma 22b).

Moses was the epitome of kindness and mercy, of goodheartedness. Yet the first sign he showed Pharaoh was the turning of his staff into a serpent. He wished to allude that when the need was there he was capable of the vengeance and harshness of a snake.

*(Deggel Machaneh Ephraim)*

■ ■ ■

One's environment influences him to a great extent, whether for better or for worse. A righteous person placed in the company of corrupt individuals will tend to be adversely affected. An evil person who associates with good people will change for the better.

The staff which was transformed into a serpent alludes to this idea. The staff, with God's name inscribed on it, became a serpent — a poisonous animal — when thrown in front of Pharaoh: when placed within the environment of the evil king. However, when a poisonous snake was put in Moses' hand (see 4:4), it became a staff.

*(R. Meir Shapira of Lublin)*

■ ■ ■

## VaEra

וַיֹּאמֶר ה' אֶל־מֹשֶׁה כָּבֵד לֵב פַּרְעֹה מֵאֵן לְשַׁלַּח הָעָם.
*God said to Moses, "Pharaoh is obstinate. He refuses to let the people leave. . . ."*
(7:14)

Ohr HaChayyim asks: Didn't Moses already know Pharaoh's position? Why did God find it necessary to reiterate the king's refusal to release the Israelites?

Ohr HaChayyim answers that when Moses performed the miracle of the staff Pharaoh never actually said that the Israelites could not leave. In fact, Scripture does not record any reaction at all by Pharaoh. God now informed Moses that Pharaoh's silence was due to his obstinacy — his refusal to free the Israelites.

■ ■ ■

לֵךְ אֶל־פַּרְעֹה בַּבֹּקֶר הִנֵּה יֹצֵא הַמַּיְמָה וְנִצַּבְתָּ לִקְרָאתוֹ עַל־שְׂפַת הַיְאֹר וְהַמַּטֶּה אֲשֶׁר־נֶהְפַּךְ לְנָחָשׁ תִּקַּח בְּיָדֶךָ.
*". . . Go to Pharaoh in the morning, when he goes out to the water. Stand so that you will meet him on the bank of the Nile. Take in your hand the staff that was transformed into a snake. . . ."* (7:15)

Avitul Safra said in the name of R. Papa: The Pharaoh who was Moses' contemporary was an *amgoshi*, as it says, "when he goes out to the water" (Moed Kattan 18a).

Rav and Shmuel differ regarding the definition of the word *amgoshi*. Rav holds that an *amgoshi* is a blasphemer — someone who cleaves to idol worship and continuously blasphemes God — while Shmuel holds that an *amgoshi* is a sorcerer (Shabbath 75a).

Rav and Shmuel would interpret the present verse to support their respective views. According to Shmuel, the explanation of "when he goes out to the water" is that Pharaoh went there to practice sorcery. However, we would have to qualify this by pointing out that Pharaoh stayed on the river bank. He could not actually have gone into the water, as sorcery is ineffective in water (Sanhedrin 67b). Rav, who considers Pharaoh a blasphemer, would explain "when he goes out to the water" in accordance with the Sages' statement that Pharaoh proclaimed himself to be a god,

saying, "The Nile is mine, I created it" (Ezekiel 29:3).
*(Torah Temimah)*

Torah Temimah's explanation is merely a restatement of Rashi's exposition of the debate between Rav and Shmuel. Aruch and Maharsha, as well, advance the same explanation. Tosafoth, however, is of a different mind. He asserts that Rav and Shmuel are not arguing regarding R. Papa's declaration about Pharaoh (undoubtedly because Rav and Shmuel lived well before R. Papa, and it is illogical that a statement of his would be the subject matter of a dispute between them). Instead, Tosafoth says that Rav and Shmuel disagree regarding the word *amgoshi* as it appears in the Mishnah or in the Beraithoth — these having been authored before the time of Rav and Shmuel.

While Rashi in Tractate Moed Kattan asserts, as mentioned, that, according to Rav, Pharaoh went to the Nile to reinforce his claim that he created it, Rashi on the present verse gives a different explanation. He quotes the Midrashic view that Pharaoh asserted he was a god — as indeed is Rav's opinion. His purpose in going to the Nile, however, was not to assert his claim to divinity, but to relieve himself, so that no one would observe him doing so and prove he was not divine. This is why he went "in the morning" — when one needs to relieve oneself.

■ ■ ■

וְאָמַרְתָּ אֵלָיו ה' אֱלֹהֵי הָעִבְרִים שְׁלָחַנִי אֵלֶיךָ לֵאמֹר שַׁלַּח אֶת־עַמִּי וְיַעַבְדֻנִי בַּמִּדְבָּר וְהִנֵּה לֹא־שָׁמַעְתָּ עַד־כֹּה.

". . . Say to him, God, Lord of the Hebrews, has sent me to you with the message: 'Let My people leave, so that they may worship Me in the desert.' But so far you have not paid heed. . . ." (7:16)

"But so far *(ad koh)* you have not paid heed" — R. Levi Yitzchak of Berdichev asks: At present, the Egyptians had not yet suffered any plagues. How was it possible, then, to tell Pharaoh that he had not heeded God's word until now? The implication is that he should have been moved to obey God.

## VaEra

In answer, R. Levi Yitzchak cites the statement by the Sages that Moses prophesied with the word *zeh*, while the other prophets utilized the word *koh* (Yalkut Shimoni on Numbers 30:2). (Both words may be translated as "this," in identification of a particular object or thought, such as "This *(zeh)* is the word" [Numbers 30:2], or "This *(koh)* is what God says" [11:4]. In the subsequent explanation, R. Levi Yitzchak assumes that *zeh* carries a more definite connotation than *koh*.) Nonetheless, we do observe occasions when Moses used the word *koh* (e.g., 11:4). Why is it said that Moses prophesied with the word *zeh*?

R. Levi Yitzchak advances the view of Rivash regarding God's comment to Moses before He spoke to the Israelites at Mount Sinai: "so that the people will hear when I speak to you. They will then believe in you forever" (19:9). Rivash differentiates between the degree of belief one attains when he actually sees something and that which he attains when he calculates something to be true. Although a person may become completely certain of something based on logical deduction, absolute belief is attained only through direct observation. And so it was with the Israelites. The Israelites witnessed God's wonders in Egypt, but their absolute faith in Him was firmed only at Mount Sinai, where God actually spoke to them. As it says regarding Mount Sinai, "You have been shown, so that you will know that God is the Supreme Being" (Deuteronomy 4:35). This is what God meant when He told Moses that the Israelites will "believe in you forever."

R. Levi Yitzchak continues that *zeh* is utilized to connote that one may point to something he sees and say, "This is it." The Israelites personally witnessed God at Mount Sinai, and could point to Him and say, "This — *zeh* — is God." In Egypt, however, having experienced God through His wonders but not by direct observation, they would not have used the word *zeh*, but rather the word *koh*, in saying, "It is certainly *koh*, as this."

Hence, says R. Levi Yitzchak, there were indeed times when Moses prophesied with the term *koh*, but these occurred before the Revelation at Sinai. After Moses saw God face to face at Sinai, he prophesied with the word *zeh*.

## The Eternal Heritage

R. Levi Yitzchak continues that, if Pharaoh had not kept the Israelites in Egypt against their will, they would have left Egypt much earlier and immediately gone to Mount Sinai. God would not have punished Egypt with the Ten Plagues. The Israelites would not have witnessed God's wonders in Egypt — they would not have needed to experience the *koh* level of observation of God, but would have gone directly to the *zeh* level. This is why Moses now told Pharaoh, "But so far *(ad koh)* you have not paid heed." God, in His mercy, did not wish to afflict the Egyptians, and hoped they would immediately free the Israelites. But He now told Moses that the Egyptians were not going to obey ("you have not paid heed") until *koh* ("so far") — until the Ten Plagues, with the *koh* level of observance, had been administered.

■ ■ ■

כֹּה אָמַר ה' בְּזֹאת תֵּדַע כִּי אֲנִי ה' הִנֵּה אָנֹכִי מַכֶּה בַּמַּטֶּה אֲשֶׁר־בְּיָדִי עַל־הַמַּיִם אֲשֶׁר בַּיְאֹר וְנֶהֶפְכוּ לְדָם.

"... *God now says, 'Through this you will know that I am God.' I will strike the waters of the Nile with the staff in my hand, and they will turn into blood...*" (7:17)

A similar statement is made in the Torah regarding each of the first plagues in the three sets of plagues. [The Sages divide the plagues into three groups. The first consists of Blood, Frogs, and Lice. The second includes Wild Animals, Pestilence, and Boils. The last consists of Hail, Locusts, Darkness, and Killing of the Firstborn.] God said, before the Plague of Blood, "Through this you will know that I am God." He said, regarding Wild Animals, "You will then realize that I am God in the midst of the land" (8:18). And referring to Hail, He said, "so that you will know that there is none like Me in all the world" (9:14).

Abravanel explains that Pharaoh disputed God's power on three counts. Firstly, he argued that God does not exist — "I do not know God" (5:2). God responded, before bringing the first plague upon Egypt, that "Through this you will know that I am God."

## VaEra

Pharaoh's second argument was that, even if God does exist, He does not involve Himself with earthly matters in a detailed fashion. To this God said, before bringing the fourth plague, "You will then realize that I am God in the midst of the land" — that He is intimately involved with the earth.

Finally, Pharaoh contended that God is limited in capability, that He is unable to defy the Laws of Nature. God responded, before bringing the Plague of Hail, that Pharaoh would "know that there is none like Me in all the world" — that God can do as He pleases.

I would like to expound this view, and explain how all the plagues in their respective groupings had identical goals. The first three plagues served to confirm God's existence. The Egyptians held that the Nile River was divine. God smote the Nile, turning it into blood, in order that the Egyptians should "know that I am God." God then had the Nile spawn the frogs, demonstrating that the very river which the Egyptians worshiped testified to God's existence by producing creatures that sanctified His name. That they did so is related in the Talmud (Pesachim 53b). Remarking on the fact that Chananiah, Mishael, and Azariah were thrown alive into Nebuchadnezzar's fire (Daniel 3:19-21), thereby sanctifying God's name, the Talmud asserts that they used the frogs as their paradigm, and deduced that they too should be prepared to die in order to sanctify God's name. The frogs entered the ovens of the Egyptians (verse 28) even though they believed they would be burned to death. If the frogs, who were not commanded to sanctify God's name, were eager to do as much — concluded Chananiah, Mishael, and Azariah — they, as human beings, certainly had to be prepared to do so. And just as the frogs who went into the ovens did not die when God destroyed the other frogs (Yalkut Shimoni), neither did Chananiah, Mishael, and Azariah.

Finally, when the Plague of Lice was brought upon Egypt, even the magicians, who had previously duplicated God's feats, were forced to admit that "It is the finger of God" (8:15).

The second set of plagues, in accordance with Abravanel's view, confirmed that God involves Himself with human beings on an individual basis, not merely with the human species as a whole.

## The Eternal Heritage

According to the Egyptians, God would not, in bringing a plague, have differentiated between the Israelites and themselves. It made no difference to them that the Israelites worshiped God while they did not. In response, God brought upon Egypt the Plague of Wild Animals and said, "On that day I will separate the land of Goshen, where My people live, so that there will not be any harmful creatures there" (8:18). This miracle indicated that there is a difference between righteous people and evil people, and that God takes heed of that difference. Hence God concluded that "You will then realize that I am God in the midst of the land" — that He is involved with each action of every human being.

The same held for the Plague of Pestilence, which brought death to Egypt's animals. Scripture says, "God will make a distinction between Israel's livestock and Egypt's livestock" (9:4).

The boils, too, afflicted the entire land of Egypt (9:9), but did not affect the Israelites. Now, the boils first afflicted the magicians, and only later the rest of the Egyptians ("as the boils had attacked the magicians along with the rest of Egypt" [Ibid., verse 11]). This was because the magicians were the ones who had been causing Pharaoh to be obstinate, using their magic to reproduce the plagues. Therefore, they were smitten first [another sign that God judges every person individually, and rewards or punishes him commensurate with his behavior]. This is why the Torah points out that the magicians were unable to stand before Moses during the Plague of Boils (Ibid.). This means that their arguments against him no longer stood. They had tried to explain away the previous plagues, but having been singled out in Boils, it became clear that they were in the wrong.

The final four plagues served, according to Abravanel, to demonstrate that, contrary to Pharaoh's view, God's capabilities know no limits. However, I believe that Pharaoh had a different contention: that there is more than one God. It is to counter this that God said, before bringing the Plague of Hail, that Pharaoh would "know that there is none like Me in all the world." The implication is that Pharaoh claimed there was more than one God, and God now challenged him.

## VaEra

It seems that Pharaoh held the sun, along with the sign of Aries, which is the first of the Zodiac signs, to be deities. To demonstrate that Pharaoh was wrong, God blocked the light that these heavenly bodies give off to the earth. During Hail the skies were overcast, thereby obscuring sunshine and starlight. In the Plague of Locusts, Scripture states [in the literal reading] that the "eye" of the earth was concealed (10:5). This refers to the sun, which is the earth's eye; therefore, the earth was darkened (Ibid., verse 15). Of course, the Plague of Darkness was a direct inhibition of light. And the final plague, during which the firstborn were killed, occurred at midnight. All this disproved Pharaoh's contention that there existed more than one deity.

Scripture says regarding Hail that "Never before in Egypt, since the day it was founded, has there been anything like it" (9:18); and about Locusts it says, "Never had there been such a locust plague" (10:14), as these proved that "there is none like Me in all the world" (9:14). The final plague especially served as a rebuff to Pharaoh's claim that Aries was powerful. Aries is the "firstborn" of the Zodiac signs, and yet could not prevent the advent of the plague in which the firstborn were killed. Hence, these four plagues were a refutation of Pharaoh's claim that there are other deities along with God. *(Kli Yekar)*

■ ■ ■

וַיַּעֲשׂוּ־כֵן חַרְטֻמֵּי מִצְרַיִם בְּלָטֵיהֶם וַיֶּחֱזַק לֵב־פַּרְעֹה וְלֹא־שָׁמַע אֲלֵהֶם כַּאֲשֶׁר דִּבֶּר ה'.

*The magicians of Egypt were able to do the same with their hidden arts. Pharaoh became obstinate, and would not listen to [Moses and Aaron], just as God had said. (7:22)*

At first glance, it seems inexplicable that God commanded Moses to perform feats which the Egyptians were capable of duplicating, such as the turning of the Nile into blood and the swarming of the frogs. How would this demonstrate God's power?

One may compare this with a scholar who announces that he has discovered a new theory. The scholar asserts that he explained the theory to a group of unknown, simple people in a small town, and that they were astounded by the profundity of the theory. Such a proclamation would be met with little fanfare, as the acceptance by ignorant people of a scholarly presentation is not evidence of its soundness. If, on the other hand, the theorist were to propound his thoughts before learned men of renown, and they accepted his thesis and admitted they were incapable of producing work of a like caliber, this would lend credence and repute to the scholar.

God chose for His proving ground Egypt, a country recognized as a bastion of sorcery and magic (Rashi). In order that future generations would be aware of the ability of Egypt's magicians, God first chose to perform wonders that they had the ability to duplicate — to transform a staff into a serpent and water into blood, and to fill Egypt with frogs — feats which even experts are unable to perform. Having thereby established the credentials of these magicians, God then brought the Plague of Lice. When the magicians were unable to do likewise, they were forced to announce that "It is the finger of God" (8:15). They did not duplicate the remaining plagues either. This was proof that the plagues in Egypt were supernatural — the work of God.

*(Shemen HaMaor)*

■

Whereas the Sages have said that all of the waters in Egypt became blood, where did the magicians find water to demonstrate their ability to transform it?

Ohr HaChayyim opines that only the waters which were above ground (rivers, lakes, and the like) became blood. Underground water sources were not transformed, and the magicians took water from there. He finds a basis for this in the Torah's statement that the Egyptians dug for water (verse 24). Alternatively, says Ohr HaChayyim, the Midrash asserts that the Israelites became wealthy due to the Plague of Blood. The Israelites sold water to the Egyptians, and the magicians transformed some of that water into blood.

R. Bachya proposes that the magicians did not actually transform

## VaEra

water into blood. Rather, having heard Moses and Aaron warn Pharaoh of the impending transformation of the water, they hastened to find a spot where the change had not yet taken place, and made it seem as if they were altering the water. It was, however, the act of Aaron that actually transformed it.

Sforno is of the opinion that the magicians created an optical illusion to make it appear that they transformed the water into blood. In reality, however, they were unable to perform the feat.

Ibn Ezra points to three differences between the accomplishment of Moses and Aaron, and that of the magicians. Firstly, Aaron transformed all of the Nile that was before him, and the waters which were out of his sight as well, into blood. Secondly, he changed flowing waters. Finally, the waters remained blood for seven days. The magicians were able to transform only small amounts of stagnant water, for a short duration — until Pharaoh left their presence.

■

There exists a difference of opinion regarding the nature of the Plague of Blood. Sforno maintains that the waters actually became blood. Da'ath Zekenim MiBa'alei HaTosafoth contends that the waters did not become blood. They merely took on the *appearance* of blood, and this alone would not have prevented the Egyptians from drinking it. However, due to the death of the fish in the Nile, the waters became foul (verse 18) and undrinkable.

This being the case, why is the plague referred to as "Blood" and not "Putridity"? Da'ath Zekenim answers that the bloody color was recognizable to the eye, while the putridity of the water was not.

■

Why is it that today sorcery does not exist? Moreover, we no longer find demons or dybbuks, or the practice of hidden arts. Why is this the case?

R. Yaakov Kamenetsky says that God makes certain that free will always exists among men. To ensure this, God created a balance between good and evil forces. This balance has changed over the generations. For example, in Moses' time there was an extremely vivid manifestation of God. Pharaoh had to be allowed the choice of heeding or ignoring God's wishes. If there had been no other force but God to which Pharaoh could have attributed the plagues and wonders that occurred in Egypt, he would have had no choice but to acknowledge God's mastery and would have freed the Israelites. Pharaoh would not have had the free will he needed to choose whether or not to obey God. Therefore, God allowed sorcery to exist, permitting Pharaoh — if he so chose — to attribute the plagues to witchcraft. The ability of the sorcerers to create supernatural phenomena balanced the readiness of God to display His powers. And even during the Plague of Lice, when Pharaoh's magicians asserted that only God could have brought such a plague (8:15), Pharaoh retained the option of rejecting God. He was able to tell himself that Moses was merely a more powerful sorcerer than his own magicians — that Moses was capable of turning dust into lice, and that God was not involved.

R. Yaakov continues that it was because of this — the balance of forces — that Joseph took care to tell Pharaoh that God, not he, had interpreted the king's dreams (Genesis 41:16). Since there were men with the ability to interpret dreams, Joseph had to make it clear that God was the interpreter in Pharaoh's case.

After prophecy ceased, the connection between God and men was loosened. There did remain, however, the *bath kol*, the Heavenly voice, which occasionally spoke to men. It was no longer necessary for sorcery to exist, as its counterforce, blatant manifestation of the Divine will, was not in existence either. Still, in order that one would have the free will to reject the *bath kol* as Godly, God permitted corresponding evil forces — demons and spirits — to exist. One could, if he wished, attribute evidence of God to them.

When the *bath kol* ceased, there still existed miracle workers, and so demons with evil power in corresponding proportion to the miracle workers existed.

Today we do not witness supernatural events, and so, concludes R. Yaakov, it is unnecessary for any evil balancing force to exist. In

## VaEra

our time, therefore, there are neither sorcerers nor spirits and demons.

■ ■ ■

וַיִּפֶן פַּרְעֹה וַיָּבֹא אֶל־בֵּיתוֹ וְלֹא־שָׁת לִבּוֹ גַּם־לָזֹאת.
*Pharaoh turned away and went to his palace, refusing to pay attention to this as well.* (7:23)

"To this as well" — Rashi says that Scripture is referring to Pharaoh's disregard of two signs God had sent: the changing of the staff into a serpent, and the Plague of Blood.

Ramban contends that the verse is not referring to the miracle of the staff. Rather, "to this as well" comes to emphasize that Pharaoh ignored the transformation of the water into blood even though it constituted not only a wonder, but a plague as well. Pharaoh should have recognized the seriousness of his predicament and the possibility that God might directly smite him in the future.

Sforno says that "to this as well" refers to the fact that there was a qualitative difference between Aaron's accomplishment in transforming the water and that of the magicians, just as there was a difference when both changed their staffs into serpents. In the case of the staffs, Aaron's serpent was animate, while the magicians' serpents were inanimate. In the case of the blood, Aaron changed the water into actual blood, while the magicians succeeded only in creating an optical illusion. But Pharaoh ignored "this as well."

R. Yitzchak HaLevi Horowitz, commenting on Rashi's view, wonders why the miracle of the staff merits allusion at this point, when the issue is the Plague of Blood. In answer, R. Yitzchak cites the Zohar's statement that Pharaoh and his sorcerers were amazed when Aaron's staff swallowed their staffs, because it is impossible, by sorcery, to have an inanimate object consume another object. However, the magicians, who, at the Plague of Lice, acknowledged God's hand, did not do so here. This was because they believed that Aaron's staff had originally been a serpent and that he had transformed it into a staff before the confrontation at Pharaoh's

## The Eternal Heritage

palace. It could thus, through sorcery, swallow their staffs.

Now, the Talmud (Sanhedrin 67b) remarks that items produced through witchcraft are put to the test by water. When coming in contact with water, they revert to their natural state. The Plague of Blood was begun by Aaron smiting the Nile with his staff. Had the staff originally been a serpent, it would have reverted to its original state when it struck the water. The fact that it did not was proof of God's hand in the swallowing by Aaron's staff of the other staffs — as it was a feat which could not be accomplished by sorcery.

This, says R. Yitzchak, is the connection between the miracle of the staff and the Plague of Blood.

■ ■ ■

וְשָׁרַץ הַיְאֹר צְפַרְדְּעִים וְעָלוּ וּבָאוּ בְּבֵיתֶךָ וּבַחֲדַר מִשְׁכָּבְךָ וְעַל־מִטָּתֶךָ וּבְבֵית עֲבָדֶיךָ וּבְעַמֶּךָ וּבְתַנּוּרֶיךָ וּבְמִשְׁאֲרוֹתֶיךָ.

"... *The Nile will swarm with frogs. They will come up into your palace, into your bedroom, and onto your bed, as well as into the homes of your servants and your nation, and into your ovens and kneading bowls. ...*" (7:28)

R. Akiva said, "There was one frog, which multiplied until it covered the entire land of Egypt." R. Eleazar b. Azariah retorted, "There was one frog, which called to the other frogs, and they came" (Sanhedrin 67b). [The debate centers around the words *vata'al hatzefardea* (8:2), literally, "the frog emerged," in singular form.]

The Talmud (Pesachim 53b) reports the words of Todos of Rome, who says that Chananiah, Mishael, and Azariah were moved to allow themselves to be thrown into Nebuchadnezzar's furnace, in order to sanctify God's name, by the actions of the frogs. The frogs entered the ovens of the Egyptians at risk to their lives, although they were not enjoined by the halacha to sanctify God's name. Certainly, then, men, who are required to sanctify God's name, had to be willing to die for Him.

God apparently made the frogs decide to enter the ovens, as frogs do not think for themselves. We may assume that God would not have done this unless He wanted us to conclude that it is proper to

## VaEra

sacrifice one's life for the sake of His name. Chananiah, Mishael, and Azariah thus properly derived the correct course of action from the deportment of the frogs.

However, the inference Chananiah and his friends made was valid only if the frogs already existed. If, on the other hand, they were created for the specific purpose of afflicting the Egyptians, it did not necessarily follow that Chananiah, Mishael, and Azariah, who, as it is with all righteous men of Israel, were created to fulfill a number of purposes, should sacrifice their lives to hallow God's name. Perhaps it was better for them to remain alive so that they could fulfill the other purposes for which they had been born.

Hence, according to R. Eleazar b. Azariah, the inference was a logical one. He was of the opinion that no frogs were specifically created at this point in time; they were already in existence. However, R. Akiva opined that the frogs were created miraculously, just for the purpose of plaguing Egypt. Having been created with the very intention that they sanctify God's name by assisting in the administration of the plague, even at the cost of their lives, their self-sacrifice would not lead to the inference that men are bound to act similarly. This was R. Eleazar's objection to R. Akiva's view. *(Chatham Sofer)*

■ ■ ■

וַיִּקְרָא פַרְעֹה לְמשֶׁה וּלְאַהֲרֹן וַיֹּאמֶר הַעְתִּירוּ אֶל־ה' וְיָסֵר הַצְפַרְדְּעִים מִמֶּנִּי וּמֵעַמִּי וַאֲשַׁלְּחָה אֶת־הָעָם וְיִזְבְּחוּ לַה'.

*Pharaoh summoned Moses and Aaron and said, "Pray to God that He should get the frogs away from me and my people. I will then let the nation leave and sacrifice to God." (8:4)*

Ohr HaChayyim notes that while Pharaoh took no notice of the Plague of Blood — "Pharaoh turned away and went to his palace, refusing to pay attention to this" (7:23) — he did seek relief from the Plague of Frogs: "Pray to God that He should get the frogs away from me." What was the difference between the plagues? Whereas the magicians were able to duplicate Frogs just as they did Blood, and from the sequence of verses it seems that this was the reason

Pharaoh rejected the message of Blood, why did he have a greater appreciation for the message of Frogs?

Ohr HaChayyim answers that Pharaoh exhibited a willingness to recognize the lessons of those plagues which posed a threat to life. He asked Moses to pray and he promised concessions only when his life was in danger. This was true not only with the first two plagues, but with the others as well. Blood did not constitute a life-threatening plague, as the Egyptians were able to find water in sources other than the Nile, or by purchasing it from the Israelites. The frogs did endanger life, because they generated a great deal of frightening noise by their croaking; in addition, the frogs actually entered the bodies of the Egyptians.

The Plague of Lice did not pose a threat to life. Thus, although the magicians were unable to duplicate the plague, and acknowledged that God had created it (verse 15), Pharaoh was obstinate in his refusal to free the Israelites (Ibid.). By contrast, the Plague of Wild Animals was a source of great fear for Pharaoh, and so he sent for Moses and offered to allow the Israelites to sacrifice to God in Egypt (verse 21). And when Moses insisted that the Israelites leave the land in order to sacrifice, Pharaoh agreed (verse 24).

The Plague of Pestilence affected only the animals, and so, despite the fact that Pharaoh knew the Israelite animals were not affected (9:7), he was not moved to make any concessions. Similarly, the Plague of Boils did not constitute a threat to life. In fact, notes Ohr HaChayyim, the Torah never says that Pharaoh himself suffered from the boils; it says only that they affected the magicians and all of Egypt (Ibid., verse 11). It is possible that Pharaoh did not contract the boils, which would be an added reason why he did not demonstrate any leniency due to that plague (Ibid., verse 12).

The Plague of Hail was marked by thunder, and by fire falling from heaven with the hail. The Egyptians were terrorized by this, thinking God might do to them what He had done to Sodom and Gomorrah. Pharaoh admitted God was righteous while he was wicked, and asked Moses to intercede for him, promising to release the Israelites (Ibid., verses 27, 28).

## VaEra

Regarding the Plague of Locusts, Pharaoh pleaded with Moses to pray for him, describing the plague, which led to hunger, as "death" (10:17). Clearly, the fear of death was what caused him to ask Moses to pray for the cessation of the plague.

As for the Plague of Darkness, which certainly struck terror into the hearts of the Egyptians, Ohr HaChayyim writes that we do not find Pharaoh pleading with Moses to intercede with God on his behalf. Ohr HaChayyim conjectures that during the first three days of the plague the Egyptians were able to blunt its impact by kindling lanterns. During the next three days, the darkness was so thick that it became tangible, and no one was able to move (Ibid., verse 23). Pharaoh was simply unable to call for Moses. However, immediately after the plague ended Pharaoh sent for Moses, offering to release the Israelites. He asked only that they leave behind their animals as a surety that they would return (Ibid., verse 24). Pharaoh had no reason to ask Moses to pray, because the plague had come to a halt.

■ ■ ■

וַיֹּאמֶר מֹשֶׁה לְפַרְעֹה הִתְפָּאֵר עָלַי לְמָתַי אַעְתִּיר לְךָ וְלַעֲבָדֶיךָ וּלְעַמְּךָ לְהַכְרִית הַצְפַרְדְּעִים מִמְּךָ וּמִבָּתֶּיךָ רַק בַּיְאֹר תִּשָּׁאַרְנָה.

*Moses said to Pharaoh, "Test me. That which I pray for you, your servants, and your people to remove the frogs from you and your homes, so that they will remain only in the Nile — when should this take effect?" (8:5)*

R. Yaakov Kamenetsky points out that Moses was forced to pray exceedingly for the removal of the frogs — *atir*, lit., "shall I pray," denotes a great amount of prayer (see Rashi on Genesis 25:21). Now, whereas the purpose of the plagues was to assist the Israelites by weakening Pharaoh's resolve to keep them in Egypt, it should have sufficed for Moses to say that a particular plague was no longer necessary. Why did he have to engage in increased prayer to move God to kill the frogs?

We see — says R. Yaakov — that when the plagues were inflicted they were not merely a supernatural imposition. Rather, they became part of nature. Moses' request was thus that the natural way be circumvented, and this demands increased prayer.

■

There is a dispute between Mizrachi and Divrei David regarding Rashi's understanding of the different forms of the word *athor*. Commenting on the present verse, Rashi says that Scripture chose the *hiphil* (causative) form for the word *athor* — *atir*, instead of the *kal* (simple) form, *etar* — because *athor* connotes a great amount of prayer. Large amounts are better expressed in the *hiphil* form, as the causative form infers a certain urgency. For example, says Rashi, "I will increase" is expressed in the *hiphil* form — *arbeh* — not in the *kal* form, because it refers to an abundance.

Mizrachi explains that, according to Rashi, wherever Scripture uses the *kal* form for *athor*, the word does not denote a great deal of prayer, but, rather, intense prayer. Therefore, commenting on Scripture's description of Moses' prayer to God to stop the Plague of Wild Animals — "he entreated (*va'yetar* — *kal* form) God" (verse 26) — Rashi says, "he concentrated *(nith'ametz)* in prayer." Rashi adds that Scripture could have written *va'yater*, the *hiphil* form, and it would have denoted that Moses prayed a great deal. However, in the *kal* form it means that Moses prayed fervently. Apparently Rashi sees a difference between the *kal* and *hiphil* forms.

Divrei David takes issue with Mizrachi's exposition of Rashi's view, based on Rashi's explanation, in Genesis 25:21, of the word *va'yetar* (referring to Isaac's prayer that he be given offspring). Rashi says that Isaac "increased [his prayers] and urged with his prayers." Were Mizrachi correct, Rashi should have explained that Isaac prayed fervently, as *va'yetar* is the *kal* form. Divrei David thus avers that there is no difference between the *kal* and *hiphil* forms of *athor*. The word always refers to an increased amount. The *hiphil* form is chosen merely because it better connotes a large amount than does the *kal* form, but both forms may be used. As for Rashi's explanation of *va'yetar* as *nith'ametz*, Divrei David does not translate *nith'ametz* as "he concentrated." The word literally infers a

## VaEra

strengthening, and Divrei David takes Rashi to mean: "he was strong in praying a great deal."

■

Rashi says that Moses told Pharaoh he would pray immediately for the frogs to be killed at whatever time Pharaoh requested. Rashi's view is based on the words *lemathai atir lecha,* lit., "For when should I pray for you?" Were Moses saying that he would commence prayer at whichever time Pharaoh desired, he would have said: *mathai atir lecha,* "When should I pray for you?" The letter *lamed,* when attached to the word *mathai,* changes its meaning from "when" to "for when."

Ramban disagrees with Rashi. Ramban opines that Moses asked Pharaoh to appoint the time at which Moses was to entreat God. Ramban proves this by pointing to the description of the actual prayer. Scripture says that "Moses cried out to God," and "God did as Moses requested, and the frogs . . . died" (verses 8, 9). It does not say that the frogs perished on the next day. According to Rashi, that is what occurred, as Pharaoh told Moses that the frogs should die on the next day (verse 6). Evidently, the prayer was followed immediately by the death of the frogs.

As for the *lamed* in the word *lemathai,* Ramban lists several cases where a *lamed* is used as a prefix without changing the meaning of the word to which it is attached, being utilized only as a stylistic device (see, e.g., *lemachar,* verse 19).

■

Oznayim LaTorah writes that Moses offered three proofs to dispel any thought on Pharaoh's part that the frogs were the work of sorcery.

Firstly, Moses offered to remove the frogs at an appointed time set by Pharaoh. This cannot be accomplished through wizardry. Secondly, Moses foretold the order of the frogs' removal — "for you, your servants, and your people." Sorcerers cannot control their creations in such a fashion. Thirdly, Moses said that the frogs would remain in the Nile. Creatures created by wizardry cannot remain extant indefinitely.

## The Eternal Heritage

Oznayim LaTorah adds three more reasons why the frogs in the river were left alive. Firstly, Moses did not want Pharaoh, who held that the Nile was divine, to attribute to it the destruction of the frogs. Therefore, he mandated that the frogs in the Nile would remain. If the Nile were divine, it certainly would have been capable of eradicating the frogs from its midst along with the other frogs. Secondly, Moses feared that the Egyptians might reinstate their policy of throwing the Israelite children into the Nile. He left the frogs in the Nile so that their croaking would serve as a warning to Egypt that such an attempt would result in the renewal of the plague. Finally, some of the frogs had sanctified God's name by entering the ovens of the Egyptians. They were now able, as their reward, to enter the Nile and be saved, while the other frogs died.

■ ■ ■

וַיֹּאמֶר לְמָחָר וַיֹּאמֶר כִּדְבָרְךָ לְמַעַן תֵּדַע כִּי־אֵין כַּה' אֱלֹהֵינוּ.
*He replied, "Tomorrow." [Moses] responded, "As you wish, so that you will know that there is none like God our Lord. . . ." (8:6)*

Regardless of whether one maintains that Moses prayed now (Rashi's view), or whether one believes that he prayed on the day after his conversation with Pharaoh (Ramban's view), there exists a glaring problem. Pharaoh and Egypt were clearly suffering from the frogs. Why did Pharaoh want the frogs eradicated on the following day, as opposed to immediately?

Mishkenothecha Yisrael, by R. Yisrael Eli Kohn, advances two answers by R. Yosef Dunner to this question. Firstly, he says that Pharaoh believed Moses knew (by virture of sorcery) that the plague was to cease at the time he came to the palace. Moses asked Pharaoh when he wanted the plague to stop, expecting the king to request that it cease immediately. Whereas the frogs were to be eradicated at this moment anyway, it would have appeared that Moses had the power to grant Pharaoh's request, when in reality all Moses did was align the cessation of the plague with the time of Pharaoh's request for such. Therefore, Pharaoh asked that the plague be stopped on the morrow. He believed that it would stop

## VaEra

today, and that Moses would thus be revealed as a fraud.

Moses replied to Pharaoh, "As you wish, so that you will know that there is none like God our Lord." Pharaoh would see that God was the power behind the plague, that it was not the result of sorcery. God would cause it to cease only on the morrow, as per Pharaoh's request.

Secondly, R. Dunner says that Pharaoh may have had a different calculation in mind. The Israelites were in Egypt for only 210 years, not the 400 years to which they were sentenced. One reason for this was that the extraordinary harshness of the slavery which the Israelites endured compensated for the missing 190 years.

Pharaoh was aware of the principle that if, during a particular period of punishment, one suffers more than usual, the duration of the punishment is shortened. He was concerned that, were he to request that the Plague of Frogs end immediately — perhaps prior to the time when it was supposed to cease — its intensity would be increased to make up for its abbreviated length. Therefore, he told Moses that he would prefer that it end on the next day. He was prepared to endure an additional day of the plague if that meant that its intensity would not be increased.

■ ■ ■

וַיֵּצֵא מֹשֶׁה וְאַהֲרֹן מֵעִם פַּרְעֹה וַיִּצְעַק מֹשֶׁה אֶל־ה' עַל־דְּבַר הַצְפַרְדְּעִים אֲשֶׁר־שָׂם לְפַרְעֹה.

*Moses and Aaron left Pharaoh, and Moses cried out to God concerning the frogs He had brought upon Pharaoh. (8:8)*

R. Avraham Broda once lodged at a certain inn. There were present some *maskilim*, adherents to the trend of Enlightenment. When R. Avraham began to pray, the *maskilim* made a great deal of noise in order to disturb his concentration. In turn, he raised his voice and began to pray loudly.

The *maskilim* asked him why he was praying loudly. He responded by pointing to a discrepancy in the way Moses' prayers to God during the plagues are described. Regarding the Plague of Frogs, it says that Moses "cried out," *vayitz'ak*, while elsewhere it states that he "prayed" — *va'yetar* (verse 26) — or "he spread his hands out to God" (9:33), or uses other similar terms. Why was it only in the case of Frogs that Moses had to cry out? R. Avraham explained that because the frogs were croaking very loudly Moses was unable to hear himself praying. In order to conform with the dictum that one should hear himself as he prays, Moses had to cry out. This was what R. Avraham was now doing as well.

*(Cited by Iturei Torah)*

■

Why is it that in the case of the frogs Moses had to cry out, while regarding the other plagues this was not necessary?

Sforno answers that Moses desired the eradication of the frogs which were afflicting the Egyptians, but not those that were in the Nile — "Moses cried out to God concerning the frogs He had brought upon Pharaoh." The Talmud (Sanhedrin 64a) states that God does not generally grant a request in such a fashion — "Heaven does not grant half." If Moses wanted the frogs killed, then God would have been willing to kill them all, but not just some of them.

To override this restriction, Moses had to cry out, to be especially urgent in his request.

■ ■ ■

וַיַּעַשׂ ה׳ כִּדְבַר מֹשֶׁה וַיָּמֻתוּ הַצְפַרְדְּעִים מִן־הַבָּתִּים מִן־הַחֲצֵרֹת וּמִן־הַשָּׂדֹת.

*God did as Moses requested, and the frogs in the houses, courtyards, and fields died. (8:9)*

Although Scripture previously stated (7:28) that the frogs were in the ovens as well as in the houses, courtyards, and fields, no mention is made here that those in the ovens perished.

Da'ath Zekenim MiBa'alei HaTosafoth explains that the ones which went into the ovens were not killed. They had risked their lives by entering the ovens in accordance with God's command. In return, God now left them alive.

■

*VaEra*

Why, in the Plague of Wild Animals, were the beasts removed (verse 27) — brought back to their habitats alive — while the frogs were killed?

The beasts were not specially created for the Plague of Wild Animals. They were already alive, and were brought from the forests into the inhabited areas. These animals were part of the world's ecosystem, and were necessary for the continued proper functioning of the earth.

By contrast, the frogs were specifically created at this juncture. "The Nile will swarm with frogs" (7:28) implies that new frogs were now created. [This accords with the Talmudic view that every time the Egyptians struck a frog, seeking to kill it, it split, creating a new frog.] These frogs were superfluous in the natural order, and, not being needed to help the world function properly, were killed when the plague ended. *(Metziath Yitzchak)*

■ ■ ■

וַיַּרְא פַּרְעֹה כִּי הָיְתָה הָרְוָחָה וְהַכְבֵּד אֶת־לִבּוֹ וְלֹא שָׁמַע אֲלֵהֶם כַּאֲשֶׁר דִּבֶּר ה׳.

*Pharaoh saw that there was a respite, so he hardened his heart and would not listen to [Moses and Aaron], as God had said. (8:11)*

It is difficult to understand why Pharaoh became obstinate after relief was granted from the Plague of Frogs. [Why didn't he recognize that Moses was speaking in God's name and submit to Moses' demands?]

It seems that Pharaoh was uncertain whether Moses was God's messenger or whether he was a mere sorcerer. In order to test Moses, Pharaoh asked him to pray for the cessation of the plague, promising to send away the Israelites if Moses succeeded. At the same time, Pharaoh decided privately not to release the Israelites. If Moses were truly God's messenger — reasoned Pharaoh — he would see beyond Pharaoh's words and know he was lying; Moses would then refuse to pray for the removal of the frogs. Since Moses did arrange for their eradication, Pharaoh decided that Moses was merely a sorcerer, and not God's agent. Therefore, despite his promise to the contrary, Pharaoh refused to allow the Israelites to leave. *(Arvei Nachal)*

■ ■ ■

וַיֹּאמֶר ה' אֶל־מֹשֶׁה אֱמֹר אֶל־אַהֲרֹן נְטֵה אֶת־מַטְּךָ וְהַךְ אֶת־עֲפַר הָאָרֶץ וְהָיָה לְכִנִּם בְּכָל־אֶרֶץ מִצְרָיִם.
*God said to Moses, "Tell Aaron: Hold out your staff and strike the dust of the earth. It will turn into lice throughout Egypt." (8:12)*

The Plague of Lice occurred before the Plague of Wild Animals. Yet, in Psalms, Wild Animals is mentioned before Lice: "He commanded, and wild animals came, lice in all their boundaries" (105:31).

The explanation is that the lice actually came twice: first in the Plague of Lice, and then as part of the Plague of Wild Animals, among which were included all kinds of creatures. This second visitation of lice is reflected in the verse in Psalms.

*(Kehillath Yitzchak)*

■ ■ ■

וַיַּעֲשׂוּ־כֵן הַחַרְטֻמִּים בְּלָטֵיהֶם לְהוֹצִיא אֶת־הַכִּנִּים וְלֹא יָכֹלוּ וַתְּהִי הַכִּנָּם בָּאָדָם וּבַבְּהֵמָה.
*The magicians attempted to do the same with their hidden arts — to bring forth lice — but they could not. The lice were attacking man and beast. (8:14)*

"The lice were attacking man . . ." The implication is that all the people — Egyptians and Israelites alike — were affected by the lice. Rambam, in his Commentary on the Mishnah, and R. Yonah say this as well (Avoth 5:4), explaining that the lice were found in the Israelite district of Goshen — which was not the case with the other plagues — but nevertheless did not afflict the Israelites.

It seems that the source for the above contention is in Bereshith Rabbah (Ch. 96). It states that Jacob ordered Joseph not to bury him in Egypt because in the end it would be struck by lice, and the lice

## VaEra

would swarm over his body. One may ask: Why didn't Jacob ask to be buried in Goshen? It must be that even Goshen was victimized by the lice.

Now, we must explain why this plague differed from the others, in that the Israelites were affected by it.

It was during the Plague of Lice that Pharaoh's magicians acknowledged the role of God (verse 15). Hence, it was possible that Pharaoh might have chosen to free the Israelites at this juncture. Desiring to make Pharaoh obstinate, God brought the plague upon the entire Egypt, including Goshen. This gave Pharaoh the ability to justify the plague as a natural disaster which had struck his entire land, and he refused to believe that the Israelites were not actually being afflicted by the lice.

Another explanation may be advanced, based on the assertion in Mishnath D'Rabbi Eliezer that, beginning at the time of this plague, the Israelites were no longer forced to make bricks for the Egyptians. This was because the lice infested the earth, and suitable brick-making material could no longer be found. If the plague had not affected the land of Goshen, the Egyptians would simply have compelled the Israelites to use *its* earth to make the bricks. Therefore, the plague struck Goshen along with the rest of Egypt.

*(Oznayim LaTorah)*

■ ■ ■

כִּי אִם־אֵינְךָ מְשַׁלֵּחַ אֶת־עַמִּי הִנְנִי מַשְׁלִיחַ בְּךָ וּבַעֲבָדֶיךָ וּבְעַמְּךָ וּבְבָתֶּיךָ אֶת־הֶעָרֹב וּמָלְאוּ בָּתֵּי מִצְרַיִם אֶת־הֶעָרֹב וְגַם הָאֲדָמָה אֲשֶׁר־הֵם עָלֶיהָ.

". . . For if you will not let My people leave, I will send swarms of wild animals to attack you, your servants, your people, and your homes. The houses of Egypt, and even the land upon which they stand, will be filled with the wild animals. . . ." (8:17)

The end of the verse literally reads: "The houses of Egypt will be filled with the wild animals, as well as the land upon which they stand." It appears that "upon which they stand" refers not to the houses, but to the animals. The significance of this is hard to understand.

## The Eternal Heritage

Chanukath HaTorah points to the Rabbis' assertion that there exists an animal, the *adnei hasadeh,* which has human form and is attached to the earth (see Kilayim 8:5). The *adnei hasadeh* is nurtured by the ground, and if it is detached from the earth, it dies.

Chanukath HaTorah says that the *adnei hasadeh* were among the wild animals which afflicted Egypt. In order to remain alive, these creatures had to come with the "land upon which they stood," as detachment from the soil would have resulted in their death.

■ ■ ■

וְהִפְלֵיתִי בַיּוֹם הַהוּא אֶת־אֶרֶץ גֹּשֶׁן אֲשֶׁר עַמִּי עֹמֵד עָלֶיהָ לְבִלְתִּי הֱיוֹת־שָׁם עָרֹב לְמַעַן תֵּדַע כִּי אֲנִי ה' בְּקֶרֶב הָאָרֶץ.

". . . *On that day, I will set apart the land of Goshen, where My people live, so that there will not be any wild animals there. You will then realize that I am God in the midst of the land. . . .*" (8:18)

Ramban says that the first three plagues were localized, and so it was not astonishing that the Israelite section remained unscathed. The blood, frogs, and lice all sprang from particular areas in Egypt. The Nile became blood, thus affecting the areas dependent upon the river. The frogs came from the Nile, so they too only affected particular locations. The lice came from the earth, and so that plague was also confined to the particular sections where the ground was transformed.

However, the wild animals came from their natural habitats and swarmed toward the cities. It was to be expected that they would attack Goshen along with the rest of Egypt. This is why God said here, "I will set apart the land of Goshen." The Israelite section would be spared through a miracle.

Ramban says that the words of the next verse, "I will thus make a distinction between My people and your people," refer to a further miracle. Even in the sections which were attacked by the animals because they had a majority of Egyptians, the local Israelites who were there remained unharmed by the beasts.

■ ■ ■

## VaEra

וַיֹּאמֶר מֹשֶׁה לֹא נָכוֹן לַעֲשׂוֹת כֵּן כִּי תּוֹעֲבַת מִצְרַיִם נִזְבַּח לַה' אֱלֹהֵינוּ הֵן נִזְבַּח אֶת־תּוֹעֲבַת מִצְרַיִם לְעֵינֵיהֶם וְלֹא יִסְקְלֻנוּ.

*Moses replied, "It would not be proper to do that, because what we will sacrifice to God our Lord is sacred to the Egyptians. Could we sacrifice what is sacred to the Egyptians before their very eyes without them stoning us? . . ." (8:22)*

*To'avath Mitzrayim*, "sacred to the Egyptians," literally means "the abomination of Egypt." While the common explanation is that the Egyptians worshiped animals — these being among their deities — and so their slaughtering would be abominable to the Egyptians, Ibn Ezra has a different view. He says that the Egyptians were very careful to avoid mistreating animals. They desisted from consuming meat and despised anyone who did so.

R. Yosef Shaul Nathanson says that for this reason Moses objected to Pharaoh's plan that the Israelites offer their sacrifices in Egypt. Moses said, "It would not be proper to do that." The halacha is that an object which is unappealing to human beings is unacceptable for a sacrifice to God (see Sukkah 50a). Since the Egyptians abhorred the thought of killing animals, it would have been wrong to conduct sacrificial worship in their midst. Therefore, said Moses, the Israelites had to travel three days' distance (verse 23), lest they offend the Egyptians, in violation of the halacha.

■ ■ ■

דֶּרֶךְ שְׁלֹשֶׁת יָמִים נֵלֵךְ בַּמִּדְבָּר וְזָבַחְנוּ לַה' אֱלֹהֵינוּ כַּאֲשֶׁר יֹאמַר אֵלֵינוּ.

*". . . We will take a three-day journey into the desert, and sacrifice to God our Lord as He commands us." (8:23)*

R. Avraham of Sochachev says that every man who wishes to become close to God must first rid himself of any bad attributes. Thus, Moses told Pharaoh that before sacrificing to God the Israelites had to "take a three-day journey." This was similar to the three days of preparation that God ordered the Israelites to undergo before receiving the Torah (19:11). Before performing the sacrifices, the Israelites had to leave the materialistic surroundings of Egypt and take the time to purify themselves from any unholiness.

*The Eternal Heritage*

Pharaoh was not of the same mind as Moses. The king maintained that the Israelites could "sacrifice to your God here in this land" (verse 21). He saw no need for spiritual preparation. Despite any impurities or a materialistic bent (*aretz*, "land," is taken as a reference to physical desires), one could engage in sacrificing to God.

*(Ma'ayanah shel Torah and Iturei Torah,*
*citing Shem MiShmuel)*

■ ■ ■

וַיֹּאמֶר ה׳ אֶל־מֹשֶׁה בֹּא אֶל־פַּרְעֹה וְדִבַּרְתָּ אֵלָיו כֹּה־אָמַר ה׳ אֱלֹהֵי הָעִבְרִים שַׁלַּח־אֶת עַמִּי וְיַעַבְדֻנִי.

God told Moses, "Go to Pharaoh. Say to him that God, the Lord of the Hebrews, has said: Let My people leave and serve Me. . . ." (9:1)

Ohr HaChayyim says that the term *bo el,* "Go to," or, more literally, "Come into" or "Enter into," indicated that Moses was to enter Pharaoh's palace without obtaining permission. Moses was to ignore the palace guard. As the Sages say, Pharaoh had many armed guards, as well as lions and dogs, but none of them prevented Moses from going to the king.

Ohr HaChayyim continues that proof for the Sages' words may be adduced from Pharaoh's admonition to Moses: "Don't you dare see me again! The day you appear before me, you will die!" (10:28). Why did Pharaoh find it necessary to warn Moses? Why didn't he simply instruct his guards to prevent Moses from gaining access to him? Evidently, due to a miracle, the guards and animals were powerless to stop Moses from coming in.

Ohr HaChayyim points out that God used a different word when instructing Moses to meet Pharaoh at the Nile. Moses was told, *lech,* "Go" (7:15). When Pharaoh was not in his palace, surrounded by guards, it was not necessary to order Moses to "come in," to "enter." No extraordinary means were called for in order for Moses to meet Pharaoh. It was only necessary to tell him to "go" — that although Pharaoh went to the river to relieve himself, and this was generally

## VaEra

an inappropriate moment for conversation, Moses was to approach him.

■ ■ ■

וְלֹא־יָכְלוּ הַחַרְטֻמִּים לַעֲמֹד לִפְנֵי מֹשֶׁה מִפְּנֵי הַשְּׁחִין כִּי־הָיָה הַשְּׁחִין בַּחַרְטֻמִּם וּבְכָל־מִצְרָיִם.

*The magicians were unable to stand before Moses due to the boils, as the boils had attacked the magicians along with the rest of Egypt.* (9:11)

"The magicians were unable to stand before Moses, due to the boils." The implication of these words is that the magicians *were* able to stand before Moses during the preceding plagues.

Chatham Sofer says that the Torah explicitly relates how the magicians duplicated the Plagues of Blood and Frogs, and how they were unable to duplicate Lice. No mention, however, is made of their prowess regarding Wild Animals or Pestilence. Now, there was no need for them to attempt to reproduce the Plague of Wild Animals, because the animals were already spread over the entire Egypt, with the exception of Goshen, where the Israelites resided. And for the magicians to try and spread the plague to Goshen as a demonstration of their abilities served no purpose. If Moses had been unable to make the plague effective there, why should they be compelled to do so as a demonstration of their powers? Perhaps Goshen had been spared by good fortune. But the Plague of Pestilence presents a difficulty. Whereas the present verse implies that, before the Plague of Boils, the magicians availed themselves of every opportunity to challenge Moses, why are they not mentioned in regard to Pestilence? Why didn't they attempt to spread it to the flocks of the Israelites?

(This difference between Wild Animals and Pestilence is somewhat difficult to understand. One would think that, just as Moses would not afflict the Israelite flocks with Pestilence, so would he not have caused Goshen to be overrun by the Wild Animals. Why, then, didn't the magicians attempt to make the Wild Animals spread to Goshen?)

To resolve this problem, Chatham Sofer makes reference to the

Talmudic assertion that the forced labor policy to which the Israelites were subject was abandoned on Rosh HaShanah, six months before their redemption, which occurred in the month of Nissan (Rosh HaShanah 11a). And the Midrash states that the labor ceased at the same time that the plagues commenced. Additionally, the Midrash says that a month's time elapsed between the beginning of one plague and the beginning of the next. Thus, the Plague of Blood commenced on Rosh HaShanah, Frogs on the first day of Cheshvan, Lice on the first of Kislev, Wild Animals on the first day of Teveth, and Pestilence on the first of Shevat. Evidently there was a leap month, Adar II, with Boils commencing on the first day of Adar I and Hail at the onset of Adar II. Locusts began on the first of Nissan (see Ramban on 10:4). Darkness started several days before Passover, which begins on the fourteenth day of Nissan. And the Plague of the Killing of the Firstborn occurred on the night of the fifteenth of Nissan.

The Talmud states that the Israelites left Egypt on a Thursday, which was the fifteenth of Nissan. We may now calculate that the first day of Shevat fell on a Sabbath. (Nissan began on a Thursday. Hence, Adar II commenced on a Wednesday, and Adar I on a Monday. Shevat thus began on a Sabbath. Such a sequence occurred in the year 5746 — 1986 — and in the year 5749 — 1989.)

On the Sabbath, the magicians were powerless to perform any sorcery. This is clear from the Talmud's assertion that a *ba'al ov*, a certain kind of sorcerer, is unable to perform any feats on the Sabbath (Sanhedrin 65b). They were therefore incapable of duplicating the Plague of Pestilence by spreading it to the flocks belonging to the Israelites. This — says Chatham Sofer — is why no mention is made of the magicians in regard to that plague.

According to Chatham Sofer, the plagues commenced on Rosh HaShanah. This is not, however, the view advanced by Tosafoth (Rosh HaShanah 11a). Taking note of the fact that the Mishnah (Ediyoth 2:10) says that the Egyptians were judged for twelve months, Tosafoth asserts that the slavery did not cease when the plagues began, but rather several months later.

## VaEra

Ra'avad, in his commentary on the Mishnah, proves that the plagues began a year prior to the Exodus from the fact that the Israelites were forced to gather straw in order to make bricks (5:12). Straw is found in abundance in Egypt in the month of Iyar, which follows Nissan. Hence the plagues continued for twelve months, from Iyar to the following Nissan.

As for Chatham Sofer, he maintains that the Mishnah, in saying that the Egyptians were judged for twelve months, is calculating from the time that Moses first went to confront Pharaoh. However, the first plague did not actually begin until Rosh HaShanah.

■ ■ ■

כִּי בַּפַּעַם הַזֹּאת אֲנִי שֹׁלֵחַ אֶת־כָּל־מַגֵּפֹתַי אֶל־לִבְּךָ וּבַעֲבָדֶיךָ וּבְעַמֶּךָ בַּעֲבוּר תֵּדַע כִּי אֵין כָּמֹנִי בְּכָל־הָאָרֶץ.

". . . This time I will send all My plagues against your very heart, your servants, and your people, so that you will know that there is none like Me in all the world. . . ." (9:14)

Why does Scripture say, in the case of Hail, that God would dispatch "all My plagues" against the Egyptians?

The Midrash says that God uses three phenomena to exact punishment from those who transgress His commands — fire, wind, and water. Sodom was punished with fire. The Generation of the Flood was destroyed by water. And the Generation of the Division of Mankind was afflicted by wind, which scattered the people who attempted to build a tower up to the heavens.

In Egypt, too, fire, wind, and water were utilized by God to dispense punishment. The Plagues of Blood and Frogs were rooted in the water of the Nile. The locusts were driven to Egypt by wind. And the Plague of Boils was a punishment of heat — which is the essence of fire. But the Plague of Hail differed in that all three of these elements were present. "I will cause it to rain tomorrow at this time" (verse 18) indicates the presence of water. "There was fire darting within the hail" (verse 24) demonstrates the presence of fire. And "God caused it to thunder" (verse 23) reveals the presence of wind. This is why it says that "all" of God's plagues were utilized in the Plague of Hail. God's three carriers of retribution — fire, wind, and water — were all involved in the application of the plague.

*(Vilna Gaon)*

■

"This time I will send all My plagues" — According to Rashi, we glean from these words that the Plague of the Killing of the Firstborn, *Makkath Bechoroth,* was equivalent in its severity to all the other plagues.

It is very difficult to understand what Rashi means by this. What does the Plague of the Killing of the Firstborn have to do with the Plague of Hail, which is the actual subject of discussion in the present verse?

Many commentators have striven to clarify Rashi's view.

R. Tam of Orleans asserts that Rashi is not referring to *Makkath Bechoroth,* the Plague of the Killing of the Firstborn. Rather, he is simply using another name for *Makkath Barad,* the Plague of Hail. The term Rashi utilizes is *Makkath Bakuroth,* which is spelled identically to *Makkath Bechoroth,* but is vowelized differently. (There are no vowels in Rashi, making the confusion over the vowelization possible.) *Bakuroth,* "the ripe ears," refers to the ripe crops which were destroyed by the hail, while the unripe crops remained standing (verses 31, 32). This view of R. Tam of Orleans is also accepted by Mizrachi.

However, the difficulties with this approach are glaring. Firstly, why would Rashi invent a new term to describe the Plague of Hail, and not be content with the term *Barad?* Secondly, if a new term were appropriate, why would Rashi select one that could so easily be confused with an already-established term? Thirdly, Maharal, in his work Gur Aryeh, points out that according to Rashi earlier (4:23), at Moses' first confrontation with Pharaoh, he threatened the king with death for the Egyptian firstborn, although that punishment was not actually meted out until the end; it constituted the final plague. The reason Moses did so at such an early juncture was because the last plague was so harsh (4:23). If, as R. Tam insists, the Plague of Hail was the harshest of the plagues, why didn't Moses use *it* to threaten Pharaoh? Finally, Maharal says that it would not be

## VaEra

logical to believe that when God brought the harshest plague, Hail, upon the Egyptians, Pharaoh still refused to release the Israelites, while after He brought a more lenient plague, the Killing of the Firstborn, Pharaoh yielded.

Maharal contends instead that Rashi is referring to *Makkath Bechoroth*, the Killing of the Firstborn. What, however, does it have to do with the present verse, which says, "This time I will send all My plagues," apparently referring to Hail, which occurred immediately after the warning given here? Maharal explains that the words "This time" do not refer to the Plague of Hail. They refer, rather, to the general matter at hand, the topic of this entire section — Pharaoh's refusal to permit the Israelites to leave Egypt. *Bapa'am hazoth*, "This time," should be translated somewhat less literally. It should be rendered: "Due to this matter" — due to the fact that Pharaoh was acting in an obstinate fashion. God now told Pharaoh that his stubbornness would result in "all My plagues," in a plague equivalent to all the others combined, being brought upon Egypt. There would still be other plagues to reckon with before that final plague, but it was the Plague of the Killing of the Firstborn concerning which Pharaoh was now admonished.

Maharal continues that God was not adopting a new tactic in warning Pharaoh of a plague which was not to occur for some time. God had already done this once before, when He warned Pharaoh about the final plague before even the first plague was implemented (4:23).

Why, however, did God choose this particular moment — the time preceding the Plague of Hail — to administer His warning about the demise of the firstborn? Maharal answers that, because the Plague of Pestilence harmed only the animals of the Egyptians and not the people themselves, Pharaoh might have concluded that God would not cause the Egyptians bodily harm. God wanted Pharaoh to know that such was not the case, that He was indeed prepared to physically afflict them, by killing the firstborn. He had allowed them to escape the Plague of Pestilence only so that His name would be spread across the earth, which would occur with Hail, a plague unprecedented in the annals of Egypt.

Maharal adds that the verses in this section now follow one another splendidly. God warned Pharaoh of the eventual doom of the firstborn. He continued that "I could have unleashed My power, killing you and your people with the Pestilence" (verse 15). "The only reason I let you survive was to show you My power, so that My name will be spread all over the world" (verse 16). All this, said God, should have made Pharaoh reconsider his position, and yet Pharaoh was "still oppressing My people" (verse 17). Therefore, God would "bring a very heavy hail," the likes of which had not been experienced in the history of Egypt (verse 18). As a result, God's name would be spread throughout the earth.

Maharal offers a second theory as to why reference is made to the final plague when the subject of discussion is apparently the seventh plague. The Haggadah quotes R. Yehuda, who divides the Ten Plagues into three sets. Maharal says that each set had a particular goal in mind. The first three plagues were a challenge to Pharaoh's belief that there was no God calling for the release of the Israelites. Pharaoh called in his magicians to duplicate the plagues, but they were forced, at the third plague — Lice — to admit that it was administered by the hand of God (8:15).

The next three plagues had a different purpose. The first plagues had been land-wide phenomena, and so Pharaoh was convinced that God did not assert *hashgachah prattith*, providence over particulars. Pharaoh held that God's interest in the earth was a general one. Hence, the fourth plague, Wild Animals, did not strike the land of Goshen, where the Israelites had their primary residence (Ibid., verse 18). The same occurred with the Plague of Pestilence (verse 4). And while no mention is made of a separation between Goshen and the rest of Egypt as concerns the Plague of Boils, Maharal assumes that such was the case.

The final four plagues were a sign that "there is none like Me in all the world." The previous plagues had demonstrated God's awesome capabilities, but not necessarily His uniqueness. This was the task of the last four plagues. Thus, Hail and Locusts are both described as plagues which were beyond anything seen in the history of Egypt (verse 18, 10:6). As for Darkness, says Maharal,

## VaEra

there is no question that it was a unique event (given the prolonged period of night and the Midrashic assertion that there was substance to the darkness; it could actually be felt). Finally, Scripture explicitly states that the Plague of the Killing of the Firstborn brought unprecedented anguish to Egypt (11:6).

Maharal says that when Scripture speaks of "This time" it is referring to the set of four plagues which commenced with Hail. It is therefore very pertinent to mention here that "This time all My plagues" would be unleashed, as it was now that the final set of plagues began. However, says Maharal, "all My plagues" refers only to the Killing of the Firstborn.

It would be wrong, he says, to conjecture that one of the other plagues in the set is the subject of "all My plagues," because it was certainly the final one that was the harshest. The plagues did not diminish in intensity. Neither could one posit that the four, when combined, equaled the intensity of the other six plagues, since each plague occurred separately. Finally, one would be unable to maintain that each of the final four plagues was equivalent to the other plagues, for, were that the case, Pharaoh would have released the Israelites after the Plague of Hail, there being as much intensity to it as there was to the plagues that followed.

Sifthei Chachamim comes to the defense of R. Tam of Orleans — with his view that Rashi's words are *Makkath Bakuroth*, referring to Hail, not *Makkath Bechoroth*. As for Rashi's earlier statement that the harshest plague was that of the Killing of the Firstborn, Sifthei Chachamim resolves the contradiction by saying that Pharaoh found the Killing of the Firstborn to be the harshest plague. However, the general public was stricken most by Hail, which destroyed food. Pharaoh, as the king, was still able to access sufficient food, and thus was not as harshly affected by the Plague of Hail. Earlier Rashi spoke concerning which plague was to affect Pharaoh himself the most, while here he is asserting that the Plague of Hail was the harshest for the general public to endure.

Alternatively, says Sifthei Chachamim, the Torah, in saying that Hail was equivalent to all the plagues, is comparing it only with the first six plagues — the plagues which had already been visited upon

Egypt. However, the last three plagues were harsher than Hail. Levush HaOhrah advances this thesis as well.

Ohr HaChayyim also considers this last approach, but rejects it. Instead, he posits a completely different explanation of the words "all My plagues against your very heart." He avers that Pharaoh had not, as of the sixth plague — Boils — conceded that the plagues were the work of God. He still harbored the belief that Moses was a sorcerer. The proof of this — Pharaoh contended — lay in the fact that his own magicians had been able to duplicate the plagues. And while these magicians had acknowledged the hand of God during the Plague of Lice, Pharaoh himself felt that Moses was simply a better magician than they. God now said that "This time," with the Plague of Hail, He would send "all My plagues" — the six plagues previous to Hail — "against your very heart." The Plague of Hail would finally convince Pharaoh that it had been God who had been the power behind the plagues. Pharaoh could not reasonably argue that the hail, in which water and fire mixed (verse 24), was anything but the work of God. Magicians do not have the capability to produce such a marvel. This is why Scripture uses the term "*My* plagues"; it would now become clear that the previous plagues had been wrought by God.

Divrei David rejects R. Tam's view and maintains that it is the Plague of the Killing of the Firstborn which was as powerful as the rest of the plagues combined. What, then, is the connection to the Plague of Hail? Divrei David explains that Scripture terms Hail "all My plagues" because the seventh plague was indeed more powerful than the other plagues. And yet, when God threatened Pharaoh at the onset of their confrontation, He warned the king that the firstborn Egyptians would die. (Divrei David's source for this is not 4:23, but the Midrashic exposition of 7:16.) Obviously, then, this last plague was more powerful than the Plague of Hail, else God would have threatened Pharaoh with Hail. Therefore, while Hail was equivalent to the other plagues, with the exception of the final one, the Killing of the Firstborn was as powerful as all the other plagues, *including* Hail. Since this derives from the present verse, Rashi mentions it here.

## VaEra

There are two other opinions which, like R. Tam, amend the text of Rashi away from the words *Makkath Bechoroth*. Abravanel asserts that the correct reading is *Makkath Batzoreth*, which translates as a "plague of scarcity." The reference is to Hail, which caused a shortage of food in Egypt.

Chida cites R. Heschel, who insists that Rashi wrote *Makkath Barad*, Hail. However, he wrote the words acronymically, and the first letters of the two words, *mem* and *beth*, are the same as the letters of the words *Makkath Bechoroth*. Those who recopied Rashi's commentary erred, and in spelling out the acronym wrote *makkath bechoroth*. Maharsha shares this opinion.

■ ■ ■

וַיֹּאמֶר אֵלָיו מֹשֶׁה כְּצֵאתִי אֶת־הָעִיר אֶפְרֹשׂ אֶת־כַּפַּי אֶל־ה' הַקֹּלוֹת יֶחְדָּלוּן וְהַבָּרָד לֹא יִהְיֶה־עוֹד לְמַעַן תֵּדַע כִּי לַה' הָאָרֶץ.
וְאַתָּה וַעֲבָדֶיךָ יָדַעְתִּי כִּי טֶרֶם תִּירְאוּן מִפְּנֵי ה' אֱלֹהִים.

*Moses said to [Pharaoh], "When I go out of the city, I will spread my hands [in prayer] to God. The thunder will stop, and there will not be any more hail. [This will occur] so that you will know that the whole world belongs to God.*
*"But as for you and your servants, I realize that you still do not fear God the Lord."* (9:29, 30)

Chatham Sofer questions the order of the verses in this section. After detailing Moses' discussion with Pharaoh, in which Moses promised to pray to God for the cessation of the hail, Scripture interrupts to relate that the hail destroyed the flax and the barley but did not destroy the wheat and spelt (verses 31, 32). Then it says that Moses prayed to God, who brought the plague to a halt (verse 33). Wouldn't it have been more orderly to place Moses' prayer immediately after his discussion with Pharaoh, and to discuss the crop damage earlier, where the hail's destructive power was portrayed (verse 25)?

Chatham Sofer bases his answer to this problem on the Midrash's view of the words "But the wheat and spelt were not destroyed, because they are late in sprouting" (verse 32). The Midrash understands the word *afiloth*, "late," to allude to the word *pelaoth* or *pelaim,* "wonders." Although the wheat and spelt should have been destroyed, a miracle was wrought and they were spared.

It is known, Chatham Sofer says, that the ancient philosophers asserted that there were two gods. They maintained that it would be impossible for one god to act, at the same instant, in contradictory capacities. God could not be merciful and a dispenser of justice simultaneously. Hence, there had to be two deities.

Chatham Sofer continues that Pharaoh was just such a philosopher and heretic, and so the plagues were orchestrated to demonstrate God's oneness. This is indicated in several verses. "You will then know that there is none like God our Lord" (8:6) affirms that there is but one God. "You will then realize that I am God in the midst of the land" (Ibid., verse 18) establishes that God observes and rules the world. And "so that you will know that there is none like Me in all the world" (verse 14) again affirms the unity of God.

The Plague of Hail demonstrated that God can display compassion at the same time that He metes out justice. While the flax and barley were smitten, as should naturally have occurred given the severity of the hail, the wheat and spelt were spared. At the same instant in which He was implementing the plague, God exercised mercy and performed a miracle in order to spare the wheat and spelt.

This, concludes Chatham Sofer, serves to explain the order of the verses. Moses said, "I realize that you still do not fear God the Lord." *Ado-nai,* "God," alludes to God's merciful aspect, while *Elokim,* "Lord," connotes His attribute of justice. Even though Pharaoh had seen both attributes exercised simultaneously by God — in that the flax and barley were destroyed while the wheat and spelt were spared — he had yet to acquire fear of God. And, indeed, Pharaoh continued to remain obstinate (verse 35).

■

"When I go out of the city" — Moses did not pray within the city because it was full of idols (Rashi). Why was he careful not to pray within the city limits specifically during the Plague of Hail? Why wasn't this a concern during the other plagues as well?

## VaEra

As we know, the Egyptians worshiped sheep as gods. Regarding the Plague of Hail, Scripture states that those among Pharaoh's servants who feared God brought their livestock into their houses (verse 20). The animals were at this moment within the city, while during the other plagues they were outside the city, in the fields. Moses did not pray within the city limits now because Egypt's gods had been taken into the city. *(Rebbe R. Heschel)*

R. Shlomo Kluger approaches the above question in a different fashion. The halacha is that a non-Jew has the ability to nullify the status of an object which was worshiped as a god by non-Jews. This nullification is effectual even if it was merely done orally (Yoreh De'ah 146:1, 7); no tangible action is necessary.

R. Shlomo Kluger avers that Moses *always* left the city in order to pray, due to the presence of idols in the city. However, now Pharaoh admitted that "God is the just one" (verse 27). This statement amounted to a nullification of the status of the idols in the city. Pharaoh knew that Moses had not, until now, prayed inside the city. However, having now declared God to be the true Divine being, Pharaoh pressured the Israelite leader to entreat God immediately, since there was no longer an obstacle to prayer in the city.

Moses retorted that Pharaoh did not yet fear God. Rashi explains that Moses knew Pharaoh would resume his wicked ways once a respite had been granted. The acknowledgment that "God is the just one" was thus a coerced one; it had been prompted by the plague. The halacha is that the non-Jew's renunciation of an idol does not take effect if he was forced to pronounce it; the renunciation must come of his own volition. Therefore, Moses had to leave the city for prayer even on this occasion, and that is why it is emphasized here that he did so.

■ ■ ■

וְהַפִּשְׁתָּה וְהַשְּׂעֹרָה נֻכָּתָה כִּי הַשְּׂעֹרָה אָבִיב וְהַפִּשְׁתָּה גִּבְעֹל.
*The flax and barley were destroyed, because the barley was ripe and the flax had formed stalks. (9:31)*

There exists a difference of opinion regarding the identity of the

## The Eternal Heritage

speaker in this verse and in the following verse. Ibn Ezra says that Scripture is narrating, and that the information regarding the damage to the crops was not part of the conversation between Moses and Pharaoh. However, Sa'adiah Gaon and Ramban contend that Moses told Pharaoh about the crop damage.

Ohr HaChayyim accepts Ibn Ezra's view that Moses' speech ended in the previous verse, and that Scripture is now narrating regarding the extent of the crop damage. Why, however, does Scripture choose to interject this information now?

Ohr HaChayyim answers that Scripture wishes to supply the reason why, as Moses said, Pharaoh did not as yet fear God (verse 30). The Midrash states that the wheat and spelt were spared miraculously. Instead of recognizing that God had overridden the natural order of things, Pharaoh asserted that God was not omnipotent, for although His hail was capable of destroying some of the crops, it had not succeeded in destroying all of them.

Ohr HaChayyim adds that God performed this miracle for the very purpose of hardening Pharaoh's heart, as He had said He would do (4:21).

■ ■ ■

וְהַחִטָּה וְהַכֻּסֶּמֶת לֹא נֻכּוּ כִּי אֲפִילֹת הֵנָּה.

*The wheat and spelt were not destroyed, since they are late in sprouting. (9:32)*

Why were the wheat and spelt left undamaged?

It is possible to threaten someone only as long as he possesses something which he does not desire to lose. If someone has nothing, he has nothing to lose, and threats become ineffective. Pharaoh was left with the wheat and spelt so that he would continue to have a stake in the confrontation. *(Yad Yosef)*

■ ■ ■

וַיֵּצֵא מֹשֶׁה מֵעִם פַּרְעֹה אֶת־הָעִיר וַיִּפְרֹשׂ כַּפָּיו אֶל־ה' וַיַּחְדְּלוּ הַקֹּלוֹת וְהַבָּרָד וּמָטָר לֹא־נִתַּךְ אָרְצָה.

*Moses left Pharaoh's presence and went out of the city. He spread his hands out to*

## VaEra

God. *The thunder and hail ceased, and rain stopped falling to the ground.* (9:33)

Pharaoh asked that the thunder and hail cease (verse 28). He did not desire that the rain also stop. The rain would have been beneficial for the ground, since Egypt does not receive much rainfall and is reliant upon the Nile for irrigation. But Pharaoh's wish was not honored. Not only was there a halt to the thunder and hail, but the "rain stopped falling to the ground."

*(R. Yaakov of Lissa)*

∎

The commentators wonder how it is that, despite observing that Moses' prayer caused this awesome plague to cease entirely, Pharaoh remained firm in his refusal to release the Israelites (verse 35).

Divrei Shaul agrees with R. Yaakov of Lissa that Pharaoh did not want the rain to stop. The Rav Peninim commentary adds that Moses evidently agreed to comply with Pharaoh's request; Moses said, "The thunder will then stop, and there will not be any more hail" (verse 29). Moses did not call for the rain to stop.

When Pharaoh saw that the rain *did* stop along with the thunder and hail, he concluded that Moses did not have the ability to control the weather, and that it had been coincidental that the thunder and hail stopped after he had prayed.

This, says the Rav Peninim commentary, is why God subsequently had to tell Moses, "Go to Pharaoh" (10:1). Moses was embarrassed to see the king, because he had promised Pharaoh to arrange for the continuation of the rainfall, and had failed. Therefore, he had to be coaxed to go to Pharaoh.

■ ■ ■

וַיַּרְא פַּרְעֹה כִּי־חָדַל הַמָּטָר וְהַבָּרָד וְהַקֹּלֹת וַיֹּסֶף לַחֲטֹא וַיַּכְבֵּד לִבּוֹ הוּא וַעֲבָדָיו.

*Pharaoh saw that the rain, hail, and thunder had ceased, and so he continued to sin. He and his servants continued to be obstinate.* (9:34)

Rashbam says that until now Pharaoh had not sinned

presumptuously. However, he had now admitted that he and his nation had acted wickedly (verse 27). By remaining obstinate even after this acknowledgment, he was sinning intentionally.

# 3

## Bo

וַיֹּאמֶר ה' אֶל־מֹשֶׁה בֹּא אֶל־פַּרְעֹה כִּי־אֲנִי הִכְבַּדְתִּי אֶת־לִבּוֹ וְאֶת־לֵב עֲבָדָיו לְמַעַן שִׁתִי אֹתֹתַי אֵלֶּה בְּקִרְבּוֹ.

*God said to Moses, "Go to Pharaoh, for I have hardened the hearts of him and his servants so that I may demonstrate these miraculous signs among them...."* (10:1)

Why does it say here *bo*, "Go," to Pharaoh, while elsewhere the word *lech* is used to denote "go"? [*Bo* implies "going in," achieving a closer proximity to the person to whom one is going.] Secondly, why is it specifically at the Plague of Locusts that God told Moses He had "hardened the hearts of him and his servants"?

God performs two sorts of miracles for the Jewish people. In the first type, He harms the enemies of the Jews so that they are forced to cease to harm the Jews. In the second type, God causes the enemies of the Jews to have second thoughts — He turns their hearts so that they willfully abandon their campaign against the Jews and become benevolent towards them. Such was the case with King Achashveirosh. While Haman was punished, we do not find any indication that Achashveirosh was penalized for his role in the Purim episode. This is because God caused Achashveirosh to have a change of heart regarding Haman's plan to exterminate the Jews.

The allusion to God's interference in Achashveirosh's thought process is found in the present verse. The Sages say that the duration of every plague [including the time period during which warning was served to Pharaoh] was a month. Whereas the Plague of the Killing of the Firstborn occurred midway through the month of Nissan, the Plague of Locusts must have commenced midway through Shevat — one month before Purim, which occurs on the fourteenth of Adar. At the time of this plague, God said that He had hardened Pharaoh's heart, causing him to assume a harsh posture towards the Israelites. It is a principle that God accentuates positive aspects over negative ones. If He is willing to sway a ruler's heart towards evil, as He did with Pharaoh, He is certainly ready to sway a ruler towards good.

Now, it is stated that one is required to begin studying the laws of a festival thirty days before the festival occurs (Pesachim 6a). Thus, thirty days before the celebration of Purim takes place — i.e., in the middle of Shevat — Scripture informs us that God is willing to sway the heart of a king in favor of the Jews. This is why it is here that God says: "I have hardened the hearts of him and his servants."

*(Kedushath Levi)*

■

R. Yehoshua Leib Diskin advances an explanation concerning the use of the word *bo* and the reason that God told Moses that He had made Pharaoh stubborn. R. Yehoshua Leib asks: If God made Pharaoh stubborn, what purpose was there in having Moses go to him?

In answer, he points out that before bringing the Plague of Hail God announced that He was sending "all My plagues" against Egypt (9:14). Certainly no one could remain truculent in the face of such an onslaught, and Pharaoh would have had to recognize the truth and be ready to release the Israelites. Indeed, this is what transpired. Pharaoh admitted that God was just, and he agreed to send out the Israelites (Ibid., verses 27, 28).

Having witnessed this change of heart, Moses expected that Pharaoh would send for him, in order that they could make the arrangements for the departure of the Israelites. God now informed

*Bo*

Moses: *bo*, "Go." Pharaoh would not call for him; he would have to take the initiative and go to Pharaoh, as the king had been made obstinate.

■

"I have hardened the hearts of him and his servants" — Ramban explains why it was that God found it necessary to inform Moses that *He* had made Pharaoh obstinate. Pharaoh had just admitted that he and his nation were wicked, while God was just (9:27). Given that concession, how could Pharaoh have now made such an about-face, and resumed his stubborn posture? Hence, God said that He had made Pharaoh obstinate, in order to demonstrate His might to the Egyptians, as well as to make known His might for all time (verse 2). The Egyptians were not, however, to suffer additional punishment for their obstinacy, as their ability to choose freely had been taken from them.

■

"I have hardened the hearts of him and his servants" — Moses was amazed by Pharaoh's stubbornness in the face of all that had transpired. Such an attribute, felt Moses, was worthy of one who was God-fearing; one should have the desire to be "fierce as a tiger" in heeding God's will (Avoth 5:20).

God thus explained to Moses that Pharaoh was not truly this obstinate; God had forced him to be stubborn.

*(R. Yechiel Meir of Gostynin, as cited by Iturei Torah)*

■

"I have hardened the hearts of him and his servants" — How was the hardening of the hearts of Pharaoh's servants manifested? On the contrary, didn't they implore Pharaoh to release the Israelites (verse 7)?

The servants told Pharaoh, "Let the *men* go." They did not tell him, "Let the *nation* go." The servants held that only the males were to be released, as it is not the nature of women and children to be present at a religious service. Since Moses had insisted that the purpose of the Israelite journey was to worship God, there was no reason to send the females.

This advice to hold back the women and children was given because the servants' hearts had been hardened.

*(Moshav Zekenim)*

■ ■ ■

וַיָּבֹא מֹשֶׁה וְאַהֲרֹן אֶל־פַּרְעֹה וַיֹּאמְרוּ אֵלָיו כֹּה־אָמַר ה' אֱלֹהֵי הָעִבְרִים עַד־מָתַי מֵאַנְתָּ לֵעָנֹת מִפָּנָי שַׁלַּח עַמִּי וְיַעַבְדֻנִי.

Moses and Aaron went to Pharaoh. They said to him: God, the Lord of the Hebrews, says: "How long will you refuse to submit to Me? Let My people leave and serve Me. . . ." (10:3)

When a Jew sins and does not heed God's desires, his heart is broken. He regrets that he was unable to withstand temptation and, deep in his heart, he yearns and prays to be given the desire to do God's will. This is regarded as a step that is above the simple will to heed God's word, and is termed *ra'ava dera'ava*, "the will to have the will."

Pharaoh was different. Not only did he lack regret that he had not submitted to God, but he was pleased at his ability to maintain his obstinacy. He was happy in his lack of desire to repent. And this was his primary transgression: "How long will you refuse to submit before Me?" Pharaoh did not seek to acquire the will to heed God's will, to become submissive.

*(Sefath Emeth)*

■

"How long will you refuse to submit to Me?" — There are some sins which are so severe that the Sages say about the transgressor, "He is not given the opportunity to repent" (Sanhedrin 107b); all the paths to repentance are closed to this sinner. And yet, if he considers his desperate plight — seeing the bottomless pit below him and knowing that there is no escape — and his heart is broken and he is humbled, God has mercy on him. God opens a special gate through which his prayers may be received. In the words of the Sages, God digs a hole under His Throne of Glory in order to accept the man's

## Bo

repentance (Ruth Rabbah 5). The repenter's humbleness creates the path to his return by the digging of a hole, since the normal paths are sealed before him.

However, if one "refuse[s] to submit" to God — if he is not humbled despite having sinned so severely that the paths to return are closed to him — then there is no longer any hope for him. He remains among those who are not given the opportunity to repent.

*(Yismach Yisrael, in the name of his father, R. Yechiel of Aleksandrow)*

■ ■ ■

כִּי אִם־מָאֵן אַתָּה לְשַׁלֵּחַ אֶת־עַמִּי הִנְנִי מֵבִיא מָחָר אַרְבֶּה בִּגְבֻלֶךָ.
". . . For if you refuse to let My people leave, I will bring locusts within your boundaries tomorrow. . . ." (10:4)

The Midrash derives from this verse that the locusts afflicted only the Land of Egypt. They made no entry into any of the surrounding lands, which, like Egypt, were the possessions of the various descendants of Ham. These had been at odds over the precise location of their respective borders. The Plague of Locusts resolved this dispute, as the insects went to the outer reaches of Egypt, but stopped upon reaching the border.

Chatham Sofer poses a difficulty concerning the Midrash. It is, he says, certain that the people in the disputed territories also enslaved the Israelites. These territories must have been under Egyptian dominion, and the Israelites were there to make bricks for the inhabitants. If Egypt did not control these lands then the previous plagues would also not have affected them. Whereas Egypt did control these lands, and the Israelites were oppressed therein, why was it specifically the Plague of Locusts that was selected to delineate Egypt's borders?

Chatham Sofer says that in order to resolve this we must first examine an apparent inconsistency in Scripture. In confronting Pharaoh at this time, Moses first told him, in God's name, "How long will you refuse to submit to Me? Let My people leave and serve Me" (verse 3). Moses continued, "If you refuse to let My people leave . . ." Why did he not say: "If you refuse to submit to Me . . ."? The lack of submission was the criticism that Moses first heaped on Pharaoh. Why didn't Moses continue with the same criticism?

Chatham Sofer answers by advancing the Sages' view that during the Plague of Hail, when Pharaoh said, "God is the just one. It is I and my people who are in the wrong" (9:27), he meant that he and God were righteous, while the nation was wicked. The verse is to be read: "God is the just one and I," but "my people are in the wrong." Chatham Sofer contends that the "people" to whom Pharaoh referred were not the Egyptians, but the Israelites, and that he called them "my people" because they were his servants. Pharaoh asserted that the Israelites were wicked, for, if they were not wicked, God would not have permitted their enslavement. Pharaoh thus had no choice in this but to comply with God's wishes. As Scripture says, the hearts of kings are in God's hands (Proverbs 21:1).

Chatham Sofer adds that Pharaoh had made the same contention at his first confrontation with Moses. He had said, "I do not know God, and I will not let Israel leave" (5:2). Besides being unfamiliar with the God in whose name Moses and Aaron had spoken, Pharaoh said he had not been moved to free the Israelites. He claimed that this was an indication that, whoever the true God might be, He desired their enslavement, with Pharaoh being merely an instrument of the Divine plan.

Chatham Sofer continues that, as is known, Pharaoh lost his free will during the last five plagues. This was especially the case with the Plague of Locusts. Seven plagues had already been inflicted, and God does not generally inflict more than seven penalties on a nation. If the people still do not repent, He destroys them. God now told Moses to go to Pharaoh, but not to be astonished at the continued obstinacy of the king, because God had hardened his heart (verse 1). Hence, Pharaoh had room to assert that it was God who was forcing him to keep the Israelites imprisoned — evidently due to their evil deeds — since Pharaoh knew that he himself actually desired to free them.

*Bo*

In order to determine Pharaoh's true position regarding the Israelites, God elected to test him by having the locusts define the borders of Egypt. If the king finally desired to behave in a righteous manner, he would relinquish control of the disputed areas, having seen that the locusts did not strike there. Pharaoh's refusal to do this would demonstrate that it was his evil nature which had caused the Israelites to suffer; it was not the plan of God. This is why it was at the Plague of Locusts — the eighth plague — that God delineated Egypt's borders.

This, concludes Chatham Sofer, also explains why God first reprimanded Pharaoh for his lack of humility and then shifted His attack to the king's refusal to release the Israelites. God said: Why do you refuse to be humbled before Me? And if you deny this charge, asserting that you treat people humanely and that the Israelites' oppression is due to their wickedness, then this can be verified. If "you refuse to let My people leave" — if you heed God's word regarding everything, but cannot release the Israelites — I will bring locusts in your land, but not in the lands around Egypt. You will then have the opportunity to demonstrate your righteousness, by relinquishing the illegally held territories, but you will refuse to do so.

■ ■ ■

וּמָלְאוּ בָתֶּיךָ וּבָתֵּי כָל־עֲבָדֶיךָ וּבָתֵּי כָל־מִצְרַיִם אֲשֶׁר לֹא־רָאוּ אֲבֹתֶיךָ וַאֲבוֹת אֲבֹתֶיךָ מִיּוֹם הֱיוֹתָם עַל־הָאֲדָמָה עַד הַיּוֹם הַזֶּה וַיִּפֶן וַיֵּצֵא מֵעִם פַּרְעֹה.

"*. . . They will fill your quarters, as well as the quarters of all your servants and the houses of all Egypt. It will be something that your fathers and your fathers' fathers never saw, from the day they settled the land until today." [Moses] turned away and left Pharaoh. (10:6)*

"Moses turned away and left Pharaoh." The Midrash says that Moses turned away and left because he saw Pharaoh's servants whispering.

R. David Luria was arrested in Pressburg, due to the work of an informer. After spending several days in confinement, R. David was brought before a magistrate. During the proceedings, whenever the judges wished to talk privately among themselves, they would speak in French so that the defendant would not be able to understand the conversation.

However, R. David knew French, and he turned away from the judges.

One of the judges reprimanded R. David, saying that he was displaying a lack of respect by turning away from the bench. Protocol called for him to stand at attention.

R. David countered, in French, that he had turned away in order to display respect. Whereas the judges assumed he was not conversant in French, while he actually was, it would have been improper for him to listen to their conversation.

The judges were very impressed by this unexpected explanation, and released R. David.

Later, R. David explained that his role model in this regard was Moses. The Midrash states that Moses exited Pharaoh's palace when he saw the king's servants whispering. Evidently, Moses realized that they did not want him to hear their conversation, and so, out of respect, he moved away.

*(MeOtzareinu HaYashan)*

■

Scripture states that Moses "turned away and left Pharaoh." Why is it that only after delivering the warning concerning the Plague of Locusts — as opposed to the other plagues — did Moses comport himself in this fashion?

God had informed Moses that Pharaoh's heart had now been hardened so that He could inflict the plagues upon Egypt (verse 1). Pharaoh would remain truculent; he would not be moved by the upcoming plague to change his position. Moses saw no purpose in waiting for Pharaoh to respond to the warning, as he knew what Pharaoh's reaction would be, and so he left immediately upon completing his speech. *(Maggid of Dubno)*

■ ■ ■

*Bo*

וַיֹּאמֶר מֹשֶׁה בִּנְעָרֵינוּ וּבִזְקֵנֵינוּ נֵלֵךְ בְּבָנֵינוּ וּבִבְנוֹתֵנוּ בְּצֹאנֵנוּ וּבִבְקָרֵנוּ נֵלֵךְ כִּי חַג־ה׳ לָנוּ.

*Moses replied, "We will go with our young and old alike. We will go with our sons and daughters, and with our sheep and cattle, as it is a festival to God for all of us."* (10:9)

"Young and old" — The first group that had to be rescued from Egypt was the youth. Because of their lack of a proper spiritual upbringing, the young Israelites were more susceptible than their elders to being caught up by the impurity of Egypt. After the youth had left would go the older generation, which still had some roots in Judaism and was more likely to survive spiritually in Egypt.

*(Sefer HaDerush)*

■ ■ ■

וַיֹּאמֶר אֲלֵהֶם יְהִי כֵן ה׳ עִמָּכֶם כַּאֲשֶׁר אֲשַׁלַּח אֶתְכֶם וְאֶת־טַפְּכֶם רְאוּ כִּי רָעָה נֶגֶד פְּנֵיכֶם.

*[Pharaoh] replied, "May God only be with you just as I will let you leave with your children. You must realize that you will be confronted by evil. . . ."* (10:10)

According to the Midrash, Pharaoh told Moses that it was not standard for children to participate in sacrificial service. Moses' insistence that the children be allowed to accompany the men had made clear his actual, evil plan: he intended to flee. But, said Pharaoh, Moses' plan would backfire, and the Israelites would not be freed.

Chatham Sofer explains that there are two kinds of worship. Firstly, there is the worship whereby one engages in Torah study, and in prayer and sacrifices. The presence of infants and children during such endeavors is undesirable, as the play and chatter of young people disturb one's concentration. As an example, Chatham Sofer cites the story told in the work Chovoth HaLevavoth, by Rabbeinu Bachya, of a city where the women and children lived in a separate district so that they would not distract the men from their worship of God.

The second form of worship is that of celebration, such as is demonstrated on a festival. For such worship, it is desirable that women and children participate along with the men. As Scripture says, "You shall rejoice on your festival along with your son and daughter" (Deuteronomy 16:14). This sort of worship, however, is not established without good reason. It is introduced only to mark a momentous event such as the redemption of a person or a nation.

Chatham Sofer continues that the first type of service is termed *laShem*, "for God," while the second type is termed *lachem*, "for you." The fact that these two categories exist is expressed by the Talmud (Beitzah 15b), which points to a contradiction in Scriptural verses regarding the nature of a festival. One verse asserts that the seventh day of Passover is "a retreat dedicated to God, *laShem*" (Deuteronomy 16:8), while another says that Shemini Atzereth is "a time of retreat for you, *lachem*" (Numbers 29:35). R. Yehoshua resolves the difficulty by saying that half of a festival should be spent in Torah study — "a retreat dedicated to God" — while the other half is reserved for eating and drinking, for physical celebration — "a time of retreat for you." Although it is a commandment from God to engage in physical enjoyment, this is termed *lachem*, "for you." And despite the fact that God has no need for our sacrifices or prayers, the first kind of service is termed *laShem*, "for God," because it contains no physical benefits for the worshipers.

Chatham Sofer says that Pharaoh asked Moses: Will God be with you if I send your children along with you? Won't they distract you from the service, causing God to be dismayed? Moses, however, said that it is "a festival to God for all of us" (verse 9). This would be a worship service of the second kind, a public celebration, in which it is necessary to include the children as well as the adults.

To this Pharaoh retorted that Moses obviously was conspiring to flee. The worship of the second type takes place only to rejoice in an event such as a redemption, and so it could only be that Moses did not intend to return.

■■■

## Bo

וְעַתָּה שָׂא נָא חַטָּאתִי אַךְ הַפַּעַם וְהַעְתִּירוּ לַה' אֱלֹהֵיכֶם וְיָסֵר מֵעָלַי רַק אֶת־הַמָּוֶת הַזֶּה.

"... *Now forgive my sin just one more time. Pray to God your Lord that He should take just this death away from me.*" (10:17)

Likutei Yehoshua points out that we do not find Pharaoh describing any of the other plagues as "death." What made the Plague of Locusts so outstanding that such a harsh term was needed to describe it?

Likutei Yehoshua answers this problem based on the Talmud's prescribed courses of action in cases of hunger and epidemic. The Talmud says that when confronted with hunger the people of a city should scatter — they should depart for another city. In the event of an epidemic, the converse is advised; people are told to remain within the city's confines (Bava Kamma 60b).

The Midrash says that an epidemic accompanied each of the other plagues. Hence, the Plague of Locusts posed a particular difficulty. The hunger brought about by the destruction of the crops called for people to leave the cities, while the accompanying epidemic was best combated by citizens remaining in their homes. This dilemma was the cause of Pharaoh's assessment of the plague as "death" — neither remedy would suffice.

■

"Pray to God your Lord that He should take just this death away from me." Why does Pharaoh ask that God remove "just" the locusts, the implication being that there was something else for which Pharaoh could have asked Moses to pray, but didn't?

We may resolve this based on the Talmud's instructions regarding how to pray when one is faced with hunger and epidemic simultaneously. In the days of R. Shmuel b. Nachmani, such a situation occurred. It was inappropriate to request the alleviation of both, for that was seen as asking too much (the Talmud cites a Scriptural verse to support this). R. Shmuel b. Nachmani advised the people to ask for relief from the hunger. He said that, if God would ease the conditions which had led to the lack of food, He would do so only because there were living people to enjoy it. As it says, God "provides sustenance for all living beings" (Psalms 145:16); food is given to the living, not the dead. Thus, the answering of the prayer for relief from hunger would necessarily be accompanied by the cessation of the epidemic (Ta'anith 8b).

The Plague of Locusts was actually one of hunger, as the grasshoppers consumed all of the produce in the fields (verse 15). And the Midrash says that an epidemic accompanied each of the plagues, including that of Locusts. Thus, hunger and epidemic existed simultaneously at this time. It was improper to request relief from both of these, so Pharaoh asked Moses to obtain relief from "just this death" — only from the hunger. If God would consent, the epidemic would by necessity come to a halt, else there would be no one to enjoy the new produce which would be available.

The other plagues did not consist of coincident hunger and epidemic. The invocation of the promise that God "provides sustenance for all living beings" did not apply, and so the cessation of those plagues did not necessarily include the cessation of the epidemic. Therefore, when Pharaoh requested the alleviation of those plagues, he had to ask God to halt the epidemic that went with them. He did this by not limiting his request to "just" the main plague. His requests were general, and included the epidemic as well. *(Torah Temimah)*

■ ■ ■

וַיֹּאמֶר ה' אֶל־מֹשֶׁה נְטֵה יָדְךָ עַל־הַשָּׁמַיִם וִיהִי חֹשֶׁךְ עַל־אֶרֶץ מִצְרָיִם וְיָמֵשׁ חֹשֶׁךְ.

*God said to Moses, "Reach out toward the sky with your hand, and there will be darkness in Egypt. The darkness will be intense." (10:21)*

The Midrash relates that God asked the angels if the Egyptians deserved to be smitten by a Plague of Darkness. There was unanimous consent that they merited being stricken with such a plague. The Midrash continues by asking why a Plague of Darkness in particular was selected. It answers that, firstly, there existed wicked Israelites, who did not desire to leave Egypt. They died during the Plague of Darkness so that the Egyptians would not be

## Bo

able to observe their downfall. Secondly, the Israelites used the period of darkness to seek out the hidden valuables of the Egyptians. When the Israelites later sought to borrow these valuables, the Egyptians were unable to deny their existence.

It is asked: Why do we find that a reason is sought for the selection of the Plague of Darkness, while a reason is not sought for the selection of the other plagues?

The Rebbe R. Heschel responds by citing a Talmudic injunction regarding the verdict of a court of law. The law is that if a court, in deciding a capital case, votes unanimously for conviction, the defendant is not executed (Sanhedrin 17a). The halachic decisors qualify this law by asserting that it applies only if each of the judges rendered the guilty verdict for the identical reason. It may then be assumed that there was not a conscientious search for contrary evidence. However, if the judges had different bases for their respective verdicts, the defendant is executed.

The Midrash's approach may now be clarified. Having established that all the angels agreed regarding the plaguing of Egypt with Darkness, it proceeds to ask why the plague was visited upon Egypt. If every angel concurred, the law is that Egypt should have been spared. The Midrash responds that the angels were unanimous in their opinion, but disagreed on the reasons for the carrying out of the plague. While some supported its implementation because the Egyptians deserved it, others believed the plague was necessary in order to permit the killing of the wicked Israelites, or so that the Israelites could search, unimpeded, for the Egyptians' valuables.

Because the reasons behind the votes of the angels varied, the plague could be carried out. *(Iturei Torah)*

■

The Midrash says that the angels agreed unanimously with God's plan to afflict Egypt with darkness. Why is it emphasized that there was no dissent among the angels?

There are three differences between the judicial proceedings in capital cases and those in monetary cases. Firstly, in capital cases the youngest of the judges is the first to render his opinion, and the vote proceeds in reverse age order. This is done so that the younger jurists will not be intimidated by the opinion of their seniors. In cases other than capital ones, the oldest judge announces his opinion first. Secondly, in capital cases the opening arguments must support the innocence of the defendant, while in other cases there is no such requirement. Lastly, a unanimous verdict to convict a defendant in a capital crime case results in an acquittal. This does not obtain in other cases.

When the angels heard God, the head of the Heavenly Court, announce His vote to afflict Egypt with the Plague of Darkness, they surmised that the case before them was not a capital one. Had it been a capital case, the voting procedure would have commenced with the angels, not with God. The same conclusion resulted from the fact that God's opening argument was accusatory — the Midrash says that He told the angels, "The Egyptians deserve to be smitten." Given this assumption, their arrival at a unanimous verdict did not prevent the administration of the plague, as a unanimous decision in a non-capital case does not preclude a guilty verdict. That is the reason that the angels' lack of dissent is emphasized.

*(Malbim)*

■

Normal darkness occurs due to the absence of light. It is not an entity unto itself. Darkness is prepared to accept light when the latter arrives.

The darkness in Egypt during the plague differed. It was palpable — it had substance to it. This was not merely a case of the absence of light; the darkness constituted a distinct entity. This darkness was not capable of accepting light. Not even a candle or torch could be lit. Therefore, "People could not see each other" (verse 23). *(Sforno)*

■

Why did God afflict the Egyptians with darkness? Because there were wicked Israelites who did not wish to leave Egypt; these died during the three days of Darkness (Midrash).

## Bo

Tosefeth Berachah explains the Midrash's question as follows: During the other plagues, the Egyptians were able to confirm the miraculous fact that the Israelites were unaffected. Indeed, the purpose of the plagues was to emphasize the protection by God of the Israelites. This was not the case with Darkness. The Egyptians could not see whether or not the land of Goshen was struck by the plague. They had room to assume that the Israelites, too, were being victimized by the plague, and that it was not a plague sent by God, but a natural occurrence. What, then, was the purpose of the Plague of Darkness? Why did God inflict this plague upon them? This is the Midrash's question.

■ ■ ■

וַיֵּט מֹשֶׁה אֶת־יָדוֹ עַל־הַשָּׁמָיִם וַיְהִי חֹשֶׁךְ־אֲפֵלָה בְּכָל־אֶרֶץ מִצְרַיִם שְׁלֹשֶׁת יָמִים.

*Moses lifted his hand toward the sky, and there was a thick darkness in Egypt, which lasted for three days. (10:22)*

A certain man began criticizing a particular person (in the man's absence). When R. Chaim of Sanz reprimanded the speaker, the latter responded that the subject of the evil talk was wicked — indeed, an atheist — and that it would be a meritorious deed to be involved in his burial (that he deserved to die).

R. Chaim harshly condemned the man's posture toward his fellow human being. As proof, he cited the Midrash's statement that the Plague of Darkness was inflicted upon Egypt so that God could kill the wicked Israelites. The surviving Israelites were able to bury their fallen comrades without the Egyptians noticing.

R. Chaim continued by pointing to the Midrash's view of the words "You shall hold it in safekeeping" (12:6). The Midrash cites a verse in Ezekiel (16:8) which states, "I passed over you and saw you. This time was a time of love for you." The Midrash explains that when the time for redemption came — for keeping God's promise to Abraham, Isaac, and Jacob to free the Israelites from Egypt — God realized that the Israelites did not possess commandments to merit being freed. They were "naked and bare" (Ibid., verse 7).

## The Eternal Heritage

Hence, He gave them two commandments, the Paschal Lamb and circumcision, and so they were "wallowing in your blood" (Ibid., verse 6). *Damayich*, "your blood," is in plural form, indicating two sets of blood — that of the Paschal Lamb and that of circumcision.

If — asserted R. Chaim — it is meritorious to bury wicked people, why does the Midrash say that the Jews were devoid of merit? Having buried the many wicked people who died during the Plague of Darkness, they should have had in their possession a plethora of meritorious deeds! Rather, we see that there is no merit acquired for being involved in the burial of wicked people — that it is not proper to pray for their death.

*(Iturei Torah)*

■ ■ ■

לֹא־רָאוּ אִישׁ אֶת־אָחִיו וְלֹא־קָמוּ אִישׁ מִתַּחְתָּיו שְׁלֹשֶׁת יָמִים וּלְכָל־בְּנֵי יִשְׂרָאֵל הָיָה אוֹר בְּמוֹשְׁבֹתָם.

*People could not see each other, and neither could anyone leave his place, for three days. The Israelites, however, had light in the areas where they lived.* (10:23)

The Sages say that during the Plague of Darkness the Israelites searched the homes of the Egyptians for valuables. When the Israelites later asked to borrow these valuables and the Egyptians denied having them, the Israelites were able to point them out.

Scripture says earlier, "God saw that the light was good, and God divided . . ." (Genesis 1:4). Rashi explains that God realized that evil men had no right to benefit from the special light of Creation. Therefore, God elected to store it for the use of the righteous in the future.

R. Menachem Mendel of Kotsk says that, whereas the Egyptians were blinded, they would have been unable now to see the light of Creation, and so God released it for the use of the Israelites. It was with the help of this special light that they were able to detect the Egyptians' hidden valuables. The light of Creation was able to penetrate everywhere, revealing everything to the Israelites. This is the meaning of "The Israelites, however, *had light* in the areas where they lived" — they had the light of Creation.

*(Cited by Iturei Torah)*

■

## Bo

"The Israelites, however, had light in the areas where they lived." Every Jewish soul possesses a spark of the primordial light, the light of Creation. Much of the effect of these sparks, however, depends on the Jews' environment: "where they live." The Jews may be compared with precious stones, which, when located in sand and dirt, may not be recognized as valuable, but upon being placed in gold settings are appreciated for their worth.

Because each Jew has this spark, it is prohibited to criticize a Jew for being in a lowly spiritual state.

*(R. Yisrael of Ruzhin)*

■ ■ ■

וְגַם־מִקְנֵנוּ יֵלֵךְ עִמָּנוּ לֹא תִשָּׁאֵר פַּרְסָה כִּי מִמֶּנּוּ נִקַּח לַעֲבֹד אֶת־ה' אֱלֹהֵינוּ וַאֲנַחְנוּ לֹא־נֵדַע מַה־נַּעֲבֹד אֶת־ה' עַד־בֹּאֵנוּ שָׁמָּה.

"... *Our livestock must also go along with us. Not a single hoof can be left behind, for it is from them that we must take to serve God our Lord, and we won't know what we will need to serve God until we get there.*" (10:26)

The Talmud says that, had the Torah not been given, we would have learned not to steal from the ant, not to engage in illicit sexual relations from the dove, and how to behave modestly from the cat (Eruvin 100b).

Malbim, in his work Eretz Chemdah, believes that the present verse accords with the Talmud's view. "It is from [the animals] that we must take to serve our Lord" — we must take examples from animals of how to act properly. This is because "we won't know what we will need to serve God until we get there" — we have not yet gotten "there," to Mount Sinai, and do not yet have the Torah to guide us.

Similarly, Scripture says, "If you do not know, most beautiful of women, go after the heels of the sheep" (Song of Songs 1:8) — learn from the behavior of the animals. And the Talmud says (Yoma 18a) that, on the day preceding Yom Kippur, bullocks, rams, and sheep would be brought before the High Priest to familiarize him with them, so that he would do the Yom Kippur service properly. This is yet another allusion that animals set an example for human beings regarding proper behavior. *(Cited by Iturei Torah)*

■ ■ ■

דַּבֶּר־נָא בְּאָזְנֵי הָעָם וְיִשְׁאֲלוּ אִישׁ מֵאֵת רֵעֵהוּ וְאִשָּׁה מֵאֵת רְעוּתָהּ כְּלֵי־כֶסֶף וּכְלֵי זָהָב.

". . . *Please speak to the people that each man should borrow from his friend, and each woman from her friend, silver and gold articles.*" (11:2)

What is the connection between this verse and the content of the previous verse, which says, "When he lets you leave, he will drive you out of here completely"?

In dealings between a proprietor and his worker, the law is that if either one of them changes the terms of their agreement, or backs out of it, that party is at a disadvantage. If the worker is hired for a full day and the proprietor fires him at midday, he must pay the worker an entire day's wages. Conversely, if the worker quits after half a day, the proprietor does not have to pay him at all if he cannot find a replacement for the employee.

The Sages explain the right of the Israelites to take silver and gold from the Egyptians as stemming from the services rendered by the Israelites to their hosts without recompense. The Israelites were even entitled to take their pay by deception.

There is, however, an argument which could be made in the Egyptians' behalf. It was decreed that the children of Abraham would be slaves for 400 years. God shortened this period, and the Israelites were in Egypt for only 210 years. Since they had not worked the entire period for which they were contracted — 400 years — it was the Israelites who had broken their contract with the Egyptians. Given this, the Israelites should not have been entitled to any pay whatsoever.

It is to counter this line of reasoning that Scripture says, "When he lets you leave, he will drive you out of here completely." The departure of the Israelites would, in the end, be ordered by Pharaoh. He, not they, would break the service agreement. The

## Bo

Egyptians would thus have to pay the Israelites' hire for 400 years. Therefore, the Israelites were entitled to ask for silver and gold.

*(Mishnath D'Rabbi Eliezer)*

■

*Na* denotes a request — "Please" (Berachoth 9a).

Why did the Israelites have to be exhorted to take valuables from the Egyptians? Did they despise silver and gold? Furthermore, the Talmud says that God did not want Abraham to contend that, although the promise to enslave his descendants had been kept, the assurance that they would leave with great wealth had not been kept. Why is it relevant that Abraham would have adopted an accusatory stance towards God? Is God only interested in keeping His promises so that He will not be faulted by others? Wouldn't He, at any rate, desire to keep His word?

These questions have been asked in the past, but remain unresolved. Today, however, the answer has been revealed by the debate over whether Jews should accept reparations from Germany for the property the Nazis confiscated from them. There is a difference of opinion. One camp supports the acceptance of reparations, maintaining that since the Germans exterminated six million Jews it would be even more abominable for them to keep the Jews' property. The second camp counters that the receipt of compensation for property would be looked on differently — as reparation for the people who were killed, as an agreement that the money would atone for the lives that were destroyed.

The same debate doubtless existed in Egypt. Many Israelite children had been killed by the Egyptians. Some were thrown into the Nile, while others were sealed inside the walls of buildings during construction.

A number of Israelites were unwilling to accept valuables as compensation for their children, as that would have implied that the money was a sufficient atonement. Others held that the payment was coming to the Israelites in return for the work they had performed for the Egyptians.

God did not desire to force those Israelites who abhorred the thought of reparations to take money from Egypt. This is why He phrased His wish as a request: "*Please* speak to the people." And yet, He did make the request, rather than saying nothing, because if the Israelites had not left with valuables Abraham would have had a legitimate complaint — that God had kept His promise to enslave them, but not His promise to enrich them. For this reason, it was appropriate for the Israelites to put aside their reservations and ask for valuables.   *(Oznayim LaTorah)*

■

The Israelites were being told to ask for silver and gold. However, their doing so would have constituted a fulfillment of God's wishes. A person is not necessarily so eager to heed God's command, and so Moses had to exhort the Israelites — God told him, "Please speak to the people."   *(Sefer HaDerush)*

■

The Talmud says that God urged the Israelites to get valuables from the Egyptians, so that Abraham would not say that God kept His word regarding the enslavement of the Israelites, but had reneged regarding His promise to give them wealth when He freed them (Berachoth 9a).

According to the halacha, when someone is liable for the death penalty and a simultaneous monetary penalty, he suffers only the former. The monetary obligation is subsumed under the death sentence (Gittin 52b). The question thus arises: Whereas the Egyptians were liable for death and for a monetary penalty, why were both punishments imposed on them [death with the tenth plague and at the Red Sea, money with the riches they gave the Israelites]? The answer is that the subsuming of the smaller penalty under the larger applies only if the defendant is liable for both due to his actions against one party. The Egyptians had two separate obligations. They deserved the death penalty for their treatment of the Israelites. However, the monetary assessment was owed to Abraham — who would inveigh against an attempt to send the Israelites out of Egypt without riches.

*(Iturei Torah, citing R. Naftali Horowitz)*

■

*Bo*

The house of study of R. Yannai said: *Na* denotes a request — "Please" (Berachoth 9a).

Another statement by R. Yannai's house of study (Berachoth 32a) is that Moses interceded for the Israelites when they sinned with the Golden Calf. He told God that they had made the idol because He had overwhelmed them with silver and gold. As Scripture says, "Jeshurun thus became fat (rich) and rebelled" (Deuteronomy 32:15). Riches cause one to rebel against God.

The Talmud does not explain the manner by which God provided the Israelites with silver and gold. We may explain that the reference is to the assertion by the same house of R. Yannai that God told the Israelites to "Please" ask the Egyptians for silver and gold. Moses asserted that God Himself had implored the Israelites to request valuables, and that they were not entirely to blame for the making of the Golden Calf. *(Torah Temimah)*

■ ■ ■

וַיִּתֵּן ה' אֶת־חֵן הָעָם בְּעֵינֵי מִצְרָיִם גַּם הָאִישׁ מֹשֶׁה גָּדוֹל מְאֹד בְּאֶרֶץ מִצְרַיִם בְּעֵינֵי עַבְדֵי־פַרְעֹה וּבְעֵינֵי הָעָם.

God allowed the nation to find favor in the eyes of the Egyptians. Moses was also very highly respected in Egypt — both by Pharaoh's officials and by the people. (11:3)

"Moses was also very highly respected . . . by the people." Ramban says that "the people" were the Israelites. They had at first doubted Moses' capabilities (5:21, 6:9). Now, however, they saw that he was God's faithful prophet, and he gained respect among them.

Ramban records an alternate view, that "the people" were the Egyptians. This is in accord with the simple explanation of the verse, and is also the opinion of Ibn Ezra.

■

It is rare that a ruler will be popular among the elite of a people and among the common folk as well. Generally, someone who is loved by the elite is hated by the simple people, and a ruler whom the people love is not liked by the leaders. This is because leaders and commoners place different demands upon their ruler, and expect him to possess different skills.

Moses was unique in that he gained respect in the eyes of "Pharaoh's officials" — the ranking members of Egyptian society — as well as among "the people," the common folk.

*(HaDerash VeHaIyun)*

■

"Moses was also very highly respected." This means that in Moses' honor the Egyptians gave the Israelites additional gifts.

*(Sforno)*

■ ■ ■

וַיֹּאמֶר מֹשֶׁה כֹּה אָמַר ה' כַּחֲצֹת הַלַּיְלָה אֲנִי יוֹצֵא בְּתוֹךְ מִצְרָיִם.
Moses said (to Pharaoh): This is what God says — "At midnight, I will go out into the midst of Egypt. . . ." (11:4)

*Kachatzoth,* "At midnight," may also be translated as "Around midnight." The Rabbis say that Moses did not specify the exact time for the infliction of the plague; *kachatzoth* implies that it might occur a short time before or after midnight. Moses suspected that Pharaoh's astrologers might err in calculating the time, and think the plague had struck before or after midnight. If he had said *bachatzoth,* which could only be translated as "At midnight," the astrologers might claim that Moses had lied. For this reason, he approximated the time. God, however, who knows the exact time, actually said *bachatzoth.*

R. Yonathan Eybeschuetz objects that, even lacking an accurate timekeeping method, the astrologers should have been able to calculate the arrival of midnight. The Talmud says that there are three phases during the night (*mishmaroth,* literally, "watches") (Berachoth 3a). The middle phase is marked by the barking of dogs. The Egyptians should have been able to fix the arrival of midnight at the middle of the second phase — the halfway mark of the barking of dogs. Why was Moses concerned that they would think he had lied about the onset of the plague?

## Bo

R. Yonathan answers by saying that on that particular night the dogs did not bark. As Scripture says, "among the Israelites, no dog will bark" (verse 7).

Chatham Sofer explains Moses' decision to approximate God's arrival — "Around midnight" — as deriving from the time difference between the Land of Israel and Egypt. Midnight arrives in Egypt several minutes after it arrives in Israel, and God's calculation was based on Israel-time. The Egyptians, on the other hand, would calculate based on Egypt-time, and so they would believe that Moses had lied.

Chatham Sofer proves that God calculated based on Israel-time from the Sages' statement that the night during which Abraham defeated the Four Kings was split in two. Half was accorded for Abraham's miracle, and the second half for the Exodus (Rashi on Genesis 14:15). Now, Abraham's miracle occurred in the Land of Israel, and so the calculation for the miracle in Egypt was also based on Israel's midnight.

Hence, the Plague of the Killing of the Firstborn actually occurred several minutes before midnight, Egypt-time.

∎

Rashi says earlier (2:11) that the Egyptian taskmasters forced the Israelite slaves to arise and go to work at the call of the rooster.

It may be that Rashi's source for this is the present verse. It says that God would strike the Egyptians *kachatzoth halailah*, which may also be translated: "like midnight," i.e., similar to another midnight. We find that God punished the Egyptians measure for measure with how they oppressed the Israelites. In alluding to another midnight, God may have been referring to the time at which the Israelites were wakened for work. Just as the taskmasters, who were among the elite, awakened the Israelites at midnight — the hour when the rooster first calls — so did God punish the firstborn, who were also of the elite, at midnight.

Alternatively, the allusion to another midnight may be to the defeat by Abraham of the Four Kings, which occurred at midnight. Just as Abraham had smitten the kings at that hour, so would God

## The Eternal Heritage

destroy the Egyptians at midnight. [This is based on the Midrash's understanding of Genesis 14:15. The verse says that Abraham "divided," *Vayechalek*, his forces and attacked the kings on "that night." The Midrash understands *Vayechalek* to denote that the night itself was divided, the first half being allocated for Abraham's miracle, and the second half being stored for the miracle of the Exodus.] *(Kli Yekar)*

■

Why does God say "I will go out into the midst of Egypt" and not "I will go out into the *Land of* Egypt"?

God's first act was to destroy the guardian angel of Egypt. This God did Himself, as no angel had the power to defeat Egypt's guardian. Afterward, God dispatched His messengers — the Angel of Death and his coterie — to slay the firstborn Egyptians. Thus, Scripture first says, "I will go out into the midst of Egypt." God did not go into the *land* of Egypt, but into *Egypt* — against the heavenly representative of Egypt. Scripture then says, "All the firstborn in the Land of Egypt will die" (verse 5); the Angel of Death took up the fight and went into Egypt itself.

This resolves a contradiction about who was actually the agent of destruction in Egypt. The Sages say that God Himself smote Egypt, as is written in the Haggadah: "I, not an angel." But the verse in Scripture reads: "God . . . will not permit the destroyer (meaning the Angel of Death) to enter your houses to strike" (12:23). This problem is now resolved; God Himself defeated Egypt's guardian angel, while the Angel of Death destroyed the firstborn sons.

*(Kli Yekar)*

■ ■ ■

וּלְכֹל בְּנֵי יִשְׂרָאֵל לֹא יֶחֱרַץ־כֶּלֶב לְשֹׁנוֹ לְמֵאִישׁ וְעַד־בְּהֵמָה לְמַעַן תֵּדְעוּן אֲשֶׁר יַפְלֶה ה' בֵּין מִצְרַיִם וּבֵין יִשְׂרָאֵל.

". . . But among the Israelites no dog will bark, at man or at beast. You will thus realize that God is making a miraculous distinction between Egypt and Israel. . . ." (11:7)

The Midrash, commenting on Moses' assertion that "Now it is

## Bo

known" (2:14), explains that Moses was not referring to the situation at hand — his killing of the Egyptian who had struck a Hebrew — but to the reason the Israelites had been kept in slavery. Moses was told by one of the two quarreling Israelites he confronted, "Do you intend to kill me as you killed the Egyptian?" (Ibid.) The Midrash comments that this Israelite threatened to reveal Moses' deed to Pharaoh. Upon hearing this, Moses concluded that the Israelites did not merit redemption because they engaged in slanderous talk. "Now," Moses said, the reason the Israelites have been enslaved "is known."

R. Mordechai Banet avers that the Israelites could not have been redeemed until they exorcised the evil trait of slander from among them. They accomplished this in regard to Moses' request that they borrow fine objects from the Egyptians (verse 2, 12:35). The Sages say that the Israelites knew of Moses' request for twelve months, but did not reveal it to the Egyptians prematurely. Their fortitude in keeping this secret, which, had it been revealed early, could have prompted a violent reaction from the Egyptians, demonstrated that they had rid themselves of the propensity to engage in slanderous talk.

This, says R. Mordechai, is the thrust of the current verse, which states that "among the Israelites no dog will bark." The Sages write that one who speaks slanderously deserves to be thrown to the dogs (Pesachim 118a). Whereas the Israelites had purged themselves of this characteristic, they were safe from attack by dogs.

■

What is the significance of the fact that no dog would bark at the Israelites? Given the incredible events that were to unfold on the night of the redemption, this seems rather unimportant.

It is known that, among all the animals which are kept in the house, the dog is the most loyal to its master, and the most attuned to what occurs around the house. If someone in the house dies, or even if some minor accident occurs, the dog begins to bark or howl, signaling its sorrow and its participation in the pain afflicting the household.

Scripture first describes the level of sorrow which will exist in Egypt: "There will be a great cry of anguish throughout all of Egypt. Never before has there been anything like it, and never will there again be" (verse 6). However — it continues — in the Israelites' sector "no dog will bark." There would be quiet, with not even the smallest incident to cause the most sensitive beasts, the dogs, to bark. *(R. Yeshayah Horowitz)*

■

Why does the Torah take the pains to promise that the dogs would be at peace with the Israelites — that no dog would bark at them on this night? Moreover, the implication is that the dogs *would* bark at the Egyptians. Why is this significant?

The Talmud (Bava Kamma 60b) states: If the dogs are howling, it is a sign that the Angel of Death has entered the city. If the dogs are playing, it is a sign that Elijah the Prophet has entered the city.

This night is the paradigm for Jewish redemption through the ages. Furthermore, the Exodus from Egypt was the turning point in the establishment of Israel as God's nation. And the ultimate end for which the Jewish people was founded was to serve God unstintingly, under the protection of the Messiah, whose coming will be heralded by Elijah. It is this night which set the stage for the unfolding of Jewish history and for its glorious climax with the Messiah's arrival.

Elijah is the symbol for the Israelites of the final redemption, but he is more than that. He *has a part* in every redemption, however minor, that the Jews have ever experienced or will ever experience. This is because Jewish history is not a series of unrelated incidents — a rise, followed by a fall, then again a rise. It is, rather, a continuum, and every redemption accorded the Jews is connected with the final redemption we will enjoy.

Hence, Elijah was present, at least in a symbolic sense, at the redemption of the Israelites from Egypt. As stated by the Talmud, if the dogs are not howling, but playing, it is a sign that Elijah is present. This is why "among the Israelites no dog will bark." The dogs did, however, bark among the Egyptians. This was the night of

## Bo

the Plague of the Killing of the Firstborn; as the Talmud says, if the dogs are howling, it is a sign that the Angel of Death is present.

With this in mind, we can shed new light on the practice, during the Passover Seder, to open the door to one's house so that Elijah can enter and drink from the wine poured for him (the Cup of Elijah). What is the significance of having Elijah at the Seder? One may argue that he represents the future, final redemption for which the Jews pine, and this is certainly true. There is more, however. Elijah is invited to the Seder not only because of the role he *will* play, but also due to the role he *did* play. As the heralder of any redemption, his involvement was crucial for the redemption of the Israelites from Egypt. At the Seder, he is honored for this involvement, as we pour a cup of wine for him and invite him to grace our table.

R. Yosef Dov Soloveichik of Brisk also invokes the Talmudic passage regarding the conduct of dogs and Elijah's presence in order to explain the present verse. However, his approach differs in two respects from the above. Firstly, he assumes that the dogs were absolutely quiet, while the preceding allows that they were playing. Secondly, he avers that the dogs did not howl at the Egyptians just as they did not howl at the Israelites.

R. Yosef Dov says that the dogs were in a quandary. On the one hand, Elijah was present in Egypt, which should have prompted them to be playful. And such frolicking is accompanied by happy barking. On the other hand, the Angel of Death was present too, which should have caused the dogs to howl. Unable to make a decision as to how to behave, they remained silent — "no dog will bark."

R. Yosef Dov's view is difficult to accept. Firstly, the Torah does not say that the dogs maintained silence. It says they did not bark (lit., whet their tongues). Obviously, the reference is to the sort of barking which would be frightening. It does not say that the dogs refrained from joyful barking, as that would not have been distressful. Secondly, according to R. Yosef Dov, the dogs were silent throughout Egypt — they did not disturb the Egyptians just as they did not disturb the Israelites. However, the implication of the verse is otherwise: "among the Israelites no dog will bark." The dogs would, evidently, bark at the Egytians. Hence, his view that they were silent, as a compromise, does not accord with the tone of Scripture.

■

MeOtzareinu HaYashan relates a story of two men who came to a rabbi in order to resolve a dispute. One of the men, knowing this particular rabbi was amenable to accepting bribes, whispered that he desired to delay the trial, and was prepared to bestow favors upon the rabbi if he agreed. The rabbi consented to postpone the case.

In the interim, the second man discovered that his opponent had bribed the rabbi. The second man also went to the rabbi and proposed an even larger sum of money if the latter would decide in his favor. The rabbi agreed.

When the case was finally argued, the rabbi sat silent, not knowing what to do.

The second man smiled, and told the rabbi that he had always been puzzled by the fact that the dogs did not bark at the Israelites on the night of their redemption from Egypt. Now, however, he realized that the explanation is based on the Talmud's statement that dogs bark when the Angel of Death is present and frolic when Elijah is present. Both were in Egypt on that night, and so the dogs, not knowing how to act, kept silent (in accordance with R. Yosef Dov Soloveichik's view above).

You too — said the complainant — are caught in such a dilemma, and, unable to please both sides, are maintaining your silence.

■

Another explanation may be posited for Scripture's emphasis on the fact that the dogs did not bark at the Israelites. The Talmud (Bava Kamma 83a) relates that a certain pregnant woman went to her neighbor's house in order to bake bread. The neighbor's dog barked at the woman, but her neighbor told her not to fear the animal, as it had no teeth. The woman responded, "Take your kindness and throw it on the thorns, for the embryo has already been

## Bo

moved." The Talmud utilizes this episode to demonstrate that a dog is capable of causing death by its barking.

The night of the redemption from Egypt is termed *leil shimurim*, a "night of vigil" (12:42). It is a night when Jews are given special providence so that they are safe from harm. God here assured Moses that, although the Egyptians were to die, the Israelites would remain protected. God would alter nature so that death would not come to them even by the barking of a dog.

■

Why did the Israelites need assurance that no dog would bark at them? What reason would there be to believe that the dogs would be prone to barking?

The Talmud states that there are three phases during the night. During the second phase, dogs bark (Berachoth 3a). The Plague of the Killing of the Firstborn occurred at midnight, which is during the second phase. This is why the Israelites needed assurance that the dogs would not bark at them.

*(Ketoreth Sammim)*

■

"But among the Israelites no dog will bark." The Midrash says that, because the dogs did not bark at the Jews on this night, Scripture reserved a reward for them. Regarding a *terefah*, an animal which is terminally ill — and thus unsuitable to be slaughtered and eaten — Scripture orders, "Cast it to the dogs" (22:30). This teaches that God does not withhold reward from any creature which does His will.

Now, in the case of a *nevelah*, an improperly slaughtered animal, Scripture asserts that "You may give it to the resident alien in your settlement so that he can eat it" (Deuteronomy 14:21). Such an animal may not be eaten by a Jew, but he may otherwise derive benefit from it — such as by selling it or by giving it away to a non-Jewish friend. It is Scripture's intent to teach the same with regard to a *terefah*.

Torah Temimah asks how we may assume that all manner of benefit may be enjoyed in the case of a *terefah*. In light of the

Midrash, perhaps one may feed a *terefah* to his dog, but do nothing else with it. If the reason for Scripture's instruction to feed a *terefah* to one's dog is that God rewards all creatures, is it not possible that all other uses are prohibited, with feeding it to one's dog the exception?

Torah Temimah answers that this conjecture is certainly not plausible. The rules regarding *nevelah* are stricter than those applying to *terefah*. While *nevelah* contaminates someone who carries it to a greater degree than someone who merely touches it, this is not the case with *terefah*; there is no increased level of contamination if one carries it. Despite this, the halacha is that *nevelah* is eligible for all manners of use. Certainly, then, *terefah*, which imparts a lenient degree of contamination, is eligible for all uses. But Scripture chooses to demonstrate this suitability by saying *terefah* is permitted as dog food, in order to teach that God rewards all creatures for their deeds.

■ ■ ■

וְיָרְדוּ כָל־עֲבָדֶיךָ אֵלֶּה אֵלַי וְהִשְׁתַּחֲווּ־לִי לֵאמֹר צֵא אַתָּה וְכָל־הָעָם אֲשֶׁר־בְּרַגְלֶיךָ וְאַחֲרֵי־כֵן אֵצֵא וַיֵּצֵא מֵעִם־פַּרְעֹה בָּחֳרִי־אָף.

"... All your officials here will come and bow down to me. They will say, 'Leave! You and all your followers.' That is when I will leave." He left Pharaoh in great anger. (11:8)

Why did Moses become angry in warning Pharaoh about the final plague? There seemingly was more reason for him to be incensed at other times. For example, when Pharaoh pleaded for the cessation of the Plagues of Frogs, Wild Animals, Hail, and Locusts, he promised in each case to free the Israelites. [Actually, he did not say so explicitly in the case of Locusts, but he admitted to having sinned, so this may be inferred (10:17).] After each plague subsided, Pharaoh went back on his word. Moreover, he once actually expelled Moses from his presence (10:11). Why was Moses' wrath kindled here in particular?

We may explain Moses' anger at this time in accordance with the commentators' view as to why God specifically wanted Moses, and nobody else, to redeem the Israelites. God had promised Jacob, "I will also bring you back up" (Genesis 46:4); God Himself, and not an intermediary, would be the redeemer of Israel. Had any prophet but Moses been God's agent, this would not have been the case. But contrary to the way it was with the other prophets, God spoke directly through Moses. Thus, with Moses as the redeeming prophet, it was considered as if God Himself freed the Israelites.

The commentators apply the identical idea to explain why, when Moses attempted to extract water from the rock in the desert, he hit the rock, rather than speaking to it as he had been commanded by God (Numbers 20:7-11). The Sages (Bava Metzia 86b) say that God supplied water to the Israelites through an intermediary — Moses' earlier striking of the rock, on God's command, to create a well (17:6) — because Abraham, in providing water for the angels who visited him, did not bring it himself, but had someone else fetch it (Genesis 18:4, "Let water *be brought*"). Had Moses, in the later incident, spoken to the rock, the extraction of the water would have come about by a direct act of God, since He spoke directly through Moses. Therefore, Moses had to strike the rock.

Nevertheless, he was punished — God told him he would not lead the Israelites into Canaan. Yet the punishment was not for hitting the rock, but for becoming angry and scolding the Israelites for their challenge to God, terming them "rebels" (Numbers 20:10). Once Moses became angry, God no longer spoke through him, because anger causes the Divine Presence to depart (see Pesachim 66b). With the Divine Presence gone, Moses could have obeyed God's command to speak to the rock, as the extraction of the water would not have come about directly through God. Due to Moses' anger, he became liable for not speaking to the rock.

Scripture says (Psalms 106:32, 33): "They angered at the waters of Merivah, and it went badly for Moses because of them. This was because they angered [God's] spirit and He pronounced [an oath] with his lips." These words may be similarly understood. "It went badly for Moses" due to the fact that he smote the rock. Now, there was a necessity for him to act thusly — so that the miracle of extracting the water would be accomplished through an

## The Eternal Heritage

intermediary — and one may wonder where Moses' sin lay. The answer is that the Israelites "angered his" — Moses' (rather than God's) — spirit, and so "He could have pronounced with his lips." Since God's presence had left him because of his anger, his speaking to the rock would not have changed its status as an intermediary, as God would not have been speaking directly through Moses. He should therefore have obeyed God's command to speak.

We can now comprehend why there was no anger on Moses' part regarding the other plagues. Those plagues were rendered through the agency of Moses, or by Aaron in behalf of Moses. By contrast, the final plague was the direct doing of God; as the Haggadah states, "I, not an angel." Hence, had Moses become riled during the other plagues, the Divine Presence would have departed from him, and there would have been no direct involvement at all by God. But in the case of the final plague, with God directly involved, Moses was able to become angry. While the anger would preclude the Divine Presence speaking through him, God was to be present in a different fashion — as He, not an angel, was to administer the plague. Thus, God's oath to Jacob that He would personally redeem the Hebrews would remain inviolate.

*(Lechem Abirim, by R. Elimelech Fischman)*

■ ■ ■

וַיֹּאמֶר ה' אֶל־מֹשֶׁה וְאֶל־אַהֲרֹן בְּאֶרֶץ מִצְרַיִם לֵאמֹר.
הַחֹדֶשׁ הַזֶּה לָכֶם רֹאשׁ חֳדָשִׁים רִאשׁוֹן הוּא לָכֶם לְחָדְשֵׁי הַשָּׁנָה.

*God said to Moses and Aaron in Egypt as follows:*
*"This month shall be the first month to you — the first month of the year. . . ."*
(12:1, 2)

The commentators ask why this particular commandment was addressed to both Moses and Aaron. In the name of R. Naftali Katz, the following answer, based on the Midrash, is given.

The Midrash says that the necessity to occasionally add a month to the year is implied in this command. Now, the Talmud (Sanhedrin 18b) rules that a king and a high priest cannot be part of the court of law which is ruling on the issue of intercalating the year,

## Bo

as both of these men may be biased regarding the subject. A king has a large group of soldiers, for whom he must provide daily necessities. Their salary is based on the entire year; it is not calculated by the number of months. If a king were to sit on the court which is considering whether or not to intercalate the year, he would be inclined to vote in the positive, thereby stretching a year's wages over thirteen months.

A high priest is also biased. He has to perform the Yom Kippur rituals, which include five ritual immersions, as well as the hallowing of his hands and feet in water ten times. He would prefer not to have to perform these rituals in cold water, and would thus favor the arrival of Yom Kippur at an early date, when the weather is warmer. He would be inclined to vote against intercalation, as adding a month delays the onset of Yom Kippur.

Logic dictates that it is only when a king or a high priest alone is on the court that a potential conflict of interest would exist. If they were both to serve on the court, there would be no conflict, because each of them has the opposite inclination — the king toward intercalation, the priest away from it. With both possibilities represented, it may be assumed that the correct decision will be made.

Moses, as it is known, was considered a king, while Aaron was the first high priest. God addressed this portion — which deals with the leap year — to both of them in order to indicate that a king and a high priest may serve together on a court to determine the suitability of intercalation. However, they may not do so separately.

*(Yalkut HaUrim)*

■

The Midrash says that the verse "He tells His words to Jacob, His statutes and ordinances to Israel" (Psalms 147:19) relates to the present verse. "He tells His words to Jacob" refers to the Torah, while "His statutes and ordinances to Israel" refers to the hallowing of the new moon. [*Chukim*, "statutes," are commandments for which the basis is not known. *Mishpatim*, "ordinances," are those for which the reason is known.] The statutes are the holidays, of which

## The Eternal Heritage

it is said, "It is a statute *(chok)* to Israel" (Psalms 81:5). The date upon which a holiday falls depends on when the moon of that month has been hallowed. The ordinances are the monetary laws. If someone sells a field or house to his fellow man, or lends or borrows, and desires to steal from him, the other party can show the judges his deed of ownership, which contains the date of the transaction. Using this information, which, again, depends on when the new moon falls, the judges may be able to determine who is in the right.

We see from the Midrash that not only the structure of the calendar, but the actual laws of day-to-day living, which assure the righteous conduct of worldly affairs, are dependent upon the hallowing of the new moon.

This, says one Torah scholar, is why we say, when celebrating the new moon, "David, King of Israel, is alive and established." David is a symbol for righteousness and justice; as Scripture says, "David did justice and righteousness" (Samuel II, 8:15). When acknowledging the new moon, we emphasize the connection between it and righteous behavior. *(Cited by Iturei Torah)*

■

The Midrash infers from the fact that the Jewish people calculate time based on the lunar year that the moon symbolizes them. After the moon is full, it decreases continually until it is invisible, at which time one might conclude that it is gone forever. However, it again becomes visible and begins to increase in size. Similarly, even when the Jewish people are in such a lowly state that it appears they will never recover, they rise again to their full height.

Moreover, just as in the future the moon will be as bright as the sun, and as bright as the light which shone during the seven days of Creation (see the Prayer for the Hallowing of the Moon), so will the Jewish people rise to their full glory.

Sefath Emeth, pointing out that the nations of the world calculate a solar year, says that they share characteristics with the sun. Just as the sun is powerful only during the daytime, so too do the nations have influence only when they dominate. A nation which ceases to be powerful — it enters a period of darkness — also ceases to be influential.

## Bo

The Jews are different. Although they may be mired in darkness — in a state where they wield no power — they continue to be influential, just as the moon, which is radiant at night.

One must object to Sefath Emeth's explanation. Whereas the Muslims also base their calendar on the moon, it would seem impossible to use this line of reasoning.

■

On the Sabbath before the week during which a new moon occurs, a special prayer is recited. Part of the liturgy reads: "He who performed miracles for our forefathers, and took them from slavery, should redeem us speedily." Tosefeth Berachah questions the connection of this recollection about our ancestors' redemption along with the plea for our own redemption to the blessing of the new month.

Tosefeth Berachah explains that the relationship derives from the fact that the blessing of the new month was the first commandment given the Israelites at the time of their redemption. Hence, we pray every month that just as our ancestors were redeemed upon being given this commandment, so should God seize the moment of our blessing of the new month to redeem us.

■

Once, a particular rabbi who was outstanding in Torah study went for an audience with R. Chaim of Sanz. However, word was passed around that the visiting rabbi did not exhibit fear of Heaven in a corresponding measure with his scholarship, and R. Chaim thus accorded him a cool reception.

At the same time, a wealthy, materialistic Jew, whose outward appearance indicated that he did not excel at keeping the commandments, also went to R. Chaim, and the latter received him wholeheartedly.

In consternation, the visiting rabbi asked R. Chaim how it was that the wealthy visitor had merited a more genial reception than he. Was it — asked the rabbi — because the other was a man of means?

R. Chaim replied that this was not at all the reason. He pointed out that, in the text of the Blessing of the Month, we request "a life which contains fear of Heaven and fear of sin." Further in the text, we ask for "a life in which we will possess a love for the Torah and fear of Heaven." Why is the appeal for fear of Heaven repeated? The answer, said R. Chaim — staring sternly at the rabbi — is that the trait of "love for the Torah" demands a special degree of fear of Heaven. *(MeOtzareinu HaYashan)*

■

The Torah does not identify the various months by name. Instead, they are referred to by number; Nissan, being the month of the Exodus, is the first month — as established in this verse — and the other months follow accordingly. Thus, for example, Av is the fifth month (Numbers 33:38) and Tishrei is the seventh month (Ibid., 29:1).

Years are also reckoned based on the time of redemption from Egypt, not on the time since Creation (e.g., Numbers 10:11 and 33:38).

Ramban writes that the calendar thereby serves as a reminder of our redemption from Egypt. This is similar to how the days of the week are often numbered in relation to the Sabbath (in the daily liturgy we say, "Today is the first day of the Sabbath," "Today is the second day of the Sabbath," etc.).

Ramban continues that the calculation of the month differs from the calculation of the years. The year begins in Tishrei, not in Nissan (see 23:16, 34:22). This is why Scripture says here, regarding Nissan, "This month shall be the first month *for you*." While not the first month of the year, the Israelites were to reckon it as the first month, because that was the month when they were liberated — it was *for them* the first month.

Ramban continues that the connection between the months and redemption is also seen in the names by which we call the months. The months now have Babylonian names, as a result of the Babylonian exile. Until the exile to Babylon, the months had no names, and the Jews identified them by number. However, the return from Babylon fulfilled the Biblical prophecy that "No longer

## Bo

will it be said, 'God . . . who brought the Israelites out of the Land of Egypt,' but 'God . . . who brought up the Israelites from a land to the north'" (Jeremiah 16:14, 15). The reference point for the Jews had become the new miracle — their return from exile in Babylonia. To serve as a reminder of this, the months were given the names by which the Babylonians knew them.

■ ■ ■

דַּבְּרוּ אֶל־כָּל־עֲדַת יִשְׂרָאֵל לֵאמֹר בֶּעָשֹׂר לַחֹדֶשׁ הַזֶּה וְיִקְחוּ לָהֶם אִישׁ שֶׂה לְבֵית־אָבֹת שֶׂה לַבָּיִת.

". . . Speak to the entire community of Israel, saying: On the tenth of this month, every man must take a lamb for each extended family — a lamb for each household. . . ." (12:3)

It is known that the heavenly representative — the angel — of Egypt is chief among the representatives of the seventy nations. And the heavenly bodies — the stars and constellations — are categorized according to these representatives. Thus, Aries the Lamb, which is the chief sign, is in the province of Egypt's angel. The Egyptians worshiped Aries because they held it to be their ruler and the supplier of all their needs. For this reason, the Egyptians loathed shepherds (Genesis 46:34).

Aries has dominion in the month of Nissan. Therefore, God selected it as the month for the Israelites' redemption, and He commanded them to slaughter a lamb for the Paschal sacrifice in order to humble the Egyptians' god. Also, He wanted the lamb to change from an attacker to a defender. *(Shlah)*

■

"Every man must take a lamb" — R. Yitzchak said: A man can be an agent *(shaliach)*, but a minor cannot be an agent (Pesachim 91b).

Although it is a general principle that minors may not act as agents, Tosafoth (Kiddushin 42a) explains that the Torah must specifically exclude them in this instance. Since a minor is permitted to join a group of subscribers in order to partake of the sacrifice, and indeed *must* join if he wishes to eat, one might speculate that he may also act as an agent to procure a lamb for others. To obviate such speculation, the Torah specifically excludes a minor from acting in the capacity of an agent for the Paschal sacrifice.

This, however, contradicts Tosafoth elsewhere (Nedarim 36a), where, in explanation of R. Zera's statement that "'A lamb for each household' is not a Torah law," Tosafoth says that a minor is not obligated, Scripturally, to subscribe to one of the groups formed for the purpose of eating the Paschal Lamb; he may eat without having joined a group.

In answer, we must say that R. Zera's view is a minority one, and that a minor is indeed obligated by Scripture to subscribe to a group if he wishes to eat. Hence, while Tosafoth expounded R. Zera's view, we do not decide the law according to that view. Thus, there is no contradiction in Tosafoth.

In truth, the Torah's words do seem to indicate that a minor is obligated to subscribe to a group before partaking of the sacrifice. Scripture describes the requirement to partake of the lamb as follows: "Individuals shall be assigned to a lamb according to how much each one will eat" (verse 4). It would seem that even a minor, if he has the ability to consume an olive-sized portion [the minimum requirement], can eat, but would have to join a group in order to do so.

This is also implied elsewhere in the Talmud (Succah 42b). There it states that a minor who has the ability to consume an olive-sized portion can be included among those for whom the Paschal Lamb is sacrificed, because Scripture says that "Individuals . . . according to how much each one will eat" are included (verse 4). Rashi explains that the minor may be enumerated as a subscriber because he is capable of eating. Now, it would be wrong to assume that the Talmud and Rashi are describing not the minor's ability to fulfill the commandment of eating the Paschal sacrifice, but the obligation of his father to educate him *(chinuch)*. If that were the case, it would be enough to speak of the minor eating from the sacrifice. It would not be a reason to require him to subscribe to a group, for, while only those who include themselves in a group may partake of the lamb slaughtered by that group, this rule applies only to people

## Bo

eligible for group participation — adults. Obviously, then, the requirement to subscribe extends to a minor as well as to an adult.

Further proof of a minor's obligation to enlist in a group before eating of the Paschal Lamb may be adduced from yet another Talmudic dictum. The Talmud says, in exposition of the verse "If anyone kills a human being" (Numbers 35:30), that "human being," *nefesh,* includes a minor. If one killed even a minor, he is liable for the death penalty (Sanhedrin 84b). Now, in regard to the Paschal Lamb, Scripture speaks of taking a lamb "according to the number of persons," *nefashoth* (the plural of *nefesh*). Since the word *nefashoth* is used, minors are evidently included.

*(Torah Temimah)*

■

Shulchan Aruch (Orach Chaim 430) records that the Sabbath before Passover is celebrated as *Shabbath HaGadol,* the "Great Sabbath." The reason for this is the miracle which took place in Egypt on that day, which was the tenth of Nissan. Each Israelite took a lamb for the Paschal sacrifice and tied it to the foot of his bed. The firstborn Egyptians asked why this was being done, and the Hebrews responded that it was for the Paschal sacrifice, and that God would slay the firstborn Egyptians.

The firstborn sons went to their fathers and to Pharaoh, complaining that they were about to be killed and asking that the Israelites be released. The request was refused, and the firstborn physically assaulted their elders. The result was that many Egyptians were killed.

It is asked: Although this did take place on the Sabbath, wouldn't it be more accurate to commemorate the event on the tenth of Nissan, the date of its occurrence? After all, the general procedure is to celebrate on the date that an event occurred, not on the day of the week.

Taz records the answer of R. Moshe Charif, who says that the tenth of Nissan was also the date on which the Jordan River miraculously split for the Israelites, allowing them to cross into the Land of Canaan. Had the commemoration of the miracle in Egypt been established on the tenth of Nissan, people might have mistakenly assumed that the miracle of the Jordan River was the object of celebration. Therefore, the day of the week — the Sabbath — was chosen instead for the commemoration.

Magen Avraham proposes a different answer. He points out that the tenth of Nissan coincides with yet another event: the death of Miriam, Moses' sister (Orach Chaim 580). A fast day was established on that date in her memory, thereby precluding the celebration of a holiday.

Chatham Sofer asserts that, although Taz makes no mention of the death of Miriam as a factor, he too actually considers it significant. If, as Taz says, the tenth of Nissan was eschewed as the date for celebration of the miracle of the Paschal Lamb because it was also the date on which the Jordan split, why wasn't it declared a holiday in light of the miracle at the Jordan? The answer, according to Chatham Sofer, is that Miriam died on that date. Her death preceded the Jordan miracle. The Talmud rules that if one takes upon himself to fast on a particular date, and that date is later declared a holiday by the Rabbis, the person is still to fast, even though fasting on a holiday is forbidden (Ta'anith 12a). Hence, once Miriam's death initiated a fast day, there was no place for a holiday commemorating the splitting of the Jordan River.

■ ■ ■

וְאִם־יִמְעַט הַבַּיִת מִהְיוֹת מִשֶּׂה וְלָקַח הוּא וּשְׁכֵנוֹ הַקָּרֹב אֶל־בֵּיתוֹ בְּמִכְסַת נְפָשֹׁת אִישׁ לְפִי אָכְלוֹ תָּכֹסּוּ עַל־הַשֶּׂה.

" . . . Now, if the household is too small for a lamb, then he and a neighbor can obtain [a lamb together] according to the number of persons. Individuals shall be assigned to a lamb according to how much each one will eat. . . ." (12:4)

"Now, if the household is too small for a lamb, *Ve'im yimat habayith*" — Ohr HaChayyim avers that this verse is consistent with both the views of R. Yehuda and R. Yossi, as recorded by the Midrash. R. Yehuda says that, while people are permitted to withdraw from one group assigned to a particular lamb and join

## Bo

another group, at least one subscriber of the original group must remain; the group cannot entirely disband. R. Yossi contends that no one of the original group need remain. However, all the assignees to a particular lamb may not withdraw at one time and leave the animal without any subscribers. Once designated, a lamb must remain with at least one subscriber, but this need not be an original subscriber.

It is from the words *Ve'im yimat habayith*, which may be translated as "if the number in the household decreases" — if there is a withdrawal from the group — that the right to switch groups is derived. The implication of "decrease" is that the original group may become smaller, but cannot disband completely. Thus, R. Yehuda maintains that the original group can "decrease" as long as someone remains in the group. Hence, so long as one member of the group remains with the lamb, the group stays intact.

R. Yossi would derive his ruling from the words "for a lamb." Scripture is not concerned with whether or not any original group members remain with the lamb. Its concern is only that the lamb not "decrease," that it remain one to which people have subscribed. If new subscribers have replaced the original ones, that is fine.

■ ■ ■

וְהָיָה לָכֶם לְמִשְׁמֶרֶת עַד אַרְבָּעָה עָשָׂר יוֹם לַחֹדֶשׁ הַזֶּה וְשָׁחֲטוּ אֹתוֹ כֹּל קְהַל עֲדַת־יִשְׂרָאֵל בֵּין הָעַרְבָּיִם.

"*. . . You shall hold it in safekeeping until the fourteenth day of this month. Then the entire community of Israel shall slaughter [their sacrifice] in the afternoon. . . .*" (12:6)

"You shall hold it in safekeeping" — Rashi records that R. Mathia b. Charash said: Scripture says, "I passed over you and saw you. This time was a time of love for you" — the time had arrived to honor My vow to Abraham that I would redeem his children. However, they had no commandments to fulfill which would have permitted them to merit redemption — "You were naked and bare." Therefore, God gave the Israelites two commandments: the blood of the Paschal sacrifice and the blood of circumcision — "I said to you, 'You will live through your blood,' I said to you, 'You will live through your blood'" (Ezekiel 16:6-8).

Why were the Israelites specifically given these two commandments? We are able to answer this based on the Sages' declaration that "There is no reward in this world for fulfilling a commandment" (Chullin 142a). This pertains only to positive commandments. Whereas their violation does not incur a penalty [such as flogging or death] in the present world, neither does their fulfillment earn a reward. However, negative commandments, and those few positive commandments which do incur a penalty in this world for their abrogation, carry a reward if they are fulfilled.

God wished to endow the Israelites with commandments whose fulfillment would entitle them to a reward — redemption. Therefore, He instructed them to observe the two positive commandments which, if violated, incur a penalty in this world: *kareth*, extinction, which includes one dying before his allotted life span has passed. These two commandments are the Paschal Lamb and circumcision. *(Lev Aryeh)*

∎

"You were naked and bare" — We may explain the difference between "naked," *erom,* and "bare," *eryah,* as follows: *Erom* denotes the state when one is lacking his outer clothing. Scripture says, "Just as my servant Isaiah went naked, *erom* . . ." (Isaiah 20:3). Since it is inconceivable that Isaiah actually went about without any clothing, we must conclude that he was only partially dressed — he did not have on his outer garments, but wore his undergarments. For this reason, he was termed "naked." *Eryah,* on the other hand, denotes a state of complete nudity.

To counter these two spiritual states in which the Israelites were mired, God gave them the commandments of the Paschal sacrifice and circumcision. The Paschal sacrifice is a commandment of temporary duration, having significance only once a year. It is similar to the state of *erom,* of having outer garments, which one may discard.

Circumcision finds allusion in undergarments. Just as they may

## Bo

not be removed, so too circumcision is a commandment which, when fulfilled, leaves a permanent impression.

*(Tzvi Yisrael)*

■ ■ ■

וְאָכְלוּ אֶת־הַבָּשָׂר בַּלַּיְלָה הַזֶּה צְלִי־אֵשׁ וּמַצּוֹת עַל־מְרֹרִים יֹאכְלֻהוּ.

". . . *They shall eat the meat that night: roasted over fire, with matzoh and bitter herbs.* . . ." (12:8)

A disciple of R. Menachem Mendel of Kotsk came to inform him that his life was bitter, and that he was praying that the harsh times would quickly end.

The Rebbe of Kotsk told him that he should not seek a hasty end to his suffering. The rule is that one who swallows *maror*, the bitter herbs, on Passover eve has not fulfilled the requirement to eat them (while in the case of matzoh one may swallow it). A person has to chew his *maror*; he has to eat his bitter portion carefully. One has to ponder why he has been allotted a bitter portion; he should try to discover what it means and what God is seeking from him.

*(MeOtzareinu HaYashan)*

■

"That night" — What are we taught by the word "that," *hazeh*, which denotes exclusivity? It comes to exclude another night. Whereas the Paschal Lamb has the status of a holy sacrifice of lesser degree *(kadashim kallim)*, and peace offerings also have that status, we might think that since peace sacrifices are eaten for two days and one night, the Paschal Lamb may be eaten for two nights. These would take the place of the two days allotted for peace offerings, and so the Paschal Lamb would be eaten for two nights and one day. Hence, we learn here that it is eaten only on "that night," and not on another night (Berachoth 9a).

Rashi is of the opinion that the Talmud is not proposing the right to eat of the Paschal sacrifice during the daytime, since Scripture specifically permits its consumption only at "night." Rather, the Talmud wonders if the sacrifice can be held over from the first night of Passover until the second, at which time it might again be eaten. This the Torah precludes with its interpretation of the word *hazeh*, "that" — only on that night.

Rashbam (Pesachim 120b) takes issue with Rashi, maintaining that the Talmud is indeed contemplating the permissibility of eating of the Paschal Lamb even during the daytime. As for the word "night," Rashbam says that the Talmud understood it to exclude the day upon which the lamb was sacrificed — the fourteenth of Nissan. Once, however, the sacrifice becomes permitted, on the subsequent night, it is possible to conjecture that it would be permitted on the next day, the fifteenth of Nissan.

■ ■ ■

אַל־תֹּאכְלוּ מִמֶּנּוּ נָא וּבָשֵׁל מְבֻשָּׁל בַּמָּיִם כִּי אִם־צְלִי־אֵשׁ רֹאשׁוֹ עַל־כְּרָעָיו וְעַל־קִרְבּוֹ.

*". . . Do not eat it raw or cooked in water, but rather roasted over fire, including its head, its legs, and its internal organs. . . ."* (12:9)

R. Chisda said: If one eats a Paschal sacrifice which was cooked in the hot springs of Tiberias, he is liable, for he did not eat it roasted over a fire (Pesachim 41a).

Torah Temimah points out that Mareh Kohen asks how one could conceive that the Paschal Lamb would be cooked in Tiberias, when the law mandates that the sacrifice not be taken out of Jerusalem. Neither could one transport the water of the hot springs to Jerusalem, as they would cool during the trip.

Rashi, however, explains the reference to the Tiberian springs as denoting "boiling fountains."

Now — says Torah Temimah — Rashi's gloss seems superfluous; everyone is surely aware of the famous "Hot Springs of Tiberias." Rather, Rashi intends to say that this term includes all hot springs, not just those in Tiberias. Torah Temimah notes his own astonishment at Mareh Kohen's negligence to take Rashi's view into account.

Torah Temimah advances proof for Rashi's opinion from R. Yochanan's assertion that three sources of water which had been opened to produce the Flood remained open even after the Flood ceased. One of these three was the Tiberian hot springs (Sanhedrin 108a). Now, R. Yochanan himself maintains that the Flood did not affect the Land of Israel (Zevachim 113b); how, then, did the hot springs in Tiberias have any connection with the Flood? We thus see that the term "hot springs of Tiberias" refers to hot springs in general.

■ ■ ■

וְכָכָה תֹּאכְלוּ אֹתוֹ מָתְנֵיכֶם חֲגֻרִים נַעֲלֵיכֶם בְּרַגְלֵיכֶם וּמַקֶּלְכֶם בְּיֶדְכֶם וַאֲכַלְתֶּם אֹתוֹ בְּחִפָּזוֹן פֶּסַח הוּא לַה'.

". . . You must eat it in the following fashion — with your waist belted, your shoes on your feet, and your staff in your hand. And you must eat it in haste. It is the Passover offering to God. . . ." (12:11)

When a person resolves to follow God, he must act in haste. In trying to separate himself from the materialism to which he is bound, he has to vigilantly await the moment when he is able to summon the desire to follow God, and to quickly seize that moment. This allows him to break free from his worldly desires. This idea is symbolized by the first Passover, when the Israelites [in breaking free from the materialistic quagmire of Egypt] were told to eat *bechipazon*, "in haste."

But once a person has succeeded in finding the proper path, he should proceed slowly. This is symbolized by the Passover of all other years, where the Jews are not commanded to eat in haste.

(R. Tzaddok HaKohen of Lublin)

■ ■ ■

וְהָיָה הַדָּם לָכֶם לְאֹת עַל הַבָּתִּים אֲשֶׁר אַתֶּם שָׁם וְרָאִיתִי אֶת־הַדָּם וּפָסַחְתִּי עֲלֵכֶם וְלֹא־יִהְיֶה בָכֶם נֶגֶף לְמַשְׁחִית בְּהַכֹּתִי בְּאֶרֶץ מִצְרָיִם.

". . . The blood will be a sign for you on the houses where you are located. I will see the blood and pass you by. There will not be a deadly plague among you when I strike Egypt. . . ." (12:13)

In one of his responsa, the medieval Sage Rashba relates that he was asked the following question by a certain philosopher.

Regarding the Second Temple, Scripture says: "The honor of this last temple will exceed that of the first" (Haggai 2:9). Since the Second Temple is here termed "the last *(ha'acharon)* temple," why do Jews believe there will one day be a Third Temple?

Rashba responded that *acharon* is not to be translated as "last," but as "latest." Proof of this — he asserted — may be adduced from Exodus 4:8, 9. There, God said to Moses, "If they do not believe you, and do not pay attention to the evidence of the first sign, then they will believe the evidence of the second *(ha'acharon)* sign. And if they also do not believe these two signs . . . then you shall take some water from the Nile and spill it on the ground. The water you will take from the Nile will become blood on the ground." Although the second sign (Moses' hand turning leprous) was termed *ha'acharon*, there followed another sign — the water turning into blood. Obviously *ha'acharon* cannot be translated as "the last"; it must be translated as "the second." Similarly, in the case of the temples, *ha'acharon* is not to be translated "the last," but "the latest."

R. Yeshayah Horowitz contends that Rashba's response to the philosopher's question is alluded to in the present verse. It says, "The blood will be a sign for you on the houses"; the miracle of the blood will be a sign regarding the houses — meaning the temples. Just as in the case of the water becoming blood the word *ha'acharon* does not mean "the last," so too in the case of the temples it does not mean "the last," as there will be a Third Temple.

*(MeOtzareinu HaYashan)*

■

"The blood will be a sign for you" — Why did God need a sign on the houses of the Israelites? He certainly knew where the Israelites lived!

The primary obstacle to the redemption of the Israelites was that they had imitated their hosts and become idol worshipers (Shemoth Rabbah 21). God wished to eradicate this blemish. Hence, the Israelites were commanded, in taking a lamb for the Paschal sacrifice, with the word *mishchu* — literally, "drag along" (verse 21). The implication was that they were to drag the lamb through the streets to their homes. The Egyptians, seeing their god being prepared for slaughter, would doubtless take on a threatening posture. And yet, the Israelites were enjoined to have no fear of being attacked.

Then came the actual slaughter of the lambs. The Israelites were to gather in large groups for this — as many families could share one lamb — in the public squares. The Egyptians would thus be forced to watch their gods being slaughtered by the Israelites, who again were to evince no fear at all.

The final ignominy for the Egyptians was that, when the time came to eat the sacrifice, the Israelites would publicize the ritual by painting the blood on their doorposts for all to see. When the Egyptians would pass by an Israelite house and see the blood, and know that at that moment their god was being eaten, they would certainly be moved to group together for an attack on the Israelites. Despite this, the Israelites were not to have any fear.

This conduct on the part of the Israelites would serve as proof that they had rejected idolatry, and had fully repented, returning to the worship of God. This is Scripture's intent when it says, "The blood will be a sign *for you.*" It was not a sign for God, but a sign regarding the Israelites' repentance. And seeing this sign, God would be moved to spare the Israelites — although they too were liable for death, due to the fact that they had also worshiped the lamb as a god.

In instructing the Israelites regarding all this, Moses added that they were to remain in their homes for the entire night. He asserted that the purpose of the blood was to incite the Egyptians to violence so that, by remaining fearless, the Israelites would merit God's mercy. The Hebrews might be tempted to leave their houses in order to escape an attack. And indeed — said Moses — God had not forbidden this. However, by going beyond the letter of His commandment and signaling with this self-imposed restriction that they did not fear the Egyptians, the Israelites would establish even more strongly their commitment to God.     *(Binah LaIttim)*

וְהָיָה הַיּוֹם הַזֶּה לָכֶם לְזִכָּרוֹן וְחַגֹּתֶם אֹתוֹ חַג לַה' לְדֹרֹתֵיכֶם חֻקַּת עוֹלָם תְּחָגֻּהוּ.

". . . *This day is one that you must remember. You must keep it as a festival to God for all generations. It is a statute forever that you must celebrate it. . . .*" (12:14)

If Passover is perceived as the celebration of a physical redemption, there is room for people to claim that it should not be celebrated at a time when the Jews are subjugated by the nations.

However, Passover must be seen as marking a *spiritual* redemption — the release by God of the Israelites from the spiritual impurity of Egypt, and His taking them as His treasured nation, upon whom He would manifest His Divine Presence and holiness. Viewed in this light, it becomes an eternal holiday, one worthy of celebration even when the Jews are oppressed in their exile.

Scripture's intent in the present verse may now be understood. "You must keep it as a festival to God for all generations" — If you see Passover as a "festival *to God*," a spiritual holiday, then "It is a statute forever that you must celebrate it," even during the harshest moments of the exile. *(Ma'ayanah shel Torah, based on Meshech Chochmah)*

■ ■ ■

שִׁבְעַת יָמִים מַצּוֹת תֹּאכֵלוּ אַךְ בַּיּוֹם הָרִאשׁוֹן תַּשְׁבִּיתוּ שְּׂאֹר מִבָּתֵּיכֶם כִּי כָּל־אֹכֵל חָמֵץ וְנִכְרְתָה הַנֶּפֶשׁ הַהִוא מִיִּשְׂרָאֵל מִיּוֹם הָרִאשֹׁן עַד־יוֹם הַשְּׁבִעִי.

". . . *You shall eat matzos for seven days. By the first day, you must remove all leaven from your homes, because whoever eats leaven from the first day to the seventh day will have his soul cut off from Israel. . . .*" (12:15)

"That soul" (the literal translation of *hanefesh hahi*) — when it is in its full soul (faculties) and mind, but excluding one who eats leaven because he is forced to do so (an *annus*) (Rashi).

Why must the Torah include a verse to spare one who is forced to eat leaven from the penalty of excision? Isn't it a rule throughout Jewish law that an *annus* due to force or accident is not held liable for the sin he commits? This is deduced from the case of the rape of a betrothed woman, who is not punished (Nedarim 27a).

## Bo

At the present time, the Israelites were still considered Noahides. They were not yet Jews. It is the opinion of Ritva (Makkoth 9a) that Avimelech, who wished to have relations with Sarah, thinking she was unmarried, was liable for death at the hands of Heaven ("You will die because of the woman you took, since she is already married [Genesis 20:3]). While a Jew is not liable at Heaven's hand in such a case, a Noahide — as was Avimelech — *is* liable. We see that the status of *annus* does not mitigate the sin of a Noahide. We would have applied the same rule in the case of the Israelites and leaven. Hence, Scripture teaches that the liability of a Noahide *annus* exists only when he sinned due to a lack of knowledge. [Avimelech was going to have relations with Sarah because he did not know she was married.] When a Noahide sins because of ignorance of circumstance, he is liable, since it is up to him to be aware of the facts. But someone who is an *annus* due to force is not held responsible.

*(Har Tzvi)*

■

The medieval Sages (Tosafoth and Rabbeinu Nissim, Pesachim 2a) propose two reasons why the Torah goes further in stigmatizing *chametz* than it does regarding other prohibited foods — in ordering that *chametz* be burned and forbidding its very presence on one's property. One reason is that *chametz* is permitted during most of the year. Hence, it would be simple to forget that it is forbidden on Passover. Its removal from the home minimizes the likelihood of one coming to eat it. The second reason is that the transgression of this prohibition incurs a greater penalty — excision (*kareth*) — than is incurred by the eating of other forbidden foods.

The Torah alludes to these two reasons in the present verse. It says: "By the first day, you must remove all leaven from your homes." Why? Because "whoever eats leaven," which may be translated as "all eat leaven." Everyone consumes leaven during the year, and, being accustomed to it, might err on Passover.

Scripture continues that such a person "will have his soul cut off from Israel"; in addition to the possibility of error, since the penalty

## The Eternal Heritage

for eating leaven on Passover is so severe, the laws governing it are extraordinarily stringent. *(R. Nathan Adler, as cited by Chatham Sofer)*

After citing the above in the name of his teacher, R. Nathan Adler, Chatham Sofer suggests that there is an additional pitfall in the case of *chametz*. One might object that *chametz* should be no different than the case of Yom Kippur. While one is permitted to eat food all year, one may not do so on Yom Kippur. Additionally, the penalty for violating this rule is excision, the same penalty which applies in the case of *chametz*. Why, then, didn't the Torah find it necessary to create an extra precaution on Yom Kippur, by forbidding the presence of food in the home? The answer, Chatham Sofer says, is that the prohibition to eat *chametz* continues "from the first day to the seventh day." Yom Kippur is only one day, and so there is less chance that one will transgress the rule against eating on that day. But Passover lasts for seven days, and so extra precautions are necessary.

■ ■ ■

וּבַיּוֹם הָרִאשׁוֹן מִקְרָא־קֹדֶשׁ וּבַיּוֹם הַשְּׁבִיעִי מִקְרָא־קֹדֶשׁ יִהְיֶה לָכֶם כָּל־מְלָאכָה לֹא־יֵעָשֶׂה בָהֶם אַךְ אֲשֶׁר יֵאָכֵל לְכָל־נֶפֶשׁ הוּא לְבַדּוֹ יֵעָשֶׂה לָכֶם.

"... *The first day shall be a sacred holiday, and the seventh day shall [also] be a sacred holiday to you. No work may be done on them, except for what is needed so that everyone will have food — this alone may be done by you. . . .*" (12:16)

"No work may be done on them" — This includes work done by others (Rashi).

Da'ath Zekenim MiBa'alei HaTosafoth objects that we find, regarding the Sabbath, that the prohibition to have a non-Jew do work for a Jew is Rabbinic in origin. Yet, it seems that Rashi understands the stricture here as being Scriptural. (The "others" referred to by Rashi must be non-Jews, as there is nothing novel about the fact that a Jew cannot work on Passover.)

Da'ath Zekenim answers that Rashi does not intend to say that having a non-Jew do work for a Jew on a holiday involves a

## Bo

Scriptural transgression. Rashi is merely using the verse as an *asmachta*, as Biblical support for a Rabbinic dictum.

Alternatively, says Da'ath Zekenim, Rashi's statement that Scripture precludes having one's work done by others refers not to gentiles, but to one's own children. Children are not liable to keep the commandments, and so one might think it permissible to have them do his work. Scripture instructs contrarily — "No work may be done on them," even by minors.

Now, one is already enjoined from commanding a minor to do work which is prohibited on the Sabbath. This law is derived from the words "Do not do any manner of work — you, your son, your daughter . . ." (20:10). However, one might think that such is the case only regarding the Sabbath, which is bound by stricter guidelines than are the holidays. Therefore, concludes Da'ath Zekenim, Rashi declares that the same stricture applies to the holidays.

■ ■ ■

וּלְקַחְתֶּם אֲגֻדַּת אֵזוֹב וּטְבַלְתֶּם בַּדָּם אֲשֶׁר־בַּסַּף וְהִגַּעְתֶּם אֶל־הַמַּשְׁקוֹף וְאֶל־שְׁתֵּי הַמְּזוּזֹת מִן־הַדָּם אֲשֶׁר בַּסָּף וְאַתֶּם לֹא תֵצְאוּ אִישׁ מִפֶּתַח־בֵּיתוֹ עַד־בֹּקֶר.

*". . . You shall take a bunch of hyssop and dip it in the blood [which will be placed] in a basin. You will touch the lintel and the two doorposts with some of the blood in the basin. No one of you may go out the door of his house until morning. . . ." (12:22)*

"You will touch the lintel and the two doorposts" — When God commanded Moses regarding the blood on the doors, He said, "They must take of the blood and place it on the two doorposts and on the lintel" (verse 7). Why did Moses now reverse the order, mentioning the lintel before the doorposts?

The following answer has been given: We see here that God is humble. He indicated to Moses that the Israelites had no merit except for the presence among them of Moses and Aaron, who were the "doorposts" upon which the House of Israel stood. And the lintel represents God's kindness, which rests upon the doorposts.

Moses realized that God was being humble in placing Moses and

## The Eternal Heritage

Aaron before Himself. Moses believed this was not respectful of God, that He should be mentioned first. Hence, Moses changed the order and placed "You will touch the lintel," representing God, before "and the two doorposts," representing himself and Aaron.

*(Tzeror HaMor)*

■

R. Yecheskel of Kuzhmir understands this verse as an allusion to the spiritual state of the Israelites. The hyssop is a small plant, and represents a lowly state, while the lintel represents a high spiritual level. Moses said that even if the Israelites were in a lowly spiritual state, as long as they were united — symbolized by the bunch — and prepared to sacrifice their lives for Judaism — represented by the dipping in blood — they could reach the highest spiritual levels.

■ ■ ■

וְעָבַר ה' לִנְגֹּף אֶת־מִצְרַיִם וְרָאָה אֶת־הַדָּם עַל־הַמַּשְׁקוֹף וְעַל שְׁתֵּי הַמְּזוּזֹת וּפָסַח ה' עַל־הַפֶּתַח וְלֹא יִתֵּן הַמַּשְׁחִית לָבֹא אֶל־בָּתֵּיכֶם לִנְגֹּף.

"... *God will then pass through to strike Egypt. He will see the blood on the lintel and on the two doorposts. God will then pass over that door, and will not permit the destroyer to enter your houses to strike....*" (12:23)

The Haggadah states, "I will pass through Egypt": I — God and not an angel — will smite the Egyptians. This being the case, why does Moses say that God will not allow the "destroyer to enter your houses to strike"? How does the destroyer — the Angel of Death — play a role here?

The Killing of the Firstborn did indeed occur directly through the hand of God. There were, however, other deaths that were to occur on that night — natural deaths, of which the Angel of Death was in charge. Scripture asserts here that, during the hour that the plague struck, God would not permit the Angel of Death to claim, among the Israelites, the lives which otherwise would have been taken at that time. In this way, the Egyptians would be unable to declare that the Israelites had also been struck by the plague.

*(Vilna Gaon)*

■

## Bo

Although the verse "I will pass through Egypt" shows that the Plague of the Killing of the Firstborn was carried out by God Himself, permission was granted to the Angel of Death to kill other Egyptians on Passover night. As the Rabbis say, "When the bull falls, the knife is whetted" (Shabbath 32a). [If the bull is on the ground, that is the time to slaughter it, rather than wait till it gets up, at which time it would have to be calmed again. Similarly, when people are dying, the Angel of Death can take the lives of those who were not truly meant to die at that time.] For this reason the Egyptians were crying, "We are all dying" (Rashi on verse 33). God killed only the firstborn, but the Angel of Death was slaying others as well.

This is why Scripture says that God will "not permit the destroyer to enter your houses to strike." The Angel of Death was to be present in Egypt — slaying those who were not firstborns. But due to the merit of smearing the blood on the doorposts, the Israelites would be saved from the Angel of Death, who would otherwise have been able to strike among them.

*(R. Yaakov Moshe Charlop)*

"God will pass over that door" — Heaven does not come to the aid of a person unless he first takes a step toward repentance. As the Sages say: Open for Me a doorway of repentance the width of a needle and I will open for you doors through which wagons can pass (Shir HaShirim Rabbah 5). The first step, no matter how small, must be taken by the man.

The Israelites of Egypt were so ensconced in the mire of impurity that they were unable to take the first step toward repentance — to open the doorway. Despite this, God had mercy upon them and opened a doorway for them. He ignored the fact that they did not even open a doorway the width of a needle.

This is Scripture's intent when it says, "God will pass over that door." God by-passed the usual requirement that a "door" be opened by one who needs His aid.

*(Botzina D'Nehora)*

## The Eternal Heritage

וְהָיָה כִּי־יֹאמְרוּ אֲלֵיכֶם בְּנֵיכֶם מָה הָעֲבֹדָה הַזֹּאת לָכֶם.
". . . When it comes to pass that your children will ask you, 'What is this service to you?' . . ." (12:26)

"When it comes to pass that your children will ask you" — The Midrash says, regarding these words: The Israelites received the good news here that they were destined to have children and grandchildren.

It is asked: The verse makes reference only to "your children." How does the Midrash derive that grandchildren were included?

The Torah wouldn't have commanded the Israelites to teach their children about the Exodus only upon being asked about it. This is because the halacha mandates that "a man is required to teach his son Torah." One is not supposed to wait for his son's questions before teaching him. Therefore, the Rabbis deduce that grandchildren are the subject of this verse. *(Zeith Ra'anan)*

■

According to the Haggadah, there are four prototypical sons — a wise son, a wicked son, a simple son, and a son who is incapable of making an inquiry.

Each of the four is represented in Scripture. The present verse, in asking "What is this service to you?" reflects the question asked by the wicked son. However, the reply to him occurs not in the words of the following verse — "You must say, 'It is the Passover sacrifice to God'" — but later in Scripture (13:8): "It is because of this that God acted for me when I left Egypt." The implication of the response is that God "acted for *me*," but not for the wicked son, who has rejected God. He would not have been redeemed.

Why does the author of the Haggadah eschew the simple explanation — that the response to the wicked son is located immediately after his question — in favor of the view that the response to his question is elsewhere?

Vilna Gaon avers that "It is the Passover sacrifice to God" is not an appropriate response to the wicked son. Since this individual has rejected God, one is not to enter into a discourse with him, by describing what transpired in Egypt. Instead, the wicked son is to

## Bo

be curtly informed that he would have played no part in the Exodus, and, in the words of the Haggadah, one is to "set his teeth on edge" while telling him this.

Vilna Gaon continues that we may derive from Scripture itself that "It is the Passover sacrifice to God" is not a response to the posed question. The verse in the present section begins, "You must say." It does not read, "You must say *to him.*" Evidently, "It is the Passover sacrifice to God" is not a response to the question which precedes it. Rather, these words are meant to strengthen the faith of the father, lest he be swayed by the derisive attitude of his son.

Thus, "You must say" means that you must remind yourself of the miracle God performed for the Israelites.

■

R. Meir Simcha of Dvinsk points to an inconsistency in the phrasing of the questions posed by the four sons. Elsewhere, Scripture says, "When your child later asks you, *lemor* . . ." (13:14). The word *lemor,* literally, "saying," is used in that verse, which concerns the simple son. Regarding the wise son, *lemor* is also used (Deuteronomy 6:20). (Of course, there is no verse for the fourth son, who does not know how to ask.) Yet, in the present case, that of the wicked son, *lemor* is omitted.

R. Meir Simcha resolves this dissimilarity by making note of the Midrash's understanding of *lemor.* The Midrash on Deuteronomy (3:23) asserts that *lemor* indicates a demand by the questioner for a response. Thus, the other sons all seek an answer to their question. However, the wicked son does not desire a response. His words — "What is this service to you?" — are meant not as an earnest query, but as a scornful denigration of the commandment. Therefore, *lemor* is not written here.

Furthermore, the wicked son does not actually ask. The literal reading is: "When it comes to pass that your children will *say* to you." This is not a question on his part, but a statement.

■

Iturei Torah cites a view which finds an optimistic note in the portion discussing the wicked son. The section concludes, "The

## The Eternal Heritage

people bent their heads and prostrated themselves" (verse 27). Now, since the questioner here is the wicked son, why did the people bow? Where is there room for happiness and thanksgiving in this context?

The optimism, says Iturei Torah, occurs because this son, while wicked, is nevertheless inquisitive about the ways of Judaism. There is a wicked type who is at an even lower level. One may be so wicked that he has no interest whatsoever in God's Torah and laws.

■

"What is this service to you?" — The Haggadah asserts that this question is that of the prototypical wicked son. However, instead of giving the answer proposed in the succeeding verse — "You must say, 'It is the Passover sacrifice to God'" — the Haggadah records a different answer. It quotes the words "you must tell your child, 'It is because of this that God acted for me when I left Egypt'" (13:8).

Kli Yekar notes two commonly asked questions. Firstly, why did the Haggadah eschew the answer given in the next verse? Secondly, isn't the answer given to the wicked son the same as that given the son who is incapable of asking questions? And yet, while the Haggadah derives that the wicked son would not have escaped Egypt — the answer to him being "God acted for *me*," implying that only the father, but not the son, would have been saved by God — the same deduction is not made regarding the son who cannot ask. He apparently would have participated in the redemption.

Kli Yekar posits three answers to these questions. The first answer is that "You must say, 'It is the Passover sacrifice to God'" cannot be the response to the wicked son's query. These words are not structured to be a response. Scripture does not command, "You must say *to him*," along the lines of the responses to the other sons, but rather, "You must say."

This is evidently a command in its own right, having nothing whatever to do with the question posed in the previous verse. Kli Yekar says that it serves instead as the basis for R. Gamliel's ruling that one must speak of the Paschal sacrifice during the Passover Seder. R. Gamliel says that three items must be mentioned at the

## Bo

Seder: the Paschal sacrifice, the matzoh, and the bitter herbs (*maror*). If mention of any of these is omitted, one has not fulfilled the requirement (Pesachim 116a). Kli Yekar says that the source for the obligation to mention the Paschal Lamb is in the words "You must say, 'It is the Passover sacrifice to God.'" And the verse which mandates the discussion of matzoh and *maror* is "It is because of this that God acted for me when I left Egypt," whence it is derived that "this" refers to the matzoh and *maror*, as the Haggadah itself explains.

As for the wicked son's question, Kli Yekar says it is connected with the previous verse, not the subsequent one. The previous verse states, "you must keep this service." *Ushemartem*, "you must keep," is an unusually strong term. Additionally, the wicked son is referred to in the plural — *b'naichem*, "your children" — while the other sons are identified in the singular (13:8, 14, Deuteronomy 6:20). Kli Yekar explains that "you must keep this service" deals with a time when many rebellious people will arise and challenge the integrity of the Passover service — hence the plural form. At that time — the Torah instructs — the Passover service will require *shemirah*, "keeping." Extra care will have to be taken to protect the Passover's legitimacy.

The verse regarding the wicked son is a clarification of the previous verse. When will the Paschal sacrifice require keeping? When "your children will ask you" — at a time that a multitude will scoff at the Passover service.

Thus, we still lack an answer to the wicked son's question. Kli Yekar proceeds to explain that the author of the Haggadah deduced that "God acted for me" is the appropriate response. And while this is the same response given to the son who cannot ask, that very fact is the reason the Haggadist chose it. How — wondered the Haggadist — can we give this answer to the silent son, without making the deduction as well that God acted for "me, but not for him" as regards this son? The deduction is not made because we know that the son's reticence is due to ineptness. But is it not conceivable that he doesn't ask because he is so evil that he has no interest whatsoever in the ritual?

The answer, according to the Haggadah, is that we indeed have

## The Eternal Heritage

doubts about this son's position, and this is why "God acted for me" is the ideal phrase with which to address him. The derivation that God would have acted "for me, but not for him" is not one which *must necessarily* be made. This derivation is dependent upon the character of the son to whom it is being addressed. If the son who is speechless actually is wicked, then the deduction is to be made. If, however, he does not speak because he is incapable of posing questions, then we are to assume that he would have participated in the service in Egypt and would have been redeemed. "God acted for me" includes the speaker and all others who would have heeded God's directive. However, whereas this verse could also serve as a rejoinder to the wicked son, the Haggadist selected it as the answer to the query posed by that son.

This, continues Kli Yekar, is why, in its answer to the son who doesn't speak, Scripture chose the word *vehigadta*, "you must tell," instead of *ve'amarta*, "you must say," which it uses regarding the other sons (13:14, Deuteronomy 6:21). *Vehigadta* can indicate either a harsh tone or a mild tone (Rashi on 19:13, and Chaggigah 14a), and it is used here to allow for both the positive and the negative nuances.

Kli Yekar's second proposal is that "It is the Passover sacrifice to God" is indeed the response to the wicked son's question. Why, then, did the Haggadist record a different response — "God acted for me"? Kli Yekar explains that the latter verse's inference — that the evil son would not have been saved — is rooted in the implication of the former verse. The wicked son jeers: "What is this service to you?" He implies that there is no spiritual substance to the Paschal ceremony. Rather, its entire purpose is to be a "service *to you*"; it is meant so you can enjoy a meal. The father answers, "It is the Passover sacrifice *to God*" — it is meant for God's benefit, not for ours. Proof of this follows in the next verse — that "He passed over the houses of the Israelites in Egypt when He smote Egypt, thereby sparing our houses." How can one say that there is no substance to this service when all who engaged in it were saved during the Tenth Plague, while the Egyptians, who did not perform the service, were killed?

Now, the wicked son readily admits that he would not have participated in the Paschal service. Therefore, he would not have been redeemed with the other Israelites. It is from "It is the Passover sacrifice to God" that we are able to infer that the wicked son would have died in Egypt. We glean from "It is the Passover sacrifice to God" that we are to make the deduction of "God acted for me, but not for him." And so — says Kli Yekar — it is the former verse which answers the wicked son. We tell him, "It is the Passover sacrifice to God." But, in the Haggadah's words, the father is to "set [his son's] teeth on edge." That is accomplished with the disclosure that the wicked son would have perished in Egypt, and this information is inferred from "God acted for me." Therefore, the Haggadah records these words. The wicked son will be set on edge, dismayed, when he understands that God would not have acted in his behalf.

To summarize, according to Kli Yekar's first answer, "God acted for me" is the response given the wicked son. According to his second answer, "It is the Passover sacrifice to God" is the actual response.

Kli Yekar's third explanation reconciles the two possible responses to the wicked son. He says that the Haggadist had *both* answers in mind as retorts to the wicked son. The son is first to be told, "It is the Passover sacrifice to God." Only if that fails is he to be reprimanded with "God acted for me." The Haggadist derives that the latter verse serves as an answer to the wicked son as well as to the son who is unable to ask from the word *vehigadta*, "you must tell." Scripture had two alternative words it might have used — *ve'amarta* and *vedibarta*. The former indicates a mild tone, while the latter lends a harsh tone (see Rashi on 32:7). *Vehigadta*, by contrast, can indicate either a harsh or a mild tone (as explained earlier). By utilizing *vehigadta*, Scripture intimates that both sons are the objects of discussion. As stated earlier, one would infer that the wicked son would not have been saved, while the same inference would not be made concerning the inept son. And "you must tell" does not follow the evil son's question because the first answer to be given him is the one in the next verse: "You shall say, 'It is the Passover sacrifice to God.'" The word *va'amartem* dictates a soft

## The Eternal Heritage

tone, and it is with such a tone that the wicked son should first be approached. Only if this fails is a strict tone to be taken.

Why, then, does the Haggadist omit any reference to "It is the Passover sacrifice to God"? Kli Yekar answers that there may be an allusion to this verse in the statement "You shall also *(af)* set his teeth on edge." The word *af*, also, seems unnecessary. Kli Yekar explains, therefore, that the Haggadist says: Along with the obvious answer — the one recorded by Scripture immediately following the wicked son's question — you shall "also" give him a second answer, if the first is ineffectual.

■ ■ ■

וַאֲמַרְתֶּם זֶבַח־פֶּסַח הוּא לַה' אֲשֶׁר פָּסַח עַל־בָּתֵּי בְנֵי־יִשְׂרָאֵל בְּמִצְרַיִם בְּנָגְפּוֹ אֶת־מִצְרַיִם וְאֶת־בָּתֵּינוּ הִצִּיל וַיִּקֹּד הָעָם וַיִּשְׁתַּחֲווּ.

". . . You must say, 'It is the Passover sacrifice to God, for He passed over the houses of the Israelites in Egypt when he smote Egypt, thereby sparing our homes.'" The people bowed and prostrated themselves. (12:27)

"The people bowed and prostrated themselves" in gratitude for the news (in verse 26) that they were to have children — "your children will ask you" (Rashi).

One may ask: Why would the Israelites have thought until now that they would not have children?

B'nai Yissaschar answers this question based on the fact that the children mentioned in the present section refer to wicked sons, as explained in the Haggadah. Still, Scripture says of them, "*Vehaya*, When it comes to pass" (verse 26). *Vehaya* is taken by the Rabbis as a word which connotes happiness (see VaYikra Rabbah 11). And we find the Talmud saying (Bava Bathra 133b) that a father should not direct an inheritance away from his son, even from an evil son to a good son. This, says B'nai Yissaschar, is because the evil son may have worthy children. Thus, even when one has a wicked son, there is reason to rejoice. This was the news here.

B'nai Yissaschar adds that, while the Haggadah says that the wicked son would not have been redeemed, we find that in fact

*Bo*

wicked people *were* redeemed. The reason was that they were destined to have righteous descendants.

*(Cited by Iturei Torah)*

■ ■ ■

וַיֵּלְכוּ וַיַּעֲשׂוּ בְּנֵי יִשְׂרָאֵל כַּאֲשֶׁר צִוָּה ה' אֶת־מֹשֶׁה וְאַהֲרֹן כֵּן עָשׂוּ.
*The Israelites went and did as God had instructed Moses and Aaron. They did it exactly.* (12:28)

"The Israelites went and did" — The Torah makes note not only of the fact that the Israelites *did* as they were commanded, but also of the fact that they *went* to do God's bidding. Rashi says that they earned credit for the act of going itself, separate from the credit earned for the actual doing of the mitzvah.

Going to do a mitzvah is also considered a mitzvah. For this reason, the evil inclination tries to convince a person not to go. Therefore, those who do go receive a reward. As the Sages say, "He who goes but does not do receives credit for going" (Avoth 5:14).

*(Imrei Shammai)*

■

"The Israelites went and did as God had instructed Moses and Aaron" — This is meant as praise of the Israelites, for they did not neglect any part of the service, as commanded by Moses and Aaron (Rashi).

Why are the Israelites praised for this? Is it conceivable that they would violate the first commandment given them?

When God commanded Moses and Aaron, He first revealed the various details of the service — that the lamb was to be taken on the tenth of the month and slaughtered on the afternoon of the fourteenth, that the blood was to be smeared on the lintel and doorposts (verse 7), and that the lamb was to be eaten in a certain manner. Only much later did God say that the blood on the houses would serve as a sign for the Israelites (verse 13). The implication of this was that the Israelites were to perform the service in a purely altruistic fashion — entirely for the purpose of fulfilling God's

## The Eternal Heritage

wishes. The service was not to be done with the goal of achieving redemption. However, the performance of the service would result in redemption — "The blood will be a sign for you on the houses."

Moses, however, relayed the information in a different fashion. After instructing that the blood was to be smeared on the doorposts, he immediately added, "Not a single one of you may go out the door of his house until morning," and that God would see the blood and spare them (verse 22, 23). The implication was that the Israelites should put the blood on their doors *for the purpose* of having a defense against the imminent plague.

Rashi tells us here that the Israelites concluded that God's intent was that they were not to have an ulterior motive when performing the service. They acted "as God had instructed Moses," not as Moses had told them himself.

Rashi is saying that the Israelites neglected nothing of "the commandment of Moses and Aaron" — of what the two had been commanded *by God.*

*(Maor VaShemesh)*

■

"They did it exactly" — These words are extra, and come to add that Moses and Aaron also did as God had instructed (Rashi).

What does the Torah intend to emphasize here? Would anyone think that the Israelites in general performed the Paschal service but Moses and Aaron did not?

R. Menachem Mendel of Kotsk responds that the Israelites fulfilled this precept with such precision and in such a perfect manner that "Moses and Aaron also did so" — even Moses and Aaron were unable to fulfill the commandment in a better fashion.

*(Gedulath HaTzaddikim)*

■ ■ ■

וַיְהִי בַּחֲצִי הַלַּיְלָה וַה' הִכָּה כָל־בְּכוֹר בְּאֶרֶץ מִצְרַיִם מִבְּכֹר פַּרְעֹה הַיֹּשֵׁב עַל־כִּסְאוֹ עַד בְּכוֹר הַשְּׁבִי אֲשֶׁר בְּבֵית הַבּוֹר וְכֹל בְּכוֹר בְּהֵמָה.

*It was midnight, and God killed every firstborn son in Egypt — from the firstborn son of Pharaoh, sitting on his throne, to the firstborn of the prisoners in the dungeon, and every firstborn animal.* (12:29)

According to the Midrash, we glean from the present verse that on this night the sun shone as if it were noon. How is this derived?

On the verse "God named the light 'day,' and the darkness He named 'night'"(Genesis 1:5), the Midrash points out that it does not say, "and the darkness God named night." God's name is explicitly associated with the light, which symbolizes good, but not with the darkness, because God does not attach His name to evil. He associates His name only with good.

With this Midrash in mind, one may wonder why God's name is mentioned in the present verse — "It was midnight, and God killed every firstborn son in Egypt" — given that it was nighttime. In answer, the Midrash says that we may conclude from the mention of God's name that the sun shone as if it were noon, although it was actually midnight. *(Rebbe R. Heschel)*

■

Among the nations of old, the firstborn were considered sacred, so much so that at crucial moments they were brought as sacrifices in order to acquire atonement for their people and to ward off predicted catastrophes. Thus we find that when the king of Moab fought against the Jews he sacrificed his firstborn son — "He brought him as a burnt offering on top of the wall" (Kings II, 3:27). And this was the Prophet Micah's thinking when he said, "Shall I give up a firstborn son for my sin?" (Micah 6:7). He asked, sardonically, if it were possible to achieve atonement by sacrificing a firstborn son.

In Egypt, the firstborn sons were so revered that they were treated as idols. People bowed down to them and ministered to them. It was against this background that God punished Egypt by killing its firstborn sons. As the Sages say, "When God exacts retribution from a nation, He first exacts retribution from its gods" (see Rashi on 11:5). *(MeOtzareinu HaYashan)*

■ ■ ■

## The Eternal Heritage

וּבְנֵי־יִשְׂרָאֵל עָשׂוּ כִּדְבַר מֹשֶׁה וַיִּשְׁאֲלוּ מִמִּצְרַיִם כְּלֵי־כֶסֶף וּכְלֵי זָהָב וּשְׂמָלֹת.

*The Israelites did as Moses had asked; they requested silver and gold articles, and clothing, from the Egyptians. (12:35)*

"As Moses had asked" — regarding his asking the people to let each man "borrow from his friend" (11:2) (Rashi). What is Rashi coming to add? Isn't it clear from the verse what the Israelites did: "They requested silver and gold articles, and clothing, from the Egyptians"?

Vilna Gaon says that Moses had really made a different request of the Israelites: he had told them that every man should "borrow from his *friend*." The word *re'ehu*, "his friend," denotes a Jew. Moses had asked the Israelites to become involved in *gemilath chessed*, the doing of kind acts for one another. It is for this reason that God, in directing Moses regarding this, said, "Please speak to the people." If the instruction to have each man borrow from his friend referred to the Israelites borrowing from the Egyptians, the word *na*, "Please," would have been unnecessary. The urgency expressed by *na* was that the Israelites needed to be kind to one another. In the merit of doing this, "God allowed the nation to find favor in the eyes of the Egyptians" (11:3).

This is Rashi's point here. Because the Israelites had done "as Moses had asked," in letting each man "borrow from his friend," they earned the right to request "silver and gold articles, and clothing, from the Egyptians." *(MeOtzareinu HaYashan)*

■ ■ ■

וּמוֹשַׁב בְּנֵי יִשְׂרָאֵל אֲשֶׁר יָשְׁבוּ בְּמִצְרָיִם שְׁלֹשִׁים שָׁנָה וְאַרְבַּע מֵאוֹת שָׁנָה.

*The time the Israelites spent in Egypt was 430 years. (12:40)*

Rashi says that there were 400 years from Isaac's birth until the Exodus, and that the 430 years are numbered beginning with the Pact Between the Halves made by God with Abraham (Genesis 15:13). This means that the pact was concluded thirty years before Abraham had Isaac.

*Bo*

This, however, presents a grave difficulty. The Torah states that Abraham was seventy-five years old when he left Charan for Canaan (Ibid., 12:4). This is recorded in the beginning of the portion Lech Lecha. The Pact Between the Halves was made toward the end of Lech Lecha. Abraham was 100 years old when Isaac was born (Ibid., 21:5). It would turn out that Abraham was seventy-five at the beginning of Lech Lecha and seventy toward the end.

Now, Da'ath Zekenim MiBa'alei HaTosafoth (Ibid., 12:4) asserts that Lech Lecha is out of chronological order, and that Abraham came twice from Charan to Canaan. The second half of the portion — the war with the Five Kings and the Pact Between the Halves — took place on Abraham's first trip, while the first half — his descent to Egypt and the parting of ways between him and Lot — occurred on his second trip.

However, Rashi says that, upon his separation from Lot, Abraham promised to be available if Lot needed his assistance (Ibid., 13:9). Rashi continues that Lot later did need help, when he was captured by the Five Kings. Hence, the war followed the descent to Egypt and the separation of Abraham and Lot. And Rashi also says that the Pact Between the Halves followed the war (Ibid., 15:1). Therefore, Rashi believes that the entire Lech Lecha *is* in chronological order, and that Abraham did not come to Canaan from Charan twice. Hence, the question remains: How could Abraham have been five years younger when he made the pact than he was when he first came to Canaan?

It should be noted that according to Ibn Ezra the 430 years are enumerated from the time Abraham first arrived in Canaan, not from the Pact Between the Halves.

■ ■ ■

לֵיל שִׁמֻּרִים הוּא לַה' לְהוֹצִיאָם מֵאֶרֶץ מִצְרָיִם הוּא־הַלַּיְלָה הַזֶּה לַה' שִׁמֻּרִים לְכָל־בְּנֵי יִשְׂרָאֵל לְדֹרֹתָם.

*It was a night of vigil for God, so that He might take them out of Egypt. This night is to God a vigil for the Israelites for all generations. (12:42)*

Ohr HaChayyim says that this verse alludes to five miracles which took place in history on the fifteenth night of Nissan.

## The Eternal Heritage

On this night, Abraham defeated the four kings who had captured Lot, as it says, "He divided [his forces] against them and [attacked them] that night" (Genesis 14:15). The Israelites left Egypt on this night: "It was midnight" (verse 29). In King Hezekiah's day, the Angel Gabriel defeated the army of Sennacherib, as it says, "That night, God's angel went out . . ." (Kings II 19:35). In Mordecai and Esther's time, King Achashveirosh became aware of the fact that Mordecai had turned in the conspirators Bigthan and Teresh, as it says "On that night, the king's sleep was elusive" (Esther 6:1). That event marked the beginning of Haman's downfall. The fifth and final miracle is the future redemption, which will occur on the fifteenth of Nissan.

The allusion to Abraham's miracle is found in the words "It was a night of vigil for God." The Rabbis say that some people had not believed that God miraculously saved Abraham from the furnace into which Nimrod had thrown him. However, upon observing how Abraham miraculously defeated Cedarlaomer and the three other kings, they became convinced regarding God's existence and power. Thus, "It was a night of vigil *for God*," a night which confirmed God's supremacy.

The Exodus from Egypt is reflected in the words "so that He might take them out of Egypt." The defeat of Sennacherib by Gabriel is hinted at by the words *hu halailah*, "This night." The implication is that this is a particular night, one referred to elsewhere; hence the definite identification — "*This* night," rather than "It is a night." The reference is to the battle with Sennacherib, about which Scripture says, "*That* night, God's angel went out . . ." Achashveirosh's experience finds allusion in the words *hazeh laShem*, literally, "this is to God." (Ohr HaChayyim does not make clear how this refers to Achashveirosh.)

The final redemption, concludes Ohr HaChayyim, is alluded to by the words "a vigil for the Israelites for all generations" — at the end of all the generations, at the time of the Messiah's coming.

It is interesting to note that the five allusions are in the same order in the verse as the events they represent are ordered historically.

■ ■ ■

## Bo

וַיֹּאמֶר ה' אֶל־מֹשֶׁה וְאַהֲרֹן זֹאת חֻקַּת הַפָּסַח כָּל־בֶּן־נֵכָר לֹא־יֹאכַל בּוֹ.
God said to Moses and Aaron, "This is the law of the Paschal sacrifice. No outsider may eat of it. . . ." (12:43)

"No outsider may eat of it" — The Targum says that this refers to an Israelite who has become an apostate. Why are these words taken to refer to an apostate?

There are two other possible explanations for the "outsider" of the verse: a non-Jew who is fed by a Jew, and a non-Jew who takes for himself. R. Meir Simcha of Dvinsk asserts that neither is a suitable subject for the verse. Were the Torah referring to a gentile who is fed of the lamb by a Jew, it would have to say, "*Do not feed* any outsider." And as for a non-Jew having his own Passover sacrifice, the commandments were not given to gentiles, making it unnecessary to exclude them from participation in this particular one. Thus, the only remaining possibility is a Jew who has become an apostate.

■

Before reciting *Kol Nidre* on Yom Kippur, we express the thought that the sinners of Israel are included among the Jewish community. Similarly, the Sages declare that sinners are to be included in the prayer gatherings which were convened on fast days (Kerithuth 6b). Yet regarding the Paschal sacrifice apostates are excluded from the community. Why is this the case?

When an apostate or sinner indicates his desire to participate with us in prayer and fasting, we take this as a sign that he is serious about becoming more attached to Judaism. We do not distance ourselves from such a man. However, if the sinner does not participate in fasting, leaving the crying to others, and seeks only to join in a festive meal, he is not earnest. For such a man we have no need.

*(Pardes Yosef)*

■ ■ ■

בְּבַיִת אֶחָד יֵאָכֵל לֹא־תוֹצִיא מִן־הַבַּיִת מִן־הַבָּשָׂר חוּצָה וְעֶצֶם לֹא תִשְׁבְּרוּ־בוֹ.
". . . It must be eaten in one house. Do not take any of the meat outside the

*house. Do not break any of its bones. . . ."* (12:46)

The part of the verse which speaks about not taking the meat out of the house is addressed to the individual *(lo thotzi).* However, the part which forbids the breaking of any bones is written in the plural *(lo thishberu).*

An explanation for this lack of symmetry is proposed in the name of R. Zalman of Vilna. He points to Rambam's halachic ruling that *ein motzi achar motzi* — once a person has taken a piece of Passover meat out of its locale, transgressing the stricture "Do not take any of the meat outside the house," if he removes it a second time he has not violated the law twice. By contrast, *yesh shover achar shover.* If someone breaks a bone of the Paschal sacrifice, violating the precept "Do not break any of its bones," and then makes a second break in that bone, he does transgress the rule twice.

Thus, a multitude of transgressions may occur in the breaking of a bone, but only one can occur in removing meat from its assigned place. This, says R. Zalman, is why the instruction regarding the location of the meat is in the singular, while the one concerning the breaking of bones is in the plural. *(MeOtzareinu HaYashan)*

■ ■ ■

וַיְהִי בְּעֶצֶם הַיּוֹם הַזֶּה הוֹצִיא ה' אֶת־בְּנֵי יִשְׂרָאֵל מֵאֶרֶץ מִצְרַיִם עַל־צִבְאֹתָם.

*On that very day, God took the Israelites out of Egypt by their hosts.* (12:51)

Kli Yekar points out that this same thought is expressed earlier (verse 41), but he notes significant differences between the two verses. The earlier verse states that "all of God's hosts *left* Egypt." The word "left" indicates that the Israelites went out of their own volition — they were not taken out. The present verse seems to indicate the contrary, that "God *took* the Israelites out of Egypt." Secondly, the earlier verse says that "all of God's hosts left Egypt." The Israelites are not mentioned by name. The present verse mentions *b'nai Yisrael,* "the Israelites." Additionally, the present verse declares that the Israelites went out "by their hosts." It would

## Bo

appear there were two distinct groups — the Israelites, and their "hosts."

In resolution of these differences, Kli Yekar avers that the "hosts" were the Mixed Multitude who left Egypt with the Israelites (verse 38) and converted to Judaism. God has a special affinity for proselytes, because although they are not actually *b'nai Yisrael*, literally, "children of Israel (Jacob)," they are still among the "hosts of God." And they do have the status of Jews. Hence, the earlier verse, which says that "all of God's hosts left Egypt," refers to the Mixed Multitude. These people *"left* Egypt." God had not come to bring them out; they elected on their own to join up with the Israelites. The present verse discusses the Israelites themselves, whom "God *took* . . . out of Egypt"; God came to Egypt to redeem them. And they departed "by their hosts" — *along* with the Mixed Multitude.

■ ■ ■

וַיֹּאמֶר מֹשֶׁה אֶל־הָעָם זָכוֹר אֶת־הַיּוֹם הַזֶּה אֲשֶׁר יְצָאתֶם מִמִּצְרַיִם מִבֵּית עֲבָדִים כִּי בְּחֹזֶק יָד הוֹצִיא ה' אֶתְכֶם מִזֶּה וְלֹא יֵאָכֵל חָמֵץ.
Moses said to the people, "Remember this day, when you left Egypt, the house of slavery — when God brought you out of here with a mighty hand. No leaven may be eaten. . . ." (13:3)

Rashi says: The words "Remember this day" teach us that it is obligatory to recall the Exodus every day.

R. Yosef Dov Soloveitchik of Boston points out that Rambam deduces the requirement to recall the Exodus every day from a different verse. Rambam writes (Hilchoth Kriyath Shma 1:3): It is a commandment to recall the Exodus from Egypt every day, as it says, "in order that you will remember the day you left Egypt all the days of your life" (Deuteronomy 16:3).

As for the present verse, Rambam says that it applies to the special law regarding the retelling of the Exodus on Passover night. Rambam writes (Hilchoth Chametz U'Matzoh 7:1): It is a positive Torah command to relate the miracles and wonders which were

## The Eternal Heritage

done for our forefathers in Egypt on the fifteenth night of Nissan, for it says, "Remember this day, when you left Egypt."

R. Soloveitchik continues that the Mishnah (Berachoth 12b) clearly supports Rambam's view. It says: We recall the Exodus at night. R. Eleazar b. Azariah said, "I am about seventy years old, but I did not merit that the Exodus should be mentioned at night, until Ben Zoma gleaned it from the fact that it says, 'in order that you will remember the day you left Egypt all the days of your life.' 'The days of your life' refers to daytime, and so '*all* the days of your life' refers to the nights."

The subject of R. Eleazar b. Azariah's pronouncement is the daily requirement to mention the Exodus, not the special one which occurs on Passover night, and yet he uses the verse in Deuteronomy as his source. Why, then, does Rashi comment that the present verse refers to the year-round commandment, when it is obviously the verse in Deuteronomy which does so?

R. Soloveitchik answers that without a doubt the present verse is the actual source of the year-round commandment, as Rashi notes here. The present verse speaks in an injunctive tone: "Remember this day"; it gives a command. The objective of the verse in Deuteronomy is not to give a commandment regarding the recollection of the Exodus. Rather, its purpose is to teach the prohibition of eating leaven and the concomitant requirement to eat matzoh on Passover: "Do not eat any leaven with [the Paschal Lamb]. You will eat matzoh — bread of affliction — with it for seven days." The Exodus is mentioned only to point out the reason for the laws of leaven and matzoh: "Do not eat any leaven . . . You will eat matzoh . . . because you left Egypt in a hurry, [which was] in order that you will remember the day you left Egypt all the days of your life." Thus, the purpose of the present verse is to mandate recollection of the Exodus, while that of the verse in Deuteronomy is to mandate the withdrawal from leaven and the eating of matzoh.

However, continues R. Soloveitchik, the present verse is not specific about the times when the Exodus must be mentioned. This information is found in Deuteronomy, where it says the words "all the days of your life." In order to make the regulations of the

## Bo

commandment clear, the Mishnah and Rambam record the latter verse instead of the present verse.

R. Soloveitchik notes in closing that the Midrash Mechilta, which was Rashi's source for his comment, utilizes these two verses in tandem. After quoting the present verse, it asks how we are to know that the Exodus must be recalled twice a day — at night as well as in the daytime — and answers that this teaching comes from the verse in Deuteronomy.

■ ■ ■

הַיּוֹם אַתֶּם יֹצְאִים בְּחֹדֶשׁ הָאָבִיב.
"... *You are leaving this day, in the month of Aviv.* ..." (13:4)

"In the month of Aviv" — Rashi asks: Would we not have known in which month they left Egypt? Why did the Torah have to inform us that it was in the month of Aviv? Rashi answers that Moses told the Israelites that they should appreciate the kindness God accorded them by staging the Exodus in the spring, when the weather is ideal.

Levush HaOhrah wonders what Rashi's question was in the first place. Rashi says that we would have known which was the month of the Exodus even if it were not recorded by the Torah. This, however, would be true only as long as an accurate oral transmission of that information existed. If the tradition were lost or corrupted, we who live in later generations would not know the month of the Exodus. Whereas we see today that we have lost many oral transmissions, what was Rashi's objection? Furthermore, although Scripture says, "This month shall be the first month to you" (12:2), and the Exodus took place in the first month, we would not have known which month was the first if the Torah had not told us it is the month of Aviv.

In answer, Levush HaOhrah amends the content of Rashi's comment to read, "Did *they* not know in which month they left Egypt?" Moses told the Israelites, "You are leaving this day, in the month of Aviv." Rashi's objection is not that there is no purpose in informing future generations, but that *the Israelites* themselves certainly were aware which month it was, and should not have needed to be told. And if the intent was to inform future generations, the month's name should not have been mentioned here, but at the end of the next verse, which says, "You will perform this service in this month." Obviously, later generations would need to know which is the month being discussed. But Scripture would not need to insert an additional verse here. Moreover, if the sole purpose of the verse is to inform us when the Exodus took place, then the words "You are leaving this day" are superfluous. To this Rashi answers that Moses was not merely telling the Israelites that they were leaving Egypt in the month of Aviv; rather, he wished to emphasize the good climate of Aviv. However, whereas he said this, later generations are also made aware via this verse that the Israelites departed Egypt in Aviv.

■ ■ ■

וְהִגַּדְתָּ לְבִנְךָ בַּיּוֹם הַהוּא לֵאמֹר בַּעֲבוּר זֶה עָשָׂה ה' לִי בְּצֵאתִי מִמִּצְרָיִם.
". . . On that day, you must tell your child, 'It is because of this that God acted for me when I left Egypt.'. . ." (13:8)

There are two distinct commandments which involve the retelling of the Exodus. Firstly, one is required to mention the Exodus every morning and night; this is accomplished with the recitation of the third paragraph of the *Shma*. Secondly, there is a requirement to discuss the Exodus on the night of the fifteenth of Nissan, which is derived from the present verse.

R. Yosef Dov Soloveitchik of Boston says that his grandfather, R. Chaim Soloveichik, makes four distinctions between these two commandments. The first distinction is the one already mentioned: that the second mitzvah is unique to the fifteenth night of Nissan. The second difference is that the first mitzvah mandates just a mention of the Exodus, while the second mitzvah includes a retelling of the miracles God performed for the Israelites. The third difference is that one can fulfill the daily requirement by mentioning the Exodus to himself, while the annual command is fulfilled by one telling over the Exodus to his children or to others via a question-and-answer process. If necessary, one asks the

*Bo*

questions to himself and provides the answers. The requirement to tell over the Exodus is derived from the words of the present verse: "On that day, you must tell your child, 'It is because of this that God acted for me when I left Egypt.'" The fourth difference is that the daily mitzvah is not actually a commandment in itself; it is part of the requirement to read the *Shma*. The annual mitzvah is a separate one, and is enumerated among the 613 commandments.

R. Soloveitchik adds a fifth difference between the two commandments. The telling of the Exodus on the fifteenth of Nissan includes not only mention of the wonders performed by God, but also praise and thanks for the fact that God freed His people. As the Haggadah says, "Therefore, we are required to offer thanks and praise." This is the basis of the requirement to recite Hallel at the Seder.

However, in the printing of R. Chaim's commentary on the Talmud, a somewhat different list of differences is recorded in his name. The first and third differences are the same. But regarding the second difference, the commentary does not limit itself to saying that on Passover night one must speak of the miracles wrought for the Israelites. It adds that, to fulfill the annual mitzvah, one must begin with the unsavory past of the Jewish people and end with the praiseworthy news of their acceptance as God's people and the miracles performed for them.

R. Chaim says that an additional part of the Passover mitzvah is to discuss the reasons for the laws that pertain to Passover night. This refers to R. Gamliel's dictum that, to fulfill one's obligation, one must speak of the Paschal Lamb, the matzoh, and the bitter herbs (Pesachim 116a).

■ ■ ■

וְכָל־פֶּטֶר חֲמֹר תִּפְדֶּה בְשֶׂה וְאִם־לֹא תִפְדֶּה וַעֲרַפְתּוֹ וְכֹל בְּכוֹר אָדָם בְּבָנֶיךָ תִּפְדֶּה.

"... *Every firstling donkey must be redeemed with a sheep. If you do not redeem it, you must decapitate it. You must also redeem every firstborn among your sons....*" (13:13)

"If you do not redeem it, you must decapitate it." This teaches that the mitzvah to redeem is preferred over the mitzvah to break the neck (Bechoroth 13a).

The Torah prefers that one redeem his donkey, by giving a sheep to a priest. If, however, he desires to retain the sheep, he has a second option: to break the donkey's neck, thereby exempting him from giving a sheep to the priest.

Rambam records these as separate positive commandments. Whereas the Talmud says that the commandment to redeem is preferred over the commandment to break the neck, there are apparently two commandments. Ra'avad, Rambam's primary disputant, argues that there is only one commandment — to redeem the donkey by giving a sheep to the priest. The option to destroy the donkey is not a mitzvah, but is, in fact, a transgression, which results from the owner's refusal to part with his sheep, leading to the priest's being deprived of property gain.

As for the Talmud's description of the second option as a mitzvah, Ra'avad contends that this was not meant literally. However, since the first option was termed a mitzvah, it followed to term the second option in the same manner.

Torah Temimah defends Rambam's view, noting that a similar situation is found in the case of *yibbum* — where a husband has died and left no descendants. The husband's brother is commanded to marry his sister-in-law in order to maintain his brother's lineage. If the living brother declines to do so, he must perform a ceremony called *chalitzah*, which serves to separate him from his sister-in-law, so that she may marry someone else. Now, the refusal to perform *yibbum* results in the loss of a husband to the widow, as, by law, she is entitled to be married to her dead husband's brother. This loss is certainly greater than the priest's loss of property in the case of redemption. And yet, *chalitzah* — the second option in this case — is enumerated as a separate mitzvah from *yibbum*. By Ra'avad's logic, only *yibbum* should be counted among the commandments.

■

A donkey lacks both of the signs that qualify an animal as kosher. It does not chew its cud and it does not have split hooves. A donkey's

## Bo

non-kosher status is thus more glaring than that of a camel or a pig, each of which possesses one of the two symbols of kashruth. And yet, it is only the donkey which is to be sanctified to God and redeemed.

This is because there are times when it is easier to take someone who is openly impure and draw him to holiness than it is to do the same for one whose impurity is concealed — who has a symbol of purity which masks his true nature. *(Yalkut Margalioth)*

■ ■ ■

וְהָיָה כִּי־יִשְׁאָלְךָ בִנְךָ מָחָר לֵאמֹר מַה־זֹּאת וְאָמַרְתָּ אֵלָיו בְּחֹזֶק יָד הוֹצִיאָנוּ ה' מִמִּצְרַיִם מִבֵּית עֲבָדִים.

*". . . When your child later asks you, 'What is this?' you will tell him, 'God brought us out of Egypt, the place of slavery, with a show of power. . . .'"* (13:14)

Chatham Sofer expounds this verse based on a statement by Tosafoth (Pesachim 116b). Tosafoth discusses the blessing made on the second cup of wine on Passover night, wherein we say, "We said before Him a new song." Tosafoth declares that the words "new song" should be written and said in the feminine form — *shirah chadashah,* not the masculine *shir chadash.* This is because the Exodus had a feminine aspect to it. Just as a woman suffers from birth pains, so was there suffering after the Egyptian exile: the three subsequent exiles of the Jewish people (the Babylonian, Persian, and Roman exiles). When the final redemption arrives, it will contain a male aspect. There will be no pain afterwards, and so the masculine form, *shir chadash,* will be used.

Chatham Sofer continues by citing the view that the Israelites were supposed to have stayed in Egypt longer; they were redeemed early. It is for this reason, say the Sages, that the other exiles were decreed upon them — to make up for the early release from Egypt. The early redemption is indicated by the word *bechozek,* "with a show," in the present verse. The word literally means "with strength," which can infer an early act.

The present verse contains the question of the simple son in the Haggadah. He asks: "What is this?" using the feminine form of "this," *zoth*, instead of the masculine *zeh*. His question therefore is: Why does Passover have a feminine aspect? And one is to reply that God took the Israelites from Egypt with strength — prior to their intended date of departure. This led to the other exiles, which gave the Exodus the character of a woman, who has birth pains.

∎

The Haggadah states that "What is this?" is the question posed by the simple son. Kli Yekar wonders how the Haggadist knew that the simple son is the questioner here, and why he would ask about the redemption of the firstborn and not about the Passover rituals.

Kli Yekar answers that the simple son is not one to scoff at God's commandments. Therefore, as long as the Passover ritual involves the consumption of food — the lamb, matzoh, and bitter herbs — he is not moved to question the ceremony.

However, the redemption of the firstborn accrues no benefit to him. Conversely, he is instructed to give money to the priest as a redemption. Even a simpleton is wise when it comes to holding on to his money, and will not relinquish funds without a good reason. This is why he asks his question at this point.

As further proof that it is the simple son who is speaking, Kli Yekar points out that the question is posed "later," literally, "tomorrow." This son is not wicked, and fulfills the commandment upon hearing it. In fact, he delays his question one day — until "tomorrow" — lest one suspect that he is challenging the commandment; were he doing so, he would ask immediately.

∎ ∎ ∎

וְהָיָה לְאוֹת עַל־יָדְכָה וּלְטוֹטָפֹת בֵּין עֵינֶיךָ כִּי בְּחֹזֶק יָד הוֹצִיאָנוּ ה' מִמִּצְרָיִם.

". . . [These words] shall be a sign on your arm and frontlets between your eyes, because God brought us out of Egypt with a show of power." (13:16)

Our Sages instruct that *tefillin*, phylacteries, are to be worn on the left hand. This is gleaned from the spelling of the word *yadchah*, "your arm," to which an extra letter, *heh*, is added at the end. Generally no *heh* is added, since the pronunciation of the word is the same with or without it. The addition of the *heh* permits the treatment of *yadchah* as the contraction of *yad*, hand, and *kehah*, weak. The weaker hand, the left one, is to be used for the donning of *tefillin*.

Why is the right hand, which usually takes precedence in ritual, shunned in the case of *tefillin*? The Sages answer that the *tefillin* should be placed against the heart, which is on the left side.

Kli Yekar explains that the intellectual and physical aspects of a man are in opposition. When one gains ground, the other must of necessity falter. If one's physical side is oppressed, then his intellectual aspect becomes stronger. This is why God brought the Israelites into Egypt — to allow their intellect to improve as they underwent physical oppression.

Kli Yekar cites as evidence the difference between young and old people. Young people possess strength, but their intellect is relatively weak. As people age, their strength decreases, while their intellect improves.

So it is — says Kli Yekar — with a man's hands. The left — weaker — hand is positioned nearer to the heart than is the right hand. The heart is the habitat of wisdom, while hands are the repositories of strength. It is the wisdom in the heart which causes the weakness of the left hand. By contrast, the right hand is on the side of the body which contains the liver, which is the abode of desire, and so there is nothing to undermine that hand's strength.

Kli Yekar continues that, in instructing one to wear *tefillin* on his weak arm, so that "It shall be a sign," Scripture is actually ordering that the sign be placed on the heart, as the heart causes the weakness of the left arm. The purpose of *tefillin* is to be a remembrance of God for a person at the place where his intelligence lies. Similarly, the phylacteries for the head are placed "between your eyes." The eyes and heart are the body's two seekers of sin (see Numbers 15:39), and so they need to be reminded of God's existence and power.

■

*Totafoth*, "frontlets," is a contraction of *tot*, which in Coptic is two, and *poth*, which in African is two, as there are four compartments in the phylacteries worn on the head (Sanhedrin 4b).

Why does the Torah use foreign languages in this instance?

The phylacteries are meant to serve as a reminder — "a reminder between your eyes" (verse 9). The mitzvah of *tefillin* was the first commandment given to the Israelites after the exile in Egypt. God indicated here that although the exile had been harsh, and despite the fact that "there is no Torah like the Torah of the Land of Israel" (Bereshith Rabbah 16), it is nevertheless important to remember the Torah one has studied outside of Israel. This is because Jewish history is a continuum. The use of foreign languages serves to emphasize the importance of remembering the Torah studied in exile. *(Cited by Iturei Torah)*

■

Why does Scripture discuss the commandment of phylacteries immediately before stating, in the next verse, "When Pharaoh let the people leave"?

R. Yonathan Eybeschuetz points to the Midrash, which says that Pharaoh said *vei*. This is an expression of hopelessness, and is derived from the word *Vayehi*, "When," whose first two letters, taken alone, read *vei*. Pharaoh had given up hope of keeping the Israelites enslaved. The Talmud rules that if a slave owner gives up hope of recapturing his runaway slave the slave becomes liable to don phylacteries, as a freed slave is considered a full-fledged Jew. Thus, since Pharaoh had said *vei*, the Israelites were commanded regarding phylacteries. *(MeOtzareinu HaYashan)*

Kthav Sofer says that it was Moses who said *vei*, because "God did not lead [the nation] by way of the land of the Philistines" (verse 17). Had the Israelites been brought through the desert via inhabited areas, they would have had water, and would not have needed access to the well which was created miraculously for them. Moses would not have sinned regarding that well (Numbers 20:12), and would have entered the Land of Israel. Therefore, Moses was distressed and said *vei*.

# 4
# Beshalach

וַיְהִי בְּשַׁלַּח פַּרְעֹה אֶת־הָעָם וְלֹא־נָחָם אֱלֹהִים דֶּרֶךְ אֶרֶץ פְּלִשְׁתִּים כִּי קָרוֹב הוּא כִּי אָמַר אֱלֹהִים פֶּן־יִנָּחֵם הָעָם בִּרְאֹתָם מִלְחָמָה וְשָׁבוּ מִצְרָיְמָה.

When Pharaoh let the people leave, God did not lead them by way of the land of the Philistines, although it was the shorter route. This was because God said that the people might reconsider [leaving] if they had to do battle, and would return to Egypt. (13:17)

"When *(Vayehi)* Pharaoh let the people leave" — The term *vayehi* always indicates distress (Megillah 10b). The distress here was that Pharaoh released "the nation," the *am*. The term *am* always refers to wicked people (Rashi on Numbers 11:1). Examples are: "What shall I do for this people *(la'am)*?" (17:4) and "This evil nation *(ha'am)*" (Jeremiah 13:10).

Pharaoh sent the Mixed Multitude along with the Israelites, and they are the *am* referred to here. Due to their evil inclination and poor character, the Mixed Multitude influenced the Israelites toward evil, and caused them trouble on several occasions.

*(Agra D'Kallah)*

■

*Beshalach*, "let leave," literally means "when [he] sent." *Shiluach*, "sending," always denotes escorting, as Scripture says (Genesis

18:16), "Abraham went with them to send them *(leshalcham)* on their way" (Midrash). This would mean that Pharaoh escorted the Israelites out of Egypt.

The purpose of escorting someone is, according to Maharal, to establish a tie, a connection, with that person. This means that, even at this late stage, Pharaoh still believed he could draw the Israelites into his sphere. He tried to establish a connection with them by escorting them from Egypt, hoping to inject them with the corruptness of Egypt.

*(R. Avraham of Sochachev)*

"When Pharaoh let the people leave" — Pharaoh expelled the Israelites; they did not leave due to their own desire (as it also says, "They had been *driven out* of Egypt" [12:39]). Therefore, "God did not lead them by way of the land of the Philistines," because "the people might reconsider." God did not have faith in them; He suspected they did not truly wish to leave.

*(Mussar HaYahaduth)*

The Exodus from Egypt is the source of all the exiles. Therefore, the manner in which the Israelites left Egypt had symbolism for the future diasporas. God did not lead the Israelites through the Philistine country "*because* it was the shorter route" (*ki*, "although," may also be translated as "because"). He wanted to teach the Israelites how to travel difficult distances, so that they would have experience when it came to negotiating their wanderings in the winding roads of their exiles.

*(Iturei Torah, citing Sefath Emeth)*

"God said that the people might reconsider [leaving]." The last impression of something is the one which leaves its mark on a person. If it is good, he forgets the bad that preceded it.

The final hours in Egypt left a good impression on the Israelites. Pharaoh took his leave of them with pleasant words — "Bless me too" (12:32) — and the Egyptians gave the Israelites gold and silver.

*Beshalach*

It was due to these good last few moments that God feared the Israelites might desire to return to Egypt.

*(Sha'ar Bath Rabbim)*

■

The bad traits of the Philistines were levity and scoffery. R. Simcha Bunem of Pshischa has already derived this from the words of the Philistines themselves: "Call in Samson and let him make sport for us" (Judges 16:25). It also says, in the Midrash, that the words "in the company of scoffers" (Psalms 1:1) refer to Avimelech, king of the Philistines (Bereshith Rabbah 61). This is why Isaac was sent into exile in the land of the Philistines (Genesis 26:1). Isaac's great attribute was his fear of Heaven, as Scripture says, "the God of Abraham and the dread of Isaac" (Ibid., 31:42). When someone is exiled, he is placed in confrontation with characteristics that are in opposition to his own, and levity and scoffery are in opposition to fear of Heaven.

Egypt's flaw was its inclination toward illicit sexual liaisons. About Egypt we read, "Do not follow the ways of Egypt" (Leviticus 18:3), after which appears a list of forbidden sexual relationships. It also says regarding Egypt, "The spraying [of semen] of horses is their spray" (Ezekiel 23:20) — the Egyptians are compared with animals as regards sexual matters.

The Mishnah declares, "Levity and lightheadedness lead a person to licentiousness" (Avoth 3:13). The defects of the Egyptians and the Philistines — levity and sexual immorality — are therefore connected. The Torah says, "God did not lead them by way of the land of the Philistines because it was close" (the literal reading). The bad trait of the Philistines was connected — closely related — to that of the Egyptians, as levity leads to licentiousness. God feared that since the Israelites had been influenced by Egypt they might "reconsider if they had to do battle." This refers to a spiritual war; faced with the Philistine expressions of levity and scoffery, the Israelites might be unable to win a spiritual battle against moral corruptness — their moral behavior could degenerate.

*(Shem MiShmuel)*

■

"It was the shorter route," lit., "it was close by." Da'ath Zekenim MiBa'alei HaTosafoth proposes several explanations for these words. Firstly, he says they mean that the people of Israel were "close" to, relatives of, God, in accordance with the verse "To the children of Israel, the nation that is related to Him" (Psalms 148:14). The Jewish people, as God's nation, are not guided in the same manner as the rest of the world; God sets a different course for them.

Alternatively, he says that the Philistines were related to the Egyptians. Mitzrayim, Ham's second son and the progenitor of Egypt, was also the ancestor of the Philistines (Genesis 10:14). God was concerned that the Philistines might "reconsider," might take umbrage at, the fact that the Israelites were fleeing from the Philistines' cousins the Egyptians. The Philistines would "do battle" against the Israelites and "return" the Israelites to Egypt.

In this context, the entire verse takes on a different meaning than a simple reading would indicate. The Philistines, not the Israelites, might "reconsider," and the Israelites would not decide to return to Egypt, but would be brought back against their will.

Da'ath Zekenim posits yet another interpretation: that "it was close" refers to the time frame surrounding the Exodus. Abraham had been promised that the Israelites would return to Canaan four generations hence (Ibid., 15:16). That time had not yet arrived, and until then the Canaanites were to rule the land. As there were not yet Israelites of a fourth generation, the period of Canaanite rule in the Land of Canaan was still too "close by" for them to be expelled.

Rashi explains that the land of the Philistines was "close" to Egypt physically. God feared that, if the Israelites were confronted with the choice of fighting a war or retreating, they would go back to Egypt. It would appear that Da'ath Zekenim avoids this explanation, although it is simpler than those he gives, because *karov hu*, "it was the shorter route," is written in masculine gender. *Eretz*, "land," is a feminine word, and so *karov hu* cannot modify *eretz*. In each of Da'ath Zekenim's explanations, *karov hu* modifies a masculine noun: in the first case, *ha'am*, "the people"; in the second case, *Pelishtim*, Philistines; and in the third case, *z'man*, time (although this is an implied subject, as Da'ath Zekenim does not

## Beshalach

actually use the word in his commentary).

■ ■ ■

וַיַּסֵּב אֱלֹהִים אֶת־הָעָם דֶּרֶךְ הַמִּדְבָּר יַם־סוּף וַחֲמֻשִׁים עָלוּ בְנֵי־יִשְׂרָאֵל מֵאֶרֶץ מִצְרָיִם.

*God made the people take a roundabout route — by way of the desert to the Red Sea. The Israelites were armed when they left Egypt (13:18).*

*Chamushim* means "armed" (Rashi).

Why did the Israelites bring arms into the desert? Don't we find that, when they were confronted by the Egyptians at the Red Sea, "The Israelites cried out to God" (14:10)? They did not resort to weaponry!

On Jacob's words "which I took from the Amorites with my sword and my bow" (Genesis 48:22), Onkelos translates, "with my prayers and requests." Prayers and requests constitute the "arms" of the Jewish people; these were the arms they brought out of Egypt.

*(Seer of Lublin)*

■

*Chamushim*, lit., "one-fifth." Twenty percent of the Israelites left Egypt, while the other eighty percent died during the three days of the Plague of Darkness (Rashi).

We are taught here how careful one must be to avoid sin. Although only one-fifth of the Israelites — the righteous ones — left Egypt, God took them on a circuitous route, suspecting that even these select ones would wish to return to Egypt.

*(Sha'arei Simcha)*

■

Chatham Sofer points to the Midrash, which makes two calculations as to the percentage of Israelites who left Egypt. One opinion has one-fifth of the Israelites participating in the Exodus, while another has only one-fiftieth participating. Additionally, there is the simple meaning of the verse: that *chamushim* means "armed."

In order to resolve the differences among the various interpretations, Chatham Sofer notes that, in the present verse and in the previous verse, the Israelites are termed the *am*, "people,"

## The Eternal Heritage

several times. Only once are they identified as the "Israelites" — when it says that the "Israelites were armed when they left Egypt." Chatham Sofer explains that the term "Israelites" — literally, "children of Israel" — was applied to the righteous ones. These were eager to fight God's wars, and left Egypt with arms. And they *desired* to depart Egypt; they were not among those who had to be expelled (12:39). But the simple folk, the *am*, "people," left Egypt unwillingly; had the Egyptians not banished them, they would have remained. These people did not arm themselves, as they were prepared to return to Egypt rather than become involved in a conflict.

With this in mind, Chatham Sofer clarifies the meaning of these two verses. "When Pharaoh let the *people* leave" — the simple "people," who would have stayed were they not expelled — "God made the people take a roundabout route" — God feared they would return to Egypt at the first hint of war, and so did not lead them on a direct route. However, the "*Israelites* were armed when they left Egypt" — the righteous people were prepared to fight, and would have been able to take the direct route.

Chatham Sofer avers that the one-fifth figure in the Midrash refers to the actual percentage of Israelites who left Egypt, the remaining four-fifths having perished during the Plague of Darkness. Of the one-fifth who left, one-fiftieth were righteous, and took arms with them; this accounts for the one-fiftieth figue mentioned in the Midrash.

■

The Talmud (Sanhedrin 111a) states that only two out of every six hundred thousand Israelites left Egypt, while the others died during the Plague of Darkness. Since 600,000 males came out of Egypt, this would mean that there were 180 billion male Israelites in that country.

There is no doubt that this figure is not to be taken literally, and so it is reasonable to say that the one-fifth and one-fiftieth figures are also not meant literally. This fact becomes even more obvious when considering that those who did not leave are said to have perished during the Plague of Darkness, as God wanted to conceal their death from the Egyptians. Even if one were to use the figure of one-fifth, the smallest of these numbers, that would mean that four-fifths of the Israelites — about two-and-a-half million men alone — died during the Plague of Darkness. How would it have been possible to conceal the death of so many people? There is no doubt that, when the plague ended, the Egyptians would have realized that the population of Israelites had diminished alarmingly. Furthermore, it would mean that the Plague of Darkness was more a plague upon the Israelites than it was upon the Egyptians, a thought which is simply untenable.

It must be, therefore, that the Israelites did not suffer losses of the magnitude indicated by these figures. Rather, the Sages have some other point in mind when they say that four-fifths or more of the Israelites died before the Exodus. They teach this lesson by use of these extraordinary calculations. While it is hard to say what that lesson is, there is a likely candidate. We are taught that the Israelites had become so spiritually bereft that they were mired in forty-nine levels of impurity, out of a possible fifty levels. Perhaps, by saying that few Israelites survived to participate in the Exodus, the Sages are hinting at the low spiritual level of the Israelites — that they did not truly deserve to be redeemed.

With this thought, the figure of one-fiftieth takes on new significance. It serves as an allusion that the Israelites had descended to forty-nine out of a possible fifty levels of impurity, with only one-fiftieth of their spiritual existence remaining untainted.

■

*Chamushim* means "armed" (Rashi). If the Israelites were armed and prepared for war, why, when they were faced with a potential battle at the Red Sea, didn't God order them to fight? He could have helped them win, and they would have defeated Egypt by natural means. Why did God resort to a miracle — the splitting of the sea and the drowning of the Egyptians therein — to save the Israelites?

The answer is that it would not have been proper for the Israelites to fight the people who had been their hosts. As it says, "Do not despise the Egyptian, since you were a sojourner in his land" (Deuteronomy 23:8). The Sages derive from here (Bava Kamma 92b): "Do not throw a stone into a well from which you have drunk water." Since the Israelites could not fight the Egyptians, God resorted to a miracle. *(Chatham Sofer)*

∎

Although the Israelites took a detour through the wilderness in order to avoid war, they nevertheless were armed. Why did they need the arms if they were steering clear of possible conflict?

Ohr HaChayyim says that it was the combination of both factors — the avoidance of war and the armed status — that guaranteed the Israelites would not be tempted to turn back toward Egypt. Had they not had arms, they would have felt imperiled and would have gone back.

∎ ∎ ∎

וַיִּקַּח מֹשֶׁה אֶת־עַצְמוֹת יוֹסֵף עִמּוֹ כִּי הַשְׁבֵּעַ הִשְׁבִּיעַ אֶת־בְּנֵי יִשְׂרָאֵל לֵאמֹר פָּקֹד יִפְקֹד אֱלֹהִים אֶתְכֶם וְהַעֲלִיתֶם אֶת־עַצְמֹתַי מִזֶּה אִתְּכֶם.

*Moses took Joseph's remains with him, because Joseph had bound the Israelites by an oath, as follows: "God will surely remember you, and you must then bring my remains out of here with you." (13:19)*

The Midrash (Shemoth Rabbah 33) says: A name is better than wealth; Moses' name was better than Korach's wealth.

Chatham Sofer quotes the Zohar's statement that, when Joseph collected all the money of Egypt and Canaan (Genesis 47:14), he also collected all the holy sparks which were to be found there — the Godly energy that gives life and is present in all things. And when the Israelites departed Egypt, they took these sparks along with Egypt's wealth. Hence, one who assembled more money also assembled more holy sparks.

This, says Chatham Sofer, was Korach's complaint to Moses when he asserted that Moses and Aaron had allotted too much power to themselves. Korach said, "All the people in the community are holy" (Numbers 16:3). They had all collected of Egypt's booty; indeed, they had collected more than Moses. Korach himself had taken

## Beshalach

more spoils than anyone, as implied by the Talmud (Pesachim 119a). He therefore had possession of more sparks than anyone.

However, Chatham Sofer points out, it is said that one who buries a *tzaddik*, a righteous person, draws to himself an abundance of holiness. Since Moses was involved in burying Joseph, and Joseph had been the cause of the Israelites' coming into possession of the holy sparks, Moses also obtained the sparks.

Chatham Sofer continues that the Sages explain the words "David acquired a name" (Samuel II, 8:13) by saying that he acquired a good reputation because he buried the dead. We thus see that being involved in burial duties earns oneself a "name." This is the Midrash's intent when it says that Moses' name was better than Korach's wealth. By being involved in Joseph's burial, Moses acquired greater holiness than Korach had in taking of Egypt's booty. This is also the Midrash's thinking in ascribing the verse "One who is smart at heart takes commandments" (Proverbs 10:8) to Moses' burial of Joseph. Moses discerned the importance of this particular deed.

Korach did not believe that burial imparts any holiness. He thus held that "All the people in the community are holy" — by obtaining the sparks through taking the booty, they were holier than Moses.

Chatham Sofer concludes that Korach was punished in corresponding measure to his crime. He did not merit burial, but was swallowed by the earth (Numbers 16:32). There he will stay until he arises in the future, as R. Yitzchak Luria gleans from the words "The righteous one will sprout like the palm tree" (Psalms 92:13), the last letters of which spell out Korach — *tzaddiK katamaR yifraCH*.

■

What is the connection between this verse, which speaks of Joseph's remains, and the previous one, which states that the Israelites were armed when they left Egypt?

Kli Yekar cites the Midrash, which says that two cabinets were taken through the desert: the ark, which held the Two Tablets with the Ten Commandments written upon them, and Joseph's coffin.

## The Eternal Heritage

The nations asked: Why is the coffin of a dead man placed near an ark containing the words of the Eternal One? The Israelites responded that Joseph kept the Ten Commandments that were written on the Two Tablets.

Kli Yekar continues that the Israelites' "arms" was the Holy Ark, which accompanied them when they did battle (see Numbers 14:44, Samuel I, 4:3). Still, that was only after the Ten Commandments were given. How were the Israelites armed when they left Egypt?

The answer, says Kli Yekar, is that "Moses took Joseph's bones with him." Joseph's coffin was the "arms," the defense, of the Israelites; since Joseph kept the Ten Commandments, it was as if they were inscribed on his coffin. That is the connection between the verses.

■ ■ ■

דַּבֵּר אֶל־בְּנֵי יִשְׂרָאֵל וְיָשֻׁבוּ וְיַחֲנוּ לִפְנֵי פִּי הַחִירֹת בֵּין מִגְדֹּל וּבֵין הַיָּם לִפְנֵי בַּעַל צְפֹן נִכְחוֹ תַחֲנוּ עַל־הַיָּם.

"Speak to the Israelites and tell them to turn back and camp before Pi Hachiroth, between Migdol and the sea — before Ba'al Tzefon, opposite it, near the sea you shall encamp. . . ." (14:2)

Ba'al Tzefon was left standing, although the other Egyptian idols were destroyed during the Tenth Plague, so that the Egyptians would mistakenly think that God could not destroy it (Rashi).

Why was Ba'al Tzefon, of all the idols, left standing?

The Egyptians worshiped many gods, because they believed each god had dominion in a particular field. Ba'al Tzefon [which translates to Lord of the North] was the god which had influence regarding wealth. As Scripture says, "Gold (wealth) will come from the north" (Job 37:22).

God left this idol standing to cause the Egyptians to err and think that Ba'al Tzefon was demanding justice for the fact that the Israelites had taken their wealth (12:35, 36). Pharaoh had accepted the other indignities suffered by Egypt, thinking that the country and its gods deserved punishment. But he held that the Israelites had done wrong in taking the Egyptians' wealth. And the fact that Ba'al

## Beshalach

Tzefon had not been destroyed was proof to Pharaoh of the correctness of his view.

This is why, in explaining the words "Pharaoh and his officials had a change of heart regarding the people" (verse 5), Rashi says they wished to take back their money. And while the Torah states that Pharaoh regretted the loss of the Israelites as slaves (Ibid.), and does not mention the loss of money, his primary concern was actually the loss of wealth. However, since a slave's acquisitions become his owner's property, Pharaoh expressed his chagrin in terms of the Israelites' status as slaves.

*(Kli Yekar)*

■ ■ ■

וְחִזַּקְתִּי אֶת־לֵב־פַּרְעֹה וְרָדַף אַחֲרֵיהֶם וְאִכָּבְדָה בְּפַרְעֹה וּבְכָל־חֵילוֹ וְיָדְעוּ מִצְרַיִם כִּי־אֲנִי ה' וַיַּעֲשׂוּ־כֵן.

"... I will harden Pharaoh's heart and he will come after them. I will be glorified through Pharaoh and his entire army, and Egypt will know that I am God." [The Israelites] did [as they had been instructed]. (14:4)

Ramban says that when the firstborn Egyptians were killed Pharaoh became so frightened that he was prepared to let the Israelites leave permanently. He did not hold Moses to the latter's declaration that the Israelites were leaving only temporarily, and, in fact, he even asked Moses to obtain a blessing for him (12:32). Pharaoh had no intention of chasing the Israelites of his own volition; therefore, God had to impel him to do so.

The same scenario occurs later, when God tells Moses that He will harden the Egyptians' hearts so that they will follow the Israelites into the parted Red Sea (14:17). Certainly — says Ramban — the Egyptians, having witnessed the miracle whereby the sea split, would not have been so foolish as to continue the pursuit. It was now obvious to them that God was intent on helping the Israelites. It was only because He hardened the Egyptians' hearts that they went into the sea.

■ ■ ■

## The Eternal Heritage

וַיֻּגַּד לְמֶלֶךְ מִצְרַיִם כִּי בָרַח הָעָם וַיֵּהָפֵךְ לְבַב פַּרְעֹה וַעֲבָדָיו אֶל־הָעָם וַיֹּאמְרוּ מַה־זֹּאת עָשִׂינוּ כִּי־שִׁלַּחְנוּ אֶת־יִשְׂרָאֵל מֵעָבְדֵנוּ.

*The king of Egypt was informed that the people had escaped. Pharaoh and his officials had a change of heart regarding the people, and said, "What have we done in releasing Israel from doing our work?" (14:5)*

Kli Yekar asks several questions concerning this verse. Firstly, whereas Pharaoh had sent the Israelites of his own free will, why does Scripture write that they "had escaped"? Wouldn't it be more correct to say that they "were escaping" — in that they were not returning, as promised, after three days, but continuing on their way? Secondly, why does Scripture twice refer to the Israelites as "the people," and then identify them as "Israel"? Thirdly, how did Pharaoh propose to defeat the Israelites with only 600 chariots (verse 7)? Although the Torah does add that Pharaoh took along "all of Egypt's chariots," this certainly does not mean to include the chariots of the entire land, as it would have been impossible to mobilize them at such short notice. Rather, it includes those of the city named Egypt, and actually only the chariots of the people who had feared the coming of the Plague of Hail and taken their horses in from the fields, as the other horses had died (Rashi on 14:7).

Kli Yekar answers that the term "the people" refers to the Mixed Multitude, who had recognized the importance of the Israelites and left Egypt with them. These people truly "had escaped" from Egypt; they had not been given permission by Pharaoh to leave even for a short time. It was about them that Pharaoh was now thinking. He insisted that, having seen how the Israelites had become lost in the desert (verse 3), the Mixed Multitude had certainly concluded that God no longer supported the Israelites. The Mixed Multitude doubtless desired to return to Egypt, but were being prevented from doing so by the Israelites. Pharaoh believed that when the Mixed Multitude observed the Egyptians coming to assist them they would rebel against the Israelites and rejoin the Egyptians. It was for this reason that Pharaoh felt comfortable in pursuing the Israelites with such a small force — he thought the Mixed Multitude would ally with him.

*Beshalach*

With this in mind, Kli Yekar proceeds to interpret the present verse. Rashi says that Pharaoh was informed of the Israelites' escape by captains he had sent along with them. These men reported that the Israelites had not turned back after three days. Kli Yekar does not accept this, as he maintains that the verse refers to the Mixed Multitude, and not to the Israelites. According to Kli Yekar, the report given to Pharaoh here was transmitted not after the Israelites left, but at the time of their departure; it contained the news that Egyptians were leaving illegally along with the Israelites. Due to this, Pharaoh had feelings of hatred toward the Mixed Multitude. This is what is meant by "The king of Egypt was informed that the people had escaped": he had been informed at the time of the Exodus that his own people had escaped. However, now "Pharaoh . . . had a change of heart regarding the people." Thinking they regretted having betrayed him, his disposition toward the Mixed Multitude changed from hatred to love.

Kli Yekar concludes that the Israelites themselves are, however, the subject of the *end* of the verse, when Pharaoh says, "What have we done in releasing Israel from doing our work?" Therefore, the term "Israel" is used.

■

"The king of Egypt was informed that the people had escaped." Rashi explains that Pharaoh had sent officers along with the Israelites to insure that they would keep their word and return after three days (8:23). When three days passed and the Israelites did not turn back toward Egypt, the officers rode back to inform Pharaoh. This occurred on the fourth day. The Egyptians gave chase on the fifth and sixth days. On the night of the seventh day the Israelites crossed the sea while the Egyptians drowned, and in the daytime of the seventh day the Israelites sang to God (15:1). That, concludes Rashi, corresponds to the seventh day of Passover, which is why we read this section as the Torah portion on that day.

Mizrachi points to a contradiction in Rashi. Elsewhere (Numbers 15:41), Rashi quotes R. Moshe HaDarshan to the effect that there are eight strings in each corner of the ritual fringes, *tzitzith*, as a symbol of the eight days which elapsed from the time the Israelites departed Egypt until they sang at the Red Sea. Why does Rashi give a number of seven days in the present verse and eight days in the section discussing *tzitzith*?

Mizrachi suggests that R. Moshe HaDarshan disagrees with the Aggadah quoted by Rashi here, and maintains that the Israelites did not sing until the eighth day.

Sifthei Chachamim avers that there is no dispute between R. Moshe HaDarshan and the present Rashi, the two sources agreeing that the Israelites sang on the seventh day of Passover. However, R. Moshe HaDarshan is including in his count the daytime of the fourteenth of Nissan, the day on which the Paschal Lamb was slaughtered. Although in general a day without the night preceding it is not counted as a full day, the reverse holds in the case of sacrifices; the day consists of the daytime and the night *following* it. Since the Paschal Lamb was offered on the afternoon of the fourteenth, the count begins with that afternoon. Hence, there were seven days and nights from Passover Eve through the night of the seventh day of Passover. The eighth day commenced at daylight of the seventh day of Passover, and it was then that the Israelites sang.

Divrei David opines that all agree the Israelites sang on the eighth day of their journey, the day after Passover. While Rashi here says they sang on the seventh day, Divrei David says that Rashi is not referring to the seventh day of Passover, but to the seventh *full day* of their journey. We find, in regard to Moses' stay on Mount Sinai, that when he told the Israelites he would remain there for forty days, he had in mind forty *full* days — nights followed by days. Thus, the day he went up was not counted, as he went up during the daytime (Rashi on 32:1). The same principle applied to the three days allotted the Israelites for their journey; Pharaoh permitted them to be gone three full days. Hence, the day of their departure — the first day of Passover — did not count, as they left in the daytime of the fifteenth (Rashi on Deuteronomy 32:48). When Rashi says the officers waited three days, he is actually referring to the second, third, and fourth days of Passover — the sixteenth, seventeenth, and eighteenth of Nissan. The officers rode back to Pharaoh on the fifth

## Beshalach

day of Passover, the nineteenth of Nissan. The Egyptians chased the Israelites on the sixth and seventh days (the twentieth and twenty-first), and drowned the next night, the night after Passover. The Israelites sang the next morning — eight days after leaving Egypt, but in reality only seven full days.

As for why we read this portion on the seventh day of Passover, when the Israelites sang on the eighth day, Divrei David says that, since for the Israelites the eighth day was enumerated as the seventh day, it is proper to celebrate the seventh day of Passover as a commemoration of this event.

However, Divrei David's explanation is problematic. Rashi says, "In the morning they sang, and it was the seventh day of Passover. Therefore, we read the song on the seventh day." It is clear that Rashi believes the Israelites sang on the same day upon which we read this portion — the seventh day of Passover.

■

"Pharaoh and his officials had a change of heart." The Egyptians changed their minds and decided to pursue the Israelites to retrieve the money they had given them (Rashi). Why does Rashi introduce a reason for Pharaoh's change of heart, when the Torah itself gives a different reason — "What have we done in releasing Israel from doing our work?"

Sifthei Chachamim answers, in Maharshal's name, that the stated reason — the loss of the Israelites as slaves — was indeed cause enough for Pharaoh to elect to chase them. The king had been unwilling until the very end to release the Israelites, and so it would make sense that he regretted having done so. By contrast, Pharaoh's officials had been ready to free the Israelites (10:7). Yet the Torah says that "his officials" also "had a change of heart." Why would the officials suddenly have regretted the decision? It is for this that Rashi seeks an explanation, and asserts that the officials were distressed at having lost their wealth.

Levush HaOhrah gives another answer. He points out that the Torah makes reference to the Egyptians' thoughts — "a change of heart" — and to their spoken words: "What have we done in releasing Israel from doing our work?" If their mind and speech were in agreement, it would have been enough to mention their declaration that they regretted losing their slaves. Why was it necessary to state that there had been a change of heart? Evidently, in their hearts lurked a different, unspoken reason for their regret — that the Israelites had taken their money.

■ ■ ■

וַיִּקַּח שֵׁשׁ־מֵאוֹת רֶכֶב בָּחוּר וְכֹל רֶכֶב מִצְרָיִם וְשָׁלִשִׁם עַל־כֻּלּוֹ.

He took 600 chariots with chosen crews, as well as the entire chariot corps of Egypt, with supporting infantry for them all. (14:7)

Why did Pharaoh send exactly 600 chariots?

When an enemy is able to overpower the Jewish people, due to the latter's spiritual weakness, two of the enemy give chase to 10,000 Jews — a ratio of one to 5,000 (Deuteronomy 32:30). Now, 600,000 Jews left Egypt, and at the ratio of one to 5,000, Pharaoh should have dispatched 120 chariots.

In truth, however, the population of Israelites had been much greater. Eighty percent of the Israelites died during the Plague of Darkness (Rashi on 13:18), so there had actually been 3,000,000 Israelites. Pharaoh did not know of the death of these people [God killed them during the Plague of Darkness to keep their demise a secret], and so he sent 600 chariots — a ratio of one to 5,000 for a population of 3,000,000. *(R. Chaim Rappaport)*

■ ■ ■

וּפַרְעֹה הִקְרִיב וַיִּשְׂאוּ בְנֵי־יִשְׂרָאֵל אֶת־עֵינֵיהֶם וְהִנֵּה מִצְרַיִם נֹסֵעַ אַחֲרֵיהֶם וַיִּירְאוּ מְאֹד וַיִּצְעֲקוּ בְנֵי־יִשְׂרָאֵל אֶל־ה'.

As Pharaoh drew near, the Israelites looked up to see Egypt traveling at their rear, and became very frightened. The Israelites cried out to God. (14:10)

"Egypt [was] traveling at their rear." The Torah describes the Egyptians in the singular here (*Mitzrayim nose'a*, "Egypt [was] traveling"). Rashi comments that this was because the Egyptians chased the Israelites "as if with one heart, as if they were one man"

— with singularity of purpose. Every Egyptian had the same feelings towards the Israelites.

Later, in describing the Israelites' arrival at Mount Sinai, the Torah also uses the singular form — "Israel encamped there *(Vayichan)* opposite the mountain" (19:2). Rashi makes the same comment there about unity, but with the clauses reversed — "as if they were one man, as if with one heart." Why is there this difference?

R. Avraham of Sochachev explains that there is no unity among the citizens of the world. The citizens have no true, natural connection with one another. A nation comes together only for practical purposes — to fight a war, to exact revenge, and so on. Due to a common desire — "with one heart" — the people unite — "as if they were one man." Therefore, in discussing the Egyptians, Rashi writes that they were "as if with one heart, as if they were one man."

With the Jewish people the opposite is true. Their essence is one of unity, through their common belief in one God and one Torah. Division among them occurs when the heart does not desire this unity. Their unity as "one man" continues as long as they have "one heart," meaning a commitment to Torah observance. And so, concerning the arrival of the Jews at Mount Sinai, Rashi says that they came "as if they were one man, as if with one heart."

The gentiles are separate until united by the heart. The Jews are united until the heart causes separation.

■

"Egypt [was] traveling at their rear, and [they] became very frightened. The Israelites cried out to God." Troubles do not befall a man coincidentally. Thus, one who seeks to escape his troubles by running from them may be compared to a pregnant woman who, seeking relief from her pain, moves to a different location. Of course, the pains travel along with her. The only counsel for a man seeking relief from distress is that he pray and cleave to God: "From distress I have called God, He answered me with breadth" (Psalms 118:5).

When the Israelites saw the Egyptians pursuing them — they saw

that leaving Egypt had not solved their troubles — they understood that relief would come in only one way: "The Israelites cried out to God." And salvation followed, as they were told, "While you will see the Egyptians today, you will never see them again" (verse 13).
*(Iturei Torah, citing Ba'al Shem Tov)*

∎

"[The Israelites] became very frightened. The Israelites cried out to God." They cried to God because they realized they had another fear besides the fear of God. When this occurs, it is a form of idol worship.
*(Chiddushei HaRim)*

∎ ∎ ∎

וַיֹּאמְרוּ אֶל־מֹשֶׁה הֲמִבְּלִי אֵין־קְבָרִים בְּמִצְרַיִם לְקַחְתָּנוּ לָמוּת בַּמִּדְבָּר מַה־זֹּאת עָשִׂיתָ לָּנוּ לְהוֹצִיאָנוּ מִמִּצְרָיִם. הֲלֹא־זֶה הַדָּבָר אֲשֶׁר דִּבַּרְנוּ אֵלֶיךָ בְמִצְרַיִם לֵאמֹר חֲדַל מִמֶּנּוּ וְנַעַבְדָה אֶת־מִצְרָיִם כִּי טוֹב לָנוּ עֲבֹד אֶת־מִצְרַיִם מִמֻּתֵנוּ בַּמִּדְבָּר.

*They said to Moses, "Is it because there weren't enough graves in Egypt that you took us out to die in the desert? What is this that you did to us — bringing us out of Egypt?*
*"Isn't this the matter about which we spoke to you in Egypt, saying you should leave us alone and let us work for the Egyptians? It would have been better for us to be slaves in Egypt than to die in the desert." (14:11, 12)*

Chatham Sofer points out that the Sages consider death preferable to captivity (Bava Bathra 8b). Why, then, did the Israelites insist that it would have been better for them to remain slaves rather than to die?

He answers that death is preferred only when it is accompanied by burial. To be dead and lie unburied in the desert is not preferable to captivity. Indeed, the Midrash quotes the Israelites as saying that their death in the wilderness would be a worse one than the death of their brothers who had perished during the Plague of Darkness (when the wicked Israelites died), because their corpses would be the prey of the heat during the day and the frost at night — they would not have a burial.

## Beshalach

Thus, the Israelites complained: Is it impossible to remain unburied in Egypt that you took us out to the desert? We could have suffered this misfortune in Egypt, and there was thus no reason to take us here.

■ ■ ■

וַיֹּאמֶר מֹשֶׁה אֶל־הָעָם אַל־תִּירָאוּ הִתְיַצְּבוּ וּרְאוּ אֶת־יְשׁוּעַת ה' אֲשֶׁר־יַעֲשֶׂה לָכֶם הַיּוֹם כִּי אֲשֶׁר רְאִיתֶם אֶת־מִצְרַיִם הַיּוֹם לֹא תֹסִפוּ לִרְאֹתָם עוֹד עַד־עוֹלָם.

*Moses replied to the people, "Do not be afraid. Stand firm and you will see what God will do to rescue you today. While you will see the Egyptians today, you will never see them again. . . ." (14:13)*

"Stand firm and you will see what God will do to rescue you." The Israelites were not to fight; God alone would do battle for them.

How is it that 600,000 men were afraid of the relatively few soldiers chasing them? Why weren't they prepared to fight for themselves and their families?

The Egyptians had been masters over the Israelites, and so this generation of Israelites had grown up with a subservient attitude. The Israelites could not have fought their former masters. Also, they were weak and untrained for war. This is why Amalek, with a small band of soldiers, would have triumphed over Israel if not for Moses' prayers (17:8-13). This is also why God had all the males who came out of Egypt die in the wilderness; they would have been unable to conquer Canaan. It was left to the next generation, which had not known slavery, to fight the Canaanites. *(Ibn Ezra)*

■

"What God will do to rescue you today" — The reason Moses said that God would save the Israelites "today" was because the process of redemption from Egypt had taken a year. In order to allay the Israelites' fear that the present battle would also take a long time, Moses assured them that salvation would come "today."

*(Ohr HaChayyim)*

■

## The Eternal Heritage

In the era of R. Yecheskel Landau, who is commonly known as Noda B'Yehuda, the Torah giants of Poland became involved in a halachic dispute concerning two brothers. The brothers had been very close for many years and were involved in various business ventures together. However, disagreements arose between them, leading to a complete separation. Things deteriorated to such an extent that one of the two swore an irrevocable oath never to see his brother again.

This oath depressed the other brother so deeply that he eventually became ill and died. In turn, the surviving brother was full of regret that he had been the cause of his brother's death. He desired to go to his brother's grave and beg forgiveness, but felt bound by the oath he had made not to see him.

The surviving brother went to the rabbis of his town, who, almost to a man, agreed that it was possible to nullify the oath based on the principle that, when one takes an oath, he expects it to apply in certain circumstances, but not in all circumstances. If a situation arises wherein the oath would not have been made, the oath can be nullified. Here, the surviving brother had never expected his oath to prevent his asking his brother for forgiveness, and so the oath could be nullified.

When R. Yecheskel Landau, who was still young at the time, was advised of the question, he maintained that there was no need to resort to nullification of the oath, as the Torah itself supplies the room to be lenient in a case such as this. Moses told the Israelites: "While you will see the Egyptians today, you will never see them again." God's declaration is certainly as valid as an oath taken by a human being. And yet later the Torah says, "Israel saw the Egyptians dead on the seashore" (verse 30). We have proof here that the prohibition to see a human being due to an oath continues only as long as the person is alive. Hence, the surviving brother's oath did not have effect once his brother had died.

Hearing this, another rabbi contended that there was no proof from the case of the Israelites and Egyptians. Perhaps — he said — the Israelites did not actually come face to face with the Egyptian dead. Perhaps they saw their bodies from afar.

## Beshalach

R. Yecheskel Landau responded by citing the Midrash's statement that each Israelite was able to recognize, among the Egyptian dead, the particular taskmasters who had oppressed him in Egypt. Obviously, then, the Israelites did see the Egyptians at close hand. *(Mekor Baruch)*

■ ■ ■

ה׳ יִלָּחֵם לָכֶם וְאַתֶּם תַּחֲרִשׁוּן.
". . . God will do battle for you, while you will keep silent." (14:14)

"God will do battle for you" — The Midrash says that God's promise here is not confined only to this one instance, but is meant for all time. What point is the Midrash making?

Meshech Chochmah explains that in this particular instance God was duty-bound to help the Israelites. He had brought them out of Egypt into the wilderness, and so He had to protect them; they had a right to request such help. However, asserts the Midrash, not only would God battle for the Israelites here, but even when the Jews have no right to ask for help — when they deserve punishment, when they can do no more than "keep silent" — God will fight for them.

■

R. Meir of Peremyshlyany uses a play on words to advance a homiletic explanation for this verse. *Tacharishun,* "you will keep silent," may also be translated as "you will scheme." Such a translation for the word is found in Proverbs — "Do not plot evil against your friend" (3:29) — and in Job: "As I have seen plotters of iniquity" (4:8).

God provides for everything; as R. Tachlifa says: A man's sustenance is stipulated for him from one Rosh HaShanah to the next Rosh HaShanah (Betzah 15b). In this context the verse may be read as follows: "God will do battle for you" — He provides for you — and "you will scheme?" — you nevertheless feel the need to devise schemes regarding how to make a living? *(Iturei Torah)*

Iturei Torah cites yet another play on words by R. Meir of Peremyshlyany. *Yilacheim,* "will do battle," contains the letters of the word *lechem,* bread. And *tacharishun* can be translated as "you will plow." God does battle — He provides bread, a living. However, "*you* will plow" — people must make the effort to earn money.

■

Once, during a conversation with R. Avraham Yitzchak Kook, R. Yosef Chaim Sonnenfeld remarked that he did not believe the secular Zionist pioneers, who had rejected God and the Torah, had any merits which would permit them to see the coming of the Messiah.

In response, R. Kook pointed out that, at the time of the Exodus, God gave the Israelites statutes with which to occupy themselves — in particular, the Paschal sacrifice. It was in the merit of fulfilling that law that the Israelites were redeemed. However, there is no indication that the Israelites were given an additional commandment so that they would merit being saved at the Red Sea. The reason, said R. Kook, is because no such commandment was necessary. The Talmud (Sotah 35b) states that at the Red Sea: This tribe said, "I will go into the sea first," and this tribe said, "I will go into the sea first." Their *mesiruth nefesh,* the willingness to risk their lives, sufficed to earn the Israelites the right to be saved. Therefore, God said that He would "do battle for you, while you will keep silent."

The same — said R. Kook — held for the secular Zionists, who were risking their lives in their pioneer work; even without other merits, they had earned the right to see the Messiah..

(*MeOtzareinu HaYashan*)

■ ■ ■

וַיֹּאמֶר ה' אֶל־מֹשֶׁה מַה־תִּצְעַק אֵלָי דַּבֵּר אֶל־בְּנֵי־יִשְׂרָאֵל וְיִסָּעוּ.
God said to Moses, "Why are you crying out to Me? Speak to the Israelites and let them start traveling. . . ." (14:15)

Why, indeed, did Moses cry out to God? Why didn't he have faith that God would keep His promise to the Israelites to destroy the Egyptians?

## Beshalach

Moses loved the people of Israel so much that when he saw their distress he was unable to contain himself. He lost his patience and cried out to God.
*(Sefath Emeth)*

To the same question R. Yisrael Salanter answers that it was improper for Moses to have faith, to keep his peace, at the expense of the Israelites. When the lives of Jews hang in the balance, one cannot simply stand by and do nothing.

■ ■ ■

וְאַתָּה הָרֵם אֶת־מַטְּךָ וּנְטֵה אֶת־יָדְךָ עַל־הַיָּם וּבְקָעֵהוּ וְיָבֹאוּ בְנֵי־יִשְׂרָאֵל בְּתוֹךְ הַיָּם בַּיַּבָּשָׁה.

*". . . As for you, raise your staff and extend your hand over the sea and split it. The Israelites will then be able to cross through the sea on dry land. . . ." (14:16)*

We can see from here how much God despises pride. The Midrash records that the sea did not wish to comply with Moses' request that it split. The sea told Moses: I will not split for you, for I am greater than you, having been created on the third day while you were not created until the sixth day.

When God heard the sea express this haughty attitude, He told Moses, "Raise your staff . . . and split it" — hit the boastful one over its head.
*(R. Chanoch Henoch of Aleksandrow)*

■

"Raise *(harem)* your staff and extend your hand over the sea and split it." The Midrash says that the Egyptians believed Moses would not have been able to perform the miracles in Egypt without his staff. Therefore, God told Moses, "Take away your staff and extend your hand over the sea"; *harem*, "Raise," can also mean "take away."

Why did God command Moses not to use his staff specifically at the splitting of the sea? The answer is that He wanted Moses to perform the miracles in a manner that would correspond with how they were being performed by God. Whereas all the plagues were done by the "finger of God" (8:15), God had Moses use his staff,

## The Eternal Heritage

which resembles a finger. However, at the sea, God used His entire hand to smite the Egyptians — "The Israelites saw the great *hand* that God had unleashed against the Egyptians" (verse 31). Therefore, God told Moses to split the sea with his hand instead of with the staff. As a tangential result of this, it became obvious that the power to create Moses' miracles did not come from the staff, since Moses did not use it here. That is why it says here that "They believed in God and in His servant Moses" (Ibid.).

Now we can understand what Moses' sin was at Mei Merivah. There, he did the opposite of what he did here. Scripture relates: "Moses raised his hand and struck the rock twice with his staff" (Numbers 20:11). *Vayarem,* "[He] raised," denotes removal; Moses "removed" — did not use — his hand, but rather his staff. By doing that, he caused the Israelites to lose faith in God, as they believed that the staff, not God's power, had caused the rock to split. This regression in faith was intimated by God, who charged, "You did not have faith in Me" (Ibid., verse 12). *(Kli Yekar)*

■ ■ ■

וַיִּסַּע מַלְאַךְ הָאֱלֹהִים הַהֹלֵךְ לִפְנֵי מַחֲנֵה יִשְׂרָאֵל וַיֵּלֶךְ מֵאַחֲרֵיהֶם וַיִּסַּע עַמּוּד הֶעָנָן מִפְּנֵיהֶם וַיַּעֲמֹד מֵאַחֲרֵיהֶם.

*God's angel, who had been traveling in front of the Israelite camp, moved and went behind them, and the pillar of cloud moved from in front of them and stood at their rear. (14:19)*

Rashi says that the angel moved to the rear in order to separate the Israelite and Egyptian camps. There the angel served as a shield, deflecting the arrows hurled by the Egyptians. Then, at night, when the cloud was relieved by the pillar of fire (Rashi on 13:22), the cloud did not, as at other times, depart until daylight. Instead, it also moved to the rear of the camp, in order to block any light from reaching the Egyptians (presumably the light from the fire). Hence, according to Rashi, the angel moved to the back during the day, while the cloud did not move until evening.

Rashbam disagrees with Rashi. Rashbam avers that the angel was in charge of pushing the cloud. At evening the angel went to the rear, moving the cloud with him in order to cause darkness for the Egyptians. In Rashbam's view, the verse's two clauses are related: "God's angel . . . went behind them, and so the pillar of cloud also moved . . . and stood at their rear."

Sforno opines that the angel was contained within the pillar of fire (13:21). Both pillars — fire and cloud — moved to the rear of the Israelite camp. The fire was immediately behind the camp and the cloud stood behind the fire, so that the Israelites had light but the Egyptians were enveloped in darkness. Thus, Rashi maintains that the pillar of fire went in front of the Israelites on this night, while Sforno contends that it was behind them.

■

It is known that in general, due to their holiness, the angels are at a higher level than the Jewish people. However, when God demonstrates His love for the Jews, His nation, they assume a higher position than the angels.

The splitting of the Red Sea was an occasion when God manifested His love for the Jews, and so they ranked above the angels at that time.

This is the meaning of "God's angel, who had been traveling in front of the Israelite camp, moved and went behind them." The angels, which had been "in front of the Israelite camp" — higher in rank — stood "behind them"; the Israelites moved to a higher level than the angels.  *(Kedushath Levi)*

■ ■ ■

וַיָּבֹא בֵּין מַחֲנֵה מִצְרַיִם וּבֵין מַחֲנֵה יִשְׂרָאֵל וַיְהִי הֶעָנָן וְהַחֹשֶׁךְ וַיָּאֶר אֶת־הַלָּיְלָה וְלֹא־קָרַב זֶה אֶל־זֶה כָּל־הַלָּיְלָה.

It came between the Egyptian and the Israelite camps. There was cloud and darkness [for the Egyptians] but there was light all night [for the Israelites]. All night [the Egyptians and Israelites] could not approach one another. (14:20)

The ministering angels wanted to sing praises regarding the Egyptians' demise, but God said: "My handiwork is drowning in the sea and you desire to sing?" (Sanhedrin 39b). Maharsha explains that this teaching is gleaned from the words *zeh el zeh*, "one another." We find elsewhere (Isaiah 6:3) that the angels speak *zeh el zeh* — "One calls to another." However, on the night the Egyptians drowned, "[The angels] could not approach one another"; they were not permitted to sing.

Despite this restriction on the angels, we do find that the Israelites sang (15:1). Why were they permitted to sing, while the angels were not?

R. Yehoshua of Kutno draws an analogy with a surgeon who must perform an operation. Although he is certain of success, he does not rejoice during the operation, as that is a serious moment. Happiness is expressed only when the procedure has been successfully completed. Similarly, the Torah says, "You shall . . . rid yourselves of evil" (Deuteronomy 17:7). While eradicating evil is healthy for the world, during the eradication procedure it is improper to rejoice.

The angels wanted to sing at night, at the same hour that the Egyptians were drowning. God refused their request, saying, "My handiwork is drowning in the sea." He used the present tense — "*is* drowning." At that moment, the destruction of the Egyptians was in progress, and so it was improper to sing. The Israelites were allowed to sing praises because they did so *after* the Egyptians had perished.

■

The angels wanted to sing, but God said, "My handiwork is drowning in the sea and you desire to sing?"

The common explanation is that "My handiwork is drowning in the sea" refers to the Egyptians, and that because God pitied them He prevented the angels from singing. However, a glaring question remains: If the Egyptians merited mercy, why weren't their lives spared?

To answer this, the Rebbe R. Heschel proposes a unique exposition of the discussion between God and the angels. Regarding Sennacherib and the Assyrians, Scripture says, "God's angel went out and smote within the Assyrian camp . . ." (Isaiah 37:36). The Talmud asks: How did He smite them? R. Yitzchak Napacha

## Beshalach

answers that God opened their ears so that they heard angels singing, and due to this they died (Sanhedrin 95b). R. Heschel says that the same occurred at the Red Sea. When the Egyptians were pursuing the Israelites, the angels "wanted to sing" — they wished to cause death to the Egyptians through singing, as happened with Sennacherib. However, God rejected their plan, saying, "My handiwork is drowning in the sea" — the Egyptians had drowned the Israelite children in the Nile, with Pharaoh's decree that "Every boy who is born must be cast into the Nile" (1:22). They had slain the Israelites with every manner of cruel death — said God — and you want to kill them in turn with song, with a very lenient manner of execution? That is not how it will be; rather, the Egyptians must die in corresponding measure to their treatment of the Israelites.

*(Iturei Torah)*

■ ■ ■

וַיֵּט מֹשֶׁה אֶת־יָדוֹ עַל־הַיָּם וַיּוֹלֶךְ ה' אֶת־הַיָּם בְּרוּחַ קָדִים עַזָּה כָּל־הַלַּיְלָה וַיָּשֶׂם אֶת־הַיָּם לֶחָרָבָה וַיִּבָּקְעוּ הַמָּיִם.

*Moses extended his arm over the sea. All night, God drove the sea back with a powerful east wind, transforming the sea bed into dry land. The waters were divided. (14:21)*

"The sea saw and it fled" (Psalms 114:3). What did it see? It saw the *beraitha* (teaching) of R. Yishmael (Midrash Peliah).

The following thought has been expressed in the name of R. Yosef, the head of the Rabbinical Court of Slutsk:

The verse utilizes past tense in saying that "The sea saw and fled." However, it continues, "The Jordan *will turn* backwards" — in future tense. Should it not have said, "The Jordan *turned* backwards"?

The answer is that the Red Sea foresaw that the Jordan River would, in the future, turn about — split. This would occur when the Israelites, under Joshua's leadership, crossed the Jordan into Canaan. The Red Sea drew an inference from minor to major *(kal vachomer)* from the splitting of the Jordan: Whereas the Jordan would split before Joshua, then certainly the Red Sea was obligated

## The Eternal Heritage

to split before Moses, Joshua's teacher. Thus, "The sea saw and fled" due to the fact that "the Jordan will turn (in the future) backwards."

We can now understand what the Midrash Peliah meant when it said that the sea saw the *beraitha* of R. Yishmael. In listing the types of exegesis by which the Torah is studied, R. Yishmael includes inference, *kal vachomer*. The sea utilized a *kal vachomer*, as taught by R. Yishmael, to conclude that it should split.

*(Kehillath Yitzchak)*

■

"The sea saw and it fled"; it saw the *beraitha* of R. Yishmael (Midrash Peliah).

The Midrash relates that the angel representing the sea argued against its splitting for the Israelites, asserting that both the Israelites and the Egyptians were idol worshipers. Why, asked the angel, should the sea favor one over the other? God responded that the angel was comparing willful transgressors (the Egyptians) to those who had been *forced* to sin (the Israelites).

God's rejoinder is problematic. The halacha is that the presence of compulsion is no justification for serving idols. If one is faced with the choice of engaging in idol worship or being killed, he must allow himself to be killed. Why, then, was there a difference between the Israelites and the Egyptians?

The answer must be that the Midrash, in differentiating between willful and forced idol worship, is of the same mind as R. Yishmael, who disagrees with the above rule. R. Yishmael maintains that one is not required to give up his life rather than worship an idol (Sanhedrin 74a). The sea saw the *beraitha* of R. Yishmael: his law regarding compelled idol worship. Based on this, it split for the Israelites, for their idol worship was not willful.

*(Damesek Eliezer)*

Damesek Eliezer's explanation is difficult to accept. R. Yishmael's lenient ruling applies only when the idol worship is done in private. When it would take place in public, he agrees that one must forfeit his life rather than worship the idol. The Israelites' idol worship was

## Beshalach

in all likelihood done in public, and so one cannot apply R. Yishmael's lenient ruling to this case.

∎

"The sea saw and it fled"; it saw the *beraitha* of R. Yishmael.

R. Yishmael says that if one sees a man being threatened by his enemy he must save the victim's life even at the cost of the aggressor's life (Sanhedrin 73a). To comply with this statute, the sea had to do everything in its power to save the Israelites from their Egyptian pursuers, even if the lives of the Egyptians would be forfeited in the process.

*(Avnei Ezel)*

∎

"The sea saw and it fled." What did it see? Joseph's coffin (Midrash).

At first the Red Sea refused to obey Moses' command and split, asserting that it was greater than Moses, since the ocean was created on the third day while Man was not created until the sixth day. However, when the sea saw Joseph's coffin being carried along by the Israelites for burial in Canaan, it realized that seniority is not an indication of superiority. Joseph was younger than his brothers. Nonetheless, he was their ruler and, out of respect for his position, they felt compelled to obey his order that they take along his coffin (Genesis 50:25).

Joseph's coffin served as the basis for the right of a man — despite his relative youth — to command the sea to split.

*(HaDerash VeHaIyun)*

∎ ∎ ∎

וַיָּבֹאוּ בְנֵי־יִשְׂרָאֵל בְּתוֹךְ הַיָּם בַּיַּבָּשָׁה וְהַמַּיִם לָהֶם חוֹמָה מִימִינָם וּמִשְּׂמֹאלָם.

*The Israelites entered the sea bed on dry land. The waters were as walls on their right and left. (14:22)*

R. Meir said that the Israelites quarreled with one another at the Red Sea. This tribe said, "I will jump in first," while the next tribe said, "I will jump in first." R. Yehuda told R. Meir: This was not the way it transpired. Rather, this one said, "I will not jump into the sea first," and the next one said, "I will not jump into the sea first." But Nachshon, son of Aminadav, arose and jumped in first (Sotah 36b).

Iturei Torah quotes R. Yehoshua of Kutno to the effect that there is no dispute between R. Meir and R. Yehuda. Each Sage is talking about a separate event. R. Meir is referring to the reaction of the Israelites when they began discussing the problem of the sea. He relates that every man declared his readiness to be the first to jump into the water. R. Yehuda adds that "this was not the way it transpired." While the Israelites had expressed their eagerness to rush into the sea, they were unwilling to back up their words when the time for action arrived. Everyone backed off, saying, "I will not jump in first," until Nachshon took the initiative.

∎

The Talmud states: One who sees the site of the crossing of the [Red] Sea must give thanks and praise to God, for it says, "The Israelites entered the sea bed on dry land" (Berachoth 54a). Since a miracle was performed there for our ancestors, we are obligated to acknowledge it with a blessing: "Blessed is He who performed miracles for our forefathers in this place."

R. Achai Gaon records a later verse as the basis for this halacha: "The Israelites had gone on dry land through the sea bed" (verse 29). R. Naftali Zvi Yehuda Berlin explains that the second verse is preferred because it teaches that one is to make the blessing only when a miracle has been completed. The present verse relates that the Israelites *entered* the sea. They had not yet negotiated it safely. It was only when they exited the sea bed, which is the information relayed by the later verse, that the miracle was completed.

R. Baruch Epstein, in his Torah Temimah, asserts that, according to R. Berlin (who was his uncle), one would make a blessing at the site where the Israelites came out of the sea, but not where they entered it. Torah Temimah objects that neither the Talmud nor the halachic decisors make this distinction. Rashi, for example, explains that the Red Sea "crossing" referred to by the Talmud is "the place where the Israelites *passed through* the Red Sea." It would seem that

## Beshalach

all points along the route of the crossing are included.

Furthermore, says Torah Temimah, we find cases when we are obligated to make the blessing over miracles although the miracles were not yet completed. For example, one who sees the rock upon which Moses sat while praying for the Israelites in their war with Amalek (17:12) recites the blessing, although the outcome had not yet been decided when Moses was sitting there. Similarly, one makes the blessing upon seeing the fallen wall of Jericho, although the defeat of the city had only begun when the wall fell.

■ ■ ■

וַיָּסַר אֵת אֹפַן מַרְכְּבֹתָיו וַיְנַהֲגֵהוּ בִּכְבֵדֻת וַיֹּאמֶר מִצְרַיִם אָנוּסָה מִפְּנֵי יִשְׂרָאֵל כִּי ה׳ נִלְחָם לָהֶם בְּמִצְרָיִם.

[God] made the chariot wheels fall off, and caused them to drive heavily. The Egyptians said, "Let us flee from Israel, because God is fighting for them against Egypt." (14:25)

It seems that the Israelites were still in the sea when the Egyptians went in after them. God made the sea floor muddy, and the Egyptians became bogged down in the mud, so that they were unable to chase the Israelites. At this time, the sea had not yet covered the Egyptians, since the Israelites were still in the sea bed along with them. Only when the last Israelite had left the sea bed did God order Moses to cause the waters to return to their place (verse 26).

This explains why we say in the morning prayers, "You split the Red Sea and drowned the wicked ones *(vezeidim tibata)*. The beloved ones passed through [the text in our prayer books reads: You brought the beloved ones through], and the waters covered their adversaries." The phrasing seems problematic, as it should have said that "The beloved ones passed through" before saying that "You . . . drowned the wicked ones," since the Israelites passed through before the Egyptians drowned. Furthermore, why did the liturgist interject the phrase "The beloved ones passed through" between "You . . . drowned the wicked ones" and "the waters covered their adversaries," since these last two are related phrases?

The answer is that "You . . . drowned the wicked ones" is not the proper translation of *vezeidim tibata*. *Tibata*, "drowned," can also be translated as "mired." This refers to the fact that the Egyptians went into the sea while the Israelites were still there, and became mired in the mud. This has nothing to do with their drowning. (Usages of *teviah* to denote miring are: "Your feet are mired in mud" [Jeremiah 38:22] and "I became mired in the mud of the deep waters" [Psalms 69:3].) Then, after "The beloved ones passed through," the sea covered the Egyptians: "the waters covered their adversaries."
*(Moshav Zekenim)*

■ ■ ■

וַיֵּט מֹשֶׁה אֶת־יָדוֹ עַל־הַיָּם וַיָּשָׁב הַיָּם לִפְנוֹת בֹּקֶר לְאֵיתָנוֹ וּמִצְרַיִם נָסִים לִקְרָאתוֹ וַיְנַעֵר ה' אֶת־מִצְרַיִם בְּתוֹךְ הַיָּם.

*Just before morning, Moses extended his hand over the sea, and the sea returned to its natural strength. The Egyptians were fleeing toward the water, but God overturned the Egyptians in the middle of the sea. (14:27)*

Why did God make the sea return to its strength so quickly: "Just before morning"?

Despite the miracles the Israelites had witnessed, it was still possible that they would wish to return to Egypt. Therefore, the moment daylight arrived the sea returned to its natural state, sealing off the path to Egypt.
*(MeOtzareinu HaYashan, citing R. Shmuel Mohilever)*

■ ■ ■

וּבְנֵי יִשְׂרָאֵל הָלְכוּ בַיַּבָּשָׁה בְּתוֹךְ הַיָּם וְהַמַּיִם לָהֶם חֹמָה מִימִינָם וּמִשְּׂמֹאלָם.

*The Israelites had gone on dry land through the sea bed. The waters were as walls on their right and left. (14:29)*

People are impressed only by supernatural occurrences. They do not recognize that nature itself is a miracle, through which one can

*Beshalach*

constantly perceive God's greatness. However, when people do see a supernatural miracle, they recall that God's providence is manifest in ordinary nature as well.

"The Israelites had gone on dry land through the sea bed." When the children of Israel experienced the miracle of passing through the sea bed as if it were land, they realized that when they walked on "dry land," too, it was as if they were walking through the "sea bed" — that even their everyday lives were governed by God.

*(R. Elimelech of Lyzhansk)*

∎

"The waters were as walls" — The word "walls," *chomah*, is spelled defectively, without a *vav*, enabling it to be read *cheimah*, "anger." Ba'al HaTurim says that God became angry at the Israelites because the idolater Micah brought along his idol with him through the Red Sea.

Earlier, when the sea crossing is first described, *chomah* is spelled in full (verse 22). Why does Scripture wait until the present verse to indicate God's displeasure?

Iturei Torah cites a commentator who explains that the previous verse occurred in quite a different psychological context than the present one. Earlier the Israelites were deeply distressed and confused because the Egyptians were pursuing them. Finally, with no other recourse, they jumped into the sea. The Egyptians went in after them, and so the Israelites had no idea whether they would survive the ordeal. In such a situation, it was possible to forgive the fact that they had not destroyed their idols.

The present verse, however, occurred *after* the great miracle God had performed — drowning the Egyptians while the Israelites went safely through the very same body of water. The Israelites even broke into song. If, at this moment, they could allow an idol to remain with them, they warranted God's anger.

∎ ∎ ∎

וַיַּרְא יִשְׂרָאֵל אֶת־הַיָּד הַגְּדֹלָה אֲשֶׁר עָשָׂה ה' בְּמִצְרַיִם וַיִּירְאוּ הָעָם אֶת־ה' וַיַּאֲמִינוּ בַּה' וּבְמֹשֶׁה עַבְדּוֹ.

*The Israelites saw the great hand that God had unleashed against the Egyptians, and the people were in awe of God. They believed in God and in His servant Moses.* (14:31)

Because the Israelites "believed in God" and believed that Moses was "His servant," Moses was moved to sing God's praises (15:1). The belief in a *tzaddik* uplifts the *tzaddik* himself.
*(Deggel Machaneh Ephraim)*

■

The Israelites saw how even the lowliest among them achieved great spiritual heights: "A maidservant prophesied at the sea as even Ezekiel did not prophesy" (Midrash Mechilta). This caused them to "[believe] . . . in Moses" — to realize that a man could reach the level attained by Moses. *(Kedushath Levi)*

■ ■ ■

אָז יָשִׁיר־מֹשֶׁה וּבְנֵי יִשְׂרָאֵל אֶת־הַשִּׁירָה הַזֹּאת לַה' וַיֹּאמְרוּ לֵאמֹר אָשִׁירָה לַה' כִּי־גָאֹה גָּאָה סוּס וְרֹכְבוֹ רָמָה בַיָּם.

Moses and the Israelites then sang this song to God. It went: I will sing to God for He has triumphed over the proud, horse and rider He threw into the sea. (15:1)

"Moses and the Israelites then sang."

Rashi says: "When he saw the miracle, it occurred to him that he should sing." That is why Scripture uses the future tense, as *yashir*, "sang," actually means "he will sing."

R. Levi Yitzchak of Berdichev explains that when a person witnesses God's greatness he becomes filled with feelings of fear. He cannot experience joy at the same moment, for the fear precludes the emotion of joy. Nevertheless, after the fear passes, God's goodness will be heaped upon him — he will have joy. Since a person is aware that his feelings of fear will be followed by joy, he keeps this in mind during the time that the fear, caused by his witnessing of God's power, is upon him.

Joy may be expressed through song. It says here that the Israelites "feared God" (14:31). They could not sing while they were in the throes of fear, but they were aware of the joy that would follow.

R. Levi Yitzchak says that this is Rashi's intent here. At the

## Beshalach

moment he observed the miracle, Moses could not sing. But "it occurred to him" that he would sing in the future, after the fear had passed. This is why the verb is written in future tense.

■

Moses said: I now praise You in the same fashion that I sinned against You. I sinned against You with the word *az*, as it says, "From the moment *(me'az)* I came to Pharaoh . . . he made things worse for the people" (5:23). But You drowned him in the sea. Therefore, I will praise you with the word *az*: "Moses and the Israelites then *(az)* sang this song to God." And God, too, heals through the same instrument with which He smites (Midrash).

The explanation is as follows: Moses certainly had no doubt that God would fulfill His promise to redeem the Israelites. However, he was unaware that God heals with the same instrument through which He smites — that the ultimate purpose of affliction is for the good. This is why Moses asked God, after Pharaoh had increased the Israelites' oppression when Moses first confronted the king, "O Lord, why do You mistreat this people?" (5:22). Moses did not realize that within this bad turn lay the redemption. In truth, the additional oppression served to hasten the redemption. God heals through the instrument with which He smites, and so God responded to Moses: "Now you will see what I will do to Pharaoh. He will be forced to let them go, and he will be forced to drive them out of his land" (6:1). "*Now* you will see"; the redemption was connected with "now," with the current development — the increased oppression.

At the splitting of the Red Sea, the final defeat of the Egyptians, Moses recognized this attribute of God, and in alluding to the *az* of his earlier complaint, conceded that he had sinned in not understanding that God uses bad to produce good.

*(Cited by Iturei Torah)*

■

*Az* means "then." Then, when Moses saw the miracle of the Egyptians drowning, it occurred to him to sing (Rashi).

What is the importance of Moses *seeing* the miracle?

## The Eternal Heritage

We find that when God overturned Sodom the angel who rescued Lot told him, "Do not look behind you" (Genesis 19:17). Rashi explains that Lot had sinned along with the Sodomites, and was being spared only due to Abraham's merit. Lot was therefore not worthy of seeing the destruction of Sodom.

This helps us understand King David's words "God is my help, and I will see [the punishment of] my enemies" (Psalms 118:7). David pleaded with God that the miracle which would result in the fall of his enemies be performed in his merit. If that were the case, then David would be permitted to see their fall. R. Mordechai Banet connects this with another statement by David: "I will sing to God because He dealt kindly with me" (Ibid., 13:6). One sings to God when he realizes that he has been rewarded in his own merit — the emphasis being on the word *alai*, "with me."

Moses and the Israelites were permitted to see the downfall of the Egyptians. Because of this, Moses understood that it was the Israelites' own merit that had rescued them — not as with Lot, who actually deserved to die in Sodom. Therefore, it occurred to Moses that he should sing.

*(Korban HeAni)*

■

"It occurred to him to sing" (Rashi).

What does Rashi intend to say? Every action, after all, must be thought about before it is undertaken; by human nature it is impossible to do something without first bringing it to mind.

The explanation is that, while this is true, the degree of intent and desire is what defines the quality of the performance of a mitzvah. In reality, there was absolutely no accomplishment by the Israelites in singing. The song was sung due to Divine Inspiration; the Divine Presence spoke from their throats. They had nothing to do with the actual act of singing. However, the fact that they were chosen as the instrument by which the Divine Presence spoke indicates that they had such a desire to praise God that they ascended to the level of prophecy, thereby allowing the Divine Presence to speak through them. The fact that it occurred to the Israelites to sing — that they

## Beshalach

had such a strong desire — was thus the principle deed that they performed, and is worthy of mention.

*(Shem MiShmuel)*

■

"He has triumphed over the proud" contains a repetition of the word "proud" — *ga'oh ga'ah*.

Maharsha explains that the Egyptians are termed "arrogant," proud, by Scripture (Isaiah 30:7). Horses also have this characteristic. The Talmud (Pesachim 113b) mentions six characteristics of horses, among which are a love of war and a haughty spirit. Thus, when an Egyptian rides a horse there is a double manifestation of haughtiness, one atop the other. The Egyptians were prideful, saying, "I will give chase, I will overtake, I will divide the spoils" (verse 9), and their horses, lovers of battle, were also haughty.

This is the reason for the term *ga'oh ga'ah*, which is followed by "horse and rider He threw into the sea"— God conquered both proud creatures.

■ ■ ■

עָזִּי וְזִמְרָת יָהּ וַיְהִי־לִי לִישׁוּעָה זֶה אֵלִי וְאַנְוֵהוּ אֱלֹהֵי אָבִי וַאֲרֹמְמֶנְהוּ.
*My strength and song is the Lord, and this is my deliverance; This is my God and I will glorify Him, my father's God and I will exalt Him.* (15:2)

"This is my God and I will glorify Him." This means that one should glorify God in the mitzvos, by having a beautiful *sukkah*, a beautiful *lulav*, a beautiful *shofar* . . . Abba Shaul says, "I will glorify Him" means that one should seek to imitate Him. Just as He is gracious and merciful, so should you be gracious and merciful (Shabbath 133b).

There are some Jews — God-fearing, to be sure — who are very particular in their observance of ritual, and spare no expense to purchase a beautiful *sukkah*, *lulav*, and *ethrog*. However, when it comes to commandments such as charity and good deeds, they become very stingy.

Abba Shaul intends to say that, while it is important to have beautiful ritual objects, that is not enough. One's primary obligation is to be gracious and merciful, just as God is gracious and merciful.

*(Pinoth HaBayith)*

*Ve'anvehu*, "I will glorify Him," may be taken to connote a *naveh*, a habitat. R. Shimshon Raphael Hirsch explains that Moses said: "I will make my own body a home for the Divine Presence, by cleansing myself spiritually so that my body will merit the manifestation of the Divine Presence."

ה׳ אִישׁ מִלְחָמָה ה׳ שְׁמוֹ.
*God is the master of war. God is His name.* (15:3)

*Hashem*, "God," is the name of God denoting His attribute of mercy. The phrase "God is the master of war" seems therefore to contain an internal contradiction: How can the merciful aspect, "God," wage war?

Ohr HaChayyim says that in this particular case even the attribute of mercy waged war. Nonetheless, it did not lose its essence, its merciful nature; the Torah adds that "God is His name," that this case was an exception to the rule. "God" would, in the future, continue to be "His name"; He would retain His attribute of mercy.

Rashi does not comment on the contradiction of "God is the master of war." However, regarding "God is His name," Rashi says that, even when waging war, the Lord, through His merciful aspect, continues to provide sustenance for the world, unlike flesh-and-blood kings, who are unable to attend to other matters when they are involved in a war.

Sforno asserts that a war conducted by God is itself an act of mercy. By killing those who are evil and by their actions destroy the world, God strengthens the world and gives it reinforcement, which is a merciful gesture.

## Beshalach

The verse literally reads, "God is a man of war." Rashi writes that *ish*, "man," is to be translated as *ba'al*, "master." Iturei Torah quotes R. Raphael Gold, who explains that God rises above the usual, cruel ways of war. Even when doing battle, God maintains His attribute of mercy. He fights in a merciful fashion; He masters — controls — the excesses native to war.

■ ■ ■

יְמִינְךָ ה' נֶאְדָּרִי בַּכֹּחַ יְמִינְךָ ה' תִּרְעַץ אוֹיֵב.
*Your right hand, O God, is glorious in power; Your right hand, O God, crushes the enemy.* (15:6)

"Your right hand, O God, is glorious in power." Bina LaIttim explains that, for a human being, the potential to do an act and the actual doing of the act are separate. The fulfillment constitutes an improvement over the potential.

This is not the case with God. For Him, the potential to do something and the actualization of that potential are one and the same.

■ ■ ■

אָמַר אוֹיֵב אֶרְדֹּף אַשִּׂיג אֲחַלֵּק שָׁלָל תִּמְלָאֵמוֹ נַפְשִׁי אָרִיק חַרְבִּי תּוֹרִישֵׁמוֹ יָדִי.
*The enemy said, "I will give chase, I will overtake, I will divide the spoils. I will satisfy myself against them; I will draw my sword; my hand will demolish them."* (15:9)

R. Yehoshua Leib Diskin points out that the words of this verse are seemingly out of order. Generally one first draws a sword — fights the enemy — and then divides the spoils.

In answer, R. Yehoshua Leib says that Pharaoh, the author of this declaration, had Moses' words in mind. Moses had told him, "We will go with our young and old alike. We will go with our sons and daughters, and with our sheep and cattle" (10:9). Evidently the cattle were to bring up the rear of the Israelite camp. Upon catching

## The Eternal Heritage

up to the Israelites, the Egyptians would first reach the cattle — the spoils — and only later the people.

■ ■ ■

נָטִיתָ יְמִינְךָ תִּבְלָעֵמוֹ אָרֶץ.
*You put forth Your right hand; the earth swallowed them. (15:12)*

"The earth swallowed them" — We learn from this that the Egyptians merited being buried upon their death; this was a reward for their saying (9:27), "God is the just one" (Rashi).

The Midrash says (Esther Rabbah 3): The Egyptians, upon going down in the Red Sea, were naked; as it says, "At the blast of Your nostrils the waters piled up, *ne'ermu*." The word *ne'ermu* has the same root as the word *arum*, "naked," and so the Midrash derives that the Egyptians were buried without clothing.

This is in agreement with another statement by the Midrash (Bereshith Rabbah 36). The Midrash relates that God said to Yefeth, "You covered the nakedness of your father. By your life, I will repay you"; as it says, "On that day I will give Gog a burial place in Israel" (Ezekiel 39:11). Gog, Yefeth's descendant, would merit burial because Yefeth had covered Noah's nakedness after the latter had been assaulted by Ham. However, God told Ham: "You revealed the nakedness of your father. By your life, I will repay you"; as it says, "Likewise will the king of Assyria lead the captives of Egypt and the exiles of Cush, old and young, naked . . ." (Isaiah 20:4).

Similarly, we can say that the Egyptians, being descended from Ham, were buried without clothing at the Red Sea. However, when Sennacherib and his troops, who descended from Shem, attacked Jerusalem and were killed by God, they were left with their clothing on, because Shem covered his father together with Yefeth. Thus we find in Shemoth Rabbah 18: Why did He leave them their clothing? Because they were descendants of Shem, and God said He was indebted to their father, who along with Yefeth had covered the nakedness of Noah.

*(Imrei Shammai)*

■ ■ ■

## Beshalach

נָחִיתָ בְחַסְדְּךָ עַם־זוּ גָּאָלְתָּ נֵהַלְתָּ בְעָזְּךָ אֶל־נְוֵה קָדְשֶׁךָ.
With kindness You led this nation which You redeemed, with might You led [them] to Your holy habitat. (15:13)

*Nehalta*, "You led," is a term denoting leading. While Onkelos translates it to mean "carry" and "bear," he was not careful to translate it according to the precise Hebrew meaning (Rashi).

We can defend the translation of Onkelos by saying that the two definitions — leading and bearing — are connected. Every leader has to be able to bear burdens.

*(R. Avraham Mordechai of Gur, cited by Iturei Torah)*

■ ■ ■

תִּפֹּל עֲלֵיהֶם אֵימָתָה וָפַחַד בִּגְדֹל זְרוֹעֲךָ יִדְּמוּ כָּאָבֶן עַד־יַעֲבֹר עַמְּךָ ה' עַד־יַעֲבֹר עַם־זוּ קָנִיתָ.
Fear and dread will fall upon them, at the greatness of Your arm they will be as silent as stone, until Your people will cross, O God, until the people You acquired will cross over. (15:16)

Chatham Sofer explains this and the subsequent verses as follows:
The Sages say that God told King David, "You will not build the house in My name" (Kings I, 8:19), because David had killed many people in the wars he fought and had too much blood on his hands. If not for this, he would have merited building the Temple. It was the same with the Israelites. Had they merited capturing the Land of Canaan without having to resort to the use of weapons, they would also have merited the immediate building of the Temple and the final redemption. With this, God would have "reign[ed] forever and ever" (verse 18).

However, the Israelites were not at this spiritual level. Therefore, Moses prayed that "Fear and dread" would befall the inhabitants of Canaan, causing them either to make peace with the Israelites or to flee the land. The Israelites could then take over Canaan peacefully. Not having needed to engage in war, they would then merit the immediate building of the Temple, and so Moses continued (verse 17), "Bring them in and plant them on the mount of Your

## The Eternal Heritage

inheritance . . . The Temple Your hands have founded." Finally, "God will reign forever and ever" — the final redemption would be ushered in.

■ ■ ■

ה' יִמְלֹךְ לְעֹלָם וָעֶד.
כִּי בָא סוּס פַּרְעֹה בְּרִכְבּוֹ וּבְפָרָשָׁיו בַּיָּם וַיָּשֶׁב ה' עֲלֵהֶם אֶת־מֵי הַיָּם וּבְנֵי יִשְׂרָאֵל הָלְכוּ בַיַּבָּשָׁה בְּתוֹךְ הַיָּם.

*God will reign forever and ever.*
*For when Pharaoh's horse came into the sea, along with his chariot corps and cavalry, God made the sea come back on them, while the Israelites went on dry land through the sea bed. (15:18, 19)*

Ohr HaChayyim asks why the Torah says that "God *will reign* forever and ever" rather than saying that "God *reigned* forever and ever." The inference is that the miracle at the sea did not cause recognition of God as King throughout the world; that would come only in the future.

Ohr HaChayyim proposes two answers. The first is rooted in the continuity of the verses: "God will reign forever and ever. For when Pharaoh's horse came into the sea . . . God made the sea come back on them." The battle at the Red Sea was against Pharaoh only; it was not a triumph over all the false gods worshiped by the nations. Therefore, it did not establish God's preeminence among them. In the future, however, God will exact justice from all the nations. Thus, God "*will reign* forever" — His position as King was not recognized by all at this juncture; it will be recognized only in the future.

The second answer is also based on the continuity of the verses. The Torah relates that "Pharaoh's horse (singular) came into the sea." All the Egyptian horses drowned, as if they were one horse — the destruction was total. And so it was with the Egyptians themselves — "not a single one remained" (14:28). Had any Egyptians remained alive, they could have described the awesomeness of the miracle they had witnessed. That would have brought recognition of God among the nations. But the only

## Beshalach

survivors were Israelites, and, whereas this was their God, the nations would not heed their message, since their testimony was biased. Hence, God was not accepted throughout the world, and it could not be said that "God reigned forever and ever," because all the Egyptians perished and there was no one else to tell of the miracles.

■

There is a dispute concerning the status of the verse "For when Pharaoh's horse came . . ." Rashi (Gittin 90a) appears to hold that the verse is not part of the song sung by the Israelites. Rashi reads the verse not with the preceding verses — the song — but with the following verse: "Because Pharaoh's horse came into the sea" and drowned, "Miriam the prophetess, Aaron's sister, took the drum" and led the women in song. It would seem from Rashi that the Israelites did not sing the words of the present verse.

While Rashi does not explicitly say that the song ends with the preceding verse, Ramban does say so. He opines that the present verse is actually a continuation of the preface to the song (in verse 1): "Moses and the Israelites then sang . . . Because Pharaoh's horse came into the sea" and drowned. The present verse supplies the reason that they sang. Alternatively, "Moses and the Israelites then sang . . . *When* Pharaoh's horse came into the sea . . . while the Israelites went on dry land through the sea bed" — that is, they sang while still walking through the sea.

Ibn Ezra contends that the verse *is* part and parcel of the song. The Israelites were praising the fact that the sea came back down upon the Egyptians while there were still Israelites walking through the sea bed. As the verse concludes: "God made the sea come back on them while the Israelites were going on the dry land through the sea bed."

It would appear that this dispute is reflected in a debate regarding the morning prayer service. This song — *Az Yashir* — is said as part of *shacharith*. Mishnah Berurah makes note of a debate between R. Yitzchak Luria — Arizal — and Vilna Gaon regarding the inclusion of the present verse. Arizal maintains that "For when Pharoah's

## The Eternal Heritage

horse came . . ." is to be recited, because it is part of the song. Vilna Gaon holds that the verse is not included in the prayer service, presumably because it is not part of the song.

∎ ∎ ∎

וַיֹּאמֶר אִם־שָׁמוֹעַ תִּשְׁמַע לְקוֹל ה' אֱלֹהֶיךָ וְהַיָּשָׁר בְּעֵינָיו תַּעֲשֶׂה וְהַאֲזַנְתָּ לְמִצְוֹתָיו וְשָׁמַרְתָּ כָּל־חֻקָּיו כָּל־הַמַּחֲלָה אֲשֶׁר־שַׂמְתִּי בְמִצְרַיִם לֹא־אָשִׂים עָלֶיךָ כִּי אֲנִי ה' רֹפְאֶךָ.

[God] said, "If you obey the voice of God your Lord and do what is right in His eyes — heeding all His commandments and observing all His decrees — then I will not strike you with any of the sicknesses that I brought on Egypt, for I am the God who heals you." (15:26)

What connection does the promise that the Israelites would be spared the diseases that struck the Egyptians have to do with the context in which it was made? The Israelites were concerned here, at Marah, about the lack of water, not about disease. How does the promise about diseases fit in?

The Talmudic Sage Rabbah (Pesachim 46b) declares that, although it is forbidden to cook food on a holiday for consumption after the holiday, one does not suffer the punishment of lashes, *malkuth*, for such an infraction. Since it is possible that unexpected guests may arrive, and that those guests would be given this food, there is not an absolute certainty that the food will not be consumed during the holiday itself.

Tosafoth asks that the same principle should be applied to the Sabbath. While one may not cook on the Sabbath, this rule is suspended if a critically ill person needs food. Since there is always the possibility that someone may become very ill, why is a person who cooks on the Sabbath punished? Tosafoth answers that the likelihood of someone becoming very ill is slim. It is not to be equated with the possibility of unexpected guests arriving on a holiday, and so no comparison between the two cases may be made.

The Rabbis say that the Israelites were told the laws of the Sabbath at Marah (Sanhedrin 56b). We may propose that the Rabbis were bothered by the same question that troubled Tosafoth: How

## Beshalach

do we ever apply the prohibitions of the Sabbath, since they are suspended if a sick person comes into the picture? To this the Torah responds, "I will not strike you with any of the sicknesses that I brought on Egypt" — sickness will be rare, and so the Sabbath laws will remain intact.

This is how the topic of disease relates to this section.

*(Cited by Iturei Torah)*

∎

One of the adherents of R. Mordechai of Neskhiz came to tell him that he was very ill and to ask for advice regarding a cure. R. Mordechai told him to travel to the professor of Annopol.

When the disciple arrived in Annopol and asked to see the professor, the town's citizens laughed at him. "A professor in Annopol? This is such a small town that we do not even have a doctor here," they said.

"What do you do when you become sick?" he asked.

"Our sole option is to pray to our Father in heaven," they replied.

The chassid was very upset, and returned to his rebbe to express his disappointment at his failure in Annopol. He pointed out that Annopol had no doctor, let alone a professor.

"Did you ask the Jews there what they do when they take sick?" inquired R. Mordechai.

"Certainly. They told me that they have no alternative but to trust in God."

"Fool!" exclaimed the rebbe. "That is the professor to whom I sent you — the 'God who heals you.'"

*(MiGinzei HaChassiduth)*

∎

Rambam was the physician of the court of Vizier Al-Fadil of Egypt. As long as Al-Fadil was in Rambam's charge, the vizier never became sick.

Once the vizier told Rambam that he did not know whether or not Rambam was a competent physician. Since Al-Fadil had never taken ill, Rambam's abilities had not been tested. If the vizier were to become sick, would Rambam know how to treat him?

Rambam replied that God is the greatest doctor of all. As the Torah says, "I am the God who heals you." The proof that God is the greatest healer is that "I will not strike you with any of the sicknesses that I brought on Egypt." The best doctor is not the one who is capable of healing his patients, but the one who does not permit them to become sick in the first place.

This principle is expressed by Rambam in his "Letter Regarding a Human Being's Conduct." He writes: "Most diseases that befall a man occur due to his own fault, in that he does not know how to care for himself when he is healthy. He is like a blind man, who, due to his lack of sight, constantly stumbles, injuring himself and injuring his fellow men as well." *(MeOtzareinu HaYashan)*

■ ■ ■

וַיִּלֹּינוּ כָּל־עֲדַת בְּנֵי־יִשְׂרָאֵל עַל־מֹשֶׁה וְעַל־אַהֲרֹן בַּמִּדְבָּר.
*There, in the desert, the entire Israelite community began to murmur against Moses and Aaron. (16:2)*

R. Naftali Zvi Ropshitser said: One is never able to satisfy all the Jews, and this is the meaning of the words "They were jealous of Moses in the camp, of Aaron, God's holy one" (Psalms 106:16).

Moses and Aaron had different characteristics. Moses was a loner. As Scripture testifies: "Moses would take his tent and set it up outside the camp, at a distance from the camp" (33:7). By contrast, Aaron was very much involved with his fellow human beings, "a lover of peace and a pursuer of peace" (Avoth 1:12). He lived among the people and was concerned with all their problems.

The Israelites had complaints against both of them. Regarding Moses, "They were jealous of Moses in the camp" — they asserted that he isolated himself from them and was not "in the camp," with the people. They found Aaron's manner problematic too. They said he should act as "Aaron, God's holy one." He was too holy a man to be so involved with the nation; he had to keep a certain distance from the common folk. *(MeOtzareinu HaYashan)*

■ ■ ■

## Beshalach

וַיֹּאמֶר ה' אֶל־מֹשֶׁה הִנְנִי מַמְטִיר לָכֶם לֶחֶם מִן־הַשָּׁמָיִם וְיָצָא הָעָם וְלָקְטוּ דְּבַר־יוֹם בְּיוֹמוֹ לְמַעַן אֲנַסֶּנּוּ הֲיֵלֵךְ בְּתוֹרָתִי אִם־לֹא.

*God said to Moses, "I will make bread rain down to you from the sky. The people are to go out and gather enough for each day. In that way I will test them to see whether or not they will keep My law. . . ." (16:4)*

R. Shimon b. Yochai said: From here we learn that only those who ate of the manna are permitted to interpret the Torah (Midrash).

Once, when there was a shortage of meat, R. Yosef Shaul Nathanson permitted some of the kosher meat markets in Lvov to use the hind quarters of slaughtered animals. R. Chaim of Sanz wrote to him that he was abandoning a custom that had endured for many generations. [The hind quarters contain a large amount of *chelev*, forbidden fat, and since it is difficult to remove all of it, the use of these parts is avoided.] R. Yosef Shaul responded with a lengthy letter asserting that the use of the hind quarters was permitted, and certainly in a time of shortage.

R. Chaim retorted that he now understood R. Shimon b. Yochai's statement that only those who partook of the manna had the right to interpret the Torah. If a lenient ruling emanates from a situation involving a lack of food, there is the danger that the ruling will be applied in normal times as well. Therefore, the Torah is open to exposition only by those who lacked for nothing — those who partook of the manna, which was entirely satisfying. Only they could interpret the Torah with absolute objectivity, without prejudice. *(Cited by Iturei Torah)*

∎

"In that way I will test them to see whether or not they will keep My law." Rashi says that the "law" to which God was referring concerned the laws of the manna — that the Israelites would not leave manna over, and that they would not gather it on the Sabbath.

Kli Yekar explains that both of these were tests of the Israelites' trust in God. Someone who has food but worries that he will not have food the next day lacks trust in God. By complying with the law and not leaving one day's manna for the next, the Israelites would demonstrate their trust in God.

## The Eternal Heritage

The same went for the Sabbath. By not going to collect on that day, the Israelites would show that they believed Friday's manna would suffice for two days.

The verse says, "In that way I will test them to see whether or not they will keep My law, *Torathi*." Kli Yekar adds that only if the Israelites trusted God to provide for them could they "keep My Torah." A person who constantly worries about finances does not find the time to be involved in Torah study. Only someone who has faith that he will be provided for by God finds the time to immerse himself in the Torah.

■ ■ ■

וְהָיָה בַּיּוֹם הַשִּׁשִּׁי וְהֵכִינוּ אֵת אֲשֶׁר־יָבִיאוּ וְהָיָה מִשְׁנֶה עַל אֲשֶׁר־יִלְקְטוּ יוֹם יוֹם.

" . . . On the sixth day, when they prepare what they have brought in, it will be double what they gather every other day." (16:5)

The verse literally reads: "It will come to pass *(Vehaya)* on the sixth day." The term *vehaya* is generally understood to denote happiness (see VaYikra Rabbah 11).

R. Yitzchak Meir of Gur says that the happiness which one experiences on Friday in anticipation of the Sabbath's arrival is itself part of the preparation for the Sabbath — "*Vehaya*, there is happiness, on the sixth day, when they prepare."

*(Ma'ayanah shel Torah)*

■

"On the sixth day" — R. Bachya says that this day qualified as the "sixth day" on two counts. Firstly, it was Friday; secondly, it was the sixth day that the manna had fallen. Hence, the manna began falling on Sunday.

This can be easily calculated. The Torah tells us that the Israelites complained about the lack of food on the fifteenth of the second month, Iyar (verse 1). Now, the Israelites left Egypt on Thursday, the fifteenth of Nissan, the first month (Shabbath 87b). Nissan has thirty days, and so the first of Iyar fell on a Sabbath. Thus, the

*Beshalach*

fifteenth of Iyar also fell on a Sabbath, and that was the day when the Israelites complained to Moses. The manna fell the next morning (verse 7) — Sunday.

There is an opinion recorded in the Talmud that the Israelites left Egypt on Friday, and that the first day of Iyar was a Sunday. If this calculation is used, then the sixteenth of Iyar, the first day when the manna fell, was a Monday. According to this view, the "sixth day" of the present verse refers to the fact that this day was Friday. It was not, however, also the sixth day of manna, but rather the fifth day.

According to the first, commonly accepted, calculation, we can understand why Moses promised that the Israelites would have quail in the "evening," rather than immediately (verse 6). This being the Sabbath, God would not have brought the quail until the Sabbath was over.

■ ■ ■

וּבֹקֶר וּרְאִיתֶם אֶת־כְּבוֹד ה' בְּשָׁמְעוֹ אֶת־תְּלֻנֹּתֵיכֶם עַל־ה' וְנַחְנוּ מָה כִּי תַלִּונוּ עָלֵינוּ.

"... *And in the morning you will see God's glory. He has heard your complaints, which are against God. After all, what are we that you should complain against us?"* (16:7)

Rav said, and some say it was R. Yochanan: Greater is that which was said in the case of Moses and Aaron than that which was said regarding Abraham. In Abraham's case it says, "I am mere dust and ashes" (Genesis 18:27), while Moses and Aaron said: "what are we?" (Chullin 89a). In other words, Abraham felt that he had a little worth, that of dust, while Moses and Aaron believed they had no worth at all.

One Yom Kippur, R. Yonathan Eybeschuetz heard a Jew reciting the liturgy: "I am dust while yet alive, and certainly so after I die," with a broken heart. Minutes later came the time for the Torah-reading, and the same man quarreled with the sexton, insisting he had the right to be called to the Torah. The man taunted the sexton, saying, "Are you aware of who I am as compared to you?"

R. Yonathan approached the man and reprimanded him: "Didn't

you say a few moments ago that you are to be compared to dust?" The man responded that yes, he was indeed dust when compared to God. However, he was now comparing himself with the sexton, and he was at a higher level than the sexton.

This is the essence of the Talmud's statement. Abraham was speaking to God when he termed himself "dust." Abraham saw himself as lowly, but nevertheless felt that he had some standing, even when compared to God. Moses and Aaron, who said "what are we?" — they did not even see themselves as dirt — were speaking to the murmuring Israelites. Even compared to these individuals, Moses and Aaron considered themselves worthless.

*(R. Meir Shapira of Lublin)*

■

"After all, what are we that you should complain against us?"

According to Rashi and Ramban, Moses and Aaron asserted that they were entirely unimportant and insignificant. Therefore, there was no useful purpose served by complaining against them.

However, Ibn Ezra explains that Moses and Aaron were defending their actions. They said: What can we do? We only acted in accordance with God's instructions to us.

■■■

שָׁמַעְתִּי אֶת־תְּלוּנֹת בְּנֵי יִשְׂרָאֵל דַּבֵּר אֲלֵהֶם לֵאמֹר בֵּין הָעַרְבַּיִם תֹּאכְלוּ בָשָׂר וּבַבֹּקֶר תִּשְׂבְּעוּ־לָחֶם וִידַעְתֶּם כִּי אֲנִי ה' אֱלֹהֵיכֶם.

*"I have heard the murmurings of the Israelites. Speak to them and say: In the afternoon you will eat meat, and in the morning you will have your fill of bread. You will then know that I am God your Lord." (16:12)*

"In the afternoon you will eat meat" — Ramban records the Rabbis' statement that, just as the Jews had manna through the rest of their stay in the wilderness, they also had quail the entire time. If God had only provided the meat for one day, that would not have been a great blessing; it must be that the quail was provided throughout their journey. As for why the Torah does not discuss the quail at length, while it does so with the manna, this is because the

## Beshalach

falling of the manna was a supernatural event, while the quail came in a natural fashion.

A question remains: If the Israelites had meat the entire time that they were in the desert, what was their complaint later, at Kivroth HaTa'avah, when the Mixed Multitude said, "Who is going to give us meat to eat?" (Numbers 11:4). Ramban answers that perhaps only the older folk gathered the quail, or perhaps God arranged that only the righteous people obtained quail. While in reference to the manna the Torah writes that everyone gathered, no such declaration is made regarding the quail. At Kivroth HaTa'avah, those who were unable to gather quail complained that they had no meat.

Chatham Sofer takes issue with Ramban, arguing that there was quail only on this particular night, in order to satisfy the Israelites' hunger. Once the manna began to fall — the next morning — there was no longer a need for meat. This was because, as the Sages teach, the Israelites tasted in the manna whatever food they desired. For those who craved quail, it had the taste of quail, and so actual quail was not needed.

What, then, was the complaint at Kivroth HaTa'avah? Chatham Sofer points out that the Mixed Multitude said they had "nothing but the manna before our eyes" (Ibid., verse 6). While the manna tasted like all kinds of food, it did not change its appearance. It looked like manna even when it tasted like other foods. If someone cannot see the food he is eating, he is not satisfied (Yoma 74b). It was due to the lack of satiation, not the lack of the taste of meat, that the Mixed Multitude complained.

■ ■ ■

וַיִּרְאוּ בְנֵי־יִשְׂרָאֵל וַיֹּאמְרוּ אִישׁ אֶל־אָחִיו מָן הוּא כִּי לֹא יָדְעוּ מַה־הוּא וַיֹּאמֶר מֹשֶׁה אֲלֵהֶם הוּא הַלֶּחֶם אֲשֶׁר נָתַן ה' לָכֶם לְאָכְלָה.

*The Israelites looked at it, and asked one another, "What is it?" for they did not know what it was. Moses said to them, "This is the bread that God has given you to eat. . . ." (16:15)*

*Man hu*, "What is it?" — Rashi translates the word *man* as "a preparation of food." Rashi points to Daniel (1:5), where the word is also used: "The king prepared *(Vayeman)* for them a daily portion of the king's food." Rashi continues that since the Israelites "did not know what it was," they were unable to call the manna by a specific name, and so had to use the general term *man,* "a preparation of food."

Chizkuni says that *man* is the Egyptian-language equivalent of *mah,* "what," and that the Israelites were asking one another, "What is it?" Chizkuni sees *man hu* as a question, while Rashi sees it as a statement.

Rashbam assumes that *man hu* is a question — "What is it?" — and explains that there was a particular reason for the Torah to use Egyptian here. The Israelites were familiar with and used the Egyptian language. They named this new food *man,* in the Egyptian tongue. Its name was *man,* not *mah,* the Hebrew equivalent of *man.* Had Moses translated *man* to *mah,* readers of Scripture would not have understood why the manna was called *man,* as that is not a Hebrew word. Therefore, Moses left this particular word in its Egyptian form.

Rashbam points to other examples of the use of foreign languages in Scripture. Lavan named the mound over which he and Jacob concluded a covenant Yegar Sahadutha, while Jacob called it by the Hebrew equivalent, Galed (both mean "witness mound") (Genesis 31:47). Had Lavan's choice of name been translated into Hebrew, the Torah would have had to write that both Lavan and Jacob named the mound Galed. This would have defeated the point the Torah was trying to make — that Lavan used an Aramaic term and Jacob used a Hebrew term. Yegar Sahadutha could not be translated.

Rashbam's other example is in the Scroll of Esther (3:7), which states that Haman "conducted a lottery *(pur),* that was the lottery *(goral)."* The word *pur* is merely the Persian word for the Hebrew *goral,* and Scripture could have written, "conducted a lottery *(goral)."* However, had that been done, we would not then know the meaning of the word *Purim,* the holiday celebrated in commemoration of Haman's downfall. Since *Purim* is a Persian

## Beshalach

word, deriving from *pur,* the Scroll of Esther includes the information that *pur* is the Persian word for lottery.

■ ■ ■

זֶה הַדָּבָר אֲשֶׁר צִוָּה ה' לִקְטוּ מִמֶּנּוּ אִישׁ לְפִי אָכְלוֹ עֹמֶר לַגֻּלְגֹּלֶת מִסְפַּר נַפְשֹׁתֵיכֶם אִישׁ לַאֲשֶׁר בְּאָהֳלוֹ תִּקָּחוּ.

". . . *This is what God has commanded: Each man shall gather as much as he needs, which is an* omer *for each person; according to the number of people each man has in his tent you shall take."* (16:16)

Chatham Sofer points to an apparent contradiction in the text. On the one hand, it says that each man was to gather as much manna as he needed, as would satisfy him. On the other hand, a particular measure of manna was stipulated — an *omer.* Now, if an *omer* was enough to satisfy an adult, then how could an *omer* have been gathered for a child as well? A child consumes less than an adult, and if the same amount was gathered for him he would leave over food. More than the necessary amount would have been gathered, in violation of "Each man shall gather as much as he needs."

Chatham Sofer answers that different amounts were gathered for adults and children, but, nonetheless, an *omer* was taken for every person. He explains that the size of the *omer* differs according to the person for whom it is being measured. In this respect the *omer* resembles an *amah.* The *amah,* which is a unit of length, is the sum of six handbreadths, *tefachim.* Each handbreadth is four fingers wide. Every human being, regardless of his size, will have fingers in proportion to it. A child has very small fingers, leading to a small handbreadth and a small *amah.* An adult's fingers are wider, and their measurement results in a larger *amah.*

While the *omer* is a unit of volume, not length, Chatham Sofer points out that Rashbam (Pesachim 109b) says that measures of volume can also be calculated by finger size. Hence, the volume of the *omer* varies, depending on the size of the finger used to measure it. An *omer* of manna was gathered for each person, but the size of the *omer* correlated with the size of the person, and so there is no contradiction in the instructions to the Israelites. Larger people gathered a larger *omer* and smaller people gathered a smaller *omer*.

■ ■ ■

וַיֹּאמֶר אֲלֵהֶם הוּא אֲשֶׁר דִּבֶּר ה' שַׁבָּתוֹן שַׁבַּת־קֹדֶשׁ לַה' מָחָר אֵת אֲשֶׁר־תֹּאפוּ אֵפוּ וְאֵת אֲשֶׁר־תְּבַשְּׁלוּ בַּשֵּׁלוּ וְאֵת כָּל־הָעֹדֵף הַנִּיחוּ לָכֶם לְמִשְׁמֶרֶת עַד־הַבֹּקֶר.

*[Moses] said to them, "This is what God said: 'Tomorrow is a day of rest, the holy Sabbath, to God.' Bake what you want to bake and cook what you want to cook. As for what is left over, put it aside for yourselves carefully until morning." (16:23)*

"Bake what you want to bake and cook what you want to cook" — Rashi explains that the Israelites were to bake and cook the manna on Friday, so that they would have two days' food.

Ramban points out that, according to Rashi, the instruction to the Israelites was that they bake and cook for the Sabbath on Friday if they desired to eat baked and cooked manna on the Sabbath. Ramban notes, however, that Ibn Ezra disagrees with Rashi. On Friday, each Israelite collected two measures for every member of his household. Ibn Ezra says that the Israelites were to bake and cook one measure — Friday's food. They were not to cook the remaining measure — Saturday's food. Scripture says, "As for what is left over, put it aside . . . until morning." The extra measure was to be left until Sabbath morning. At that time, Moses told the Israelites to eat it (verse 25). Ramban adds that it turns out, according to Ibn Ezra, that the manna was eaten raw on the Sabbath, when cooking is forbidden.

While the latter point would certainly be the case after the Torah was given, the Torah had not yet been given at this juncture. This being the case, it is hard to understand why Ramban believes the Israelites were forbidden to cook the manna on the Sabbath.

Furthermore, Rashi says that the Israelites were instructed at Marah regarding the laws of the Sabbath (15:25). The Israelites were at Marah shortly before moving on to Elim, where they were given the manna. If one were to assume that the Israelites had the status of Jews even before they received the Torah, as Ramban does (Leviticus 24:10), then it might be conjectured that they were obligated to keep the laws of the Sabbath after Marah.

This would explain Ramban's assumption that the Israelites were not permitted to cook the manna on the Sabbath. However, Ibn Ezra does not say that the Israelites were commanded regarding the Sabbath at Marah, and so it is difficult to attribute this view to him.

In addition, Rashi, in explaining what transpired at Marah, says, "In Marah [God] gave them a few sections of the Torah, so that they could involve themselves *(sheyithasku)* in them: the Sabbath, the Red Heifer, and the monetary laws." Rashi does not say that the Israelites were henceforth to keep these laws. He says only that they were to become involved with them. *Sheyithasku* would seem to denote a discussion of the laws, not the actual practice of them.

This is further evident from the fact that the Red Heifer *(Parah Adumah)* is included, although the Israelites did not institute the Red Heifer ritual until they reached Mount Sinai. There is no reason to think that the laws of the Sabbath were any different.

∎

Rashi says here that the Israelites were to cook on Friday so that they would have enough manna for two days.

This seems to contradict a gloss by Rashi in Numbers 11:8. There, commenting on the Torah's statement that the Israelites used to grind, crush, or cook the manna, Rashi comments: The manna did not go into a mill or a pot or a mortar. Rather, its taste changed to the taste of ground, crushed, and cooked foods.

According to Rashi in Numbers, the Israelites did not physically do anything to prepare the manna. Its flavor changed miraculously, in compliance with the Israelites' wishes.

∎ ∎ ∎

רְאוּ כִּי־ה׳ נָתַן לָכֶם הַשַּׁבָּת עַל־כֵּן הוּא נֹתֵן לָכֶם בַּיּוֹם הַשִּׁשִּׁי לֶחֶם יוֹמָיִם שְׁבוּ אִישׁ תַּחְתָּיו אַל־יֵצֵא אִישׁ מִמְּקֹמוֹ בַּיּוֹם הַשְּׁבִיעִי.

". . . *You must realize that God has given you the Sabbath. That is why He gives you food for two days on Friday. Every man must remain in his place [on the*

## The Eternal Heritage

Sabbath]; *one may not leave his home on the Sabbath." (16:29)*

"You must realize that God has given you the Sabbath."

Rabbi David Shlomo Eibenschutz of Soroki gives the following parable:

A certain queen always spent her time in the palace. Once she decided to tour her country, but could think of nobody who was important enough to deserve to escort her. Finally she remembered that an old friend lived in a particular city. The queen was certain that this friend would be honored to escort her.

The queen arrived in her friend's city. Not knowing where her friend lived, she traveled about, looking for a place where she could stay, but found nothing. By chance she met her friend, who took the queen to her home. The friend gave the queen a beautiful suite, and extended many courtesies to her.

At that moment the queen remembered how she had been unable to find anyone else in the town who would take her in. She became very angry, and vowed to tell the king, so that he would punish the city.

In the morning, as the queen was preparing to leave, the head of the house suddenly became angry at her. He began throwing her belongings into the street and shouted, "Hurry and clear my rooms, as I have no space for you."

She became very upset, and pleaded with him: "Please have pity on me and do not embarrass me before the entire town."

But the man was unmoved, and became even angrier. He ordered all the queen's belongings thrown into the street. In return, the queen was furious at the man — so furious that she forgot she had been angry at the rest of the town. She fled from the house as quickly as she could.

The Sabbath queen was given to the Jews as a fine present from God. First the Sabbath approached the other nations, hoping to be taken in, accepted by them, but they refused to take her. Israel was the only nation willing to accept the Sabbath. All during the Sabbath day the Jews are very careful regarding her laws, and honor her greatly by Torah study, and with food and drink fit for a queen.

And yet, astonishingly, in the Sabbath's final minutes, shortly

## Beshalach

before she is to leave, we hasten to throw her out and quickly usher in the weekdays. We do not take the time to make sure the Sabbath leaves us with the honor she deserves and in the manner that we brought her in.

It is no wonder that the Sabbath queen becomes angry at us due to this.

■ ■ ■

וַיִּקְרָא שֵׁם הַמָּקוֹם מַסָּה וּמְרִיבָה עַל־רִיב בְּנֵי יִשְׂרָאֵל וְעַל נַסֹּתָם אֶת־ה׳ לֵאמֹר הֲיֵשׁ ה׳ בְּקִרְבֵּנוּ אִם־אָיִן.

[Moses] named the place Massah U'Merivah, because of the strife (riv) of the Israelites, and because they had tested (nasotham) God, saying, "Is God with us or not?" (17:7)

When a person is suffering, he seeks methods by which to alleviate his pain. He asks doctors for advice and takes all sorts of medicines. In doing all this, he forgets the critical point: that the affliction has been brought upon him by God because he did not properly keep the Torah and its commandments. Instead of seeking advice about how to avoid the pain, he should be seeking ways to come closer to God. If he is able to do that, the ailment will go away by itself.

The commentators ask: Why is the portion of Amalek placed right after the words "Is God with us or not?" when there seemingly is no connection. According to the above, this problem is resolved. The Israelites had tested God, asking if He was in their midst. Amalek's coming was meant as a lesson that the enemy attacks when the Israelites have a lack of trust in God. If they trusted Him, there would be no attack of Amalek.

*(Ba'al Shem Tov)*

■ ■ ■

וַיָּבֹא עֲמָלֵק וַיִּלָּחֶם עִם־יִשְׂרָאֵל בִּרְפִידִם.

Amalek came and attacked Israel in Rephidim. (17:8)

Da'ath Zekenim MiBa'alei HaTosafoth wonders why the

Amalekites chose this moment to do battle with the Israelites. Wouldn't it have been to the Amalekites' advantage to strike when the Israelites first came to Egypt? Whereas at that time the Israelite community numbered but seventy souls (Genesis 46:27), while it now consisted of millions, why did Amalek delay?

Da'ath Zekenim answers that Amalek did not wish to initiate a war with Israel until the latter had satisfied its obligation to wander for 400 years (Ibid., 15:13). When Abraham died, that obligation had devolved upon Isaac, and then upon Jacob and Esau and their descendants. While it was Jacob's side of the family that went into exile, the decree could just as well have fallen upon Esau's branch. The Amalekites descended from Esau (Ibid., 36:12), and they believed that, if they attacked the Israelites before the latter were redeemed, they themselves would be forced into exile in order to satisfy the obligation. Therefore, they waited until the Israelites left Egypt.

Rashi uses the Midrash to explain why the portion of Amalek is adjoined to that of the Israelites' complaint about the lack of water. This was done to point out that the Israelites had questioned God's close relationship with them. Despite the fact that He was constantly at their side, they asked, "Is God with us or not?" (verse 7). Therefore, says Rashi, God "incited the dog" — Amalek — against them, so they would recognize that they always needed and received His assistance.

Mizrachi asks: Why does Rashi select the Midrashic explanation for the positioning of this portion at the expense of the simple explanation: that this chapter follows the previous one because they occurred in that sequence? Both events took place at Rephidim, one after the other — first the complaint of the Israelites and then the war.

Gur Aryeh answers that Rashi — and the Midrash — felt it necessary to deviate from the simple meaning due to the unusual phrasing of the present verse. It says that "Amalek *came*," *Vayavo*, rather than saying that "Amalek *went out*," *vayetzei*, which is the appropriate term to use when describing a military attack (see Numbers 20:20, 21:23). The emphasis seems to be on the Amalekites' *coming* rather than on their *going out*, and so Rashi understands that they came due to the previous event, which demonstrated the Israelites' lack of faith.

Sifthei Chachamim records the view of Nachalath Yaakov that there is a different reason to eschew the simple explanation for the juxtaposition of these two portions. Nachalath Yaakov avers that there is no purpose in mentioning that Amalek battled Israel "in Rephidim." Since the previous episode occurred in Rephidim (verse 1), and Scripture later writes that the Israelites left Rephidim (19:2), it should be obvious that the war with Amalek took place there. Because Scripture does add that the war occurred in Rephidim, the Midrash and Rashi see an inference that the war was the consequence of the Israelites' behavior "in Rephidim" — their complaint about the lack of water.

Proof of this, continues Sifthei Chachamim, is that Rashi says, "This portion was adjoined to this *verse*," rather than "This portion was adjoined to this *portion*." Rashi does not intend to explain the juxtaposition of the portions, as they occurred sequentially. He is, rather, attempting to justify the wordiness of the present *verse*, of the words "in Rephidim."

Divrei David agrees with Nachalath Yaakov that the basis of Rashi's view is the addition of the words "in Rephidim," but he disagrees regarding the implication of the words. Divrei David says that, since Moses had changed the name of Rephidim to Massah (verse 7), reflecting the *nisayon*, test, that was imposed by the Israelites upon God, it is odd that the place should now again be called Rephidim. In explanation, Divrei David says that the Amalekite attack served as a counter to the doubt in God expressed by the Israelites. Since their faith in God was restored, there was no longer a purpose in referring to Rephidim as Massah. The verse emphasizes that with Amalek's coming Rephidim's name was restored, and this is the connection between the two sections.

■ ■ ■

## The Eternal Heritage

וַיֹּאמֶר מֹשֶׁה אֶל־יְהוֹשֻׁעַ בְּחַר־לָנוּ אֲנָשִׁים וְצֵא הִלָּחֵם בַּעֲמָלֵק מָחָר אָנֹכִי נִצָּב עַל־רֹאשׁ הַגִּבְעָה וּמַטֵּה הָאֱלֹהִים בְּיָדִי.

Moses said to Joshua, "Choose men for us and go do battle with Amalek. Tomorrow I will stand on top of the hill with the staff of God in my hand." (17:9)

"Moses said to Joshua *(Yehoshua)*" — When Moses later sent spies to search out the Land of Canaan, Joshua was among them. Scripture says there (Numbers 13:16) that Moses changed Joshua's name at that time from Hosea to Joshua — from *Hoshea* to *Yehoshua*. Yehoshua can be read as a contraction — *Y-ah yoshia*, "may God save." Moses told Joshua, "May God save you from the evil intent of the spies" (Ibid., Rashi). This makes the present verse difficult to understand, as it appears that Joshua's name had already been changed at this point.

Ramban asserts that Moses had called Joshua by the name Yehoshua all along, doing so because he foresaw that Joshua would be among the spies. As for the verse in Numbers, it is merely reporting that Moses had, at an earlier time, changed Joshua's name from Hosea. Alternatively, says Ramban, while Moses already called Joshua by the name Yehoshua at the present juncture, the Israelites still knew him as Hoshea. When the spies were dispatched, Moses proclaimed that Joshua was to be called Yehoshua by everyone, and it is the intent of the verse in Numbers to teach that Joshua's new name was publicized when he was sent out to spy.

■

"Go do battle with Amalek."

When the Egyptians chased the Israelites after the Exodus, God said He would do battle, while the Israelites were to "remain silent" (14:14). However, now, in Amalek's case, the Israelites were called on to fight. What was the difference between the two wars?

Generally, one has to have faith that God will provide protection, and that one's own effort is meaningless. But when a battle arises over the principles of Judaism, one cannot rely on God's help; one must do everything in his power to wage war.

The Amalekites symbolized evil and atheism, and their war with the Jews was actually a fight over the principles of belief in God and

## Beshalach

Judaism. The Israelites had no right to "remain silent" in this case; they had to "go do battle."

*(Pardes Yosef, cited by Iturei Torah)*

Pardes Yosef's explanation may be amplified as follows: Later, in their war with Midian, the Israelites described it as "God's revenge" (Numbers 31:3). God, however, termed it "revenge for the Israelites" (Ibid., verse 2). The Israelites saw the war as a battle for God, while God perceived it as a war for the sake of the Israelites. There is a symbiotic relationship between God and the Jewish people; one strives to protect the other and feels the pain and joy of the other.

The war with Midian occurred due to Midian's two-pronged attack on the Israelites. Midian incited the Israelites to immoral behavior, being involved with Moab in the latter's conspiracy to have the Israelites renounce God in favor of idol worship (Ibid., 25:1, 2). In this way Midian and Moab hoped God would cease to protect the Israelites, so that they could defeat them in battle. Hence, both the Israelites, physically, and God — spiritually — were under attack. It was thus imperative that neither party "remain silent"; each had to exact the other's revenge.

By contrast, the Egyptians' pursuit of the Israelites was not an attack against God, but against the Israelites. God does battle for the Israelites, and so they were to "remain silent."

Amalek, the paradigm of atheism, was involved in a spiritual struggle with Israel; Amalek's war was actually a war only against God. The Israelites — as God's representatives on earth — were merely the medium through which Amalek attacked God. It is up to Israel to fight for God. When His very essence is under siege, He must "remain silent," while His people, the Jews, rise to His defense.

■ ■ ■

וִידֵי מֹשֶׁה כְּבֵדִים וַיִּקְחוּ־אֶבֶן וַיָּשִׂימוּ תַחְתָּיו וַיֵּשֶׁב עָלֶיהָ וְאַהֲרֹן וְחוּר תָּמְכוּ בְיָדָיו מִזֶּה אֶחָד וּמִזֶּה אֶחָד וַיְהִי יָדָיו אֱמוּנָה עַד־בֹּא הַשָּׁמֶשׁ.

*Moses' hands became weary. They took a rock and placed it under him, and he sat*

*The Eternal Heritage*

*on it. Aaron and Hur supported his hands, one on each side, and his hands remained faithful until sunset. (17:12)*

"Moses' hands became weary" — because he was lazy and appointed Joshua to fight in his stead (Rashi).

Divrei David objects that Moses was not lazy at all, and that it was necessary for him to delegate responsibility to Joshua. The Talmud (Bava Bathra 123b) says that Esau's seed will be defeated by Joseph's seed, as Scripture declares, "Jacob's house will be a fire and Joseph's house will be a flame, while Esau's house will be straw" (Obadiah 1:18). This was the reason that, after Joseph's birth, Jacob believed he was safe in returning to Canaan and confronting Esau (Genesis 30:25). Joshua was a member of the tribe of Joseph's son Ephraim (Numbers 13:8). It would thus seem quite proper for Moses to appoint Joshua to battle Amalek, a descendant of Esau. How could Moses be faulted for delegating this authority to Joshua?

Divrei David answers that Moses' laziness did not lie in his appointment of Joshua to lead the army. Rather, it lay in his telling Joshua, "Choose men for us." While Joshua was a proper selection as leader of the army, Moses should have taken upon himself the drafting of the soldiers.

∎

Aaron and Hur were opposites. Aaron was known for his unending patience and pleasant ways; he was "a lover of peace and pursuer of peace" (Avoth 1:12). By contrast, Hur was a zealot, who later fought against the makers of the Golden Calf, and was killed in the process (Sanhedrin 7a).

Moses took hold of these two attributes as his support, because the leader of the Jewish people must possess both of them. At times he must display patience, while at other times he must be zealous and harsh. *(Chochmah Im Nachalah)*

∎ ∎ ∎

וַיַּחֲלֹשׁ יְהוֹשֻׁעַ אֶת־עֲמָלֵק וְאֶת־עַמּוֹ לְפִי־חָרֶב.
*Joshua was thus able to weaken Amalek and his nation with the sword. (17:13)*

Why does it say that Joshua "weakened" the Amalekites instead of

## Beshalach

saying that he "killed" or "smote" them? Moreover, how are we to understand the phrase "Amalek and his nation"? Aren't they one and the same? As Moses commanded, "go do battle with Amalek" (verse 9); he did not say, "go do battle with Amalek and his nation." Why then the repetition?

Our Sages say that before God smites a nation He smites that nation's representative, angel, in heaven. The Zohar writes that the name of Amalek's angel is also "Amalek," and translates the present verse accordingly: "Joshua broke their heavenly soldier." Now, an angel can be weakened, but cannot be killed. It is in reference to Amalek's angel that Scripture says, "Joshua was thus able to weaken Amalek." After defeating the angel, the Israelites fought the Amalekites themselves, and killed them — "and his nation with the sword." The word "weaken" is now understood, as is the phrase "Amalek and his nation" — the angel Amalek and the nation Amalek.

The Rav Peninim commentary records another explanation for the words "Amalek and his nation." All of the leaders of Egypt were known by the same title — Pharaoh. The same, suggests this commentary, obtained with the Amalekites; their leaders were all titled "Amalek," including the leader of the Amalekite army. In saying that Joshua weakened "Amalek and his nation," Scripture means that the chief of staff, Amalek, and his army — "his nation" — were defeated.

■ ■ ■

וַיֹּאמֶר ה' אֶל־מֹשֶׁה כְּתֹב זֹאת זִכָּרוֹן בַּסֵּפֶר וְשִׂים בְּאָזְנֵי יְהוֹשֻׁעַ כִּי־מָחֹה אֶמְחֶה אֶת־זֵכֶר עֲמָלֵק מִתַּחַת הַשָּׁמָיִם.

God said to Moses, "Record this as a reminder in the book, and put it in Joshua's ears, that I will completely obliterate the memory of Amalek from under the heavens." (17:14)

According to Rashi, God told Moses to instruct Joshua regarding the elimination of Amalek because Joshua was the man destined to lead the Israelites into Canaan. Rashi says that this was an allusion to

## The Eternal Heritage

Moses that Joshua, not he, would bring the Israelites into the Promised Land.

From the above it is clear that Rashi believes God gave Moses this instruction immediately after the battle with Amalek. Ibn Ezra is of a different mind. He points out that Scripture says, "Record this as a reminder in *the* book." Evidently a specific book is intended — the Torah, which was not completed until the last year of the forty-year journey through the wilderness, and so would not have been termed a "book" until that time. Therefore, Ibn Ezra asserts that this portion was not written until the fortieth year.

Ibn Ezra does offer another option, one that could be used to defend Rashi's view. Ibn Ezra suggests that the Israelites had in their possession a "Book of God's Wars," which is no longer extant, and that it was that book to which Scripture refers, and not to the Torah. Immediately after the war, God told Moses to record His oath in the Book of God's Wars. (See Numbers 21:14, which mentions such a book. Ibn Ezra suggests there that the Book of God's Wars had existed since Abraham's time.)

Ohr HaChayyim offers a different reason why God chose Joshua to receive the order regarding Amalek. Joshua had been sent to fight the Amalekites. He had witnessed the Amalekites' viciousness, but his efforts had served only to weaken them; he had not succeeded in completely destroying them. Joshua did not understand why God had not allowed him to make an end of the evil Amalek here and now. In order to placate him, God directed the message to him. Moreover, it was to be put "in [his] ears" — it was a personal message, meant to assuage Joshua. Since what God says is as good as done, Joshua would be consoled by the certainty of Amalek's eventual destruction.

■

Ohr HaChayyim says that the Torah alludes here to the three times in history when Amalek would be defeated by the Jewish people. The first time was in King Saul's day, and the second time was in Persia, when Mordecai and Esther triumphed over Haman. These two events are the subjects of the dual reference to Amalek's

*Beshalach*

obliteration — *machoh emcheh*. The final destruction of Amalek will occur in the future, and it finds allusion in the words "from under the heavens" — Amalek will be obliterated off the face of the earth.

# 5
# Yithro

וַיִּשְׁמַע יִתְרוֹ כֹהֵן מִדְיָן חֹתֵן מֹשֶׁה אֵת כָּל־אֲשֶׁר עָשָׂה אֱלֹהִים לְמֹשֶׁה וּלְיִשְׂרָאֵל עַמּוֹ כִּי־הוֹצִיא ה׳ אֶת־יִשְׂרָאֵל מִמִּצְרָיִם.

*Jethro, the priest of Midian — who was Moses' father-in-law — heard about all that God had done for Moses and His people Israel — that God brought Israel out of Egypt. (18:1)*

"Jethro . . . heard" — What did he hear that made him come? He heard about the splitting of the Red Sea and the war with Amalek (Rashi).

Was Jethro the only man who heard of the miracles God performed for the Israelites? Does it not say, "Nations heard and trembled" (15:14)?

Some people hear, but what they have heard has no effect on them. Jethro's quality was that he was changed by what he heard, and came to the desert to be closer to God.

(*R. Menachem Mendel of Kotsk*)

■

Jethro heard about the splitting of the Red Sea and the war with Amalek (Rashi).

It is impossible to exist solely due to miracles. As the Rabbis proclaim, "How lowly is this man for whom the natural laws are violated" (Shabbath 53b). Moreover, one is not supposed to rely on miracles (Pesachim 64b); a person must exert effort in his own behalf. On the other hand, without miracles it would also be impossible to exist — especially for the Jewish people.

When Jethro heard about the splitting of the Red Sea and the victory over Amalek — the former a miracle of God and the latter an effort by the Israelites — he understood that the Israelites were aware that both factors are vital, and so he joined them.

*(Cited by Iturei Torah,
in the name of R. Shimshon Raphael Hirsch)*

■

What did Jethro hear that caused him to come? He heard about the splitting of the Red Sea and the war with Amalek (Rashi).

Why does Rashi single out the sea and Amalek? Doesn't the verse itself record that Jethro heard "*all* that God had done for Moses and His people Israel" — that he had heard about all that had happened to the Israelites?

The Rebbe R. Zusya explains that Rashi wondered why, if Jethro had heard about all God had done for Israel, he found it necessary to join them. Why didn't he simply convert to Judaism in his own country? Rashi answers this question by saying that Jethro had heard about the sea and Amalek. He realized that, despite the astounding miracle at the sea, which was heard of by the entire world, including Amalek, that nation had had the bravado and gall to attack the Israelites. It became apparent to Jethro that simply hearing about miraculous events was not enough; one had to actually experience the events for them to influence him. Therefore, he concluded that he could not stay at a distance from the Israelites; he had to unite with them.

■

Rashi says that Jethro had seven names: Re'uel, Jether, Jethro, Hovav, Hever, Keini, and Putiel, and that he was called Jether because he added a portion to the Torah (*Yether* being of the same root as *yitaron*, "addition"). That portion, says Rashi, is "You must also seek out . . ." (verse 21), the section dealing with the appointment of judges for the Israelites.

## Yithro

Once, during a meeting of the rabbis of Warsaw, a certain rabbi sharply criticized the Agudath Israel, claiming it was not being supportive enough of the Land of Israel and the Jewish people. Another rabbi responded by pointing to the present gloss of Rashi. Why, he asked, does Rashi write that Jethro's portion begins with the words "You must also seek out," when it actually starts several verses earlier: "Moses' father-in-law said to him, 'What you are doing is not good'" (verse 17)? The reason — asserted the rabbi — is that "What you are doing is not good" constitutes a criticism of past events as opposed to a plan for future conduct that corrects the past. The positive aspect of Jethro's portion, his advice regarding the future, begins with "You must also seek out." It was in the merit of this advice that Jethro's portion was added to the Torah. Criticism is not significant; a plan for future action is.

*(Likutei Yehoshua)*

■

The timing of Jethro's arrival in the desert is the subject of a Talmudic dispute (Zevachim 116a) between R. Yehoshua b. Levi and the sons of R. Chiya, whose names are Yehuda and Chizkiyah. One opinion holds that Jethro arrived before the giving of the Torah at Mount Sinai; this opinion fits well with the order of the sections in the Torah. The other contends that Jethro did not arrive until after the Torah had been given.

This debate has an impact upon a second dispute: whether non-Jews are permitted to sacrifice *shelamim*, peace offerings. While all agree that gentiles are permitted to bring an *olah*, a burnt offering, to the Temple, there is an opinion that they may not bring peace offerings. Whereas Scripture says that Jethro brought peace offerings (verse 12), the opinion that believes Jethro came before the Lawgiving — at which time everyone was a gentile — must hold that non-Jews are permitted to bring such sacrifices. A support text for this view is Genesis 4:4, which says, "Abel also brought an offering, of the firstborn of his flock, and from their fats." If Abel brought burnt offerings, why are the fats singled out for mention? A burnt offering is brought in its entirety upon the altar. Rather, Abel must have brought peace offerings, whose fats are burned while the rest is eaten (Zevachim 116a).

R. Saadiah Gaon sides with the opinion that Jethro joined the Israelites before the Lawgiving. Ibn Ezra takes the other view. He points out that, whereas Jethro brought sacrifices, but no mention is made of an altar being built, Jethro must have arrived in the second year, after the completion of the Tabernacle, and brought the sacrifices on *its* altar. Moreover, Moses, in explaining the Israelite judicial system to his father-in-law, said, "I teach God's decrees and laws" (verse 16). This would only apply after the Israelites had received God's laws at Mount Sinai.

Furthermore, Ibn Ezra points out that the Torah says that Jethro came "to the desert, where Moses was staying, near God's mountain" (verse 5). God's mountain is Horeb, Mount Sinai (3:1). And the word *choneh*, "was staying," is in present tense, inferring that the Israelites had already been there awhile.

Additionally, Moses tells the Israelites that God had said at Sinai, "You have remained at this mountain long enough" (Deuteronomy 1:6). They had been there almost a year. Moses goes on, "I said to you at that time, 'I cannot lead you all by myself' " (Ibid., verse 9), and proceeds to detail the appointment of judges, as was advised here by Jethro. Jethro gave Moses this advice the day after his arrival (verse 13). Clearly, then, Jethro came at the end of the Israelites' stay at Mount Sinai, which was in the second year of their journey in the wilderness.

Ramban advances yet another proof for this opinion. Scripture says here that Jethro went back to his land (verse 27). This — says Ramban — is the same return trip Scripture describes later (Numbers 10:30), and it is clear from the context that the trip described in Numbers took place after the Lawgiving.

Ramban nevertheless objects to the opinion of Ibn Ezra. Ramban focuses on the fact that Jethro came to the Israelites because he had heard that "God brought Israel out of Egypt." If Jethro was moved to come after the Revelation, why was that not cited as the motivator behind his initiative? After all, the Revelation was the most miraculous event in the history of mankind. And again,

## Yithro

Scripture relates that Moses reported to Jethro about all that God had done to Pharaoh and Egypt on Israel's behalf, and about the Israelites' troubles on their journey, from which God had rescued them (verse 8). Jethro responded, "Now I know that God is the greatest of all deities" (verse 11). If Jethro arrived after the Torah was given, why didn't Moses describe *that* event to him, which surely would have established the truth of God and His Torah in Jethro's mind?

Due to this objection, Ramban subscribes to the view that Jethro joined the Israelites before the Torah was given. While it says here that Jethro came "to the desert, where Moses was staying, near God's mountain," Ramban explains that Moses was in "the desert," and Jethro went to "God's mountain." From there Jethro sent word to Moses. Ramban also asserts that Jethro did return to Midian now, and that he came to the Israelites a second time, staying permanently.

■

Rashi records the Midrash, which says that Jethro had seven names: Re'uel, Jether, Jethro, Hovav, Hever, Keini, and Putiel. Rashi adds that Jethro was called Jether because, due to him, a portion was added to the Torah — the one concerning the judiciary (*Yether*, Jether, is rooted in *yitaron*, "addition"). Rashi adds that another opinion holds Re'uel to have been Jethro's father.

Divrei David points out that Rashi is inconsistent on two counts with how he broaches the same subject later (Numbers 10:29). Firstly, there Rashi regards Re'uel as Jethro's father, which he here relegates to a second opinion. Secondly, here Rashi comments that the name Jether was given to Jethro because he added a portion to the Torah, while Jethro, *Yithro*, was given him when he converted. *Yithro* and *Yether* have the same letters, but *Yithro* has an additional letter; in honor of his conversion, a letter was appended to his name. In Numbers, Rashi says that the name Jethro was given him because he added a portion to the Torah.

Divrei David resolves the latter contradiction by saying that it is rooted in Rashi's two approaches regarding the name Re'uel. In the present section, Rashi sides with the view that Re'uel and Jethro

## The Eternal Heritage

were one and the same. Now, while one must find a reason for the addition of a name, no reason need be put forth for a man's given name. The list of seven names as recorded by the Midrash has Re'uel first, followed by Jether and then Jethro. If Re'uel was Jethro, and not his father, then it is likely that Re'uel was Jethro's given name, as the given name would be listed first. Jether is the second name on the list, and so it was an added name. Rashi must supply a reason why Jethro was called Jether, and he does so by saying that Jethro added a portion to the Torah.

However, in Numbers, Rashi's gloss is based on the view that Jethro had only six names, with Re'uel being his father. Hence, Jether, the second name on the list, would likely be Jethro's actual name. Therefore, Rashi sees no purpose in finding an explanation for Jether. It is only the third through seventh names that must be explained. Therefore, Rashi says that Jethro, the third name, was given to him because he added a chapter to the Torah.

■ ■ ■

וְאֵת שְׁנֵי בָנֶיהָ אֲשֶׁר שֵׁם הָאֶחָד גֵּרְשֹׁם כִּי אָמַר גֵּר הָיִיתִי בְּאֶרֶץ נָכְרִיָּה.
[Jethro also brought] her two sons. The name of the first was Gershom, because [Moses] had declared, "I was a foreigner (ger) in a strange land (sham)." (18:3)

The names that Moses gave his sons attest to his greatness and to how much he loved his people. Having been raised in Pharaoh's palace, Moses did not know the Israelites. Additionally, the Israelites were slaves, while Moses' father-in-law was the priest of Midian. Nonetheless, Moses identified with the Israelites and perceived himself, when in Midian, as "a foreigner in a strange land." To him, Egypt, the land where his people were living, was home, while Midian was a strange land.

In fact, Moses' agony over the Israelites' plight was so great that, even though he was saved miraculously from the sword of Pharaoh, he did not acknowledge that miracle until his second son, Eliezer, was named (verse 4, and Rashi there). *(Alshich)*

■ ■ ■

## Yithro

וַיֹּאמֶר אֶל־מֹשֶׁה אֲנִי חֹתֶנְךָ יִתְרוֹ בָּא אֵלֶיךָ וְאִשְׁתְּךָ וּשְׁנֵי בָנֶיהָ עִמָּהּ.
*He sent word to Moses: "I, Jethro — your father-in-law — am on my way to you, along with your wife and her two sons with her."* (18:6)

Jethro first mentioned himself, then Moses' wife Tzipporah, and finally her sons. According to Rashi, Jethro implied: If you won't come out to greet us for my sake, do so for your wife's sake. And if you will not come out for her sake, do so for the sake of your sons. Why does Rashi advance this Midrashic explanation, when the simple one — that Jethro was merely announcing their arrival — would appear to suffice?

Likutei Besamim says, in the name of R. Shaul of Amsterdam, that Rashi was bothered by a Scriptural inconsistency. In the previous verse Moses' sons are mentioned before his wife, while in this verse his wife is mentioned first. The previous verse would seem to reflect the more appropriate order, since, when Jacob left Aram to return to Canaan, he took "his children and wives" (Genesis 31:17). Esau, by contrast, took "his wives, his sons . . ." (Ibid., 36:6). Rashi (Ibid., 31:17) makes note of this difference between Jacob and Esau.

This difference emphasizes Jacob's righteousness, since the sons of righteous men are dearer to them than are their wives. Hence, the present verse needs clarification, as it mentions Tzipporah ahead of Moses' sons. Therefore, Rashi uses the Midrash to explain that the order given in the verse is indeed proper. Jethro saved his most intense plea for last. He first implored Moses to come out for Jethro's sake; if not for his sake, then he was to greet them for Tzipporah's sake; and if not for her sake, he had to come out for his sons, whom he held most dear.

In what sense are the sons of righteous men dearer to them than are their wives? Gur Aryeh (Genesis 31:17) explains that Esau married his wives so that they would be available to him for intercourse. He had no higher moral purpose in marrying. Esau's children were a by-product of his marriage. By contrast, Jacob was not motivated by carnal desire. His motivation in marrying was to

## The Eternal Heritage

father children, the Twelve Tribes. To Jacob, the begetting of righteous children was the primary reason for marrying.

■ ■ ■

וַיִּחַדְּ יִתְרוֹ עַל כָּל־הַטּוֹבָה אֲשֶׁר־עָשָׂה ה' לְיִשְׂרָאֵל אֲשֶׁר הִצִּילוֹ מִיַּד מִצְרָיִם.
*Jethro rejoiced because of all the good that God had done for Israel, rescuing it from the hand of Egypt. (18:9)*

*Vayichad* is an unusual term for "rejoicing," and there is a dispute in the Talmud regarding the connotation of the word. The word can also be taken as a derivative of *chad*, "sharp." Rav says that it alludes to Jethro's having used a sharp knife on himself — he underwent circumcision. Shmuel says that Jethro's skin tingled, prickled, from anguish at the demise of the Egyptians. Rav then says (in support of Shmuel's view), "As people say, 'Do not insult a gentile in the presence of a convert until ten generations have passed [since the conversion took place]'" (Sanhedrin 94a).

When Grace is said at a wedding, the words *shehasimcha bime'ono*, "in Whose abode is joy," are added to the introduction: "Blessed be God, in Whose abode is joy, and of Whose portion we ate." Chatham Sofer points out that R. Shlomo Luria, in his Yam shel Shlomo commentary on Tractate Bava Kamma, rules that these words are also added to the Introduction to Grace said at a meal commemorating joyous events, such as the conclusion of study of a Talmud tractate. It is only at a meal in celebration of a circumcision that these words are not said, because the infant has suffered pain, and it is inappropriate to mention joy when the subject of the celebration has experienced pain.

Chatham Sofer asks the following question: The requirement to make a blessing in commemoration of a miracle is derived by the Talmud (Berachoth 54b) from the fact that Jethro said, "Blessed be God, who rescued you from the hand of Egypt and the hand of Pharaoh" (verse 10). Whereas Jethro and Moses enjoyed a celebratory meal in honor of this occasion, why didn't they say "Blessed be God, in Whose abode is joy"? According to Yam shel Shlomo, there is a requirement to add these words at a meal of celebration.

## Yithro

    Chatham Sofer answers that it is due to this problem that Shmuel eschews the simple explanation of *Vayichad* — "He rejoiced" — in favor of the more esoteric thought that Jethro's skin prickled. Because Jethro was uncomfortable, regretting the destruction of Egypt, he was not required to say "in Whose abode is joy." Jethro's discomfort is thus compared to that of the circumcised infant, as pain precludes the saying of *shehasimcha bime'ono*.

    By contrast, Rav believes that it would have been inappropriate for Jethro to omit these words due to his anguish at Egypt's demise. Egypt merited destruction, and so Jethro's ambivalence was due to a fault in his perception. Therefore, Rav opines that Jethro circumcised himself; he was able to ascribe his omission of "in Whose abode is joy" to the pain of circumcision, thereby concealing his anguish concerning Egypt.

    According to this explanation, Rav actually agrees with Shmuel that Jethro was pained over Egypt's annihilation.

    Chatham Sofer adds that this explains why Rav advances proof for Shmuel's view (in speaking of the prohibition to criticize gentiles in the presence of a convert). Since Rav agrees with Shmuel, it is not odd for him to defend the latter's opinion.

    As regards Rav's apparent support for Shmuel, Lechem Asher offers two alternative explanations. He says that Rav may agree with Shmuel, and actually intends to strengthen Shmuel's position. Rav is saying that Jethro was so drawn to Judaism that he became circumcised, but he nevertheless mourned for the Egyptians.

    Lechem Asher's second explanation is that Rav does disagree with Shmuel, and Rav's statement concerning the sensitivity of converts is not intended as support for Shmuel's position. Rav's words are, "As people say, 'Do not insult . . .'" Rav is asserting that Shmuel's view accords with what "people say"; it is a popular sentiment, but is no more than that. It is to be rejected, as a convert can overcome all vestiges of his former life and not be offended by an insult to gentiles. (The reference must be to an idol worshiper, as otherwise it is certainly forbidden to insult a non-Jew whether or not a convert is present.) Therefore, one must not assume that Jethro was not wholehearted in his conversion.

Maharsha notes that another text reads, "R. *Papa* said: As people say." Maharsha says that this is the correct reading, for, if it were Rav who was defending Shmuel's view, the customary phrasing would be, "Rav explained in accordance with Shmuel's opinion." This is the language used when someone is defending his disputant's view. Whereas that language is not used here, it is evident that someone other than Rav is defending Shmuel.

■

Jethro was a Midianite, and the Midianites descended from Keturah, Abraham's second wife (Genesis 25:2). Maharsha asks how it is that, according to Rav, Jethro only now underwent circumcision, since the children of Keturah were commanded regarding circumcision along with Abraham (Sanhedrin 59b). And while Rashi's opinion is that this command was limited to Keturah's sons, Rambam contends that Keturah's descendants to this day must be circumcised. Why, according to Rambam, wasn't Jethro yet circumcised?

There are two stages in a circumcision. There is the *milah*, which is the removal of the foreskin, and the *periah*, which denotes the removal of a membrane that lies below the foreskin. Maharsha answers that, while Jews must remove the membrane in order to properly fulfill the mitzvah of circumcision, the same is not the case with the descendants of Keturah; they need only remove the foreskin. (This difference is stated by the Talmud [Yevamoth 71b], and applies not only to Keturah's children, but to Abraham, Isaac, Ishmael, and all others who were included in God's command to Abraham regarding circumcision. *Periah* is incumbent only upon Jews, and there were no Jews until the Lawgiving at Mount Sinai.) Jethro had certainly complied with the law as it applied to Keturites. This, however, did not include *periah*, and Jethro now did the *periah*, so that he would have the circumcision required of a Jew.

However, Rambam himself does not mention that there is a difference in the nature of the circumcisions required of a Jew and a Keturite. The fact that he does not do so would indicate that he believes there is no difference, and that Keturites must undergo

## Yithro

*periah* as well as *milah*. (This seems to be the opinion of Rashi in Genesis 17:25, although he voices the opposing opinion in Joshua 5:2. Rosh may also hold that all circumcisions are alike. See the discussion in Vol. I, Genesis 17:25.) If that is the case, the question remains unresolved: Why, according to Rambam, hadn't Jethro undergone *periah* beforehand, since it is required of Keturites?

Etz Yosef avers that Jethro may not have been a Midianite at all. While he is termed the "priest of Midian" (verse 1), this means that he was a leader of the Midianites, but does not prove he was of Midianite stock. Evidence of this — says Etz Yosef — is the Talmud's declaration that Jethro was among Pharaoh's circle of aides who considered the issue of the exploding Israelite population in Egypt (Sotah 11a). This would seem to indicate that Jethro was an Egyptian.

If we take this approach, then the objection to Rambam's view is answered. Jethro was an Egyptian, and so never had been commanded about circumcision. Thus, he now underwent a full circumcision, including both *milah* and *periah*.

In truth, however, Rambam's position must be questioned. The Talmud (Shabbath 135a) says in R. Assi's name: "Anyone whose mother becomes impure in childbirth is circumcised on the eighth day, while anyone whose mother does not become impure in childbirth is not circumcised on the eighth day." A Jewish woman is impure for seven days when she gives birth to a son in the normal way (Leviticus 12:2), while a gentile woman, or a Jewish woman who gives birth by Caesarian section, is not impure. According to R. Assi, only a child delivered normally must be circumcised on the eighth day; another child upon whom circumcision is incumbent need not be circumcised on the eighth day.

Abaye proceeds to question R. Assi's statement, objecting that "the previous generations prove that even one whose mother does not become impure in childbirth is circumcised on the eighth day." Abaye is referring to the generations from Abraham until the giving of the Torah. These generations were commanded to circumcise their children on the eighth day (Genesis 17:12), although there was no impurity for women who bore children at that time. R. Assi responds that "the Torah was given and the law was changed"; before the Lawgiving, circumcision was mandated for the eighth day despite the fact that no impurity was incurred during childbirth, but once the Torah was given the rule was established as stated by R. Assi.

According to Rashi, who maintains that today only Jews have the commandment of circumcision, this section presents no difficulty. However, how does Rambam, who contends that Keturites are commanded regarding circumcision even today, understand this section? Now, if the descendants of Keturah are not commanded regarding *periah*, then Rambam could say that the Talmud is referring to the type of circumcision performed by Jews. That type of circumcision is mandated for the eighth day only for Jewish children whose mothers become impure at birth. However, as explained above, it seems that Rambam believes Keturites are indeed instructed regarding *periah*. Nonetheless, there is no impurity for the mothers of Keturite children. It turns out that there is, even after the giving of the Torah, eighth-day circumcision for children whose mothers do not become impure in childbirth — Keturite children. How, then, can Rambam reconcile his opinion with R. Assi's statement that no such case exists?

"Do not insult a gentile in the presence of a convert until ten generations have passed" (Sanhedrin 94a).

Anaf Yosef quotes Ye'aroth Devash, who is puzzled by this statement in general and by its application to Jethro in particular. The Torah relates that it was due to Jethro that the Israelite justice system was founded; indeed, he merited having this portion added to Scripture in his name. How can the Talmud say that he despaired at the downfall of the enemy of Israel? Furthermore, the simple explanation of the present verse is that Jethro's emotional reaction was to the good tidings that he had heard about the Israelites. The Talmud seems to extend itself to reverse the meaning of the text. What purpose is there in doing so? Moreover, how, in general, can proselytes be derogated in this fashion: to the effect that they feel

## Yithro

badly when an idol worshiper is criticized? Whereas a proselyte has forsaken his past life of idol worship in favor of Judaism, such a comment regarding his emotions would seem untoward.

Ye'aroth Devash answers that, in actuality, the Talmud means to praise the proselyte, not to criticize him. Rambam writes that there is a difference between a proselyte who becomes Jewish at a time when the Jewish people are oppressed and one who converts when they are in a position of power. In the former case, the convert acts despite the fact that the gentiles possess power, wealth, and honor, while the Jews subsist in a poor and sorry state. Such a man deserves the greatest praise. In the latter instance, the convert's action comes when the Jews enjoy superiority and the gentiles occupy a lower station in life. To become Jewish when the Jews have an elevated position is not as laudable, and so the praise given such a man is more reserved. As the Sages say, "Proselytes were not accepted in the days of David and the days of Solomon" (Yevamoth 24b). Since the Jews were powerful in the days of these kings, the sincerity of potential converts was questioned.

Ye'aroth Devash says that we are to use Rambam's principle to solve the present problem. If one insults gentiles, it is evident that he feels the gentiles do not occupy a high station. One who converts at a time when non-Jews are not elevated is not so praiseworthy, as there is nothing remarkable about wanting to leave a despised group. Thus, one must not criticize gentiles in the presence of a convert, lest the convert feel that his conversion is not duly appreciated. On the contrary, the proselyte would prefer if the gentiles are praised, since that would allow his conversion to be seen as sincerely motivated.

Ye'aroth Devash concludes that this was precisely the case with Jethro. The Israelites had been lowly and despised in Egypt, while Jethro lived as a priest amidst the splendor of Midian. He paid no heed to his position, and departed for the wilderness to cast his lot with the Israelites. However, when he arrived, he discovered that God had heaped benefits upon the Israelites; they had merited miracles and taken possession of Egypt's wealth. Jethro became distraught, sensing that his conversion would not be accounted an altruistic one. He told himself: There is no good reflection upon me for joining a nation which is enjoying unbounded success.

Hence, the Talmud is not departing from the cause of Jethro's reaction as described by Scripture. Jethro was anguished at "all the good that God had done for Israel," in the sense that it reflected badly upon himself. He was not, however, distressed at the tidings of Egypt's fate.

■

"All the good that God had done" — This refers to the manna, the well of water, and the Torah (Rashi).

In the first verse of this portion, Rashi makes inconsistent statements regarding what Jethro heard that caused him to journey and join the Israelites. On the words "Jethro . . . heard," Rashi comments that Jethro received word of "the splitting of the Red Sea and the war with Amalek." On the words "all that God had done," Rashi says that Jethro heard how God had helped the Israelites "regarding the falling of the manna, the well, and Amalek." In the present verse, Rashi notes that the manna, the well, and the Torah were the reasons why Jethro rejoiced. Why isn't Rashi consistent, rather than listing different reasons in each of these instances?

Divrei David addresses this problem by first focusing on Rashi's two glosses on the earlier verse and then contrasting them with the present verse.

Rashi first says that Jethro heard about the splitting of the Red Sea but subsequently says that he heard about the manna and the well. According to Divrei David, Rashi sensed that the earlier verse differentiated between two categories of miracles. The first category was confined to miracles which occurred not for the good of Israel, but in order to publicize God's greatness. The splitting of the Red Sea and the war with Amalek fit into this category. The Israelites could have been brought through the desert on a route that did not require the traversal of water, but God chose to bring them via the Red Sea, in order to demonstrate His ability to split the waters. The Israelites did not derive any benefit from this detour, as they would have been quite willing to use a simple route. Similarly, they would have been quite happy not to do battle with Amalek.

## Yithro

God wanted them involved in the war so that He could display His power.

The second category of miracles included phenomena which were for the actual benefit of the Israelites. As Scripture says, Jethro heard about "all that God had done for Moses and His people Israel." The emphasis here was on the good done for the Israelites. The giving of the manna and the activation of the well were miracles intended strictly for Israel's benefit.

As for Amalek, which Rashi mentions in both categories, he first says that Jethro heard about "the war with Amalek"; in his later comment he says simply that Jethro heard how God helped the Israelites with "Amalek" — Rashi does not use the word "war." Divrei David explains that there were two aspects to the encounter with Amalek: the military defeat of the Amalekites, and the rescue of the Israelites. Rashi's first comment regarded the war, the defeat of Amalek, which was meant to glorify God, while his second comment focused on the good done for Israel — its rescue from Amalek's hand.

As for Rashi's gloss on the present verse, which mentions the giving of the Torah, Divrei David brings up the Talmudic dispute over whether Jethro arrived before or after the Lawgiving. Divrei David asserts that Rashi had no interest in siding with either of the parties, and so he tailored his glosses accordingly. The earlier verse discussed the reasons for Jethro's decision to join the Israelites. Had Rashi included the giving of the Torah, it would have meant siding with the opinion that Jethro came after the Lawgiving; therefore, Rashi omitted the giving of the Torah. The present verse, by contrast, details the reasons that Jethro "rejoiced." Here Rashi was able to include the Lawgiving, nonetheless not taking up the position of the disputant who maintains that Jethro arrived *after* the Torah was given. The present verse does not declare Jethro's joy to be confined to events that preceded the Lawgiving. Even the opinion that contends Jethro came before the giving of the Torah can concur that he rejoiced when that event took place. This opinion cannot agree, however, that Jethro *came* due to the Lawgiving, and so Rashi did not mention the Torah in the earlier verse.

Divrei David continues that Amalek was not mentioned in the present verse because, while that war was part of the reason Jethro elected to leave Midian, it was not a reason behind his rejoicing. Jethro was happy due to events which benefited him. The manna and the well benefited Jethro, as they provided nourishment for the Israelites not only when these sources of food first came into existence — before Jethro's arrival — but throughout their stay in the wilderness. The Torah, too, was a constant feature in their lives. This was not the case with the Amalekite war. It was an isolated episode in the pre-Jethro history of the Israelites; Jethro did not rejoice over it because he was not present when it occurred.

While Divrei David does not discuss the omission of the splitting of the Red Sea in Rashi's present gloss, the same idea holds true for that event as holds for the war with Amalek. Since the sea-splitting occurred prior to Jethro's arrival, he did not rejoice over it, as he derived no first-hand pleasure from it.

■

The verse literally reads, "Jethro rejoiced because of all the good that God had done for Israel, rescuing it (or him) from the hand of Egypt." Be'er Mayim Chaim objects that the Torah should have written that God rescued "them," the Israelites.

He answers that Jethro had been among Pharaoh's advisors when the king schemed to kill the firstborn Israelites (Sotah 11a). However, he left Pharaoh's company, and so he was saved.

Jethro was happy because of the good God had done in "rescuing him," Jethro himself — by giving him the idea to reject Pharaoh's philosophy.

■ ■ ■

וַיֹּאמֶר יִתְרוֹ בָּרוּךְ ה' אֲשֶׁר הִצִּיל אֶתְכֶם מִיַּד מִצְרַיִם וּמִיַּד פַּרְעֹה אֲשֶׁר הִצִּיל אֶת־הָעָם מִתַּחַת יַד־מִצְרָיִם.

Jethro said, "Blessed be God, who rescued you from the hand of Egypt and Pharaoh — who liberated the people from under Egypt's hand. . . ." (18:10)

The Talmud says: It is to the discredit of Moses and the six

## Yithro

hundred thousand that they did not say "blessed," for Jethro was the first to say "Blessed be God" (Sanhedrin 94a).

Moses and the Israelites had sung at the Red Sea, praising God and thanking Him. Was their song any less praiseworthy than Jethro's pronouncement?

The answer is that Jethro's praise contained a feature which the Israelites' praise lacked. The Israelites lauded God for the kindness and generosity He had extended to themselves. Jethro's praise was that God "rescued *you* from the hand of Egypt" — he praised God for having assisted others. That is why he is commended.

*(R. Shlomo of Radomsk)*

■

Rashbam notes that the verse seems repetitious. Having said that God "rescued you from the hand of Pharaoh and Egypt," why is it necessary to add that He "liberated the people from under Egypt's hand"?

Rashbam answers that the first part of the verse refers to Moses and Aaron. God saved them from the hand of Pharaoh and Egypt (presumably a reference to the fact that Moses and Aaron had direct contact with Pharaoh, and so were in a more dangerous position than their fellow Israelites). The second part refers to the Israelites, who were liberated from the Egyptian slavery.

■

What is the meaning of *Baruch Ado-nai*, "Blessed be God"?

R. Yosef Dov Soloveitchik of Boston notes that the Kabbalistic Sages reject the notion that, when one pronounces a blessing — for example, in the prayers or over food — he is praising God. R. Yitzchak Luria (Arizal), Vilna Gaon, and R. Shneur Zalman of Lyady (Ba'al HaTanya) join in repudiating such an approach.

R. Soloveitchik says that an analysis of blessings in the Torah bears out the view of these Sages. When God created Adam and Eve, He blessed them as follows: "God blessed them. God said to them, 'Be fruitful and multiply. Fill the land and conquer it'" (Genesis 1:28). God also blessed the seventh day: "God blessed the seventh day, and He declared it to be holy" (Ibid., 2:3). After the

Flood, says Scripture, "God blessed Noah and his children. He said to them, 'Be fruitful and multiply, and fill the earth'" (Ibid., 9:1). And God said to Abraham, "You shall become a blessing. I will bless those who bless you, and he who curses you I will curse" (Ibid., 12:2, 3).

It is quite evident from these verses — says R. Soloveitchik — that God was not praising Adam and Eve, the Sabbath, Noah, or Abraham. Neither did the patriarchs, when blessing their offspring, intend to praise them, and the same is true of Moses when he blessed the Israelites. What, then, is the purpose of these blessings? R. Soloveitchik says that, if we discover the nature of blessings given to people by God, we will also know the converse: the nature of blessings bestowed upon God by people when they say "Blessed be God."

R. Soloveitchik avers that the key to understanding the nature of blessings lies in the following words: "God created Man in His image. In the image of God He created him, male and female He created them. God blessed them. God said to them, 'Be fruitful and multiply. Fill the land and conquer it'" (Ibid., 1:27, 28). The quality of blessing is represented by the male and female. The male, who represents the *mashpia*, the giver, and the female, who represents the *mushpa*, the receiver, compose the essential relationship in which blessing is found. This is why it says, "God blessed *them*." True blessing is found only in the interaction between male and female, as only through them can come procreation. And God attaches His blessing to it: "God blessed them . . . 'Be fruitful and multiply.'" However, "Be fruitful and multiply" has its application as well in the spiritual, metaphysical world.

Moreover, the male and female are actually paradigms for states that exist in every person. Everyone, whether man or woman, possesses both male and female aspects — he/she is a giver and a receiver, a *mashpia* and a *mushpa*. R. Soloveitchik adds that this is the intent of the Sages when they say, "At the time that God created the first man, He created him with two faces (male and female)" (Bereshith Rabbah 8). Every person has the ability to create, and to exert influence upon others. This is his male aspect. On the other hand, each person is also capable of humbling himself before others and being a receptor of influence. (While these thoughts are adapted from the book *Yemai Zikkaron,* the male/female dichotomy seems to meld with R. Soloveitchik's description of two prototypical men, Adam I and Adam II, in his classic "The Lonely Man of Faith" [Tradition, Summer 1965]. Briefly, Adam I seeks to create, to conquer. Adam II observes phenomena and absorbs information. Adam I appears to represent a person's male aspect, while Adam II represents the female aspect.)

As an example, in a relationship between a teacher and his students, the teacher is the male, the *mashpia,* as he is imparting his Torah knowledge to the students; expressed in terms of procreation, he implants seeds of knowledge in their minds, and these seeds proceed to sprout. The students have the female role, as they receive information. However, it may occur that one of the students questions the teacher's line of thinking, and the latter is forced to adopt a new theory. The roles have been reversed; the student has planted a seed in his teacher's mind. The student is now the male, while the teacher has assumed the role of the female. The promise of "male and female He created them" — contends R. Soloveitchik — is that every passive person, every student, also teaches, while every active man, every teacher, sometimes assumes the female role of student, of an absorber of knowledge.

Thus, the blessing of "Be fruitful and multiply" is not just in the physical sphere, but in the intellectual and spiritual ones as well. Every person is encouraged by God to climb to greater and greater heights of knowledge. This is accomplished when one relates to others via the male/female dichotomy: at times taking the active role, by imparting knowledge to the female aspect of his counterpart, and at times taking the passive role, by allowing his friend to act in the capacity of the male, the *mashpia.*

R. Soloveitchik continues that three criteria must be met for a person to maximize his potential in terms of his female aspect. Firstly, he has to be born with the ability to absorb wisdom, knowledge, and good characteristics. Secondly, his environment must be one that leads to his development in these areas. Finally, his female aspect cannot achieve its maximum capability unless he also uses his male aspect in order to teach others. When one teaches, benefit accrues to the teacher as well as to the student. This principle is verbalized in the Talmud by R. Chanina: "I learned much from my teachers, more from my friends, and the most from my students" (Ta'anith 7a). When one imparts knowledge to his pupils, he derives extraordinary benefits.

As an example of the fact that a good environment is critical if one is to achieve his full potential, the Talmud says, "Once [the Sages] were gathered in the attic of Guria's house in Jericho. A voice from heaven said, 'There is someone here who deserves to have the Divine Spirit rest upon him in the same way it rested upon Moses, but his generation does not merit this.' The Sages looked at Hillel the Elder" (Sanhedrin 11a). Hillel had the talent to be a prophet, one of Moses' stature, but his environment precluded that possibility. R. Soloveitchik adds that, in his personal experience, he has seen extremely talented people whose growth was stunted by their environment, and people of marginal talent who have risen to great heights by maximizing their interaction with their environment in *mashpia/mushpa* terms.

In addition to the above, Ibn Ezra, in explaining the words "God blessed the seventh day," says that the blessing connotes the addition of good things, and a rebirth, both in the physical and spiritual spheres, on the Sabbath day. Ramban concurs with Ibn Ezra's assessment.

R. Soloveitchik continues that the Torah's concepts are always parallel in meaning. If God's blessing of the world infers additional good, influence, rebirth — that is, being fruitful and multiplying — the same applies when people bless God. Scripture commands, "You will eat and be satisfied. Then you must bless God your Lord for the good land that He has given you" (Deuteronomy 8:10). We are being told to bless God with additional good, with rebirth.

Yet, how can a flesh-and-blood creature bless God? Moreover, whereas blessings are unalterably bound up with the male/female relationship, how can that be applied to God?

R. Soloveitchik answers that the Kabbalah delineates male and

## Yithro

female aspects of God in His relationship with the world.

R. Soloveitchik continues that R. Shneur Zalman of Lyady once said that, just as the revealed Torah *(nigleh)* has hidden aspects, so does the hidden Torah *(nistar)* have revealed aspects. In *nigleh* terms, the Kabbalah, in ascribing a male/female dimension to God, means as follows:

God is the holy King, the creator of everything, the foundation and final purpose of the entire creation. Further, the creation of the world was not an isolated event; it is, rather, ongoing, a continuous renewal and giving of life. As we say in the morning prayer, "who, in His goodness, renews constantly the creation, every day." Were God to desert the world for even one moment, it would become again an unformed mass. God's interaction with the world, as seen in this light, is as a male vis-a-vis a female. He is the *mashpia* and we are in the role of *mushpa*. As Scripture says, "When I see Your heavens, the work of Your fingers, the moon and stars which You created, What is a man that You should remember him, and a person that You should call him to mind?" (Psalms 8:4, 5). God is everything, while Man is nothing.

However, if there were no more to the God/Man relationship than this, there would have been no room for God's revelation to the Israelites at Mount Sinai, where He concluded a covenant with them. In a covenant, each side gives and receives; each has a male and a female component. Therefore, there must be a way in which God needs Man, wherein we are in the role of *mashpia* — the male — while He is the *mushpa*, the female. The feminine aspects of God include the Shechinah — the Divine Presence — and the Kabbalistic concepts of *malchuth, matronitha*, and *kallah*. (This is not the place to explain these concepts; they are mentioned only to indicate that there are female facets to God.)

The function of God's feminine components is to allow God, who is beyond the comprehension of human beings, to dwell among them. The Torah says that God "remains *(shochein)* with [the Israelites] even when they are unclean" (Leviticus 16:17). This refers to the *Shechinah*. Now, at the same time that God comes close to Man, He remains hidden. This is expressed by the Torah as follows:

"God descended in a cloud and stood there with [Moses]" (34:5). Even at the moment when God descended, He was hidden behind a cloud.

As close as God may get to a person, this cloud remains. If the person wishes to remove the cloud, he must act to do so; God is not interested in — indeed, in a sense, cannot — disperse the cloud. The Divine Presence must be uncovered — removed from behind its cloud — by Man. God can do everything except to reveal Himself to us. In this respect — effectuating the manifestation of the *Shechinah* — Man is the *mashpia* and God is the *mushpa*; Man has the male role, God the female role. The revelation of the Divine Presence is predicated upon the search by Man for God, and that is an aspect over which God has no control. It comes under the category of "everything is in Heaven's hands with the exception of fear of Heaven" (Berachoth 33b). A person can come to fear God only when he feels that God is in his presence. Thus, a person must cause God to be revealed. This is in Man's hands, not God's hands.

R. Soloveitchik continues that a person may seek out and find God in every place and at every time, since God is the creator of everything. One can find God in the sunrise and in the sunset, in the ocean and in the plants, in the stars and in the sands — anywhere in the natural world, and within himself as well. In causing the Divine Presence to be revealed, the person is the male and God is the female. And by revealing God, the person becomes closer to Him and adds to the holiness of the world.

The same idea — says R. Soloveitchik — applies when a person eats. The Divine Presence is to be found in the foods one eats, and is also present in every action one takes while eating — not only the actual eating and drinking, but even the hand movements involved with eating. By saying a blessing over the food, the person causes the revelation of the *Shechinah*, as it is the purpose of blessings to do so. "Be fruitful and multiply" in this way manifests itself in its application to God, for here the Divine Presence is revealed, goodness and holiness proliferate, and God's attachment to the world grows. This parallels the way blessings connote the addition of good things, fruitfulness, and rebirth in Man.

## Yithro

R. Soloveitchik says, in conclusion, that the essence of Judaism is to be found in the words "Blessed are You." The nature of this essence is that God needs our assistance in order for His presence to be revealed in the world. Furthermore, this is also the foundation of the process of sin and repentance. Sin causes a person to be separated from the *Shechinah*. In this regard, the Prophet Isaiah declares: "But your transgressions have caused a division between you and your God, and your sins have caused the Face to become hidden, so that it does not hear [you]" (Isaiah 59:2). The graver the transgression, the greater is the separation from God; the cloud in which He is ensconced becomes thicker. Nonetheless, God is never completely divorced from Israel, for it says He "remains with [the Israelites] even when they are unclean" (Leviticus 16:17). The task of the sinner is to reveal God again, which he accomplishes through repentance. The Sages say that a *ba'al teshuvah*, one who has repented, is greater than an absolutely righteous person (Berachoth 34b). The reason is that the *ba'al teshuvah* has accomplished a feat which the righteous man has not accomplished: the revelation of the *Shechinah* from behind a thick division, a thick cloud.

■ ■ ■

וַיִּקַּח יִתְרוֹ חֹתֵן מֹשֶׁה עֹלָה וּזְבָחִים לֵאלֹהִים וַיָּבֹא אַהֲרֹן וְכֹל זִקְנֵי יִשְׂרָאֵל לֶאֱכָל־לֶחֶם עִם־חֹתֵן מֹשֶׁה לִפְנֵי הָאֱלֹהִים.

*Jethro, Moses' father-in-law, brought burnt offerings and [other] offerings to God. Aaron and all the elders of Israel came to share the meal with Moses' father-in-law before God.* (18:12)

Normally, when a person goes to visit a relative, the visitor brings along a gift. But Jethro's gift was the sacrifices, and they were brought not to Moses, but to God.

When Aaron and the elders saw that Jethro had defied convention and brought a gift to God, they concluded that God was certainly with Jethro. They came to eat with him so that they could partake in a meal before God. This is the Torah's intent when it says that "Aaron and all the elders of Israel came to share the meal with Moses' father-in-law *before God*."

## The Eternal Heritage

This also serves to explain why the Torah does not say that Jethro "sacrificed" or "offered" the offerings; rather, he "brought," or, more literally, "took." The significance of his act was not the actual sacrifice, but the fact that he took, selected, a gift to God. It was that aspect — the gift, as opposed to the actual sacrifice — which led Aaron to understand Jethro's greatness. And the verse mentions that Jethro was "Moses' father-in-law." Although Moses was a relative, and Jethro would have been expected to bring him a gift, Jethro's gift was to God. *(Alshich)*

■ ■ ■

וַיְהִי מִמָּחֳרָת וַיֵּשֶׁב מֹשֶׁה לִשְׁפֹּט אֶת־הָעָם וַיַּעֲמֹד הָעָם עַל־מֹשֶׁה מִן־הַבֹּקֶר עַד־הָעָרֶב.

*The next day, Moses sat to judge the people. They stood around Moses from morning till evening.* (18:13)

"The next day" — Rashi quotes the Midrash, which says that "next day" does not refer to the day after Jethro came. Rather, it refers to the day after Moses brought the second set of tablets to the Israelites. Moses came down from Mount Sinai on Yom Kippur, and so on the next day, with the laws given him by God in hand, Moses sat to judge the Israelites. Ibn Ezra says that this does refer to the day after Jethro arrived.

Rashi's proof for his contention is that Moses told Jethro (verse 16), "I teach God's laws and decrees"; Moses could not have done this before he received the Torah.

Rashi is not necessarily saying that this day was not the day after Jethro came, and that he arrived prior to Yom Kippur. Rashi's point is only that the words "next day" cannot refer to the previous event related by the Torah. Sifthei Chachamim explains that, since there is no indication from the Torah on what date Jethro arrived, it would be technically improper to go on with the term "next day." This term infers that we are aware of the calendar date. Since we do know that Moses descended from the mountain on Yom Kippur — this can be calculated elsewhere — Rashi says that the "next day" was the day following his descent.

Rashi goes on to say that, even according to the view that Jethro

## Yithro

came before the Lawgiving, this particular portion is not placed in the proper chronological order. Rashi proves this from the fact that the Torah says here that Jethro went back to his country (verse 27). We find Jethro's departure mentioned later as well, after the giving of the Torah (Numbers 10:30). Since there is no indication that Jethro left and later came back, we must assume that he only left once, after the Lawgiving, even if he arrived beforehand.

Ramban says that Rashi cannot mean that this was the day immediately following Yom Kippur. The Torah relates that Moses, Aaron, and Jethro ate a festive meal on the day Jethro arrived. If that day was Yom Kippur, how did Moses and Aaron eat? Furthermore, Moses was certainly busy on the day after Yom Kippur, teaching the Israelites the laws he had just learned with God on the mountain. He would not have had the time to sit all day in judgment of the Israelites. Therefore, Ramban says that this episode took place several days after Yom Kippur.

Mizrachi challenges Ramban's explanation, and says that the day in question was indeed the one immediately following Yom Kippur. Mizrachi has several proofs for his opinion. Firstly, Rashi says that this was *"motza'ei* Yom Kippur, the day after Yom Kippur." Additionally, the word *mimacharath,* "The next day," cannot refer to any day other than the one immediately following.

As for the fact that the Israelites ate on Yom Kippur, Mizrachi points out that they also did so the year that Solomon's Temple was completed (Kings I, 8:65). If they could eat on that occasion, then they could certainly eat in celebration of the giving of the Torah. Moreover, they were not yet commanded regarding Yom Kippur, and so would not have had to fast.

Divrei David argues that Moses and Aaron would not have eaten on Yom Kippur even if the Israelites were not yet commanded regarding the holiday. The Talmud (Yoma 28b) declares that Abraham kept even the minor commandments, despite the fact that he was not required to do so. Certainly, then, Moses and Aaron fasted on Yom Kippur even before the Torah was given.

Divrei David argues further that the Talmud (Moed Kattan 9a) is critical of Solomon for eating on Yom Kippur after the completion of the Temple. Therefore, it would be wrong to assume that Moses and Aaron also did so.

Instead, Divrei David gives his own version of how Rashi understood the sequence of events, based on the view that Jethro joined the Israelites after the Lawgiving. Divrei David says that Moses came down on Yom Kippur. On that very day, Jethro came, and Moses taught the Israelites what he had learned from God. The next night — the night after Yom Kippur — Moses, Aaron, and Jethro feasted. The next day Moses sat to judge the people.

With this calculation Divrei David resolves why Rashi could not say that "The next day" refers to the day after Jethro arrived and ate with Moses and Aaron. They had their meal at night, and the night is part of the next day. It would therefore be incorrect to term the morning following their meal the "next day."

An additional difficulty is why Rashi has a different proof for why this portion must be out of chronological order even according to the opinion that Jethro came before the Lawgiving. Why isn't the proof from "I teach God's laws and decrees" sufficient? Divrei David answers that the debate regarding the timing of Jethro's arrival actually stems from these very words. The opinion which believes Jethro arrived after the Lawgiving obtains his theory from here. Since Moses could not have taught the laws before the Lawgiving, Jethro must have come afterwards. However, the other opinion believes that these words refer to the laws Moses learned at Marah. There is thus no proof from here that Jethro came after the Lawgiving. Nevertheless, Rashi says that, even according to this opinion, the section starting with the present verse took place after Yom Kippur, because Jethro did not return home until well after the Israelites had received the Torah.

■

"From morning till evening" — R. Shmuel Salant was asked why he didn't set a particular time period to welcome visitors who had halachic questions or other problems. He responded that a Jew, and a Jewish leader in particular, must walk in God's ways and emulate His characteristics. God is prepared to answer those who turn to Him at any and every moment of the day. As the text of the Grace

## Yithro

After Meals reads, "You nourish and maintain us constantly, every day, at all times, and in every hour." *(Peninei Torah)*

■ ■ ■

וַיֹּאמֶר מֹשֶׁה לְחֹתְנוֹ כִּי־יָבֹא אֵלַי הָעָם לִדְרֹשׁ אֱלֹהִים.
כִּי־יִהְיֶה לָהֶם דָּבָר בָּא אֵלַי וְשָׁפַטְתִּי בֵּין אִישׁ וּבֵין רֵעֵהוּ וְהוֹדַעְתִּי אֶת־חֻקֵּי הָאֱלֹהִים וְאֶת־תּוֹרֹתָיו.

*Moses replied to his father-in-law, "The people come to me to seek God. "Whenever they have a problem, they come to me. I judge between a man and his neighbor, and I teach God's laws and decrees." (18:15, 16)*

One day, R. Abish of Frankfurt was informed that a certain man in the city had begun to open his store for business on the Sabbath.

R. Abish desired to meet with the man in order to convince him to mend his ways, but he was uncertain how to go about the task. He could not speak to the man in the synagogue, for the latter did not attend. If he asked the man to come and meet with him, the storeowner would refuse. If R. Abish sent a messenger with instructions to keep the store closed, the man would not obey. And if the rabbi himself went to the man, and his plea were ignored, the ramifications could be enormous, since others might see the incident as a precedent and follow in the man's footsteps.

Finally R. Abish hit upon a plan. He asked one of his friends, a well-known merchant, to buy merchandise on credit at the store. The friend was to later refuse to pay, at which time the storeowner would demand a *din Torah*, a trial, before a Rabbinical court. The case would come to R. Abish, and he would use the opportunity to admonish the man regarding the desecration of the Sabbath.

Everything went according to plan. When the storeowner came, R. Abish admitted that the incident had been a ruse, and proceeded to lecture the man. The storeowner was moved by R. Abish's words, and he promised to desist henceforth from desecrating the Sabbath. But he also expressed surprise that R. Abish had resorted to deception, creating a *din Torah* where none existed.

R. Abish replied that Moses himself had acted similarly. Moses told Jethro, "Whenever they have a problem, they come to me . . .

and I teach God's laws and decrees." There were — said the rabbi — among the Israelites those who had no interest in hearing about God's laws. Moses waited until these people had some personal matters which needed his attention. When these people had a "problem," they would come to him, and he would use the opportunity to "teach God's laws and decrees."
*(MeOtzareinu HaYashan)*

R. Menachem Mendel of Kosov makes the same deduction from this verse. He adds that Moses' example must be followed by every *tzaddik*, in every generation, for every *tzaddik* is a reflection of Moses, since Moses' spiritual influence is felt in every generation.
*(R. Menachem Mendel of Kosov)*

■

The verse literally reads, "Whenever they have a problem, *it comes* to me." The problem — not the people — would come to Moses. If the people were the subject, the plural, not the singular, should have been used.

Meshech Chochmah explains that Moses did not take personal notice of the litigants involved in the cases he adjudicated. His attention was focused solely on the problem. He did not allow the identity of the disputants to cloud his judgment.

In this vein, Ma'ayanah shel Torah relates that when a case would come before the Rabbi of Bialystok he would not look at the participants. Rather, he would sit with eyes shut and hear them out. He feared that he might recognize one of the litigants as a friend or an important person, and that his decision would be influenced by this knowledge.

■ ■ ■

וַיֹּאמֶר חֹתֵן מֹשֶׁה אֵלָיו לֹא־טוֹב הַדָּבָר אֲשֶׁר אַתָּה עֹשֶׂה. נָבֹל תִּבֹּל גַּם־אַתָּה גַּם־הָעָם הַזֶּה אֲשֶׁר עִמָּךְ כִּי־כָבֵד מִמְּךָ הַדָּבָר לֹא־תוּכַל עֲשֹׂהוּ לְבַדֶּךָ.

Moses' father-in-law said to him, "What you are doing is not good.

## Yithro

*"You are going to wear yourself out, along with this nation that is with you. Your responsibility is too great; you cannot handle it by yourself. . . ."* (18:17, 18)

Regarding the second day of Creation, Rashi asks, "Why doesn't it say 'that it was good *(tov)*' on the second day [as it does on the other days]? Because the work of creating the water was not finished until the third day, but it was started on the second day, and something that is unfinished is not considered 'good' " (Genesis 1:7).

Jethro told Moses, "What you are doing is *not good*." You will "wear yourself out" and be unable to complete the task, and an unfinished task is not termed "good." *(Imrei Shammai)*

■

"You are going to wear yourself out."

The verse literally reads, "You are going to wear yourself out also." The word "also," *gam*, is superfluous. Rashi says that it comes to include Aaron, Hur, and the seventy elders.

Rashi writes later that Hur was killed by the Israelites when he objected to their attempt to make the Golden Calf (32:5). Obviously, then, Rashi's gloss on the present verse cannot be reconciled with the opinion in the Talmud which maintains that Jethro did not arrive until after the giving of the Torah. According to that view, Hur was already dead at the time Jethro advised Moses on the judiciary.

Da'ath Zekenim MiBa'alei HaTosafoth asserts that the view which includes Hur in the present verse believes that Jethro came before the Torah was given. Additionally, Rashi must assume here that Jethro instructed Moses regarding the judicial system before the Torah was given (not as Rashi says in verse 13), because Hur was dead after the Lawgiving and would not have been mentioned by Jethro.

Maharshal adopts a different approach. He says that, although Rashi does say later that Hur died during the Golden Calf episode, there is an opinion which maintains that Hur did not die then. It is with this other view in mind that Rashi makes the present comment. If that is the case, then Rashi here may agree that Jethro arrived after the Torah was given.

Divrei David, who explains earlier that Rashi did not wish to take sides in the debate over the timing of Jethro's arrival (see verse 9), could adopt Maharshal's explanation, but not Da'ath Zekenim's, as with Da'ath Zekenim's approach Rashi does take sides here. Nevertheless, Divrei David chooses to take a different tack. He avers that Rashi does not intend to say that Hur was alive at this juncture. Rather, Hur's name is used only as an example. Jethro told Moses: Even were Aaron, Hur, and the seventy elders present, you would nonetheless wear yourself out.

Although Hur was now dead, he had been in Moses' coterie of aides, as were Aaron and the elders (24:14), and so Jethro cited him along with the others.

Divrei David points to a similar case elsewhere in Scripture. It says, "If a land sins . . . I will destroy its men and animals. Even were these three men there — Noah, Daniel, and Job — they would, in their righteousness, save [only] their own lives" (Ezekiel 14:13, 14). Now, Noah, Daniel, and Job were not alive in Ezekiel's day. It is clear that their names are mentioned as examples. So it is here with Hur.

Mizrachi suggests that Hur's name appears due to a printer's error.

∎

Mizrachi notes that Rashi here contradicts both views of the Midrash Mechilta regarding this verse. Rashi says that the word *gam*, "also," comes to include Aaron, Hur, and the seventy elders. In the Midrash, R. Yehoshua and R. Eleazar HaModai argue as to the meaning of the text. R. Yehoshua maintains that "yourself" refers to Moses, "also" refers to Aaron, and "the nation that is with you" refers to the seventy elders. R. Eleazar HaModai contends that "yourself" refers to Moses, "also" refers to Aaron and his sons Nadav and Avihu, and "the nation that is with you" refers to the seventy elders. Firstly, Rashi substitutes Hur for Nadav and Avihu. Secondly, neither R. Yehoshua nor R. Eleazar HaModai sees the word "also" as including the elders; both derive the inclusion of the elders from the words "the nation that is with you." Rashi sees "also" as referring to the elders as well.

## Yithro

Mizrachi answers that perhaps Rashi had an alternate text for the Midrash, in which "also" was seen as including the elders. And in fact it appears that the Gaon of Vilna amends the Midrash in a similar fashion.

Gur Aryeh poses the same question on Rashi, but responds differently. He says that Rashi's intent is to convey the simple explanation of the text. In the simple reading, the words "this nation that is with you" would not include the elders. Like Moses, Aaron, and Hur, the elders were separate from the general populace, in that they were judges. Jethro wished to ease two different burdens. The burden which Jethro sought to alleviate from the elders was the same one which he desired to remove from Moses and Aaron — that of judging the people. The burden carried by the general populace, "the nation that is with you," was a different one — the fact that they were forced to stand all day, awaiting the disposal of their cases (verse 14). The elders fell into the category of Moses and Aaron, and so Rashi included them with the two leaders. Rashi was not concerned with the precise method of amplification as applied to the verse — which was the Midrash's concern — but with consistent categorization. Therefore, he placed the elders together with Moses and Aaron.

■■■

וְאַתָּה תֶחֱזֶה מִכָּל־הָעָם אַנְשֵׁי־חַיִל יִרְאֵי אֱלֹהִים אַנְשֵׁי אֱמֶת שֹׂנְאֵי בָצַע וְשַׂמְתָּ עֲלֵהֶם שָׂרֵי אֲלָפִים שָׂרֵי מֵאוֹת שָׂרֵי חֲמִשִּׁים וְשָׂרֵי עֲשָׂרֹת.

". . . You must seek out from among the people wealthy, God-fearing men — men of truth, who hate improper gain. You must appoint them over [the people] as leaders of thousands, leaders of hundreds, leaders of fifties, and leaders of tens. . . ." (18:21)

There arose a dispute in the town of Lancut regarding the rabbi, a chassid, whom some members of the community sought to remove from his position. The two sides brought their disagreement to R. Shlomo Kluger of Brody for resolution.

The Rabbi of Lancut was a follower of R. Meir of Peremyshlyany. R. Meir sent a letter to R. Shlomo Kluger in support of the rabbi; R.

Meir asserted that he had seen, with the aid of Divine inspiration, that the rabbi possessed all the attributes prescribed by the Sages for his position.

R. Shlomo Kluger countered by citing a debate in the Midrash between R. Yehoshua and R. Eleazar HaModai regarding the words "You must seek out." R. Yehoshua explains that Moses was to select the judges with the aid of Divine inspiration. R. Eleazar HaModai disagrees and says that Moses was to be guided by his intellect.

Moses was the greatest of all the prophets. Nonetheless, R. Eleazar HaModai did not believe it appropriate for Moses to choose the judges with Divine inspiration. Rather, he was to use his own judgment.

The moral, said R. Shlomo Kluger, is based on the Talmud's declaration that "a leader is not appointed for a community unless the community is first consulted" (Berachoth 55a). Most people have no connection with Divine inspiration, and so their leader has to be selected based on wisdom, a quality to which the average person can relate. *(MeOtzareinu HaYashan)*

■

"Who hate improper gain" — This refers to those who hate to have their money in court (Rashi); i.e., they do not like having to go to trial for the purpose of collecting money.

There are many times when the claimant in a monetary dispute is legally correct, but would be morally wrong to demand his money. An example is when the claimant is wealthy while the defendant is poor. The importance of this principle is stressed by the Sages, who say that Jerusalem was destroyed because the people insisted on having their cases judged by the strict rule of the law, and showed no compassion (Bava Metzia 30b).

This is Rashi's intent when he says that Moses sought for the judiciary men who hated to have their money in court. The word *din*, "court," also means "law." These despised money which was coming to them only due to the law but which they were not morally entitled to take. *(MeOtzareinu HaYashan, citing R. Chaim Isaac Justman)*

■ ■ ■

## Yithro

וְשָׁפְטוּ אֶת־הָעָם בְּכָל־עֵת אֶת־הַדָּבָר הַקָּשֶׁה יְבִיאוּן אֶל־מֹשֶׁה וְכָל־הַדָּבָר הַקָּטֹן יִשְׁפּוּטוּ הֵם.

*[The judges] administered justice on a regular basis, bringing the difficult cases to Moses and judging the simple cases themselves. (18:26)*

Jethro had said, "They will bring every major case to you" (verse 22); but the Torah records that the people brought the "difficult" cases to Moses. Why did Jethro use the term "major," *gadol,* while the Torah uses the word "difficult," *kasheh?*

Among the nations of the world, the importance of a case often depends on the amount of money at stake. Cases which involve large sums are brought to higher courts, while those involving small amounts are heard in the lower courts. In a *din Torah* — a case before a Jewish court — the amount of money at stake is irrelevant; the Talmud (Sanhedrin 8a) declares that the judgment regarding a *perutah* (a small coin) is as important as one regarding a hundred *maneh* (a large sum). It is not the amount of money, but rather the nature of the case — its relative difficulty or simplicity — that is significant, with the more difficult cases being heard by more learned men. Hence, while Jethro thought that Moses should judge the "major" cases — those involving the most money — the Torah testifies that the criterion was rather the degree of difficulty involved: the Israelites brought the *"difficult* cases to Moses."

*(R. Chaim Berlin)*

■ ■ ■

וַיִּסְעוּ מֵרְפִידִים וַיָּבֹאוּ מִדְבַּר סִינַי וַיַּחֲנוּ בַּמִּדְבָּר וַיִּחַן־שָׁם יִשְׂרָאֵל נֶגֶד הָהָר.

*[The Israelites] had departed from Rephidim and arrived in the Sinai desert, camping in the wilderness. Israel encamped there, opposite the mountain. (19:2)*

"Israel encamped there, opposite the mountain." The word *vayichan,* "encamped," is in singular form. The Sages explain that the Israelites came to Mount Sinai "as one man, with one heart"; they were united in their willingness to receive the Torah. The singular form alludes to this unity of purpose.

*The Eternal Heritage*

Why is it important for us to know of the Israelites' unity?

The Torah is teaching that it would have been impossible for the Israelites to receive the Torah had they not been united; the Torah could not have been given to a divided nation. Such a nation would not have deserved to receive the Torah, whose "ways are ways of peace" (Proverbs 3:17).

This also serves to explain the tradition that not only the Israelites who were alive at the time, but all Jews ever to be born, were present at Mount Sinai for the Revelation. The Torah is the inheritance of every single Jew, and so each one had to consent to accept it.

The Revelation is marked on the holiday of Shavuoth. With the above idea in mind, it is evident that the message of Shavuoth is one of unity. A lack of unity is anathema to the spirit of the holiday.

This allows us to understand the symbolism of Sefirah, the mourning period which is observed between Passover and Shavuoth. During that time, the 24,000 students of the Talmudic Sage Rabbi Akiva died in an epidemic. The Sages say that they perished because they were not properly respectful toward one another (Yevamoth 62b). *Sin'ath chinam*, groundless hatred, is a quality which is in diametric opposition to the unity and love that are the hallmarks of Shavuoth. That holiday cannot exist in an atmosphere of hatred, and so Rabbi Akiva's disciples died in the days preceding Shavuoth.

Now, Shavuoth falls on the sixth day of Sivan. In the Midrash, the second day of Sivan is termed Yom HaMeyuchas, the "Day With a Pedigree." The day preceding the second of Sivan is that of the New Moon, while the following day is the first of the Shelosheth Yemai Hagbalah, the three days of preparation kept by the Israelites before they received the Torah. Since both the first of Sivan and the third of Sivan are significant days, the second of Sivan acquires importance as well. It is recognized as a day which is surrounded by important days; it has a lineage, a pedigree.

But this is difficult to comprehend. The fact that Yom HaMeyuchas is surrounded by significant days should not be a sufficient basis to declare it a holiday. After all, it has no significance in itself. Moreover, the name Yom HaMeyuchas would seem to magnify the day's lack of importance, by indicating that its lone claim to fame is that it follows and precedes important days.

In fact, however, there is a profound lesson in the naming of the second of Sivan. The Sages are teaching that one's environment is important, because it has a great impact upon him. If one places himself in positive surroundings — where Torah values are stressed — then he has taken a positive step, since he is bound to be affected favorably. This step merits recognition — even before the effect of the environment has actually been felt. The opposite is true if one locates in a poor environment — one where Torah values are not at a premium.

Thus, the second of Sivan, with its name denoting its position on the calendar, is not at all denigrated by the title Yom HaMeyuchas. On the contrary, the term is meant to be laudatory; because the second of Sivan is placed within a positive environment, it is praiseworthy.

Having established that the message of Shavuoth is one of unity, it is now easy to understand why Yom HaMeyuchas falls immediately before that holiday. True unity is achieved when every Jew is dedicated to the pursuit of God's will. When that occurs, the quintessential "good environment" exists. Wherever he turns in an environment of this nature, a Jew will find other Jews who are like-minded. Thus, Yom HaMeyuchas symbolizes the necessity of striving for the ultimate "good environment," for the unbreached unity of the Jewish people.

■

Rabbi Akiva's students died because they were not sufficiently respectful toward one another. Whereas Rabbi Akiva is considered the father of the Oral Law, his disciples were certainly scholars of the first order. How is it possible that they lacked the basic attribute of *derech eretz,* courtesy among men? This becomes even more perplexing when note is taken of the principle that *Derech eretz kadmah laTorah*: courtesy between men (lit., the "way of the land") takes precedence over the Torah (Tanna D'vei Eliyahu 1).

It is clear that Rabbi Akiva's disciples were not simply unattuned to one another's sensitivities. A possible explanation would be that each of the 24,000 students rode a different track in attempting to understand and absorb the Torah. Each man had his unique approach to Torah study, with his unique methods and emphases. The division among the disciples arose from these different approaches, since each student saw his own approach as superior.

Had these men not been disciples of Rabbi Akiva, there would have been no contention among them. But Rabbi Akiva is regarded as the father of the Oral Law, and this status yielded a plethora of methodologies among his students. With each man dedicated to his own approach, to the exclusion of any other, a division became inevitable.

The inability of the students to overcome this dissension brought on their punishment.

An obvious question arises in reference to the tragic story of R. Akiva's disciples. R. Akiva is the author of what is perhaps the strongest statement on human relations to be found in Rabbinic literature. Commenting on the Torah's words "You must love your neighbor as [you love] yourself" (Leviticus 19:18), R. Akiva said: "This is the cardinal principle of the Torah; all the rest is commentary" (Midrash). It seems incredibly ironic that the students of R. Akiva are the ones who erred in the matter of *derech eretz*.

We may answer that R. Akiva made his statement *after* his students died. Having seen how destructive baseless hatred could be, he declared that the cardinal principle of the Torah is love among human beings. Once that is achieved, then, as the Talmudic Sage Hillel said, "all the rest is commentary" (Shabbath 31a); i.e., it is possible to focus on studying and interpreting the Torah. Without this love, Torah study is undermined, as it was in the case of R. Akiva's students.

■ ■ ■

## Yithro

וְעַתָּה אִם־שָׁמוֹעַ תִּשְׁמְעוּ בְּקֹלִי וּשְׁמַרְתֶּם אֶת־בְּרִיתִי וִהְיִיתֶם לִי סְגֻלָּה מִכָּל־הָעַמִּים כִּי־לִי כָּל־הָאָרֶץ.
וְאַתֶּם תִּהְיוּ־לִי מַמְלֶכֶת כֹּהֲנִים וְגוֹי קָדוֹשׁ אֵלֶּה הַדְּבָרִים אֲשֶׁר תְּדַבֵּר אֶל־בְּנֵי יִשְׂרָאֵל.

" '. . . Now, if you obey Me and keep My covenant, you shall be My treasure from among all the nations, as all the world is Mine.
" 'You will be a kingdom of priests and a holy nation to Me.' These are the words that you must relate to the Israelites." (19:5, 6)

"You shall be My treasure from among all the nations, as all the world is Mine." R. Yaakov of Lissa says that these words come to emphasize the eternal chosenness of the Jewish people. Not only are they God's treasure at a time when the other nations are mired in idol worship, but also when the nations serve God — even in the days when God will be able to say that "all the world is Mine." This refers to the end of days, when "I will give all the nations clear speech, so that all may call in God's name" (Zefaniah 3:9). Even at that time the Jewish people will remain His treasure.

■

"You will be a kingdom of priests and a holy nation to Me."
The Jewish people are a nation of priests, in that they are supposed to serve as a teacher to the other nations. However, their task is not, as is believed by modern scholars, simply to translate Jewish works, making them accessible to others. Rather, they are to be a "holy nation," one whose way of life serves as an example. The Jews' life style and purity of characteristics are to be a living book. By fulfilling the Torah's precepts, Israel teaches the other nations the way to purity and holiness.

Israel can concentrate on playing this role fully only when it sits in its own land, without fear of other nations.

*(R. Avraham Yitzchak Kook)*

■

"These are the words that you must relate to the Israelites" — no less and no more (Rashi).

Kthav Sofer asks: Would it have occurred to Moses to subtract

## The Eternal Heritage

from or add to God's words? Why did he have to be admonished not to do so?

Kthav Sofer says that the answer to this question becomes evident only after another difficulty is resolved: Why did God first say, "You shall be My treasure," and then, in a separate clause, add, "You will be a kingdom of priests"? Why didn't He combine these promises in one clause: "You shall be My treasure and a kingdom of priests"?

The answer — says Kthav Sofer — is that these two promises were rewards given for different reasons. From the moment that the Israelites agreed to accept the Torah at Mount Sinai, God promised that they would be His treasure. This reward was granted regardless of whether the Israelites observed the Torah's laws properly. It was given because the Israelites took the step other nations declined to take: accepting the Torah.

The promise that the Israelites would be "a kingdom of priests and a holy nation" was not a reward for accepting the Torah. Rather, it was predicated on their rising to a higher level, by keeping the Torah's statutes. God could not assure that the Israelites would achieve this status; it was dependent upon their electing to follow in the ways of the Torah. Hence, it was not a promise, but a request; God now *asked* the Israelites to become a kingdom of priests. By contrast, He *promised* them that they would be a treasured nation, and so these two items had to be expressed separately.

With this explained, Kthav Sofer proceeds to answer his first question. God said, "These are the words that you must relate to the Israelites" — no less and no more. Moses was not being warned to relay God's words in a precise manner; he certainly would not have done otherwise. Rather, he was being told something else: to tell the Israelites "These . . . words," these two things: that they would be a treasure and that they could rise to priestly heights. And Moses was to impress upon the people that they would be "no less" than a treasure — no matter how they comported themselves, their status as a treasured nation would never be taken away. Furthermore, they could become "no more" than a priestly nation, as that is the highest level attainable.

■ ■ ■

## Yithro

וַיַּעֲנוּ כָל־הָעָם יַחְדָּו וַיֹּאמְרוּ כֹּל אֲשֶׁר־דִּבֶּר ה' נַעֲשֶׂה וַיָּשֶׁב מֹשֶׁה אֶת־דִּבְרֵי הָעָם אֶל־ה'.

*All the people answered as one, saying, "All that God has spoken we will do." Moses brought the people's response back to God. (19:8)*

There was a banker in Budapest who kept his place of business open on the Sabbath. R. Avraham Shmuel Binyamin Sofer, who is known as Kthav Sofer, asked the man to come and see him. In their conversation, R. Sofer rebuked the banker and sought to convince him to close his bank on the Sabbath. However, the banker retorted that he was not observant and had no connection to the mitzvos. R. Sofer responded that, if the banker did not heed his plea out of fear of God, he should nevertheless do so due to embarrassment.

The banker chuckled at this line of reasoning. How, he asked, did embarrassment enter the picture? What shame was there in not being observant?

R. Sofer replied that the Sages say, "If one does not have the quality of humility, it is a certainty that his ancestors were not present at Mount Sinai" (Nedarim 20a). How did the Sages know this? The answer — R. Sofer said — stems from the certainty that there were heretics among the Israelites; these people did not desire to accept the Torah, with its many obligations. Yet we know that even *they* agreed to accept it; as the Torah relates, "*All* the people answered as one." Given the overwhelming sentiment in favor of receiving the Torah, these individuals were embarrassed to be out of the mainstream. Therefore, they also proclaimed that they were willing to heed God's word.

The Sages deduced from this that, if one lacks the trait of humility and is willing to separate himself from the mainstream, it is a sign that his forefathers were not present at Mount Sinai. Thus, since the banker was Jewish, he had to respect the tradition out of embarrassment, regardless of his personal views.

*(MeOtzareinu HaYashan)*

■

There are some commandments which devolve solely upon the priests. Others are exclusive to the Levites. Yet others are obligatory

## The Eternal Heritage

only for the high priest, or the king, or the Sanhedrin, or for one who owns land or a house. Therefore, the Torah can be fully observed only by the entire Jewish people. All Jews are connected with one another, and when one Jew performs a mitzvah all Jews are rewarded. As Scripture says, "You are My sheep, the sheep which I shepherd; you are a man" (Ezekiel 34:31) — the Jewish people are considered one man. Each Jew forms a part of the body of that man and must fulfill the commandments related to his part.

Because the Jews make up one organism and therefore, each Jew becomes a full person through his participation in the community of Israel, one is supposed to study even the commandments that he is unable to fulfill. As the Sages say, "If one studies the laws of the sin offering, it is as if he offered the sin offering" (Menachoth 110a). Hence, the Israelites promised, "All that God has spoken we will do and listen to, *na'aseh venishma*" (24:7). They would "do," observe, the laws applicable to them, and would "listen to" — study and analyze — the laws applicable to others.

The present verse doesn't say *venishma*, "we will listen," because the emphasis here is on action, not on study, and on the collective aspect — that they would "do" all the commandments "as one" — that they understood their responsibility for one another, and would each act for the benefit of the whole. *(Meshech Chochmah)*

■ ■ ■

וַיֹּאמֶר ה' אֶל־מֹשֶׁה הִנֵּה אָנֹכִי בָּא אֵלֶיךָ בְּעַב הֶעָנָן בַּעֲבוּר יִשְׁמַע הָעָם בְּדַבְּרִי עִמָּךְ וְגַם־בְּךָ יַאֲמִינוּ לְעוֹלָם וַיַּגֵּד מֹשֶׁה אֶת־דִּבְרֵי הָעָם אֶל־ה'.
*God said to Moses, "I will come to you in a thick cloud, so that all the people will hear when I speak to you; then they will believe in you forever." Moses relayed the people's response to God. (19:9)*

"They will believe in you forever" is similar to God's declaration that "This is not true of My servant Moses, who is trusted throughout My house" (Numbers 12:7). The meaning of these verses would appear to lie in one of the distinctions between Moses and all other prophets. If two prophets contradict one another, both prophecies are discarded. However, if a prophet contradicts the words of

## Yithro

Moses, the prophecy of Moses stands and the other prophet's words are disregarded (Rambam, Hilchoth Yesodei HaTorah 8:3).

In saying that Moses was trusted throughout God's house and that the Israelites would believe in him forever, the Torah is asserting that only Moses' prophecies are indisputable.

(R. Yitzchak Zev HaLevi Soloveichik)

■ ■ ■

וְהִגְבַּלְתָּ אֶת־הָעָם סָבִיב לֵאמֹר הִשָּׁמְרוּ לָכֶם עֲלוֹת בָּהָר וּנְגֹעַ בְּקָצֵהוּ כָּל־הַנֹּגֵעַ בָּהָר מוֹת יוּמָת.

"... Set a boundary for the people around [the mountain], and tell them to be careful not to climb the mountain, or even touch its edge. Anyone who touches the mountain will be put to death. . . ." (19:12)

Chafetz Chaim makes the following inference: The Israelites were warned not to touch Mount Sinai because it had become holy due to the Lawgiving. This honor was extended to the mountain although it had no mind or feelings. Certainly, then, one must take extreme care not to dishonor a Torah scholar, one who has actually studied and absorbed the Torah.

R. Shmuel Greiniman, the editor of the work which collects Chafetz Chaim's Torah thoughts, relates a story that illustrates Chafetz Chaim's view of Torah Sages.

Chafetz Chaim (R. Yisrael Meir Kagan of Radin) constantly defended the leader of his generation, R. Chaim Ozer Grodzinski, from attack by less religious elements. Indeed, Chafetz Chaim once went to the city of Vilna and stayed for several weeks, calling in each of the community's leaders and impressing upon them that the honor of the Jewish people is inextricably bound up with the honor of its leader.

At a meeting of yeshiva heads and rabbis, talk turned to a proposed journey to the United States by R. Chaim Ozer for the purpose of strengthening the position of its yeshivos. R. Chaim Ozer demurred, pointing to his ill health and the effects such a trip would have on him. While Chafetz Chaim had been among those urging R. Chaim Ozer to undertake the mission, he changed his mind upon hearing the latter's objection. Chafetz Chaim said, "Since this would affect your health, I won't urge you to go, since I am as concerned about your welfare as I am about the welfare of the entire Jewish people."

■ ■ ■

וַיֵּרֶד מֹשֶׁה מִן־הָהָר אֶל־הָעָם וַיְקַדֵּשׁ אֶת־הָעָם וַיְכַבְּסוּ שִׂמְלֹתָם.
*Moses went down from the mountain to the people. He sanctified the people, and they immersed their clothing.* (19:14)

"From the mountain to the people" — This teaches that Moses paid no attention to his personal affairs. Rather, he went straight from the mountain to the people (Rashi).

R. Yecheskel of Kuzhmir asks: What personal affairs did Moses have that required tending? He was not a businessman!

The explanation — says R. Yecheskel — is that Moses neglected his own *spiritual* needs, because the spiritual needs of the people took precedence. *(Iturei Torah)*

■ ■ ■

וַיֹּאמֶר אֶל־הָעָם הֱיוּ נְכֹנִים לִשְׁלֹשֶׁת יָמִים אַל־תִּגְּשׁוּ אֶל־אִשָּׁה.
*[Moses] said to the people, "Keep yourselves in readiness for three days. Do not come near a woman."* (19:15)

On the fourth of Sivan, God told Moses that the Israelites would have to prepare for three days before they could receive the Torah (Rashi on verse 9). Thus, the third of these days was the sixth of Sivan. However, the Talmud (Shabbath 86b) records a debate concerning the actual date of the Lawgiving. While the Rabbis subscribe to the above calculation, R. Yossi contends that Moses added a fourth day of preparation, with the result that the Torah was given on the seventh of Sivan.

In saying that Moses acted on his own and delayed the Lawgiving, R. Yossi is asserting that there were two parts to the Lawgiving: that along with the Written Law was given the Oral Law. R. Yossi is

## Yithro

saying that these two are inseparable, and that the Oral and Written Laws have the same Divine origin.

The Oral Law finds its expression in the power of the Sages to interpret the Written Law. Moses analyzed the Written Torah and determined that the proper procedure was to add a fourth day of preparation. This was not an extralegal act, but rather one that was integral to the Torah system.

This also serves to explain why Shavuoth, the holiday which commemorates the giving of the Torah, falls on the sixth day of Sivan, even though the halacha is in accordance with R. Yossi, who says that the Torah was given on the seventh of the month. While it is true that the Written Law was not given until the seventh, the Oral Law was given on the sixth, when Moses elected to delay the giving of the Ten Commandments. This decision was also part of the Lawgiving, and so it is proper to celebrate Shavuoth on the sixth of Sivan. *(Heard from R. Yechiel Perr)*

■ ■ ■

וַיְהִי קוֹל הַשֹּׁפָר הוֹלֵךְ וְחָזֵק מְאֹד מֹשֶׁה יְדַבֵּר וְהָאֱלֹהִים יַעֲנֶנּוּ בְקוֹל.
*There was the sound of a ram's horn, increasing in volume to a great degree. Moses would speak, and the Lord would answer him with a voice. (19:19)*

"Moses would speak, and the Lord would answer him with a voice." One of the differences between Moses and the other prophets was that the latter were unable to speak to God; they simply heard God's message. Moses could speak to God. For example, he said to the people, "Wait here. I will hear what orders God gives regarding your case" (Numbers 9:8). And the Torah states: "Moses brought their case before God" (Ibid., 27:5). This distinction between Moses and the other prophets is made by Rambam (Hilchoth Yesodei HaTorah 7:6).

Rambam also says that the Israelites did not have faith in Moses until they witnessed the events at Mount Sinai (Ibid., 8:1). Hence, Moses' uniqueness was demonstrated at Mount Sinai, where the Israelites saw with their own eyes how he approached the mountain, and heard him speak with God.

## The Eternal Heritage

This is the meaning of the present verse. "Moses would speak" — he would ask God questions — "and the Lord would answer him with a voice": God would respond. This demonstrated Moses' uniqueness and led the people to have faith in him.

*(R. Yitzchak Zev HaLevi Soloveichik)*

■ ■ ■

וַיֵּרֶד ה' עַל־הַר סִינַי אֶל־רֹאשׁ הָהָר וַיִּקְרָא ה' לְמֹשֶׁה אֶל־רֹאשׁ הָהָר וַיַּעַל מֹשֶׁה.

*God came down onto Mount Sinai, to the peak of the mountain. He summoned Moses to the mountain peak, and Moses climbed up.* (19:20)

The Talmud (Shabbath 88a) says that at the time of Mordecai and Esther the Jewish people accepted the Torah a second time. Tosafoth explains that at Purim the Jews accepted the Torah with love — willingly; by contrast, at Mount Sinai the Torah was forced upon them. As the Talmud says, God held the mountain over their heads and threatened to bury them under it if they would not accept His Law.

Why is it that specifically during the era of Mordecai and Esther the Jews accepted the Torah with love? And why is it that up until then the Jews did not love the Torah? Given that we believe that the quality of the generations has decreased progressively since the Lawgiving at Mount Sinai, how can it be said that later generations loved the Torah more than did the earlier ones?

When one is not given the choice to reject something, then his acceptance of that thing *cannot* be out of love for it. After all, he has no alternative but to accept it.

What does the Talmud mean when it says that the mountain was held over the heads of the Israelites as a threat? At Mount Sinai, God Himself spoke to the Israelites. Furthermore, His presentation was accompanied by great thunder and lightning. An incredible spectacle occurred — the greatest contact between God and human beings that has ever taken place. It was the ultimate in *giluy panim*, the revelation of God's face. Certainly, no one could have refused to accept the Torah under such circumstances.

This is the symbolism of the mountain being placed over the

heads of the Israelites. In such a circumstance, love did not, *could not*, enter the picture. Whether or not the Israelites desired to accept the Torah was irrelevant. They had no alternative but to do so.

As the years went by, the *giluy panim* became progressively less pronounced. Yet there were prophets, who served to provide direct contact between God and the Jewish people, and the world at large as well. While the contact was not at the level achieved at Sinai, and not at the level that Moses, the greatest prophet, had with God, God did continue to communicate with human beings. Therefore, the element of love still did not enter the picture in regard to the Torah.

However, the Sages teach that the time of Mordecai and Esther coincided with the beginning of the period of *hester panim*, the "hiding of God's face." Prophecy was ceasing. The direct connection to God was being cut. In fact, Esther's name is taken as a hint of the *hester panim*, as the word "Esther" may be taken to emanate from the same root as *hester*. Additionally, we are told that God's name does not appear in the Scroll of Esther in order to hint that He had begun to hide Himself from the world.

It was only in Esther's time that the Jews finally had a choice to make regarding the Torah. Would they continue to observe the commandments, or not? Since God's presence was no longer as obvious as before, the element of fear which had forced the Jews to accept the Torah was gone. If the choice were made to continue observing the Torah, it could only be out of love for it.

This is what the Talmud and Tosafoth mean. It is not their intent to say that there was a *formal* reacceptance of the Torah by Mordecai's generation. Rather, by continuing to keep the Torah, the Jews *in effect* accepted it a second time — but this time out of love, not out of fear. The acceptance at Mount Sinai could not have full meaning for a generation which did not have direct contact with God. The Torah had to be accepted again, at a new level of awareness.

There is no comparison between the two kinds of acceptance. The first kind could occur only when there was no option, while the second one could take place only when there was a choice.

Therefore, it is not that the earlier generations did not wish to receive the Torah out of love, and it is not that they did not love the Torah. They certainly did love it. However, there was no love involved in *choosing* to accept the Torah and its commandments. The first generation where such love was possible was the generation of Mordecai and Esther.

■

When he was young, R. Chaim of Sanz was a disciple of the Rabbi of Cracow, the non-chassidic Shimon Sofer (a son of Chatham Sofer). Eventually, however, R. Chaim began to study with the chassidic R. Yisrael of Ruzhin.

One day, R. Chaim was returning from a stay in Ruzhin and was temporarily in Cracow. R. Shimon called for R. Chaim and asked why he now went to R. Yisrael to study instead of to him. "Is the Ruzhiner greater in Torah scholarship than I?" R. Shimon asked.

R. Chaim replied that there are two important mountains in the area of the Land of Israel: Mount Sinai and Mount Moriah. While the Torah was given at the former site, the Temple was built on the latter site. Why wasn't the Temple constructed on the place where the Torah had been given? The reason — asserted R. Chaim — is that Mount Moriah was where the Binding of Isaac occurred. The place where a Jew was willing to sacrifice his life to do God's will is more important than the site of the Lawgiving.

As concerns Torah scholarship — R. Chaim told R. Shimon — you are certainly greater than R. Yisrael of Ruzhin. However, in Ruzhin I have seen immense *mesiruth nefesh*, the willingness to give one's life for God. *(Shemuoth Tovoth)*

■ ■ ■

וַיֹּאמֶר מֹשֶׁה אֶל־ה׳ לֹא־יוּכַל הָעָם לַעֲלֹת אֶל־הַר סִינָי כִּי־אַתָּה הַעֵדֹתָה בָּנוּ לֵאמֹר הַגְבֵּל אֶת־הָהָר וְקִדַּשְׁתּוֹ.

Moses replied to God, "The people cannot climb Mount Sinai, because You already warned us to set a boundary around the mountain and to declare it sacred." (19:23)

R. David of Kotsk points to an apparent inconsistency in the text. In instructing the Israelites to keep away from Mount Sinai, God

## Yithro

told Moses, "Set a boundary for the *people*," or, more literally, "Keep the people within bounds" (verse 12). In contrast, Moses told God that He had "already warned us to set a boundary around the *mountain*." From Moses' words it would seem that the mountain, not the nation, was to be kept within bounds, while God had said that the nation was to be kept within bounds.

Secondly, says R. David, this dialogue between God and Moses is very long, and seems repetitive. God continues by telling Moses a second time to warn the Israelites not to approach the mountain (verse 21), Moses replies that they have already been warned, and God insists that he admonish them anyway (verse 24). This demands clarification.

Finally, Rashi comments earlier (verse 12), regarding God's original warning, that there was a sign at the boundary telling the Israelites not to approach further. What point is Rashi attempting to stress?

R. David answers that there was confusion on Moses' part whether the prohibition to approach Mount Sinai was a prohibition upon the mountain or upon the people. The former would be an example of an *issur cheftza* (a prohibition upon the object). Just as it is forbidden to eat non-kosher foods, as they are impermissible objects, so would it be forbidden to approach Mount Sinai. The latter is termed an *issur gavra* (a prohibition upon the person). In the same manner that a person is restricted from doing work on the Sabbath, the Israelites would be restricted from touching Mount Sinai. If the restriction here was an *issur gavra*, the prohibition was not upon the mountain, but upon the people.

God first told Moses, "Set a boundary for the *people*"; as Rashi explains, the purpose of the boundary was to warn the Israelites not to come closer. Moses understood this as an *issur cheftza*, as a prohibition similar to the one concerning non-kosher foods: that the mountain was a forbidden object.

It is known — says R. David — that an *issur cheftza* is stricter than an *issur gavra*, and so, when God repeated His instruction to warn the people, Moses replied, "The people cannot climb Mount Sinai, because You already warned us to set a boundary around the *mountain.*" Moses asserted that the object — the *mountain* — was the focus of the stricture, and since an object-based prohibition is of a very strict nature, there was no need to warn the Israelites a second time. They certainly would not violate such a weighty prohibition.

God replied, "Go down. You can then ascend along with Aaron. But the priests and the nation must not violate the boundary to go up toward God" (verse 24). God explained that the stricture was not object-based, for if that had been the case, Moses too would have been forbidden to ascend the mountain. Rather, it was an *issur gavra*, a person-based prohibition, extending to some persons but not to others. And in light of the relative lenience of an *issur gavra*, the people had to be warned a second time, for they might otherwise succumb to temptation and approach Mount Sinai.

*(Iturei Torah)*

■ ■ ■

וַיְדַבֵּר אֱלֹהִים אֵת כָּל־הַדְּבָרִים הָאֵלֶּה לֵאמֹר.
God spoke all these words, saying: (20:1)

"All these words" — This teaches that God spoke out all Ten Commandments simultaneously, which is something a human being cannot do. Why, then, does it add, "I am God your Lord," and "Do not have any other gods before Me"? Because God went back and detailed each commandment by itself (Rashi).

Rashi's words — which originate in the Midrash Sifre — are unclear, and several commentators strive to explain them. Levush HaOhrah asserts that God pronounced each of the Ten Commandments twice. He first said them simultaneously, and then repeated them one by one. While Moses understood God's speech when all ten were spoken together — for if nobody had understood, there would have been no purpose in saying them simultaneously — the Israelites did not understand the commandments until they were spoken separately. It is evident, however, that even after the second time the Israelites did not comprehend all of God's words, for the Torah says that Moses stood between God and the Israelites as an interpreter of the Ten Commandments (Deuteronomy 5:5). Rather, the Israelites understood the first two commandments, but not the final eight (see Makkoth 24a), which Moses had to explain again.

Levush HaOhrah says that one cannot say that God only pronounced the commandments once — simultaneously — and that Moses repeated them. This is because, according to Rashi, the word *lemor,* "saying," indicates that the Israelites answered "Yes" to the positive commandments and "No" to the negative ones. The implication is that they were responding to the direct word of God, not to Moses' repetition. Since they didn't understand God's words the first time, it must be that God repeated the commandments, at which time they were understood by the Israelites. But it was only to the first two commandments that the Israelites responded; they could not have responded to the others, since they did not understand them.

Sifthei Chachamim explains Rashi's comment as follows: If all the commandments were said simultaneously, why does Scripture state elsewhere, "God spoke one thing, but I heard two" (Psalms 62:12), implying that only two commandments — the first two — were uttered simultaneously? The answer is that God repeated only the first two commandments, and it is to this that the verse in Psalms refers. Moses repeated the remaining eight commandments.

Da'ath Zekenim MiBa'alei HaTosafoth says that the Midrash was puzzled by the fact that Moses separated the Ten Commandments into numerous sentences, even though they were all uttered together. Since this was a single pronouncement, it should have been recorded in one sentence. In answer, the Midrash says that Moses repeated the commandments. Since Moses did not speak them simultaneously, they were recorded by him in separate sentences. Hence, according to Da'ath Zekenim, Moses repeated *all* of the Ten Commandments; God said them only once.

An alternate explanation recorded by Da'ath Zekenim is that of R. Baruch. R. Baruch says that the Midrash wondered why the first two commandments — "I am God your Lord" and "Do not have any other gods before Me" — are placed in the same sentence (not in the standard text, but in the special cantillation for the Ten Commandments). By contrast, the other eight commandments are separated from one another by a section mark, the letter *samech*. And while the strictures against killing, adultery, stealing, and bearing false witness are recorded in the same sentence, they are also separated from one another by section marks. The first two commandments have no such separation. Furthermore, the first two commandments are recorded as if they were spoken by God — "*I am God your Lord*" and "*Do not have any other gods before Me*" — while the other eight are not in first person and sound as if Moses said them — e.g., "Do not take the name of God your Lord in vain" (verse 7), not "Do not take *My* name in vain."

The Midrash thus asks: Why are the first two commandments different? It answers that God Himself repeated the first two commandments, while Moses repeated the remainder.

It would seem from the above views that there is no contradiction between the statement that God spoke out all of the Ten Commandments and the statement that He spoke out only the first two commandments. The first statement refers to the original, simultaneous pronouncement by God, while the second refers to the repetition of the commandments, when He reiterated only the first two commandments.

However, Kli Yekar treats the two views as mutually exclusive. Nevertheless, he says that both views concur that only the first two commandments were uttered in first person. Even the opinion which holds that God spoke out the entire Ten Commandments agrees that the remaining eight were spoken in third person.

Kli Yekar says that the reason for differentiating between the first two commandments and the final eight was to give Moses the authority to convey God's other laws to the people. The common practice is that, once a person has seen the king and accepted him as a ruler, the person is prepared to follow the king's orders whether he hears them directly from the ruler or indirectly, from the ruler's messengers. But a person who has not yet seen the king cannot be expected to heed a messenger's edicts, for how is he to know that there actually exists a king?

For Moses to be accepted as God's messenger, God first had to demonstrate His existence to the Israelites. He did this by asserting His rulership in the first commandment: "I am God your Lord, who brought you out of Egypt." As for the necessity for God to pronounce the second commandment, this was due to the fact that one may have been misled by the phrasing of the first commandment to believe that other gods exist as well. God had said that he was the Lord "who brought you out of Egypt." One might have concluded that this God had brought the Israelites out of slavery, but that another god had created the world. The second commandment precluded this: "Do not have any other gods before Me." Once God's kingship was established, the Israelites had to heed Moses, His messenger. This is why the first two commandments were recorded in first person.

■ ■ ■

אָנֹכִי ה' אֱלֹהֶיךָ אֲשֶׁר הוֹצֵאתִיךָ מֵאֶרֶץ מִצְרַיִם מִבֵּית עֲבָדִים.
*"I am God your Lord, who brought you out of Egypt, from the house of bondage. . . ."* (20:2)

R. Simla'i said: All 613 commandments were told to Moses at Sinai. R. Hamnuna said: What verse proves this? The one which says, "Moses commanded the Torah to us" (Deuteronomy 33:4). The numerical value of the word "Torah" is 611, and "I am God your Lord" and "Do not have any other gods before Me" were heard from the mouth of the Mighty One (Makkoth 23b).

Many infer from this piece in the Talmud that only the first two commandments were heard by the entire congregation directly from God, while the remaining 611 were spoken by God to Moses, who relayed them to the Israelites. [Thus, the words "Moses commanded the Torah to us" refer to the 611 commandments which the Israelites heard from Moses, and do not include the two they heard from God.] However, Rambam disagrees and opines that the Israelites heard the entire Ten Commandments directly from God.

According to Rambam, R. Hamnuna's statement is to be understood in the following manner: Had we not been given the 611 commandments, we would not have deduced them on our own. These are laws only because "Moses commanded the Torah to us"; the emphasis is not on Moses being the *speaker* as opposed to God, but on the fact that these are statutes that came about only because they were commanded. However, the remaining two commandments — "I am God" and "Do not have any other gods" — would have been seen by us as binding even if they had not been explicitly commanded. Due to the wonders performed by God for the Israelites in Egypt, it was obvious that only He was God.

This is R. Hamnuna's intent when he says that these two statutes were "heard from the mouth of the Mighty One"; they were understood due to the demonstration by God of His might.

*(Tzvi Yisrael)*

■

"I am God your Lord" — *Elokecha*, "your Lord," is in singular form. This is because it is impossible for one man's perception of God to be identical with another man's perception. Each individual has a different level of recognition of God, with a different view of God's being, based on his spiritual level and knowledge of Torah.

*(Sifthei Kohen)*

■

"I am God your Lord" — *Elokecha*, "your Lord," is in singular form, as is the second commandment: "Do not have any other gods before Me." Rashi says that God avoided the plural form in order to provide a defense for the Israelites when they sinned by worshiping the Golden Calf. At that time, Moses was able to assert that God had not told the Israelites that He was their God, and that all other worship was idol worship; rather, this had been instructed solely to Moses.

R. Yitzchak Meir of Gur (Chiddushei HaRim) expounds Rashi's comment, saying that, at the time of the Lawgiving, the entire Israelite nation was bonded with Moses. It was thus entirely appropriate for God to speak out the commandments in singular form, because Moses and the Israelites were connected. This being the case, any command addressed to Moses applied to the Israelites

## Yithro

also. However, the sin of the Golden Calf ruptured this connection. Therefore, Moses was, at that time, correct in asserting that only he had been commanded regarding idol worship. The singular language could no longer be said to include both Moses and the Israelites.

■

"I am God your Lord, who brought you out of Egypt." The Midrash says that God took the Israelites out of Egypt on the condition that they accept His Lordship upon themselves.

R. Yehuda Aryeh Leib of Gur (Sefath Emeth) derives from the Midrash that the level of redemption from slavery attained by a man is proportional to his level of commitment to God and the Torah. The greater such commitment, the freer one becomes. That is the meaning of the dictum "There is no free man except the one who is immersed in the study of Torah" (Avoth 6:2). Similarly, in reading the *Shma*, one first accepts the yoke of Heaven's rule and the yoke of the commandments (in the first two chapters) and then mentions the redemption from Egypt (in the third chapter).

Another example of this, says Sefath Emeth, is the Sages' declaration that "one who accepts the yoke of Torah is relieved of the government's yoke" (Avoth 3:5).

■ ■ ■

לֹא־תִשְׁתַּחֲוֶה לָהֶם וְלֹא תָעָבְדֵם כִּי אָנֹכִי ה' אֱלֹהֶיךָ אֵל קַנָּא פֹּקֵד עֲוֹן אָבֹת עַל־בָּנִים עַל־שִׁלֵּשִׁים וְעַל־רִבֵּעִים לְשֹׂנְאָי.

"... *Do not bow down to them or worship them, as I, God your Lord, am a jealous God, who visits the sin of the fathers upon the sons, to the third and fourth generations, for those who hate Me....*" (20:5)

"Who visits the sin of the fathers upon the sons" — This occurs only if the sons follow in the evil footsteps of their fathers (Rashi).

Why should children be held responsible for their parents' sins and be punished for these? Even if the parents are sinners and the children copy their ways, why shouldn't the children's punishment be limited to retribution for their own sins?

R. Berachiah Nakdan, in his *Mishlei Shu'alim (Fox Parables)*, records the story of a starving wolf who, meeting a fox, wanted to eat it. The fox protested: Why would you want a weak, lean fox when you can have the large, fat man who is coming along?

The wolf responded: It is prohibited to kill a human being, as it says regarding those who kill men, "I will demand an account from the hand of every wild beast" (Genesis 9:5).

The fox replied: You have nothing to fear, since not you, but your children, will be punished, as it says, "The fathers ate unripe fruit and the teeth of the sons will be set on edge" (Jeremiah 31:28).

The wolf was convinced, and he set off to snare the man. But there was a trap set up along the road, and the wolf was caught in it.

Upon hearing the wolf's cries, the fox approached.

The wolf berated the fox: Liar! You assured me that my children — not I — would be punished for my sins.

The fox retorted: Fool! You are not being punished for your own sins, but for those of your ancestors.

The wolf was astonished: Is it possible that I should suffer due to the misdeeds of others?

The fox responded: Why, then, did you go after the man, when you knew that your children would be punished for it? This being the case, you too must suffer for the transgressions of your fathers!

This is the meaning of Rashi's comment. Children suffer for their parents' sins when the children are also sinners. If the children do not care that their own offspring will suffer for their sins, then, correspondingly, the children deserve to suffer for the misdeeds of their parents. *(Pardes Yosef)*

■ ■ ■

לֹא תִשָּׂא אֶת־שֵׁם־ה׳ אֱלֹהֶיךָ לַשָּׁוְא כִּי לֹא יְנַקֶּה ה׳ אֵת אֲשֶׁר־יִשָּׂא אֶת־שְׁמוֹ לַשָּׁוְא.

*". . . Do not take the name of God your Lord in vain, for God will not hold guiltless one who takes His name in vain. . . ."* (20:7)

The entire world trembled when God said at Sinai, "Do not take the name of God your Lord in vain" (Shevuoth 39a).

Why did the world tremble specifically at this commandment?

## Yithro

Until this commandment was given, people believed they could evade the laws against stealing, killing, and the like by claiming that their actions were for the sake of Heaven. However, the implication of "Do not take the name of God your Lord in vain" is that one may not use God's name as a screen for his actions. With the giving of this commandment, the ability to circumvent the other commandments was lost. That is why the world trembled when it was given.

*(Chezyonoth Avraham)*

■ ■ ■

זָכוֹר אֶת־יוֹם הַשַּׁבָּת לְקַדְּשׁוֹ.

"*. . . Remember the Sabbath day to keep it holy. . . .*" (20:8)

In the repetition of the Ten Commandments in Deuteronomy, the fourth commandment reads, "*Observe* the Sabbath day to keep it holy" (5:12). The Talmud (Shevuoth 20b) comments: "Remember" *(Zachor)* and "Observe" *(Shamor)* were uttered simultaneously. "Remembering" includes honoring the Sabbath with special foods, while "observing" denotes adherence to the strictures of the Sabbath.

The Maggid of Dubno explains the Talmud's dictum by saying that there are people who desire to separate *zachor* and *shamor*. For example, a poor man prefers the *shamor* aspect. As he is not a successful businessman, he loses little by abstaining from work on the Sabbath. However, he finds it difficult to uphold the *zachor* aspect, since he lacks the funds to honor the Sabbath with wine and food.

The opposite is true of a rich man. He prefers the *zachor* aspect, since he is capable of purchasing all sorts of foods in honor of the Sabbath. However, he does not enjoy the *shamor* aspect, because the inability to work leads to the loss of substantial income for him.

Our Sages therefore tell us, "*Zachor* and *shamor* were uttered simultaneously"; one has no right to divorce them from each other. The wealthy man must uphold *shamor* along with *zachor*. Furthermore, he must give assistance to the indigent man, so that the latter can also observe both aspects properly.

■

The Torah first mandates, "Remember the Sabbath day to keep it holy." It continues, "You may work during the six weekdays." It says further, "But the seventh day is the Sabbath to God," and adds, "It was during the six weekdays that God made the heaven, the earth, the sea, and all that is in them, but He rested on the seventh day."

Devash VeChalav asks: What is the need for all this repetition? Wouldn't it have sufficed to say, "You may work during the six weekdays and do all your tasks, but the seventh day is the Sabbath to God"?

In answer, Devash VeChalav points to a well-known contradiction between two Talmudic statements. In one place it says that if the Jews would observe two Sabbaths properly they would be redeemed (Shabbath 118b). Elsewhere it says that if the Jews properly observe *one* Sabbath the Messiah would come (Jerusalem Talmud, Ta'anith 1:1). The resolution given is that, in reality, only one Sabbath need be observed to prompt the Messiah's coming. This would fulfill the desired goal of duplicating God's conduct during the first week of Creation, when He created for six days and rested on the seventh.

However, this cannot actually be accomplished unless the preceding Sabbath is also observed. Only if that is done can it be said that the next Sabbath follows "six days of creation." Otherwise, the six previous days do not constitute an entity unto themselves — a separate week — but are part of the continuous series of days that preceded them.

This, says Devash VeChalav, is the thrust of the Torah in the present verses, and accounts for their verbosity. First we must "Remember the Sabbath day" — keep one Sabbath. Then we "work during the six weekdays." Finally, "the seventh day is the Sabbath day" — the second Sabbath is observed, so that there are six days of activity followed by a Sabbath. And all this must be done to emulate God's actions during Creation, as "it was during the six weekdays that God made the heaven . . . but He rested on the seventh day."

■

## Yithro

While the Torah here reads: "Remember the Sabbath day to keep it holy," the language differs when the Ten Commandments are repeated later (Deuteronomy 5:12). There it reads, "*Observe* the Sabbath day to keep it holy." The Talmud (Shevuoth 20b) says that "Remember," *Zachor*, and "Observe," *Shamor*, were uttered by God simultaneously.

Ramban asks why the Talmud makes this assertion only in regard to *zachor* and *shamor*. There are, after all, a number of other differences between the two texts of the Ten Commandments. Why isn't it said that the other discrepancies were also said simultaneously?

Ramban answers that, while the discrepancies in the reading of the other commandments are minor, *zachor* and *shamor* are substantively different. *Zachor* is a positive commandment, referring to the obligation to sanctify the Sabbath. *Shamor* is a negative commandment, as the Talmud has established that the word *hishamer* (a form of *shamor*) indicates a negative injunction (Makkoth 13b). In this case it means that one must sanctify the Sabbath by not profaning it through prohibited activity. Hence, when Moses recapitulated the Ten Commandments in Deuteronomy, he would not have changed God's words to the degree that a positive commandment was altered and became a negative one. It can only be that God used both terms when He gave the Torah, with Scripture recording one in the present verse and the other in Deuteronomy.

However, says Ramban, Moses himself made the other, minor changes — adding, for example, the conjunction "and," indicated by the letter *vav*, to the term *al shileshim* in the second commandment, so that it reads *ve'al shileshim*. This was an insignificant emendation, and so there is no need to say that God uttered *al* and *ve'al* simultaneously.

Mizrachi questions Ramban's approach. Firstly — says Mizrachi — whereas *zachor* refers to the sanctification of the Sabbath (*Kiddush*), Ramban's assertion that *zachor* is a positive command and *shamor* a negative one would yield the result that *Kiddush* is both a positive and negative commandment. What negative facet is there to *Kiddush*? There is none. Secondly, while the Talmud does say that *shamor* indicates a negative command, the Talmud makes an exception to this rule: when the term is used by Scripture in a positive form, it is considered a positive command (Yoma 81a). In the present case, the form is a positive one: "Observe the Sabbath." How, then, can Ramban categorize *shamor* as a negative command? Finally, both verses — here and in Deuteronomy — continue with the word *lekadsho,* "to keep it holy." Mizrachi asserts that this is clearly a reference to the sanctification of the Sabbath, to *Kiddush,* not, as Ramban claims, to keeping the Sabbath holy by refraining from work.

Divrei David defends the view of Ramban by saying that he is merely stating that there is a qualitative difference between the other changes found in the two texts and the *zachor-shamor* change. While the other changes made in Deuteronomy serve to clarify the Exodus text, such is not the case with *shamor.* This word supplies information that is completely new, information not found in Exodus. That being the case, how did the Israelites know of the strictures implied by *shamor* during the forty years that separated the Revelation and Moses' repetition of the Ten Commandments? Therefore, the Sages concluded that *shamor* was indeed uttered at Mount Sinai, at the same moment *zachor* was said.

Ibn Ezra has a completely different approach to the discrepancies between the two Ten Commandment texts. He challenges the view that God actually said *zachor* and *shamor* at the same instant. Ibn Ezra says that, if this were the case, one would have to say the same regarding the other differences between the texts. That, however, would result in absurdities. For example, in the first text, God says, "Do not commit murder. Do not commit adultery. Do not steal. Do not testify as a false witness against your neighbor. Do not covet your neighbor's house." The second text reads, "Do not commit murder, *and* do not commit adultery, *and* do not steal, *and* do not testify as a perjurious witness against your neighbor. *And* do not covet your neighbor's wife." The conjunction "and," signaled by the added letter *vav,* connects each of these

## Yithro

commandments in Deuteronomy, but not in Exodus. How could God have said and not said the word "and" simultaneously? Even more unfathomable, how could the Israelites have heard it and yet not heard it?

Moreover, the Exodus text refers to an *ed sheker*, a "false witness," while the Deuteronomy text refers to an *ed shav*, a "perjurious witness." Furthermore, completely different reasons for the keeping of the Sabbath are given in the two texts. And there are a host of similar discrepancies. Why don't the Sages say that all these were uttered simultaneously? Additionally, a miracle of this nature certainly should have been mentioned in the Torah, and yet it is not.

To answer all this, Ibn Ezra declares that, in the Hebrew language, it is possible to say the same thing in different ways. Two words can mean the same thing, as can two phrases. A person is not always careful to repeat the exact language of an earlier statement. For example, Eliezer, the servant of Abraham, asked Rebecca for a drink with the words *hagmi'ini na* (Genesis 24:17). When he later repeated the incident to Rebecca's family, Eliezer stated that he had asked her, *hashkini na* (Ibid., verse 43). Eliezer now used a different word, but the meaning of what he said did not change; both *hagmi'ini* and *hashkini* refer to drinking.

Moreover, a word contains a certain meaning, depending on the intent of the speaker. For example, Rebecca overheard Isaac telling Esau that he wished to bless him (Genesis 27:4). In relaying this conversation to Jacob, Rebecca said that Isaac had told Esau he wished to bless him "before God" (Ibid., verse 7). Now, Isaac did not say the words "before God." However, Rebecca did not distort his words. Rather, she understood that, when he told Esau he would bless him, Isaac meant that he would bless him through his capacity of prophecy, "before God."

According to Ibn Ezra, there is no purpose in searching for new meanings when there is a discrepancy in a repeated text. Similarly, there is no new meaning to be found if a word is spelled fully in one text and defectively in another text. These variations occur in normal usage.

So it was with the Ten Commandments. God did not utter *zachor*

## The Eternal Heritage

and *shamor* simultaneously. Neither did He make simultaneous pronouncements in any of the other instances where there are discrepancies between the texts. The only words spoken by God were the ones recorded in Exodus. When Moses repeated the Ten Commandments to the Israelites, he did so in his own words, words that brought out the meaning of what God had said. As an example, *shamor* helped define *zachor*, since part of observing the Sabbath is to keep its laws. Any other changes Moses made were also for the purpose of clarifying the meaning of the Ten Commandments.

An interesting sidelight emerges, *inter alia*, from Ibn Ezra's comment. He states: "We have seen that from the start, 'I am the Lord,' through the words 'who will take His name in vain,' there are no differences between the two texts." In point of fact, there *are* two differences between the texts of these first three commandments. Firstly, the second commandment in the present section reads, "Do not make for yourselves a molten image *and* any picture . . ." (verse 4). In Deuteronomy, the *vav*, "and," is missing. The opposite occurs in the next verse. In Exodus, God says that he "visits the sin of the fathers upon the sons, to the third and fourth generations, for those who hate Me." In Deuteronomy the reading is: "visits the sin of the fathers upon the sons, *and* to the third and fourth generations, for those who hate Me."

It seems, therefore, that Ibn Ezra had a slightly different text from ours in either the present section or in Deuteronomy, with identical readings in the texts in both of these cases. Otherwise, why did he find no difference between the two texts of the first three commandments?

While one may counter that these differences are so slight that they need not be mentioned, this is obviously not the case, since Ibn Ezra notes precisely this sort of difference in the last five commandments, as discussed before.

■

"Remember the Sabbath day" — Always keep the Sabbath in mind, so that if you come across a fine object, put it aside for the Sabbath (Rashi).

## Yithro

Ramban objects that Rashi's comment accords with the view of Shammai, in his debate with Hillel regarding this issue (Betzah 16a). Shammai's opinion is that one who comes upon a fine animal should put it aside for the Sabbath, since, if he slaughters it during the week, he may not find another, similar animal in time for the Sabbath. Hillel argues that one can slaughter the animal and have faith that he will find another with which to honor the Sabbath. The Schools of Hillel and Shammai carried forward this dispute between their mentors, and the law is in accordance with the School of Hillel. The same debate is found in the Midrash regarding a fine object that one comes upon during the week. Why, then, does Rashi here subscribe to Shammai's opinion?

Mizrachi answers that it is true that Hillel and Shammai argued regarding both foods and objects. However, the implication of the Talmudic text is that their students, the Schools of Hillel and Shammai, continued the argument only regarding foods. In the case of foods, if one eats them, they can be replaced, and so the School of Hillel holds that there is no need to desist from eating a food during the week. However, when it comes to other items, the School of Hillel dissents from its mentor's view and agrees with the School of Shammai that one should set them aside for Sabbath use, since they are not readily replaced. Rashi's comment is that if one comes upon a fine object he should set it aside for the Sabbath; as regards objects, everyone agrees that the law is according to Shammai.

■ ■ ■

שֵׁשֶׁת יָמִים תַּעֲבֹד וְעָשִׂיתָ כָּל־מְלַאכְתֶּךָ.
". . . *You may work during the six weekdays and do all your tasks.* . . ." (20:9)

Why does this verse follow the previous one: "Remember the Sabbath day to keep it holy"?

The Gaon of Vilna explains the connection based on the Talmud's ruling regarding one who has lost count and does not know which day is the Sabbath. The Talmud says that he is to count off six days and keep the seventh as the Sabbath. However, whereas it is possible that any one of the days is actually the Sabbath, he is never

## The Eternal Heritage

permitted to do more work than is necessary to keep himself alive (Shabbath 69b).

Hence, the verses may be understood as follows: If one does "Remember the Sabbath day" — if he knows which day is the Sabbath — only then is he allowed to "do *all* your tasks" during the week. However, if he loses count of the days, he can do only the minimum amount of work necessary to keep himself alive.

■

"Do all your tasks" — When the Sabbath comes, you should feel as if all your work has been completed, and should not think about work at all (Rashi).

Chiddushei HaRim avers that the state of mind described by Rashi applies not only to physical work, but to spiritual work as well. One should complete his battle with the evil inclination during the six workdays. If one serves God properly during the week, then the Sabbath provides a respite from spiritual battles as well as physical ones.

■ ■ ■

כִּי שֵׁשֶׁת־יָמִים עָשָׂה ה' אֶת־הַשָּׁמַיִם וְאֶת־הָאָרֶץ אֶת־הַיָּם וְאֶת־כָּל־אֲשֶׁר־בָּם וַיָּנַח בַּיּוֹם הַשְּׁבִיעִי עַל־כֵּן בֵּרַךְ ה' אֶת־יוֹם הַשַּׁבָּת וַיְקַדְּשֵׁהוּ.

". . . It was during the six weekdays that God made the heaven, the earth, the sea, and all that is in them, but He rested on the seventh day. God therefore blessed the Sabbath day and sanctified it. . . ." (20:11)

"If the Jews would observe two Sabbaths properly, they would immediately be redeemed" (Shabbath 118b).

If the Jewish people observe one Sabbath, it may be due to a momentary impulse. Such observance does not demonstrate a commitment on their part. However, if they keep a second Sabbath, they have evidenced a resolve to fulfill God's commandments.

As for why this resolve must be expressed through a commitment to Sabbath observance, as opposed to observance of some other law, the Sabbath serves as a sign of the connection between God and the Jewish people (31:17). Therefore, the expression of the Jews' commitment to God's Torah must be made through the Sabbath.

■ ■ ■

## Yithro

כַּבֵּד אֶת־אָבִיךָ וְאֶת־אִמֶּךָ לְמַעַן יַאֲרִכוּן יָמֶיךָ עַל הָאֲדָמָה אֲשֶׁר־ה׳ אֱלֹהֶיךָ נֹתֵן לָךְ.

". . . Honor your father and mother, so that you will live long on the land which God your Lord is giving you. . . ." (20:12)

R. Saadiah Gaon asks: Why does the Torah stipulate long life as the reward for honoring one's parents?

He answers that there are cases where parents live very long, and the burden of caring for them falls upon the children. The reward for fulfilling this obligation is long life for the children as well. However, if a child despairs that his parents are living long lives, and does not honor them, his life is cut short.

■

The Torah's laws are founded upon the principle of *middah kenegged middah* — corresponding reward or punishment for a law fulfilled or violated. Hence, one would have expected the Torah to say, "Honor your father and mother, so that you will be honored." Why is the reward long life, and not honor?

The answer is that one who attains long life also attains honor; as the Torah commands, "Stand up before a white head" (Leviticus 19:32). By promising long life to one who honors his parents, the Torah is also promising that he will receive honor.

(R. Yitzchak Caro)

■

Each of the first five commandments makes mention of God's name, while the final five commandments are recorded without mention of God.

Kli Yekar explains that the first five commandments concern Man's relationship with God (e.g., the prohibition to worship idols), while the last five concern his relationship with his fellow man (e.g., the prohibition against killing). Therefore, God is mentioned in the first five commandments.

In that case, why is God's name mentioned in the commandment to honor one's parents, which seems to belong to the second category, that of personal relations?

Kli Yekar answers with the Sages' statement that three partners are involved in the creation of a person: his father, his mother, and God. His parents provide the physical parts and God provides the soul (Niddah 31a). Now, if one must honor his parents, whose contribution is temporal — the body — then he must certainly honor God, whose gift is eternal — the soul. Therefore, this commandment includes the obligation to honor one's Father in heaven.

According to the Talmud, if one honors his parents, God considers it as if He lived with the family and has been honored by them. Where do we see the concept of God living with a family? Kli Yekar explains that this is derived from the mention of God in connection with the fifth commandment, while He is not mentioned in the last five commandments; it is evident that God places Himself within the family context, and that He is honored when one honors his parents.

Kli Yekar continues that this is why long life is the reward for the fulfillment of this particular commandment. God is the source of life, and cleaving to God results in long life. As Scripture says, "But you, the ones who remained attached to God your Lord, are all alive today" (Deuteronomy 4:4). When one honors his parents in the physical world, his soul correspondingly honors its creator, God, and this attachment to God yields long life.

■

While the reward promised here is that "you will live long," the reward mentioned in the repetition of the Ten Commandments is: "You will then live long and have it well" (Deuteronomy 5:16).

Chatham Sofer explains that, as Ramban says, one must honor his parents because they are partners with God in bringing him into the world. Yet, one might ask why it is necessary to honor parents. After all, the Sages say that it would be preferable not to be born (Eruvin 13b). Why is one obligated to honor those who caused him to suffer the misfortune of being born? The answer, says Chatham Sofer, is that Tosafoth limits the Sages' pronouncement to those people who

## Yithro

are not servants of God. For those who do serve God, it is desirable to have been born.

Now, among these servants of God there are people who count on a reward in the World to Come. But others are at such an elevated level that they have no interest in the World to Come. They would be happy to live only in the present world, in accordance with the dictum that "one hour of repentance and good works in this world is better than all of the World to Come" (Avoth 4:17).

The Ten Commandments in the present portion were recorded before the sin of the Golden Calf. At this stage, the Israelites were all at this very high level. Therefore, Scripture promises only that "you will live long," as long life in the present world was their desire. The Ten Commandments in Deuteronomy were recorded after the sin, when the Israelites had fallen from this high level. They now desired to experience the World to Come in addition to the present world, and so they were promised, "You will live long and have it well." *Yitav*, "have it well," which is derived from *tov*, "good," alludes to the next world, which is termed *kulo tov*, "completely good."

■ ■ ■

לֹא תִרְצַח לֹא תִנְאָף לֹא תִגְנֹב לֹא־תַעֲנֶה בְרֵעֲךָ עֵד שָׁקֶר.
לֹא תַחְמֹד בֵּית רֵעֶךָ לֹא־תַחְמֹד אֵשֶׁת רֵעֶךָ וְעַבְדּוֹ וַאֲמָתוֹ וְשׁוֹרוֹ וַחֲמֹרוֹ וְכֹל אֲשֶׁר לְרֵעֶךָ.

". . . *Do not commit murder. Do not commit adultery. Do not steal. Do not testify as a false witness against your neighbor.*
"*Do not covet your neighbor's house. Do not covet your neighbor's wife, his slave, his maidservant, his ox, or his donkey, or anything else that is your neighbor's.*" (20:13, 14)

In the repetition of the Ten Commandments, the text reads: "Do not testify as a perjurious witness against your neighbor. Do not covet your neighbor's wife. Do not desire your neighbor's house" (Deuteronomy 5:17, 18).

There are two differences between that text and the present one. Here the ninth commandment warns one not to testify as a "false witness" — *ed sheker* — while in Deuteronomy it warns against being a "perjurious witness," an *ed shav*. Also, the tenth commandment here first warns against coveting a neighbor's house and then against desiring his wife, while in Deuteronomy the order is reversed — the wife is mentioned first. What is the reason for these discrepancies?

Iturei Torah cites R. Mordechai Yehuda Leib Zaks's resolution for this problem. He notes that Ba'al HaTurim (Deuteronomy, Ibid.) says that these two commandments were juxtaposed in order to teach that a man must not tell a lie to a woman, saying her husband is dead, in order to marry her.

With this — says R. Mordechai — the differences in the texts may be justified. The present verse discusses a false witness — an *ed sheker*. In the Talmud (Shevuoth 21a), a *sheker* denotes a lie which is not obvious to everyone. The coveting of a house would fall under the label of a *sheker*, as, when a man makes a claim on his neighbor's house, the truth will be borne out in a court of law, with witnesses. This is not a lie of which everyone will become aware. Therefore, "Do not covet your neighbor's house" is placed immediately following the warning not to testify falsely in the present text.

The Talmud (Ibid.) says that *shav* denotes a lie which is obvious to all — such as swearing that a table is a chair. The coveting of a neighbor's wife, manifested in false testimony that her husband has died, falls under the rubric of an *ed shav*. The truth in this case does become evident to all, when the supposedly dead man comes back, alive. Hence, in Deuteronomy, "Do not covet your neighbor's wife" immediately follows the ninth commandment and precedes "Do not desire your neighbor's house."

■

"Do not covet your neighbor's house." Ibn Ezra asks how a person can be commanded not to desire other people's belongings. If one sees a beautiful object, how can he be expected to keep from thinking that it would be nice to own it?

Ibn Ezra answers that if a person knows that a certain item is beyond his reach, that he can never obtain it, then he does not even think about having it. A villager who sees the daughter of the king

## Yithro

and notices she is beautiful has no illusions that he will ever be intimate with her. Therefore, he does not even desire this in his mind.

Similarly, people must recognize that a neighbor's wife and property are off limits to him. They are not part of the portion allotted to him by God. A person who has this mindset will not covet his neighbor's wife or property.

■ ■ ■

וְכָל־הָעָם רֹאִים אֶת־הַקּוֹלֹת וְאֶת־הַלַּפִּידִם וְאֵת קוֹל הַשֹּׁפָר וְאֶת־הָהָר עָשֵׁן וַיַּרְא הָעָם וַיָּנֻעוּ וַיַּעַמְדוּ מֵרָחֹק.
*All the people saw the sounds, the flames, the blast of the ram's horn, and the mountain smoking. The people saw it and trembled, and stood far away.* (20:15)

What was the benefit of standing away from the mountain? Whereas God's glory fills the entire earth, what difference did it make how close to Mount Sinai the Israelites were?

Every Jew must believe in the One God, without needing to be convinced by miracles. It is only people of little faith who must rely upon miracles to recognize God. When the Israelites saw that God had to make use of miracles in giving them the Torah, they realized that they had not arrived at the level where belief comes without miracles.

This is the Torah's intent here: "The people saw it," the miracles, "and trembled, and stood far away" — they recognized that, spiritually, they still "stood far away" from the ideal level.

*(R. Avraham Yaakov of Sadigora)*

■ ■ ■

לֹא תַעֲשׂוּן אִתִּי אֱלֹהֵי כֶסֶף וֵאלֹהֵי זָהָב לֹא תַעֲשׂוּ לָכֶם.
"*. . . Do not make with Me gods of silver and gods of gold — do not make these for yourselves. . . .*" (20:20)

R. Yosef Patsanovski points out that, regarding silver idols, Scripture says, "Do not make with Me," while as concerns gods of gold it says, "gods of gold — do not make these for yourselves." Why does God refer to Himself — "with Me" — in connection with the silver gods, but not in connection with the golden ones?

R. Yosef answers that a wealthy man would make a golden idol, while a man of lesser means would make a silver idol. Furthermore, one who is not wealthy does not completely forsake God. The worshiper of the silver idol will pray to God as well as to the idol. Therefore, Scripture says, "Do not make *with Me* gods of silver" — idols which one will worship alongside God.

But one who is wealthy — the maker of the golden idol — will forsake God entirely, and so God is not mentioned in conjunction with the golden idols.

## CORRECTION

In the first volume of The Eternal Heritage, the translation of verse 20 on page 213 reads, in error:

God then said, "The outcry against Sodom is great, and their sin is very grave.

The correct reading is:

God then said, "The outcry against Sodom and Gomorrah is great, and their sin is very grave.